DOCTRINES
OF THE
CHRISTIAN
RELIGION

WILLIAM WILSON STEVENS

BROADMAN PRESS
NASHVILLE, TENNESSEE

4217-06
ISBN: 0-8054-1706-0

To my students
— past, present, and future —
this work is affectionately dedicated.
May its result be to the glory of God.

Dewey Decimal Classification: 230
Library of Congress Catalog Card Number, 67-13977
Printed in the United States of America

CONTENTS

Earth breaks up, time drops away,
In flows Heaven, with its new day
Of endless life, when he who trod,
Very Man and very God,
This earth in weakness, shame and pain,
Dying the death whose signs remain
Up yonder on the accursed tree,—
Shall come again, no more to be
Of captivity the thrall,
But the one God, All in all,
King of kings, Lord of lords,
As His servant John received the words,
"I died, and live for evermore!"

— ROBERT BROWNING

PREFACE

THE PURPOSE OF THIS BOOK IS TWOFOLD. IT WAS WRITTEN TO PROVIDE a Christian doctrines textbook on the college and university level. It was also written to fulfill the demand for a "layman's theology." It is sent forth with the sincere hope that this dual purpose will be adequately realized.

The book assumes only a meager knowledge of the Bible on the part of the reader; it does not purport to be a systematic theology on the seminary level. Rather, it is the outgrowth of eleven years of experience in teaching doctrines at Mississippi College on an average of more than twice a year. Evolving from this teaching was the recognition of the extreme need for a new textbook in the field of doctrines. The writer has endeavored to meet that need; not for his own use only, he hopes, but also for the use of colleagues in similar institutions.

The teaching of New Testament Greek at Mississippi College has probably influenced the writing to the extent that the book has an etymological approach. However, all Hebrew and Greek terms referred to are transliterated and fully explained. No knowledge of the original languages is assumed for the reader.

Rather than presenting a large number of biblical references relative to a subject, the writer has given only two or three and has added the corresponding passages in full. Experience has revealed that students will not stop reading the textbook long enough to refer to their Bible when biblical references are given. Therefore both the reference and passage are included, which has resulted in an enlarged format for the book; but surely the reader will welcome such a procedure. The book is fully outlined, another characteristic added owing to the study habits of students. A detailed outline precedes each chapter. The American Standard Version of the Bible is used for all biblical quotations.

Yet, with all this, the general reader has not been forgotten in the compilation of material and writing of the book. There are hundreds of preachers, deacons, Sunday school teachers, and other Christian workers who need an easily comprehended treatise on the great verities and concepts of the Christian faith. It is the writer's sincere wish that this book will supply the need of this large group. Redemption history is still the greatest story ever told. It is the story of the Bible, the unfolding of God's mighty acts in which he has not only revealed himself to alienated man but has sought to reconcile man back into his fellowship for all eternity. Begun in the Old Testament and culminated in the New, God's divine imperative is constantly present.

The writer wishes to thank all those who in any way have contributed to the development and final production of the book. Some have offered helpful criticisms and valuable suggestions, while a few have helped in other ways. A special appreciation goes out to the professors in the twelve other institutions who were gracious enough, to teach the book in its temporary mimeograph form prior to the regular publication. Finally, a word of gratitude is due all those authors, and their publishers, whose books have contributed in many and various ways to the writing of this one. From some of them direct quotations are made; others appear in the Bibliography.

— WILLIAM WILSON STEVENS

OUTLINE FOR CHAPTER ONE

I. Reasons for Expecting a Revelation
  1. Needs of man's nature
  2. Hope that these needs will be supplied
II. Two Types of Revelation
  1. Revelation in nature (natural revelation)
    (1) Relation to supernatural revelation
    (2) Scriptural evidence
    (3) Only partial, not sufficient
  2. Revelation above nature (supernatural revelation)
    (1) Preliminary revelation
    (2) Final revelation
III. Opposing Views Regarding Revelation
  1. Agnostic
  2. Pantheistic
  3. Natural religion
IV. Nature of the Biblical Revelation
  1. God's self-revelation
  2. For purpose of spiritual transformation
  3. Produced active response
  4. Historically based
  5. Experientially given
  6. Progressively presented
  7. Sufficient, but not exhaustive
V. Witness of the Revelation
  1. Differentiation of terms
  2. Divinely inspired
  3. Theories of inspiration
    (1) Naturalistic
    (2) Plenary verbal
    (3) Dynamical
  4. Authoritativeness

CHAPTER ONE

REVELATION

WHERE THERE IS NO REVELATION THERE CAN BE NO RELIGION. BY religion is meant a recognition on the part of man of a controlling superhuman power entitled to obedience, reverence, and worship. Since Brahmanism and Buddhism do not claim a revelation, they are not religions in the full sense of the term. They are speculative systems of thought, philosophies which do not satisfy. If man is to live a religious life there must be fellowship with God, which in turn presupposes that there has been a revelation from God and that man has been so created that he can receive and utilize that revelation. Therefore Christianity is a reciprocal relationship involving the self-disclosure of God and man's response to that disclosure.

I. REASONS FOR EXPECTING A REVELATION

1. NEEDS OF MAN'S NATURE

Man's nature as an intellectual and moral being requires an authoritative revelation of religious truth. Otherwise there will be deterioration instead of growth and progress. Moral and spiritual blindness would soon degenerate man to the level of bestiality. And this revelation must be higher and fuller than any knowledge man could attain with his intellectual and moral powers unaided from without. How could man's reason or intuition, without direct aid from God himself, throw any light upon the Trinity, or the love of God, or the atonement, or the afterlife? In addition to these deterring factors the matter is further complicated by the moral and intellectual perversion of man due to sin. There must be some type of special revelation of the gracious, merciful, and helpful side of God's nature if the power of sin is to be broken and man is to be emancipated. "If there be a divine Spirit of the universe, nature, such as we know her, cannot possibly be its ulti-mate word to man. Either there is no Spirit revealed in nature, or else it is inadequately revealed there, and, as all the higher religions have assumed, what we call visible nature, or *this* world, must be but a veil and surface-show whose full meaning resides in a supplementary unseen or *other* world."[1]

1 William James, "Is Life Worth Living?", *International Journal of Ethics* (Oct. 1895), p. 10.

Added to all this is the thought that in lands that have not received God's special revelation, and in ages that preceded this special revelation, the knowledge of moral and spiritual truth is crassly lacking and imperfect. The condition of man in heathen lands is one of extreme ethical depravity. There is a sense of spiritual unknown, a searching after God. Pythagoras, a Greek philosopher and mathematician who lived during the sixth century B.C., said, "It is not easy to know [duties], except men were taught them by God himself, or by some person who has received them from God, or obtained the knowledge of them through some divine means."

2. HOPE THAT THESE NEEDS WILL BE SUPPLIED

The incomplete revelation of God in the cosmic order speaks a hope that there will be a completion, in some special and distinct way, of that incomplete manifestation. It is the hope that the wants of the spirit of man will be met by a supernatural unveiling of the being of God. Does this not follow as a necessary consequence of having made man a spiritual being with the obvious purpose of a close fellowship? And does it not also follow that God will complement the work already done, the insufficient revelation of himself to man as discerned in the natural order? The highest part of the nature of man is the spiritual and intellectual, which part has not been satisfied by the complete unveiling in the natural realm. The general laws of want and supply would anticipate the granting of that which is still needed. Find in paganism anywhere a god who loves! There are vicious gods and cruel gods, but none who love. Only in the special revelation of the one true God is love manifested. Nor can reason, conscience, or natural affection discover, unaided, this wonderful facet of God's personality.

From the dim recesses of the past man has been asking himself such questions as: "From where did I come?", "Where do I go?", "Who am I?", "What is my reason for being?" The answers to these urgent questions are found only in that order of things lying outside the pale of sensory perception, where we see, feel, and hear. Precisely this is the crux of the need for revelation. Here it is that the necessity of revelation became apparent from the beginning. Men sought knowledge of that other world while still in the primer stage of seeking knowledge concerning this world. And, since they could not by their own effort discover God, would it not be reasonable, they asked, to expect that God would reveal himself?

II. TWO TYPES OF REVELATION

There are two types of revelation: one a general revelation, or revelation in nature, or natural revelation; the other a special revelation, or revelation above nature, or supernatural revelation. The Bible testifies to these two types of the unveiling of God to man. The former is derived from the natural order, man's conscience and reason, and also providence; the latter is borne in the Bible, the Word of God.

There is not only a difference in the means whereby revelation is communicated to man, one through the visible creation, with all its laws of operation, and the other in a higher, supernatural medium; there is also a difference in the nature of the subject matter revealed. General revelation is concerned with that which can be acquired by reason through a study of nature, while special revelation involves man's spiritual relation to God. It concerns that which can be apprehended only by faith. In Protestant theology revelation in nature is often termed *revelatio realis* (because embodied in things) and revelation above nature is termed *revelatio verbalis* (because embodied in words). The terms immediate revelation and mediate revelation have also been suggested for these two phases, but these terms are not too popular.

"General revelation is rooted in creation, is addressed to man as man, and more particularly to human reason, and finds its purpose in the realization of the end of his creation, to know God and thus enjoy communion with Him. Special revelation is rooted in the redemptive plan of God, is addressed to man as sinner, can be properly understood and appropriated only by faith, and serves the purpose of securing the end for which man was created in spite of the disturbance wrought by sin. In view of the eternal plan of redemption it should be said that this special revelation did not come in as an after-thought but was in the mind of God from the very beginning."[2]

1. REVELATION IN NATURE (NATURAL REVELATION)

(1) RELATION TO SUPERNATURAL REVELATION

Through the centuries there have been conflicting views concerning the relation of natural and supernatural revelation. At times the former was exalted over the latter, which was true in the rationalism of Europe. Man's ability and power were exalted and made supreme, almost to the exclusion of the authority of the Holy Scriptures. Some maintained that human reason, working through natural revelation, was all that was necessary to determine spiritual truths. Then Dersin proceeded to deny the neces-

2 Louis Berkhof, *Systematic Theology*, p. 37.

sity and possibility of supernatural revelation. F. E. D. Schleiermacher and Albert Knudson at a later period denied any distinction between natural and supernatural revelation. The latter stated in his *The Doctrine of God*, "But this distinction between natural and revealed theology has now largely fallen into disuse. The present tendency is to draw no sharp line of distinction between revelation and the natural reason, but to look upon the highest insights of reason as themselves divine revelation. In any case there is no fixed body of revealed truth, accepted as authority, that stands opposed to the truths of reason. All truth today rests on its power of appeal to the human mind."[3] Karl Barth continues the swing of the pendulum on to the opposite extreme and denies revelation in nature, recognizing as revelation only the direct action of God, God speaking, bringing something new to man, something impossible for man to have known previously. Since revelation is Christ, revelation is an act of grace. Barth says that "it is of the nature and being of this object, of God the Father, the Son, and the Holy Spirit, that He cannot be known by the powers of human knowledge, but is apprehensible and apprehended solely because of His own freedom, decision and action. What man can know by his own power according to the measure of his natural powers, his understanding, his feelings, will be at most something like a supreme being, an absolute nature, the idea of an utterly free power, of a being towering over everything. This absolute and supreme being, the ultimate and most profound, this 'thing in itself,' has nothing to do with God. It is part of the intuitions and marginal possibilities of man's thinking, man's contrivance. Man is able to think this being; but he has not thereby thought God. God is thought and known when in His own freedom God makes Himself apprehensible. . . . God is always the One who has made Himself known to man in His own revelation, and not the one man thinks out for himself and describes as God. . . . Knowledge of God takes place where there is actual experience that God speaks, that He so represents Himself to man that he cannot fail to see and hear Him. . . . Knowledge of God takes place where divine revelation takes place, illumination of man by God, transmission of human knowledge, instruction of man by this incomparable Teacher."[4]

(2) SCRIPTURAL EVIDENCE

The scriptural passages that pertain to this revelation of God in the natural order, this cosmic revelation, are as follows. "The heavens declare the glory of God; And the firmament showeth

3 Albert Knudson, *The Doctrine of God*, p. 173.
4 Karl Barth, *Dogmatics in Outline*, pp. 23, 24.

his handiwork. Day unto day uttereth speech, And night unto night showeth knowledge" (Ps. 19:1, 2). "And yet he left not himself without witness, in that he did good and gave you from heaven rains and fruitful seasons, filling your hearts with food and gladness" (Acts 14:17). "Because that which is known of God is manifest in them; for God manifested it unto them. For the invisible things of him since the creation of the world are clearly seen, being perceived through the things that are made, even his everlasting power and divinity" (Rom. 1:19, 20). These statements are quite lucid in their view of the revealing quality of the universe per se, expressing something of God's wisdom and power.

(3) ONLY PARTIAL, NOT SUFFICIENT

This revelation of God in the natural order is only partial, for there is no unfolding of the redemptive love and saving grace of God. His power, his divinity, his majesty, and his infinite wisdom may be seen, but his love required a greater unfolding. This necessitated a Calvary. Nor is there in nature alone any suggestion as to the moral and spiritual power required for victorious and Godlike Christian living. There is a striking absence of any means offered for a spiritual renewal and an impetus to holy lives. Only elementary glimpses of God are forthcoming, for there is no unfolding of a dynamic God who stoops to redeem. With this revelation alone man would tend toward deism. Paul Tillich says, "When Paul speaks of the idolatrous perversion of a potential knowledge of God through nature, he does not challenge the nations because of their questionable arguing but because of their distortion of revelation through nature. Nature in special sections or nature as a whole can be a medium of revelation in an ecstatic experience. But nature cannot be an argumentative basis for conclusions about the mystery of being."[5] Emil Brunner states it even more directly: "Thus once man has become a sinner, the general revelation is not sufficient to enable him to know the true God. The older theology, therefore, is correct in saying that the general revelation exists, but that it has no saving significance. For sinful men it is not the revelation in the Creation which is the way to God, but only the particular, historical revelation of the Old and the New Covenant."[6]

2. REVELATION ABOVE NATURE (SUPERNATURAL REVELATION)

God has spoken to man in a direct way. He has spoken through the vertical as well as through the horizontal. He has spoken through the eternal Word of God. He reveals that as the rain ful-

---

5 Paul Tillich, *Systematic Theology*, I, 120.
6 Emil Brunner, *Revelation and Reason*, p. 75.

fills the purpose for which it is sent, "so shall my word be that goeth forth out of my mouth: it shall not return unto me void, but it shall accomplish that which I please, and it shall prosper in the thing whereto I sent it" (Isa. 55:11). This Word of God, this direct and special revelation, is borne to us in the Holy Scriptures, the record of the revelation. "The Bible tells the story of God; it narrates His deeds and the history of this God in the highest, as it takes place on earth in the human sphere. The Bible proclaims the significance and the importance of this working and acting, this story of God, and in this way it proves God's existence, describes His being and His nature. Knowledge of God in the sense of Holy Scripture . . . is knowledge of His existence, His life, His action, His revelation in His work. And so the Bible is . . . the book of God's mighty acts, in which God becomes knowable by us."[7]

William Temple maintains that without natural revelation there could be no special revelation. "We affirm, then, that unless all existence is a medium of revelation, no particular revelation is possible; for the possibility of revelation depends on the personal quality of that supreme and ultimate Reality which is God. If there is no ultimate Reality, which is the ground of all else, then there is no God to be revealed; if that Reality is not personal, there can be no special revelation, but only uniform procedure; if there be an ultimate Reality, and this is personal, then all existence is revelation. Either all occurrences are in some degree revelation of God, or else there is no such revelation at all; for the conditions of the possibility of any revelation require that there should be nothing which is not revelation. Only if God is revealed in the rising of the sun in the sky can He be revealed in the rising of a son of man from the dead; only if He is revealed in the history of Syrians and Philistines can He be revealed in the history of Israel [see Amos 9:7]; only if He chooses all men for His own can He choose any at all; only if nothing is profane can anything be sacred. It is necessary to stress with all possible emphasis this universal quality of revelation in general before going on to discuss the various modes of particular revelation; for the latter, if detached from the former, loses its root in the rational coherence of the world and consequently becomes itself a superstition and a fruitful source of superstitions. But if all existence is a revelation of God, as it must be if He is the ground of its existence, and if the God thus revealed is personal, then there is more ground in reason for expecting particular revelations than for denying them."[8]

7 Barth, *op. cit.*, p. 38.
8 William Temple, *Nature, Man and God*, pp. 306-7.

This direct and special revelation has been manifested in two phases: the preliminary and the final.

(1) PRELIMINARY REVELATION

The Old Testament is the record of the preliminary revelation. The Hebrew Old Testament is composed of three sections, all of which constitute phases of God's addressing his people: the law (or *Torah*), the prophets (or *Nebiim*) and the writings (or *Kethubim*). Yet all three lead up to the final revelation found in the Word made flesh.

The contrast between this preliminary revelation and the complete revelation is discerned in the verse: "For the law was given through Moses; grace and truth came through Jesus Christ" (John 1:17). Moses, being a man, could be but the medium through whom the law, God's revelation, could be handed down. He brought a revelation from God; Jesus not only brought a revelation, he was *the* revelation. Paul states that the law revealed unto him sin, but at the same time offered no release from the enslavement of it (Rom. 7). He states that the law is a tutor to bring us to Christ, that we might be made righteous by our faith in him. Now that we are saved by faith we no longer need the tutor (Gal. 3:24, 25). Notwithstanding the erroneous thinking of the Pharisee and scribe of Jesus' day, God never intended the law to be final, and therefore a means whereby man might be justified and saved. "The law was given to the people in covenant. It was a rule of life, not of justification; it was a guide to the man who was already right in God's esteem in virtue of his general attitude towards the covenant. The law is not to Israel a law of morals on the bare ground of human duty, apart from God's exhibition of His grace. It is a line marked out along which the life of the people or the person in covenant with God, and already right with God on that ground, is to unfold itself. No assumption of sinlessness is made, nor, indeed, is such a thing demanded. The institutions of atonement provided for the taking away of sins done through infirmity, and the law was a direction to the believer how to bear himself practically within the covenant relation."[9] The law was the earliest phase of this vertical, or direct, revelation of God to his people.

The revelation that came through the prophets is also contrasted with the final revelation of Christ. "God, having of old time spoken unto the fathers in the prophets by divers portions and in divers manners, hath at the end of these days spoken unto us in his Son" (Heb. 1:1, 2). The book of Hebrews then proceeds

[9] A. B. Davidson, *The Theology of the Old Testament*, pp. 280-1.

to show the superiority of the filial revelation over the prophetic. This prophetic revelation is constantly propounded in the Old Testament. "Yet Jehovah testified unto Israel, and unto Judah, by every prophet, and every seer, saying, Turn ye from your evil ways, and keep my commandments and my statutes, according to all the law which I commanded your fathers, and which I sent to you by my servants the prophets" (II Kings 17:13). "Thus saith Jehovah, hear the word of Jehovah!" This is the recurrent theme that confronts the reader of the prophetic books. "Jehovah appeared of old unto me, saying, Yea, I have loved thee with an everlasting love: therefore with lovingkindness have I drawn thee" (Jer. 31:3). Jesus recognizes the preliminary revelation of the prophets in his parable of the wicked husbandmen (Matt. 21:33-42), where the servants sent to the husbandmen to receive the fruits represent the prophets. Paul states that the righteousness that comes through faith in Christ has previously been "witnessed by the law and the prophets" (Rom. 3:21). Stephen quotes from the prophets in his famous defense in the seventh chapter of Acts. Philip uses Isaiah to preach Christ unto the Ethiopian treasurer.

The third section of the Hebrew Scriptures, called the writings, deals with the preliminary revelation also. The psalmist declares, "He hath made known his ways unto Moses, His doings unto the children of Israel" (103:7). God speaks in the Fiftieth Psalm, "Hear, O my people, and I will speak; O Israel, and I will testify unto thee" (50:7). When Paul wishes to prove that sin is a universal factor he quotes repeatedly from the Psalms (Rom. 3:10-18). Peter quotes from the Psalms twice in his famous Pentecostal sermon (Acts 2).

That Jesus regarded the Hebrew Scriptures as clearly anticipating his coming to earth is dramatically seen in what happened as he walked with Cleopas and his anonymous friend toward Emmaus on the very day of the resurrection. "And beginning from Moses and from all the prophets, he interpreted to them in all the scriptures the things concerning himself" (Luke 24:27). And on the day of the ascension itself Jesus said, "These are my words which I spake unto you, while I was yet with you, that all things must needs be fulfilled, which are written in the law of Moses, and the prophets, and the psalms, concerning me. Then opened he their mind, that they might understand the scriptures" (Luke 24:44, 45). The Hebrew Scriptures were to Jesus both preliminary and anticipatory. They constituted God's word to man prior to *the* revelation.

(2) FINAL REVELATION

The New Testament, especially the gospels, is the record of the final revelation. Christ is the final revelation, and by "final" is meant more than the last in a series. It means complete, fulfilling. "Christianity claims to be based on the revelation in Jesus as the Christ as the final revelation.... The word 'final' in the phrase 'final revelation' means more than 'last'.... Only if 'last' means the last 'genuine' revelation can final revelation be interpreted as the last revelation.... But final revelation means more than the last genuine revelation. It means the decisive, fulfilling, unsurpassable revelation, that which is the criterion of all others. This is the Christian claim, and this is the basis of a Christian theology."[10]

So the revelation of God in Christ is primary. He is the supreme source of religious knowledge for men. He is the apex of an ascending scale, God disclosing himself to man as man is able to grasp the truth. "But when the fulness of time came, God sent forth his Son" (Gal. 4:4). This God did that he might say to men, "Ye have heard that it was said to them of old time ... but I say unto you" (Matt. 5:21-48). The Son brought a new and greater vista. He revolted against men taking his truth and attempting to force it back into an encrusted Judaism. This is like putting a new patch on an old garment or new wine into old wineskins (Matt. 9:16, 17). "For the law was given through Moses; grace and truth came through Jesus Christ" (John 1:17). He revealed to man grace and truth in that he *was* grace and truth. He brought truth, and he *was* truth. He brought the gospel, and he *was* the gospel. He not only revealed the way; he *was* the way. He not only brought life; he *was* the life. "No man hath seen God at any time; the only begotten Son, who is in the bosom of the Father, he hath declared him" (John 1:18).

The witness of this revelation in Christ is found in the New Testament, especially in the four gospels. The New Testament documents constitute the means whereby this final revelation comes to man, becoming meaningful through the aid of the Holy Spirit. Its truth is experienced in God's saving grace, of which it testifies. The gospels tell directly of this supreme revelation in Christ, while the epistles interpret his profound teaching in terms of practical Christian living and in terms of subsequent Christian thinking.

III. OPPOSING VIEWS REGARDING REVELATION

There are certain philosophies, or world-views, which deny a revelation from God.

1. Agnostic

The agnostic does not say that God exists or does not exist. Man

10 Tillich, *op. cit.*, I, 132-3.

has no way of knowing, for God has no way of communication with man. If God does exist, he is far too transcendent to reveal himself to man. The agnostic denies the fact that man is made and constituted in his entire being for fellowship with God. In fact, the whole world is incoherent and non-unitary, with the parts non-related.

The term agnostic comes from two Greek words meaning without knowledge, hence no knowledge of God. Therefore an agnostic is not an atheist, since this term means no god. An agnostic does not categorically deny the existence of God; he merely states that it is not known whether he exists or does not exist. In fact the human mind cannot know anything beyond the natural world. That which transcends natural phenomena also transcends human knowledge. It is non-knowable. Huxley was the first to call this group "agnostics," including himself in their number. Hume was another renowned member of the group. "Hume has been called the father of modern agnosticism. He did not deny the existence of God, but asserted that we have no true knowledge of His attributes. All our ideas of Him are, and can only be, anthropomorphic. We cannot be sure that there is any reality corresponding to the attributes we ascribed to Him. His agnosticism resulted from the general principle that all knowledge is based on experience."[11] Kant, Comte, and Spencer were also in this group, the last named being the great exponent of modern scientific agnosticism.

2. PANTHEISTIC

The agnostic states that God, if he exists at all, is too transcendent to be known; the pantheist states that he is too immanent to be known. He believes that God is in all things and through all things, and therefore not above all things. He is not a personal being. He is absorbed in his own universe, of which man, being a part, is as divine as any other part. The infinity of God, or his perfection by which he is free from all limitations, is necessarily denied; for he is confined to this time-space world. He is an "eternal becoming" more than an absolute being.

With such an abnormal view of God how could there be anything distinctive in revelation? If everything is revelation, how can there be a special revelation? And to say that this revelation stems from an impersonal God is virtually to deny revelation altogether. There is no distinction between God and his finite creation. His transcendence is denied, which is contrary to Scripture in every respect. Is it not true that God's personality and God's transcendence are mutually involved? Man's personality is one of the chief

11 Berkhof, op. cit., p. 31.

elements in his being made in the image of God, and this personality can develop spiritually only in fellowship with a personal God. Yet such would demand a God who is both transcendent and immanent.

3. NATURAL RELIGION

This view holds to the position that the natural order around us, along with reason and conscience, sufficiently reveals God. Hence there is no need of a revelation above nature coming directly from God. We can infer God's existence, intelligence, and power from the works of nature. Human freedom is plainly discerned in man, along with human responsibility. Immortality is inferred from the need of a future life to adjust for all the inequalities and injustices of this life.

It is objected that such a view would be merely a philosophy, not a religion. There is no experience of fellowship with God. There is no recognition of the power of sin, of guilt, of human depravity, of divine love, or of forgiveness. Natural religion does not reveal enough of God to satisfy the need of the human heart. The love, mercy, grace, and forgiving side of God are not discerned. There is no suggestion of power for righteousness and holy living. There is too much of the element of deism, God creating the world and leaving it to run itself. "For the revelation of which the Bible speaks is always such as has place within a personal relationship. It is not the revelation of an object to the subject, but a revelation of subject to subject, a revelation of mind to mind. That is the first thing that differentiates the theological meaning of revelation, the revelation that is made to faith, from the sense in which all valid knowledge has been said to be revelation."[12]

IV. NATURE OF THE BIBLICAL REVELATION

1. GOD'S SELF-REVELATION

"Through God alone can God be known."[13] It is not only God who is revealed; God himself does the revealing. God takes the initiative toward fallen man and manifests himself in redeeming love. What man receives in revelation he could never discern through his own initiative and power. God makes himself known, and so becomes both the subject and object of revelation. Man does not discover God as he discovers truth in a scientific laboratory. Man does seek after God, but that seeking could never produce sufficient knowledge of God's nature. God produces that knowledge in the heart and mind of man. In fact the very seeking itself was instilled

12 John Baillie, *The Idea of Revelation in Recent Thought*, p. 24.
13 Emil Brunner, *The Mediator*, p. 21.

in man by God. Therefore we can say that revelation is God's work throughout; it is God-centered. Revelation is not only *from* God; it is *of* God. And this "of God" does not mean merely truth about God. It is the unveiling of his essential hiddenness. It is God entering human experience that man might feel and know his presence and power. It is the offering of himself in fellowship.

What is revealed to man is not so much information about God, unless it be that concerning his mind and purpose; it is very God himself, incarnate in Jesus Christ our Lord, who is revealed. Knowledge of God comes to man in a person, rather than in the form of a doctrine, or a creed, or an impersonal faith. Faith does not relate to the holding of correct doctrines; faith undergirds fellowship with the living God. Correct doctrine expresses this faith and issues from it; incorrect doctrine hinders and perverts it. Therefore doctrine is important, even though somewhat secondary, for what is revealed for man's apprehension is not truth concerning God but the living God himself.

Generally, in man's pursuit of knowledge he places himself above the object that he is investigating, making it respond to his searching inquiry. In revelation man is under the object of knowledge, with God disclosing that which seems good to him. Man knows God in as far as God wills to reveal. "Religion springs, therefore, from the belief that God, of whom man is dimly conscious in his own soul, reveals himself. The inward knowledge of God is confirmed and interpreted from without. It belongs to the nature of this revelation that it must be given. Man is confined to his own sphere of being, and of himself can have no conception of what lies beyond it. By no exertion of his own thought can he discover God, and God must in some way come to him. There is a barrier between the seen and the unseen which must be broken through from the other side. . . . The idea of revelation answers to an instinctive knowledge on man's part that there is a sphere of being which he cannot himself discover. God cannot be known until he is revealed."[14]

2. FOR PURPOSE OF SPIRITUAL TRANSFORMATION

Revelation is for the purpose of man's spiritual transformation, not merely his intellectual enlightenment. It is for the soul, that the soul may react to God's disclosure of himself. Revelation is dynamic, God revealing himself in mighty acts that man might be a regenerate individual. It is more than communication of truth to the human mind; it is the unleashing of transforming power. It is not God as passive, becoming known, but God as active, making

[14] E. F. Scott, *The New Testament Idea of Revelation*, pp. 16, 17.

himself known. It is more than a deepened spiritual insight of God, although this is involved; it is a mighty reaching out for man's redemption, a supernatural and purposeful act on the part of the loving God.

Wilhelm Herrmann expressed this point beautifully years ago. "Only that which rescues us from our predicament, only that which lifts us out of the forlorn condition in which we have hitherto stood, makes upon us the impression of being something utterly new, that is, of being a genuine revelation."[15] Revelation not only opens men's eyes to see their dire need; it at the same time shows them how their need can be met. Only when one sees the possibility of something higher does he see the tragic sense in life. This something higher is found in Christ, the ultimate in revelation.

3. PRODUCED ACTIVE RESPONSE

The Christian revelation produced an active response on the part of man. Jesus meant that man should discover him. At a certain stage in his ministry he asked the disciples, "But who say ye that I am?" Peter answered rightly and received the commendation of our Lord (Matt. 16:15-17). The disciples responded to his revelation in a dynamic mission and church-building movement. Paul, realizing this fact, admonishes us to work out what God has worked in us. "Work out your own salvation with fear and trembling; for it is God who worketh in you both to will and to work, for his good pleasure" (Phil. 2:12, 13). We are to let our lives respond actively to his revelation in Christ. "To listen and to obey, to be alert to whatever God may have to say to us, and then to adjust our lives to what we hear — if that be all that is required of us, we cannot surely say that it is too much to ask."[16]

God at no time mechanically dictates to a passive mind that which he wants man to know, that this passive one might hand on to others the message received while in the role of an automaton. God never bypasses human experience. The human faculties are always alert and active. The revelation becomes a part of the personality of the prophet receiving it. The message, always an urgent one, compels that it be relayed to others. Amos declares, "Surely the Lord Jehovah will do nothing, except he reveal his secret unto his servants the prophets. The lion hath roared; who will not fear? The Lord Jehovah hath spoken; who can but prophesy?" (Amos 3:7, 8). God's revelation to this great prophet compelled him to preach and proclaim this new truth, God's approaching doom upon Israel. It is the same with the supreme and final revelation in

15 Wilhelm Herrmann, *Der Begriff der Offenbarung*, p. 6.
16 Baillie, *op. cit.*, p. 135.

Christ; for a small band of eleven men, afraid and apprehensive, are changed into fearless evangelists for the kingdom of their Redeemer.

4. HISTORICALLY BASED

God's revelation came to certain individuals in a point of time and on the plane of history. Jehovah made himself known to real people in Israel regarding their individual and national responsibility, and they were vividly conscious of his presence and of his speaking to them. This is seen not only in the Psalms and in the prophets but in the New Testament as well. Jesus came in a point of time and space. God's grace broke into history. "For the grace of God hath appeared, bringing salvation to all men ..." (Titus 2: 11). All history has been divided according to this great focal point, with B.C. and A.D. dates, and rightly so. The great apostolic missionary movement was one not only in history but one that highly impressed itself upon all subsequent history. God spoke to man where man lives, in space and time.

Therefore the Bible incorporates history. "It reports events which are historical in the fullest sense, because they are laden with meaning; and these events are narrated in such a fashion as to bring out clearly the meaning which they bear. According to the unanimous view of the biblical writers, the meaning of the events resides in a meeting of man with God. It is this which gives character to the history. By this I do not mean merely that the idea of a meeting with God colours the thought of the biblical writers about events; but that the course of events itself was what it was because it bore this meaning for those who participated in it. As we have seen, it was because the prophets interpreted the history of their time in this sense that the history of succeeding centuries followed the course it did. And it was so all through the Old and New Testaments."[17]

5. EXPERIENTIALLY GIVEN

God did not bypass human experience. The writers were not automatons, recording robots functioning as machines. Israel, highly conscious of the presence and guidance of God, was vividly aware of having been selected from among other nations as a peculiarity. Every Old Testament writer displayed this consciousness of God. Abraham, Isaac, and Jacob had mighty experiences of God's direction of their lives. The great deliverance from Egypt and the catastrophic happenings at Sinai burnt deep in their minds. God hewed them with the words of the prophets and melted them

---

[17] C. H. Dodd, *The Bible Today*, pp. 99-100.

through great sufferings. The Old Testament is a record of these experiences. So it is with the New Testament. The experiences of a little band of followers of our Lord while in the presence of the "glory as of the only begotten from the Father" became the impetus of a mighty missionary impact by these courageous men. The experiences of the living God, brought to a relatively unknown Jewish rabbi on the road to Damascus, at Damascus, and in Arabia, produced the world's most famous interpreter of the teaching and redeeming activity of our Lord. The New Testament records these experiences.

The fact that the revelation of which the Bible witnesses is both historically based and experientially given is what would be expected from the revelation of a personal God to personal beings who comprehend and act in a personal manner. Personal beings have experiences; functioning robots do not. The Bible is virtually the story of the great acts of God, a record of what God has done. In the New Testament is discerned a revelation through events — events with definite dates and involving definite personal characters. God visits and meets his people, and a dynamic and personal fellowship is made possible.[18]

6. PROGRESSIVELY PRESENTED

Every leading idea presented in the Scriptures becomes clearer with the expanse of the centuries. God, revealing more and more as man is able to comprehend, is first presented as one of great power and majesty. Then his holiness is discerned, especially with Isaiah. In the New Testament he is seen as the loving God, the compassionate Father who sends his Son. At first God deals just with Israel, but then his purpose is seen to be world-wide in scope. Old Testament law, fulfilling a great intention under the old covenant, is found to be merely a "tutor to bring us unto Christ, that we might be justified by faith" (Gal. 3:24). When the appropriate time came God sent his Son, the final and complete revelation. "But when the fulness of the time came, God sent forth his Son . . ." (Gal. 4:4). Even then his truth and determination for man were so revolutionary to the status quo of the spiritually blind ecclesiastics of his day that they nailed him to a cross. Man's capacity to comprehend the revelation became the measure that determined the rate at which God could proceed.

William Temple unfolds for us this thought of progressive revelation as being part of the mark of a true revelation: "a union of holiness and power, before which our spirits bow in awe, and which

18 The student is referred to C. H. Dodd's *The Bible Today*, pp. 100-104, for a fuller discussion of the validity of prophetic experience of the Old Testament and of apostolic experience of the New Testament.

authenticates itself by continuous development to some focal point in which all preparatory revelation finds fulfillment, and from which illumination radiates into every department of life and being. Whatever claims to be revelation makes good that claim in the degree in which it approximates to the ideal thus described."[19]

With this progression in mind we can better understand some of the more difficult ideas in the Old Testament: the innocent suffering with the guilty, the imprecatory Psalms, the Old Testament law of divorce, the death penalty for infractions of the law not receiving such today, etc. It is a case of God disclosing himself to a people incapable of a more rapid moral and spiritual development. Even Jesus himself says repeatedly, "Ye have heard that it was said to them of old time . . . but I say unto you . . ." (Matt. 5: 21-48). His words bring a fuller and more complete revelation. The whole book of Hebrews is written to show that the Old Testament revelation was merely preparatory to the New. God gently led his people, putting up with their childlike infirmities and infractions until he could lead them into greater areas of moral and spiritual light. When the ripening of the divine purpose was complete, as well as the maturing of human receptiveness, Christ came. "The Old Testament teaching, therefore, even in its crudest form, had in it the germ of the gospel. It required to be purified and unfolded, but from the first it was revelation, imparted to men as they were able to bear it."[20]

A revelation in the plane of history could hardly be otherwise than progressive. The very dealing with human minds and frailties would necessitate a gradual unfolding of fresh spiritual concepts. Nor is this to say that if revelation is progressive it is one of naturalistic evolution.[21] Far from it! God must provide the conditions for man to receive this revelation. God gives and man receives, but God also conditions for the reception. "We may indicate the underlying principle of progress by the following statement: at each stage there was a communication of life and truth needed for the next higher stage; the advanced stage in turn conserved the principle of the preceding stage and contained the germ which should expand into the next higher; the lines of development all converged toward fulfillment in Jesus Christ, the crowning revelation."[22]

19 Temple, *op. cit.*, pp. 324-5.
20 Scott, *op. cit.*, p. 209.
21 See E. F. Scott's *The New Testament Idea of Revelation*, pp. 209-212, for a warning against a conception of progressive revelation as purely an evolutionary process.
22 Edgar Y. Mullins, *The Christian Religion in Its Doctrinal Expression*, p. 148.

7. Sufficient, but not Exhaustive

God's revelation is sufficient for a full, rich salvation. Nothing is lacking of all the requirements for the religious life of man. If the religious experience of a certain Christian is not satisfying in any respect, or if he feels that his relationship to God is unsatisfactory in this phase or that, the fault lies not in an inadequate disclosure on God's part. Rather, the flaw is in the misinterpretation, or non-appropriation, of the revelation on man's part. And this sufficiency of revelation lies in the realm of the spiritual only, not in the realm of science, or in the arts, or in the historical, or in the field of linguistics. It is mostly in the realm of the scientific that certain men have endeavored to exact rigid tests upon the Bible, all without reason or privilege to do so.

Yet, God's sufficient revelation does not at the same time imply an exhaustive revelation. The extreme manifold richness of his person is not utterly revealed here and now. This remains for a future hope. Paul declares, "For now we see in a mirror, darkly; but then face to face: now I know in part; but then shall I know fully even as also I was fully known" (I Cor. 13:12). The knowledge that is incomplete will be complete at some future date.

The problem of suffering serves as an example of the incomplete. Job wrestles with the question of why the righteous must suffer. Paul declares, "For I reckon that the sufferings of this present time are not worthy to be compared with the glory which shall be revealed to us-ward" (Rom. 8:18). Even the revealing of heavenly glory, though to an extent experienced now, is to be consummated at the eschaton. "For the New Testament writers the messianic age has already dawned, so that they believe the glory of God to have been already revealed to them in Jesus Christ; yet because the fullness of such revelation must await the final consummation the conception of glory always has in it this forward reference. Christian theology was afterwards to go further, drawing a formal distinction between 'the state of grace' which Christians may now enjoy and 'the state of glory' which they shall enjoy hereafter; but already in the New Testament, when the words revelation and glory occur together in the same phrase ('when his glory shall be revealed,' or 'a partaker of the glory that shall be revealed'), it is the fuller and final presence of Christ that the writer has in mind."[23]

V. WITNESS OF THE REVELATION

In itself the Bible is not the revelation, but the literary vehicle for transmitting the revelation to all men. The revelation produced

23 Baillie, *op. cit.*, p. 58.

the Bible, which thus became the witness of the revelation. Since Jesus is the supreme and final revelation, the gospels, which tell of his life and teachings and miracles, constitute the heart of the Bible. The unity and meaning of the Bible lie in Jesus, the Old Testament leading up to him and the New Testament epistles looking back and interpreting him. The book of Acts records the progress of the gospel that he brought to man. Truly, the Bible is centered in Christ; for he not only brought a revelation — he *is* the revelation.

1. DIFFERENTIATION OF TERMS

There are three terms that are frequently used relative to the Bible that need to be carefully defined and differentiated. These are revelation, illumination, and inspiration. The first named is, as has been shown, God's manifestation of himself to man. God has revealed himself, has pulled back the veil, has spoken to man in a direct way. Spiritual truth became incarnate in the eternal Word of God. Illumination is the insight into this spiritual truth, this new vista, provided by the Holy Spirit, which enables the human mind to grasp and appropriate the new concepts. Inspiration is the guidance provided by the Holy Spirit enabling the messenger to deliver or record in a trustworthy manner the spiritual truth received in revelation and illumined by the Spirit. Would it not be reasonable to expect that God, in his divine providential activity, would in some miraculous way assist the biblical writers to convey to the world the illumination which, for that world, they had received? This is what is meant by the inspiration of the Scriptures.

As will be seen, the distinction involved in these terms is a psychological one; yet their use is justifiable. The term illumination is just as applicable to the one reading the record of the revelation, God's Word, as for the one originally receiving the revelation and recording it. Yet caution must be used, for the Holy Spirit illumines the mind of the one reading the Word, not the Word itself. One should not say, "God illumined for me the passage." It is the mind that is illumined. Every Christian receives spiritual insight into God's Word, though he may not receive revelation, or inspiration. Likewise, in regard to inspiration, it should be remembered that only men can be inspired, not things. Therefore the Bible is inspired because the men who wrote it were inspired. Since the distinction in these terms is on a psychological more than a theological basis, they should not be used in too categorical a manner. There is no universal agreement as to their connotations, by any means.

2. DIVINELY INSPIRED

The Bible is divinely inspired and divinely ordained. Every Old Testament prophet claims God as the source of his words, a theme so recurrent in the prophetic messages that it assumes all the prerogatives of a law (see Num. 11:23; 20:24; Isa. 55:11; 66:2; Jer. 1:12; *et al.*). The personal life of each prophet is entwined with God and his will. Jesus has the utmost respect for the Old Testament writings, referring to them repeatedly. "Ye search the scriptures, because ye think that in them ye have eternal life; and these are they which bear witness of me; and ye will not come to me, that ye may have life" (John 5:39, 40); "I was daily with you in the temple teaching, and ye took me not: but this is done that the scriptures might be fulfilled" (Mark 14:49; see Matt. 21:42; 22:29; Luke 24:27). The apostles also claim God's direction for their lives. The presence and power of the Spirit, promised them by Jesus, is a vivid reality to each. Paul states to the Christians at Corinth, "And my speech and my preaching were not in persuasive words of wisdom, but in demonstration of the Spirit and of power: that your faith should not stand in the wisdom of men, but in the power of God" (I Cor. 2:4, 5).

The *fact* of inspiration is recorded repeatedly in the Scriptures, for every "thus saith the Lord" is an indication of it. "Now Jehovah said unto Abram...." This and countless other similar statements display the fact of inspiration. The psalmist is correct when he states, "He made known his ways unto Moses, His doings unto the children of Israel" (103:7). Yet the two greatest passages revealing the reality of the inspiration of the Scriptures are as follows. "Knowing this first, that no prophecy of scripture is of private interpretation. For no prophecy ever came by the will of man: but men spake from God, being moved by the Holy Spirit" (II Peter 1:20, 21). "Every scripture inspired of God is also profitable for teaching, for reproof, for correction, for instruction which is in righteousness..." (II Tim. 3:16). The *fact* of inspiration presents no controversy; it is the *how* that brings division of opinions. This has led to what are known as theories of inspiration, which can be reduced to about three in number.

3. THEORIES OF INSPIRATION

(1) NATURALISTIC

The naturalistic theory maintains that, since God dwells in all men, all are inspired. The degree of inspiration depends upon one's natural ability and spiritual capacity. Men such as Browning, Milton, and Shakespeare are highly inspired, according to this hypothesis. The end result of such a view is that the Bible is no more divinely inspired than any other document dealing with spiritual things. This is the extremely liberal view of inspiration.

(2) PLENARY VERBAL

This theory maintains that fully every word is selected by the Holy Spirit and dictated to the writer, the latter merely recording that given to him. The drawback of this theory is that the messenger receiving the revelation becomes only a machine, a dictaphone, so to speak. Human experience is bypassed, such as Isaiah's great transforming one in the temple recorded in the sixth chapter of his book. Also, the various styles of writing found in the Bible are not accounted for. John's style is vastly different from Paul's. Then, again, the progressive element in revelation is unexplained, God progressively revealing himself as fast as man is able to comprehend and accept the new concepts. Revelation is of necessity placed altogether on one plane. This has been the view of the Roman Catholic Church through the ages.[24]

(3) DYNAMICAL

This theory holds that the thought, rather than the individual words, is inspired, and that men are able to pronounce or write down the thought, or record their experience or revelation, in a trustworthy manner. This is all accomplished through the aid of the Spirit, and therefore is inspired of God.

The virtue of such a view is that it does not bypass human experience. Peter had a tremendous spiritual experience on the Mount of Transfiguration, and this experience shines forth as he recounts it in his second epistle. "For he received from God the Father honor and glory, when there was borne such a voice to him by the Majestic Glory, This is my beloved Son, in whom I am well pleased: and this voice we ourselves heard borne out of heaven, when we were with him in the holy mount" (II Pet. 1:17, 18). Peter records for us with great feeling this tremendous display of God's glory. This theory also accounts for the various styles of writing in the biblical documents and for the idea of progressive revelation. It accords most nearly with all the data at hand.

A word of caution is in order, however, relative to such theories. They are psychological in nature, rather than scriptural; for very few, if any, biblical passages can be adduced in behalf of any one. There may be elements of truth in each; but they attempt to do the impossible. It is not in our power to grasp the means whereby God's Spirit operated in the human mind to provide a record of the revelation received. The circumstances under which the biblical

---

[24] See John Baillie's *The Idea of Revelation in Recent Thought*, pp. 111-3, for a fuller discussion of this view and the Roman Church.

writers recorded their experiences present great varieties. The men possessed varied talents and gifts, which in turn would entail varied styles of writing. Their aims were also diverse, some presenting only historical material and others giving theological interpretations. All these factors make the matter of constructing a theory of inspiration an extremely difficult one.

4. AUTHORITATIVENESS

God speaks authoritatively in the Scriptures; therefore the Bible is the book of authority for Christians. It is a vital, living authority, not a mechanical one. It is the authority for the revelation of God in Christ, final in all matters of Christian belief and practical living. It is the objective truth that saves the Christian from subjectivism.

This authoritativeness is in the realm of the spiritual. It is relative to the purpose for which it was written, the proclaiming of an animating hope to a hope-bereft world. It does not claim to be authoritative in the realm of science, and an endeavor to make it a corroborant of the exacting results of modern scientific investigation is to do it violence.

As one reads the Bible he feels this authority; he is aware that it is God speaking directly to him, decisively, demanding a response. This authority hunts man out and exposes him, making him realize his devastating plight. God does not merely offer words of advice; his every declaration is fraught with an urgency and a moral imperative. He is a God of holiness demanding holy living in his creatures. If God is to speak at all to sinful man he must speak conclusively, for his words deal with eternity and human destiny. His great divine imperative demands a response.

Karl Barth states in his *The Word of God and the Word of Man,* "It is not the right human thoughts about God which form the content of the Bible, but the right divine thoughts about men. The Bible tells us not how we should talk with God but what he says to us; not how we find the way to him, but how he has sought and found the way to us; not the right relation in which we must place ourselves to him, but the covenant which he has made with all who are Abraham's spiritual children and which he has sealed once and for all in Jesus Christ. It is this which is written in the Bible. The word of God is within the Bible."[25]

---

25 Karl Barth, *The Word of God and the Word of Man,* p. 43. The reader is also referred to C. H. Dodd's *The Authority of the Bible* for a fuller discussion of this subject.

33

OUTLINE FOR CHAPTER TWO

I. Natural Attributes of God
  1. Pertaining to his essence
    (1) Spirituality
      a. Meaning of the term as applied to God
      b. Reasons for affirming the spirituality of God
      c. Difficulties in thinking of God as Spirit
    (2) Personality
      a. Meaning of the term as applied to God
      b. Correctness of the term as applied to God
      c. Reasons for affirming the personality of God
    (3) Life
      a. Meaning of the term as applied to God
      b. Scriptural evidence
  2. Pertaining to his infinity
    (1) Absoluteness
    (2) Supremacy
    (3) Self-existence
    (4) Immutability
    (5) Unity
    (6) Perfection
    (7) Eternity
    (8) Immensity
  3. Pertaining to his creation
    (1) Omnipresence of God
      a. It is essential
      b. It is whole
      c. It is by choice
      d. Scriptural evidence
    (2) Omniscience of God
      a. It is seen in related truths
      b. It is immediate
      c. It is distinct
      d. It is not limited by time
      e. It is not limited by space
      f. It embraces the possible as well as the actual
      g. It does not embrace the absurd
      h. It does not violate the free will of man
      i. Scriptural evidence
    (3) Omnipotence of God
      a. It does not include the self-contradictory

       b. It does not include that which is contradictory to the nature of God

       c. It does not interfere with the freedom of man

       d. It is not violated by self-limitation on the part of God

       e. It does not imply the use of all the power of God

       f. Scriptural evidence

II. Moral Attributes of God

  1. Holiness

     (1) In Old Testament

     (2) In New Testament

     (3) Inclusive of other attributes

       a. Ground of righteousness

       b. Ground of love

       c. Ground of truth

  2. Righteousness

     (1) Meaning of term

     (2) Manifestations of God's righteousness

       a. Mandatory

          (a) In conscience

          (b) In Mosaic law

          (c) In revelation of Christ

          (d) In character of Christ

       b. Condemnatory

       c. Redemptive

  3. Love

     (1) Is grounded in nature of God

     (2) Shows rational and voluntary affection

     (3) Desires the best for its object

     (4) Manifests itself in regard to righteousness

     (5) Acts in behalf of its object

     (6) Seeks the love of its object

     (7) Expresses itself in various ways

     (8) Includes all mankind

  4. Truth

     (1) God not only knows truth, but is the truth

     (2) God's truth is the ground of man's truth

     (3) God as truth constitutes the ground and guarantee of revelation

III. Works of God

  1. Creation

     (1) Meaning of term

     (2) Biblical doctrine of creation

     (3) False philosophical views of creation

       a. Dualism theory

       b. Emanation theory

       c. Eternal creation theory

       d. Spontaneous generation theory

  2. Preservation

     (1) Meaning of term

(2) Theories denying the doctrine of preservation
  a. Deism
  b. Continuous creation
3. Providence
  (1) Meaning of term
  (2) Theories denying the doctrine of providence
    a. Totalism
    b. Casualism
    c. General providence only
4. Redemption

CHAPTER TWO

THE NATURE OF GOD

IN THE CHAPTER ON REVELATION WE SAW THAT GOD HAS REVEALED himself to man, and that in various ways and through a period of time, coming to the complete and final revelation in his Son Christ Jesus. "God, having of old time spoken unto the fathers in the prophets by divers portions and in divers manners, hath at the end of these days spoken unto us in his Son" (Heb. 1:1, 2). Let us look at the nature of God as he is revealed to us.

First, however, let us look at a non-biblical term which we must of necessity use (or else use its cognate): attributes. We speak of the attributes of God, meaning qualities, characteristics, or principles of God. They are the distinguishing characteristics that give rise to our total idea of God, qualities grounded in his revelation of himself to man. They cannot be separated from his essence or nature; yet they do not, in and of themselves, constitute that essence or nature. They exist because of that nature and are grounded in it. We must not think of God as sitting in heaven with attributes hanging from him. Yet there is another danger lurking here. Not only must the divine attributes not be separated from the divine nature because of being grounded in that nature; they must not be conceived as being apart from the essence of God, due to the danger of making them parts of a composite God. This would amount to thinking of God as a compound of attributes, thus making him divisible and changeable, which is exactly what happened in Greek mythology.

The attributes are so named because we must attribute them to God as fundamental faculties or qualities of his being. They help to give a rational account of God's self-revelation. We know God as he reveals to us his attributes, and we determine his attributes through his works and his words.

The attributes of God have been classified in various ways: communicable and incommunicable, relative and absolute, transient and immanent, positive and negative, and natural and moral. We will use the fifth method: natural and moral. By natural we mean the mode or manner of his existence; by moral we mean the qualities of his character.

DOCTRINES OF THE CHRISTIAN RELIGION

I. NATURAL ATTRIBUTES OF GOD

1. PERTAINING TO HIS ESSENCE

The natural attributes that pertain to the essence or being of God are three in number: spirituality, personality, and life. In fact, God may be defined, briefly, as the living personal Spirit.

(1) SPIRITUALITY

a. *Meaning of the term as applied to God*

God is Spirit. He is not matter, but is independent of matter. Matter is dependent upon him, being created by him. God is described in the Scriptures as having hands, feet, arms, eyes, mouth, etc. We call these "anthropomorphic" (from two Greek words meaning form of man) expressions of God. They are merely concepts designed to set forth vividly the activities of God, and in no way do they contradict or oppose his spirituality.

b. *Reasons for affirming the spirituality of God*

(a) The Scriptures teach it. Jesus said to the Samaritan woman at the well, "God is a Spirit: and they that worship him must worship in spirit and truth" (John 4:24). The marginal reading is "God is spirit." This latter reading is the way it should probably be translated, since there is no indefinite article in the Greek. The English article must be used or omitted as the sense dictates. Here the sense seems to imply its omission, since John means to say that God is Spirit, Spirit forming the essence of his being. He is not merely saying that God is a spiritual being. Therefore "God is Spirit" is the preferred rendering. At any rate this is the most famous passage on the spirituality of God in all the Scriptures. Paul in Romans also talks about "the invisible things of him" (1:20).

(b) Christian experience affirms it. Our spirits know and have fellowship with God as Spirit. This is the way we have experienced him in our lives. He came convicting, he came regenerating, he came sanctifying. In each of these incidents the Spirit of God was the controlling factor.

(c) Our own higher nature is spirit. Therefore God must be Spirit also, for the Creator is always greater than the created one.

c. *Difficulties in thinking of God as Spirit*

(a) The first phase of the difficulty is a theological one, for the Bible uses anthropomorphic expressions for representing God. It talks of his hands, feet, etc. Therefore we tend to think of God in terms of the materialistic, that which we can see, hear, and feel. Yet we must remember that God would have no other way to reveal himself to us except in human terms, readily conceivable by us.

(b) The second phase of the difficulty is a psychological one, for it is hard for the human mind to think abstractly. If we were to endeavor to think of God as pure Spirit he would fade off into nothingness in our minds. We must think in terms of that which we have seen or heard or felt. This was precisely Philip's difficulty when he said to Jesus, "Lord, show us the Father, and it sufficeth us" (John 14:8). It was hard for him to conceive of the spiritual God Jesus was revealing to the world. Yet at the same time Christ, God incarnate, is the very answer to this difficulty. "He that hath seen me hath seen the Father" (John 14:9).

(2) PERSONALITY

a. *Meaning of the term as applied to God*

What constitutes personality? What is necessary for one to be a person, a personal being? The word person asserts self-consciousness and self-determination. A person is a self-conscious and a self-determining being. Self-consciousness is the awareness of the self among other selves. It is the ability to look at one's self objectively, to make himself the object of thought. It is the ability to say "I am" as over against all other persons or forms of reality. It is the ability to recognize one's self as the subject of all the experiences of that self and to distinguish between the self and the experiences. The brute is conscious, but man is both conscious and self-conscious. The brute cannot objectify himself.

The second mark of personality is self-determination. It is the ability to give direction to all the activities of the self as that self lives among other beings. There are certain influences from without, but the determining factor for shaping that life is from within. It is the power to look ahead and determine a course of action. It is the power to choose an end and then to direct all energies toward achieving that end.

b. *Correctness of the term as applied to God*

With these two characteristics of personality in mind, can the term person be applied to God? Is it inadequate and misleading, implying limitation? There may be an element of truth here, but when this word asserts that God is self-conscious and self-determining it is satisfactory. There is no better word to take its place. More can certainly be said of God, but this word is true as far as it goes. It is not false.

The truth is that complete personality resides in God alone, for he is the only personality fully possessing these dual characteristics. Man is rudimentary and imperfect in these two respects. His personality is growing, becoming more self-conscious and self-determining. We are compelled to define personality in regard to ourselves, but when we do so we see that only God himself is a complete and perfect person. Man only knows and understands himself partially and can determine and fulfill his ends and purposes only partially. He is limited by his environment and by his natural abilities. However, God is complete in both these factors. He knows himself perfectly in relation to all things and is absolutely self-determining. He is dependent on nothing outside himself for what he is or does. Pantheism denies the personality of God. It says that God is the universe and the universe is God. This would eliminate self-consciousness and self-determination.

c. *Reasons for affirming the personality of God*

(a) It is inferred from the personality of man. Man's personality calls for the personality of God. God would definitely not be subordinate to created man in his qualities. Personality is the highest form of being of which we know; we attribute therefore to God this perfection of being.

(b) It is inferred from the religious life of man. Wherever man is found he is seen to be a religious person. If God is not a person the essential elements in religion would be meaningless. Every valuable thing in religion is based on the conception of God as personal. Repentance, faith, prayer, confession of sin — all point to God as personal.

(c) The Old Testament pictures God in a very personal manner. This is discerned as God speaks to Adam and Eve, to Noah, to Abraham, and to the patriarchs. It is vividly portrayed in the closeness of God to the great prophets. "And God said unto Moses, I AM THAT I AM: and he said, Thus shalt thou say unto the children of Israel, I AM hath sent me unto you" (Exod. 3:14). God did not say "It is" or "I was," but "I am," implying both personality and presence.

(d) Christ reveals God as personal. Jesus addresses his Father in the closest terms — "my Father." He looks to heaven to pray and begins with "Father." He tells Mary, "I ascend unto my Father and your Father, and my God and your God" (John 20:17). Jesus presents the Father as one with tender affection, watching over and caring for his children. Every quality that Jesus emphasized in his revelation of God is a personal quality. Love is deeply personal. Righteousness is a personal characteristic. An inanimate object, or an impersonal force, cannot love or display righteousness.

(e) Christian experience portrays God as personal. The sinner is convicted of sinning against a personal God. He repents to a personal God and expresses faith in a personal God. This same personal God regenerates and saves him, thus bringing fellowship with God in the most personal terms. God's personality is as real to the saved one as that of the man with whom he daily works.

(3) LIFE

a. *Meaning of the term as applied to God*

Life is hard to define; we know it in ourselves, yet it eludes any formal statement of signification. Life in God is not mere process, without a subject. This would entail a divine life with no God to live it. Nor is life in God a mere correspondence with an outward environment. This would entail the impossibility of God's being alive before he created the universe. Life is mental energy. Life is the energy of intellect, emotion, and volition. It is the activity of mind, heart, and will. It implies vigor, reality, intensity. It implies movement, action, motives, communication. It involves action and reaction. God is the living God, for there is within his own being a source of being and activity for himself and others. He is self-existent. He is in contrast to the gods that have no life (Jer. 10:6-11). If man's spirit implies life, God's Spirit implies an inexhaustible life, an endless, ever-abiding life.

b. *Scriptural evidence*

The Scriptures tell of a living God. After pouring ridicule on idols made of gold and silver, Jeremiah states, "But Jehovah is the true God; he is the living God, and an everlasting King" (10:10). Paul commends the Thessalonians because they "turned unto God from idols, to serve a living and true God" (I Thess. 1:9). Jesus states, "For as the Father hath life in himself, even so gave he to the Son also to have life in himself" (John 5:26). In another revealing statement Jesus talks of "the living Father" who sent him (John 6:57). Jesus could say, "I am . . . the life," because he was God in the flesh come to offer that life to man.

2. PERTAINING TO HIS INFINITY

By the infinity of God is meant that he knows no bounds or limits. It refers to the unlimited fulness of his being. His nature or essence is not lacking in any one quality. He is not limited by the universe, nor confined to the universe; for he is infinite, while the universe is finite. Relative to the universe he is both transcendent and immanent. There is an unlimited resource to his being. The infinity of God involves many factors.

DOCTRINES OF THE CHRISTIAN RELIGION

(1) ABSOLUTENESS

The absoluteness of God indicates that he is not dependent on anything outside himself. He is independent of the universe, for his relations to the universe are not necessary from his side. The world is dependent upon God, but God is not dependent upon the world. God's relations to the world are due to choice on his part, which is just the opposite to what is found in pantheism. In pantheism God is necessarily related to the world; for God is the world and the world is God. Take away the world and you take away God. In deism, which maintains that God is transcendent but not immanent and that there has been no revelation, God is unrelated to the world. Therefore deism is the exact opposite of pantheism. In deism the absoluteness of God is retained, but with the added heretical beliefs of no immanence and no revelation. In pantheism he is necessarily related to the world; in deism he is unrelated; in Christian theism he is related but not necessarily so.

(2) SUPREMACY

By the supremacy of God is meant that there is no power greater or higher than he. There is no one over him. Man cannot conceive of a being superior to God. What God wills happens. What he decrees takes place. What he wishes is fulfilled. Infinity can be shared by no other being; it can belong to only one being.

The supremacy of God was the startling factor in God's revelation of himself to the patriarchs. The prevailing idea in the minds of the people of that day was that of national gods; the god or gods of a nation reigned to the borders of that nation and no further. But the God of Abraham, Isaac, Jacob, and Moses was an international God — more, he reigned supreme over all the universe! It took ten plagues, the last a devastating one, to make Pharaoh in Egypt realize this. In fact these plagues simultaneously impressed this startling fact upon the minds of the Hebrews. Pharaoh said, "Who is Jehovah, that I should hearken unto his voice to let Israel go? I know not Jehovah, and moreover I will not let Israel go" (Exod. 5:2). He was arrogantly stating that he owed no allegiance to the God of the Hebrews. He had his own Egyptian gods down in Egypt. What was the God of the Hebrews doing down in Egypt telling him what to do? The idea of one supreme God was startlingly new in a time of polytheism, and provincial polytheism at that.

Therefore the supremacy of God does not countenance polytheism or idolatry. Since he is supreme he demands complete allegiance. Read Isaiah 40:12ff. to see the contrast between the one supreme God and vain idols, dead and helpless things. Jehovah is the supreme God, for there is no measuring of his wisdom and power. He satisfies; idols do not!

(3) SELF-EXISTENCE

God exists in and of himself. He himself is the source of his being. We have the ground of our existence outside of ourselves; God has the ground of his existence within himself. God is dependent on no one else for his existence, thus making this idea of God run parallel to that of absoluteness and supremacy.

The very name "I AM THAT I AM" (Exod. 3:14), which God gave for himself to be used of Moses in his great mission, implies self-existence. He is the "I AM" God, the God who exists in and of himself. Yet when we say that God is the cause of his own existence we do not attribute to him beginning of existence. This would imply that at some time he was not, which is not true. We are saying that the ground of his existence is not outside himself. Rather, he is the living source of all energy and all being. Nor are we saying that God willed himself into existence, for this would imply the same false conclusion, that there was a time he was not. His existence is grounded in his nature, for it is his very nature to be.

(4) IMMUTABILITY

When we say that God is immutable we are referring to his unchangeable nature. The essence of his being does not change. His attributes do not change. His will and desire do not change. This does not mean immobility or inactivity, for God is not unchangeable as a stone is unchangeable. A stone has no inner experience, is not active. This also does not mean that God cannot make free choices, for God must make choices in conformity with the changing moods and morals of man. This also does not mean that God cannot vary his method in carrying out his purposes and plans. He may be forced to alter a course due to man's vicissitudes. This also does not mean that God has no feeling in regard to our suffering and indignation in regard to our sins. Instead, immutability refers to the self-consistency that pervades all that God is or does. He is changeless in all the great attributes and powers.

Reason itself teaches no change in God. There can be no increase or decrease in God, no expansion or contraction, no development or retrogression. Any change would have to be for better or for worse. But God is perfection already, so it could not be for better. And change to worse would definitely not be consistent with perfection. In addition to this reasoning is the added verity that no cause for change exists. Why would God have to change?

Also, the Scriptures teach no change in God. The psalmist

speaks of the fact that God shall change the heavens and the earth, but of God himself he says, "But thou art the same, And thy years shall have no end" (102:27). "For I, Jehovah, change not" (Mal. 3:6). James speaks of "the Father of lights, with whom can be no variation" (1:17).

There are certain scriptural passages which at first sight might seem to denote change in God, but which, when examined closely, do not do so. In Genesis 6:6 we read, "It repented Jehovah that he had made man." This must be interpreted in the light of Numbers 23:19, "God is not a man, that he should lie, Neither the son of man, that he should repent." God's holiness does not change. Therefore when the moral conditions of man change, God must alter his treatment of man. But this is man's changing, not God's. God's dealings with man must alter simply because God himself is unchangeable. And this change in treatment is stated in an anthropomorphic manner. Likewise God's love does not change, for that love will adapt itself to the varying conditions of man. God at times may *seem* to change; but we are the ones who really change, not God.

(5) UNITY

By the unity of God is meant that God is one. It is the same idea that is expressed by the term monotheism, a word derived from the Greek, meaning one god. It is set over against polytheism (many gods). If God is infinite he is one; so this term, as in the case of the ones previously discussed, denotes an attribute inclusive of his infinity.

The most famous passage on the unity of God is found in the book of Deuteronomy. "Hear, O Israel: Jehovah our God is one Jehovah: and thou shalt love Jehovah thy God with all thy heart, and with all thy soul, and with all thy might" (6:4, 5). Because God is one he claims the entire love of Israel. "Unto thee it was showed, that thou mightest know that Jehovah he is God; there is none else besides him" (Deut. 4:35). "Thus saith Jehovah, the King of Israel, and his Redeemer, Jehovah of hosts: I am the first, and I am the last; and besides me there is no God" (Isa. 44:6).

So much for the passages from the Old Testament, for it is apparent that the unity of God is one of the greatest characteristics of Hebrew thought. It presented such a contrast to the highly polytheistic tendency of the neighboring ancient nations. Yet, the New Testament view of God presents his unity just as strongly as the Old Testament. The unity of God is not inconsistent with the doctrine of the Trinity, as will be discussed more fully later. The doctrine of the Trinity holds to personal distinctions within the *one* being of God. There are manifested three persons in the one Godhead. Jesus' teaching portrays this fact beautifully, for he quotes Deuteronomy 6:4, 5 in presenting his conception of the great commandment. "Jesus answered, The first is, Hear, O Israel; The Lord our God, the Lord is one: and thou shalt love the Lord thy God with all thy heart, and with all thy soul, and with all thy mind, and with all thy strength" (Mark 12:29, 30). So to Jesus God is one; he is a unity. Further statements in the New Testament augment this view. Jesus speaks of "the glory that cometh from the only God" (John 5:44). He also speaks of "the only true God" (John 17:3). Paul says, "There is no God but one" (I Cor. 8:4); and he also speaks of "the only God" (I Tim. 1:17). Therefore it is plainly discerned that Christianity is as monotheistic as Judaism, for the doctrine of the Trinity must not be viewed in such a way as to denote tritheism. Paul, Peter, and James did not have to depart from the belief in the unity of God when they declared their belief in the deity of Christ. They were still monotheists. The monotheism of God does not demand that he be unipersonal also. The ancient Athanasian Creed states: "We worship one God in Trinity, and Trinity in Unity; neither confounding the persons, nor dividing the substance." It is perfectly possible for God to be tripersonal and at the same time maintain his unity, disturbing as this may be to the Jews, ancient and modern.

This unity may be viewed from two angles. By unity we mean that there are no other gods besides the one infinite and perfect God. (This is denoted by the Latin word *unicus*.) By unity we also mean that God is not divided into many gods. He is undivided and indivisible. (This is denoted by the Latin word *unus*.) In regard to the former, polytheism and idolatry are knocked out. In regard to the latter, the attributes of God must not be construed in such a way as to lead to a composite God, nor must the Trinity be construed in such a way as to lead to tritheism.

(6) PERFECTION

The perfection of God relates to his qualitative excellence. His attributes are not lacking in any respect. His ways and activities with men are perfect, thereby presupposing moral perfection on his part. His intellect, affection, and will are fully complete. "Ye therefore shall be perfect, as your heavenly Father is perfect" (Matt. 5:48). Paul admonishes us so to act as to reveal the "perfect will of God" (Rom. 12:2). He also desires "that we may present every man perfect in Christ" (Col. 1:28). "As for God, his way is perfect" (Ps. 18:30). The word perfect as found in the New Testament translates a Greek word meaning complete, mature. Since

God's nature is thus, it behooves us to strive to be complete, mature also.

(7) ETERNITY

This term denotes that God transcends all limitations of time. God has no beginning or end. He is free from the succession of time, being the cause of the phenomenon we call time. God is eternal. There is no time that he has not been and no time that he will never be. When God calls himself the "I AM" God, he uses a name involving eternity (Exod. 3:14). "For I lift up my hand to heaven, And say, As I live for ever . . ." (Deut. 32:40). "Even from everlasting to everlasting, thou art God" (Ps. 90:2). "But thou art the same, And thy years shall have no end" (Ps. 102:27). "Now unto the King eternal, immortal, invisible, the only God, be honor and glory for ever and ever. Amen" (I Tim. 1:17). Jude's benediction, like that of Paul, ascribes to God "glory, majesty, dominion and power, before all time, and now, and for evermore" (Jude 25).

The eternity of God is a phase of his infinity, for it is his infinity in relation to time. God is not in time, and time is not in God. God is not under the law of time, is not conditioned by it. It came into existence from God. "God is above space and time, and we are in God. We mark the passage of time, and we write our histories. But we can do this, only because in our highest being we do not belong to space and time, but have in us a bit of eternity. . . . We belong to God; we are akin to God; and while the world passes away and the lust thereof, he that doeth the will of God abideth forever."[1] Yet we are not saying that time, as it was created by God, is not an objective reality to God. He sees it — past, present, and future — as one eternal now.

(8) IMMENSITY

This term is used to mean that God transcends all limitations of space. It is the correlative to the eternity of God, and much that was said in the previous discussion applies here. God's nature is without extension. He is not conditioned by the limitations of space. Rather, he is the cause of what is termed space. "Behold, heaven and the heaven of heavens cannot contain thee," Solomon says of God; therefore how can this temple contain him (I Kings 8:27)? The immensity of God is a phase of his infinity, for it is his infinity in relation to space. God is not in space, and space is not in God. Just as God is not subject to the law of time, he is not subject to the law of space; for he created it as well as time. With creation time began, and with creation space began. Yet, as with

---

[1] Augustus H. Strong, *Historical Discourse.*

time also, space is an objective reality to God. He sees it and recognizes it. Time and space are relations, and God sees them as such.

3. Pertaining to his creation

The universe is God's creation. Now what are the attributes of God in relation to that creation, those that exist because of that creation? These are three in number: omnipresence, omniscience, and omnipotence.

(1) Omnipresence of God

The omnipresence of God has reference to his presence in the temporal and spatial order, meaning that he is present at all points of time and space. God, in the totality of his being, penetrates the universe in all its parts, and this without being extended to do so, or expanded to do so. He does not have to be multiplied or divided to do so. He is not conditioned by time or space; rather, they are subject to him, having come into being at the time of creation.

It is to be noted that the term omnipresence is one that is used relative to creation. Eternity and immensity are terms used of God per se, not in relation to creation. God possesses the attributes of eternity and immensity prior to his creation of the universe, and still possesses them. They are much more inclusive terms than the term omnipresence, for the latter term is always used relative to the created order.

a. *It is essential*

Socinus had the heretical belief that God's essence is in heaven and that only his power is present on earth. This would be to say that God is potentially present on earth, but not essentially. This view is to be rejected. It is true that we read, "O thou that sitteth in the heavens" (Ps. 123:1), and "That hath his seat on high" (Ps. 113:5). But these words merely show his exaltation above earthly things. They merely tell us that the most glorious manifestation of himself is to the heavenly hosts and do not necessarily imply that he is present on earth only as a power. This latter would be deism.

b. *It is whole*

Likewise, God is wholly present in every part of his universe. There is no difference in God for this part or that part. The true essence of God is present in every part.

> *Though God extends beyond Creation's rim,*
> *Each smallest atom holds the whole of him.*
> —Alger, *Poetry of the Orient*

c. *It is by choice*

Also, God is present throughout his universe by choice, not by compulsion. He is there by free will, not because of necessity. The latter would be pantheism; for in pantheism God is bound to the universe by necessity, since it is claimed that God is the universe.

d. *Scriptural evidence*

The Scriptures are replete with the fact of the omnipresence of God. "Whither shall I go from thy Spirit? Or whither shall I flee from the presènce? If I ascend up into heaven, thou art there: If I make my bed in Sheol, behold, thou are there. If I take the wings of the morning, And dwell in the uttermost parts of the sea; Even there shall thy hand lead me, And thy right hand shall hold me" (Ps. 139:7-10). "Am I a God at hand, saith Jehovah, and not a God afar off? Can any hide himself in secret places so that I shall not see him? saith Jehovah. Do not I fill heaven and earth? saith Jehovah" (Jer. 23:23, 24). "He is not far from each one of us: for in him we live, and move, and have our being" (Acts 17:27, 28); so Paul informed the people of Athens. And Jesus promised his disciples to be with them "always, even unto the end of the world" (Matt. 28:20). The omnipresence of the spiritual Jesus would demonstrate the omnipresence of God.

(2) OMNISCIENCE OF GOD

The omniscience of God refers to his knowledge of the world order. He has a perfect and eternal knowledge of all things. Everything that is an object of knowledge is known by him. Both the actual and the possible are known by him. Past, present, and future are known by him. Nothing is hid from him.

a. *It is seen in related truths*

The omniscience of God is seen in prophecy. The "thus saith the Lord" of the prophets is grounded in the all-knowing of God. It is seen in his omnipresence, for an all-present God would necessarily be an all-knowing God. It is seen in creation, for if God created all he knows all. It is seen in his attribute of truth, to be discussed later.

b. *It is immediate*

The omniscience of God does not come through reasoning, through inference, through the senses, through imagination, or through induction or deduction. His knowledge is direct, for all the forces that operate in his universe are grounded in his will. The whole system of causes and effects is so grounded.

c. *It is distinct*

God's knowledge is not vague or confused or mixed up. It is sharp and distinct, true to the reality of things. It is not partial, or shrouded or distorted.

d. *It is not limited by time*

It is eternal. Past, present, and future come within its scope. They are discerned as one moment, one timeless act, in God's mind. The temporal order is real to God, for the historical order is grounded in the mind and will of God. He knows it as a whole; it is a unity in his mind. He is working out his purpose in the world order with complete control.

e. *It is not limited by space*

God knows what is taking place in every part of his created order. There is no spot, no place, no clime that is exempt from his knowledge. The spatial order is grounded in his mind and will; therefore his knowledge of it naturally follows.

f. *It embraces the possible as well as the actual*

God knows all the possibilities that exist. He knows what would have taken place under a completely different set of circumstances and environment. He knows what our lives would have been had we made other choices. He knows what would have been had he made his creation entirely different. He knows the universe as it actually exists and as he ideally would have it exist.

g. *It does not embrace the absurd*

God's knowledge does not embrace the absurd, the impossible, the self-contradictory. What would happen if a non-stoppable object came into contact with an immovable wall? There is no answer to such an absurdity.

h. *It does not violate the free will of man*

God foresees all the acts of men. He knows every choice that will be made and what will be the result of that choice. God's knowledge extends to the contingent events of the future, though many men in the past would disagree. God foreknows the motive, the choice, and the result; yet man is absolutely free to choose, for he is not coerced in doing so. This is the biblical view, for it follows from two well-known certainties: first, God knows all things, past, present, and future, and second, man is a free moral agent. Neither of these ideas can be dismissed, or violated. In fact they exist side by side. This may be hard to comprehend, but we must remember that its reality does not depend upon our understanding.

i. *Scriptural evidence*

"And there is no creature that is not manifest in his sight: but all things are naked and laid open before the eyes of him with whom we have to do" (Heb. 4:13). Paul exclaims, "O the depth of the riches both of the wisdom and the knowledge of God" (Rom. 11:33). In speaking of the knowledge of God the psalmist remarks, "Such knowledge is too wonderful for me" (139:6). Not a sparrow "shall fall on the ground without your Father: but the very hairs of your head are all numbered" (Matt. 10:29, 30).

(3) OMNIPOTENCE OF GOD

By this is meant the power of God to do anything that power can accomplish. He is all-powerful. All the power of the universe, whether physical or spiritual, has its source in God.

a. *It does not include the self-contradictory*

God cannot make a past event not to have occurred. God cannot draw a shorter line between two points than a straight line. God cannot make two and two equal five. He cannot make two mountains without a valley between. God ordained it this way; if it is a limitation it is a self-limitation. His very power is seen in the fact he planned it and executed it in this manner.

b. *It does not include that which is contradictory to the nature of God*

God cannot lie. God cannot sin. He cannot make wrong to be right. To do any of these things would be inconsistent with the moral nature of God. They would not reveal power, but the lack of it. God has all the power to do that which is consistent with his nature.

c. *It does not interfere with the freedom of man*

The fact that God has all power does not mean that man has no power. The absolute supremacy of God and the freedom of man run parallel in the Scriptures, with no thought of contradiction in the mind of the biblical writers. In fact, since the freedom of man is grounded in the will of God, and since all man's power is derived from God, man's freedom and power are manifestations, rather than contradictions, of God's power. For it must be remembered that the power God displays is a moral power, not one of sheer force. God gave man his freedom; he will not deprive him of it.

d. *It is not violated by self-limitation on the part of God*

God's power includes, not excludes, self-limitation. Such limitation is free; he may or may not employ it in his dealings with man. He is not compelled by any reason within or without himself to resort to it. Therefore it is the manifestation of his power. This self-limitation is supremely seen in the incarnation, at which time God the Son humbled himself by taking the form of human flesh. The pre-existent glory was laid aside for the limitations of the flesh. He "emptied himself" and he "humbled himself" (Phil. 2:7, 8).

e. It does not imply the use of all the power of God

His power is controlled by his will, a will that acts in accordance with his holiness and his love. He used the power that he wills at that particular time, holding in reserve all the power that he could possibly need. He is in control of that power and is not a slave of it. If necessary he "is able of these stones to raise up children unto Abraham" (Matt. 3:9), but he does not. He is able to send twelve legions of angels to Jesus, but he does not (Matt. 26:53).

f. Scriptural evidence

"I am God Almighty" (Gen. 17:1). God said, "Let there be light: and there was light" (Gen. 1:3). Paul rejoices in the "exceeding greatness of his power to us-ward who believe" (Eph. 1:19). God "giveth life to the dead, and calleth the things that are not, as though they were" (Rom. 4:17). God in his infinite knowledge "worketh all things after the counsel of his will" (Eph. 1:11). The gospel is the great evidence of his power, "for it is the power of God unto salvation" (Rom. 1:16). The Greek word translated "power" is the one from which we derive the words dynamite, dynamic, dynamo, etc. "But from henceforth shall the Son of man be seated at the right hand of the power of God" (Luke 22:69). "He hath done whatsoever he pleased" (Ps. 115:3).

II. MORAL ATTRIBUTES OF GOD

God is a moral being. In fact this constitutes the magnitude of his person to a greater extent than the natural characteristics previously discussed. This fact is easily discerned when we remember that the final and complete revelation of God is made in Christ. Nature reveals God, but not fully; the complete revelation comes through the incarnation and the atonement. Christ is the image of the invisible God.

The moral attributes of God to be discussed are holiness, righteousness, love, and truth.

DOCTRINES OF THE CHRISTIAN RELIGION

1. HOLINESS

Holiness has been rightly termed the fundamental attribute of God. It is the characteristic of God that undergirds all else, the most inclusive of the attributes.

(1) IN OLD TESTAMENT

If we are to secure a true view of holiness we must see the idea unfold throughout the Hebrew Scriptures. We are not certain as to the root meaning of the Hebrew word translated "holy," but the most accepted view is that it comes from a root verb meaning to cut off, to separate, to exalt. At no place in the book of Genesis is God termed holy; this idea does not appear until the book of Exodus, but in Exodus it is unfolded clearly. The first time God is revealed as holy is at the redemption of Israel from Egypt, where Moses in his song of praise calls God "glorious in holiness" (Exod. 15:11). Then, immediately following, at the founding of the theocracy at Sinai, God reveals himself as glorious in holiness. The stamp of holiness is imprinted on every activity at Sinai. When Israel enters into a covenant relation with God it is declared that they must be holy simply because he is holy. "For I am Jehovah your God: sanctify yourselves therefore, and be ye holy, for I am holy" (Lev. 11:44).

From these and other passages in the early sections of the Old Testament it is seen that the holiness of God refers to his deity. It designates the Godhead. It is that which constitutes him as God. It is the "numinous" quality of God, the "mysterium tremendum." It is his otherness, his transcendence, his separation from the world of his creation. It is that which distinguishes him as infinite, apart from the finite. It is a state of apartness, God being raised above all other. He is apart from other gods, imaginary gods. "Who is like unto thee, O Jehovah, among the gods? Who is like thee, glorious in holiness?" (Exod. 15:11). He is apart from his creatures. "To whom then will ye liken me, that I should be equal to him? saith the Holy One" (Isa. 40:25). He is raised above the world of his creation. The Holy One of Israel becomes his designation. This idea of transcendence, of apartness, the term holy never loses.

Then we see that things or people are considered holy when set apart or devoted to God. Belonging to God, they are holy because he is holy. The ground upon which Moses was standing when he received the theophany was holy because of God's presence. "Draw not nigh hither: put off thy shoes from off thy feet, for the place whereon thou standest is holy ground" (Exod. 3:5). The tabernacle, the ark of the covenant, the vessels of the tabernacle, the priests, the sacrifices, the Sabbath — all these are declared holy because they are set aside and dedicated to God who is holy. God's covenant people, the Hebrews, are holy because they are his. "Jehovah will establish thee for a holy people unto himself, as he hath sworn unto thee; if thou shalt keep the commandments of Jehovah thy God, and walk in his ways" (Deut. 28:9). "And ye shall be holy unto me; for I, Jehovah, am holy, and have set you apart from the peoples, that ye should be mine" (Lev. 20:26) —set apart, holy to God, for he is set apart, holy. "God as the Holy One does not remain in Himself, but gives effect to His holiness out of Himself, by instituting a separation in the world, for His own aims, electing a people out of the mass of the nations of the world, accepting them as his property, and imprinting on the ordinances which He gives to this people, and on this historical providence by which they are guided, the stamp of this separation from worldliness, and of this specific relation to Himself."[2] Israel shall be holy, for Israel's God is holy.

As yet the idea of the ethical is not so much a part of the idea of the holy. This does not happen until we come to the prophets and the Psalms. Then it is an ethical apartness, an ethical transcendence, an ethical separateness. Especially is this discerned in Isaiah, the great prophet of holiness, and supremely so in the graphic vision comprising his call and commission found in the sixth chapter of his book. He has been termed the prophet of holiness, holiness becoming the keynote of his prophetic message. The vision reveals to him God high upon a throne, with the seraphim flying back and forth and singing, "Holy, holy, holy, is Jehovah of hosts: the whole earth is full of his glory." In this display of holiness and glory he realizes his own sinfulness and the sinfulness of the people among whom he is living, which shows the ethical element in holiness; else he would not have observed his own dreadful condition. "Woe is me! for I am undone; because I am a man of unclean lips, and I dwell in the midst of a people of unclean lips; for mine eyes have seen the King, Jehovah of hosts." His conviction and confession are immediately followed by cleansing and a removal of the iniquity, thus showing the mercy part of the holiness of God along with the justice phase. Henceforth Isaiah's favorite terms for God are Holy One (10:17) and the Holy One of Israel (10:20). This ethical idea in holiness is also seen in Amos 4:2, where it is stated that God swears by his holiness to punish the wayward people of Samaria, capital of the northern kingdom, by taking them into captivity. Their oppression of the poor and needy and their lolling away their time in iniquitous living are too much for the holiness of God.

---

[2] G. F. Oehler, *Theology of the Old Testament*, p. 107.

(2) IN NEW TESTAMENT

The idea of the ethical transcendence, or ethical apartness, of God, as discerned in the Old Testament, is just as profound in the New Testament. We are told to pray, "Our Father who art in heaven, Hallowed be thy name..." (Matt. 6:9). God's being in heaven is his apartness, his otherness, his transcendence. The word "Hallowed" translates a Greek word meaning "let be holy." So we are praying that God's name shall be holy, and that we shall direct our activities to that intent. Mary was told that she would conceive of the Holy Spirit and that the child born "shall be called holy, the Son of God" (Luke 1:35, margin). Peter demands holy living for Christians and grounds his declarations in Old Testament oracles. We are to live as children of obedience, "not fashioning yourselves according to your former lusts in the time of your ignorance: but like as he who called you is holy, be ye yourselves also holy in all manner of living; because it is written, Ye shall be holy; for I am holy" (I Pet. 1:14-16). As Israel was once God's elect race and holy nation, Christians now constitute God's elect race and holy nation. "But ye are an elect race, a royal priesthood, a holy nation, a people for God's own possession, that ye may show forth the excellencies of him who called you out of darkness into his marvellous light" (I Pet. 2:9). Since God is holy, Christians are to be holy; and the idea of the ethical is highly prominent here. Throughout the epistles Christians are called saints, which is nothing but a translation for a Greek term meaning holy ones. It is true that the New Testament speaks less frequently than the Old Testament of holiness as an attribute of God, yet its presence is just as definite in these later inspired writings. The holiness of God is his supreme moral excellence; it is his moral perfection.

(3) INCLUSIVE OF OTHER ATTRIBUTES

Holiness is the ground of the other moral attributes of God: righteousness, love, and truth. These will be discussed in short order, but it must be stated here that they have their source in holiness. God's holiness is the regulating principle of his nature, for it conditions and limits the exercise of the other attributes. For instance, God wished to express his love in redeeming man, but this must be done in perfect harmony with the holiness of his character. Love made the atonement, but a violated holiness demanded it. Also, the holiness of God that requires the eternal punishment of the wicked overrides the pleading of love for the sufferers. The reason, or standard, of love is found in holiness. Not only all this, but throughout all Scripture the holiness of God is constantly and powerfully impressed upon man; it is the most prominent attribute brought to bear upon the mind of the sinner. Even in heaven itself the theme is "Holy, holy, holy is the Lord God, the Almighty" (Rev. 4:8).

a. *Ground of righteousness*

Amos, the great prophet of righteousness, bemoans the fact that God's holy name is profaned by immoral living (2:7). Isaiah, the great prophet of holiness, declares Israel to be a "sinful nation, a people laden with iniquity, a seed of evil-doers, children that deal corruptly." Their sin is that "they have despised the Holy One of Israel" (1:4). Isaiah must be cleansed to serve the holy God of Israel (6:3-7).

b. *Ground of love*

In Isaiah and Ezekiel there is a constant reminder to Israel that God's redemptive love is a manifestation of his holiness. Since God is jealous for his holy name, he will "bring back the captivity of Jacob, and have mercy upon the whole house of Israel" (Ezek. 39:25). For his holy name God will do great wonders for Israel, including returning them to their homeland, cleansing them, renewing heart and spirit, providing material blessings, etc. (Ezek. 36:22-31). In the midst of a song of comfort to Israel are found these words: "the Holy One of Israel is thy Redeemer" (Isa. 54:5). In the Magnificat of Mary, a song exalting the redeeming mercy of God, are found the words: "And holy is his name" (Luke 1:49).

c. *Ground of truth*

Jesus prays to the Father, "Sanctify them in the truth; thy word is truth" (John 17:17). The word "Sanctify" translates a Greek word meaning make holy; so Jesus is petitioning the Father to make the believers holy by means of his truth. John states, "And ye have an anointing from the Holy One, and ye know all things" (I John 2:20). So the Holy One is the source of truth. Holiness and truth are highly correlated, just as are holiness and love, and holiness and righteousness.

2. RIGHTEOUSNESS

As the keynote of Isaiah's message to Israel is holiness, so the keynote of Amos' message is righteousness. Time and again he thunders forth the great revealing truth that God is righteous, and man must react accordingly.

(1) MEANING OF TERM

The righteousness of God involves the purity of his nature, the entire freedom from his person of anything that is evil or tainted. It means that his character is upright, that it is maintained in absolute rectitude. This attribute finds God exercising himself in favor of the right as opposed to the wrong, the pure as opposed to the impure. It involves both the negative and the positive, the former in view of the absence of the impure and the latter in view of his adamant opposition to the impure wherever it is found. He is not only free from evil but is opposed to it.

The righteousness of God is grounded in his nature and is affirmed in his will. God could not affirm through his will that which his being does not sustain. Nature and affirmation of that nature — these are correlatives of the highest degree. So God's righteousness involves his self-affirming moral will against the impure and immoral. Some theologians call the righteousness of God the transitive holiness of God, which is not the holiness of God per se, but the holiness of God in relation to all moral beings, demanding of them conformity to his own moral perfection.

(2) MANIFESTATIONS OF GOD'S RIGHTEOUSNESS

There are various manifestations of God's righteousness, which can be termed mandatory, condemnatory, and redemptive.

a. *Mandatory*

God demands that man be righteous. The mandatory righteousness of God is seen in any and all means that he has used to reveal his moral requirements regarding man.

(a) It is seen in the conscience of man. Man's conscience demands that he do the right and avoid the wrong. It is true that his conscience is not infallible, that it can make mistakes, that it can be trained in an abnormal way so as to give untrue decisions. The conscience of a half-civilized denizen of the jungle is not the conscience of a refined Christian. Yet the very fact that God has placed within moral man a conscience is the first indication of his mandatory righteousness. "For the wrath of God is revealed from heaven against all ungodliness and unrighteousness of men, who hinder the truth in unrighteousness" (Rom. 1:18). Paul, in speaking of the Gentiles, states "that they show the work of the law written in their hearts, their conscience bearing witness therewith, and their thoughts one with another accusing or else excusing them" (Rom. 2:15).

(b) It is seen in the Mosaic law of the Old Testament. All the moral laws of the Mosaic system, and especially the Ten Commandments, show God's mandatory righteousness. Thou shalt not steal. Thou shalt not lie. Thou shalt not commit adultery. All these and many more manifest God's demand that man be righteous also. In the Psalms and the prophets we discern God's demands of righteousness involving the heart and soul, not just the outward act, as in the Ten Commandments.

(c) It is seen in the revelation brought by Christ. Our Lord lays stress on the subjective state of the heart and inner life; it is the motive that counts. Here is the true source of evil; for the objective act is merely the fruit of sin. The real sin is subjective. This is shown vividly concerning murder and adultery in the Sermon on the Mount (Matt. 5:21ff.). Jesus says that men are to be perfect as their Father in heaven is perfect (Matt. 5:48). The Ten Commandments are brought to a higher level in the two commandments of love to God and love to fellow man, for they constitute all that the law and the prophets endeavored to fulfill (Matt. 22:34-40).

(d) It is seen in the character of Christ himself. Here is the Christian ideal of righteousness. Here is the express image of God, and as much as men follow it and allow it to be reproduced in them, they too, to that extent, constitute the restored image of God. Jesus is the perfect man, the epitome of what God expects of redeemed humanity.

b. *Condemnatory*

But not only does God demand that man be righteous (mandatory); he also must condemn man for his lack of righteousness (condemnatory). He condemns sin in man. He deals with him in accord with strict justice, punishing the guilty for the transgression of his revealed demands. He must mete out to man the due reward of his sin. This may also be thought of as punitive righteousness.

The universality of sin shows that man falls short of the standard of righteousness set by a righteous God. "For all have sinned, and fall short of the glory of God" (Rom. 3:23). All through the Bible there is a condemnation of man's sin. Abraham said unto Jehovah, "That be far from thee to do after this manner, to slay the righteous with the wicked, that so the righteous should be as the wicked; that be far from thee: shall not the Judge of all the earth do right?" (Gen. 18:25). God is just, and condemns sin according to the full measure of his justice (Rom. 2:6-16). He does not treat the righteous and the wicked alike. Nor does he react vindictively; he merely reacts against sin and condemns it because of his righteous nature. Not to react against sin would be to violate his very nature; this would be tantamount to declaring himself to be a non-moral God. This is not so; his morality is grounded in his nature, and he must react accordingly. Nor is this to say that he does not love the sinner; he loves the sinner and condemns his sin. God can love and condemn at the same time.

The condemnatory phase of righteousness is vividly seen in Jesus' attitude toward sinners. He loved sinners, had compassion for them, wanted to help them. When they came to him, acknowledging their condemnation, showing penitence for their sin, he willingly forgave them and saved them. The sinful woman who anointed his feet with ointment in the house of Simon the Pharisee is exemplary of this type. "And he said unto her, Thy sins are forgiven" (Luke 7:48). But in antithesis to these penitent ones Jesus was absolutely unsparing in his condemnation of those who persisted in their willful unbelief. The only means of salvation from sin is to recognize God's condemnation of those sins to the fullest extent. The sinner must recognize that he is guilty and deserving of ill-desert. When he accepts God's attitude toward his sin, then and then only can he be saved by God's grace. To refuse to accept the condemnation of his sin is to remain guilty and under condemnation. This fits the case of many who came within the sphere of Jesus' teaching and life. The eighth chapter of John and the twenty-third chapter of Matthew show Jesus' unsparing and scathing denunciation of those who persisted in unbelief and in a disregard of his gracious offer of salvation. In the former passage he called them hypocrites, sons of hell, and offspring of vipers. In the latter he termed them sons of the devil, since they possessed all the characteristics of the devil. The wall of unbelief, which such recalcitrant sinners refused to remove, brought the battering ram of no-mercy.

c. *Redemptive*

Mandatory righteousness demands righteousness in man. Condemnatory righteousness deals with unrighteous man according to strict justice and is probably the phase of God's righteousness that has received the attention of theologians more than any other. Yet there is what is termed redemptive righteousness, which is the exhibition of God's righteousness in redeeming sinful man. God redeems, but at the same time he maintains the inviolability of his moral law. In all his redeeming activity God works according to the principles of righteousness. This is discussed in both the Old and the New Testaments. In the Old Testament it is found in the Psalms and in the latter half of Isaiah. "Mercy and truth are met together; Righteousness and peace have kissed each other" (Ps. 85:10). "Deliver me from bloodguiltiness, O God, thou God of my salvation; And my tongue shall sing aloud of thy righteousness" (Ps. 51:14). In the latter half of Isaiah salvation and righteousness are also used practically synonymously.

"I bring near my righteousness, it shall not be far off, and my salvation shall not tarry; and I will place salvation in Zion for Israel my glory" (Isa. 46:13). "My salvation shall be for ever, and my righteousness shall not be abolished" (Isa. 51:6). "My righteousness shall be for ever, and my salvation unto all generations" (Isa. 51:8). Other passages are Isaiah 41:10; 42:6; 45:13; 61:10. Righteousness is seen to be the ground and basis of salvation, that from which the latter evolves. Salvation is the expression of God's righteousness.

The New Testament presents the same thought. "If we confess our sins, he is faithful and righteous to forgive us our sins, and to cleanse us from all unrighteousness" (I John 1:9). "And if any man sin, we have an Advocate with the Father, Jesus Christ the righteous" (I John 2:1). Here the righteousness of God appears in the redeeming activity of Christ, which is what Paul is conveying in his statement, "Him who knew no sin he made to be sin on our behalf; that we might become the righteousness of God in him" (II Cor. 5:21). Righteousness and redeeming love are bound closely together, for God's righteousness is never neglected in the pursuit of fallen man. In fact, in the salvation that comes through Christ righteousness constitutes a prominent element. "For I am not ashamed of the gospel: for it is the power of God unto salvation to every one that believeth; to the Jew first, and also to the Greek. For therein is revealed a righteousness of God from faith unto faith: as it is written, But the righteous shall live by faith" (Rom. 1:16, 17). Man can become righteous, for God is righteous. Therefore the righteousness that comes to man in salvation is grounded in righteousness as an attribute of God. God's righteousness makes him hate sin and love the righteous; therefore God desires to save men from sin into a state of being righteous — and this even at a tremendous cost!

3. LOVE

If the keynote of Isaiah's message is holiness, and the keynote of Amos' message is righteousness, the keynote of Hosea's message is love. He is the great prophet of love, whose very domestic tragedy exemplifies this great attribute of God.

(1) IS GROUNDED IN NATURE OF GOD

The love of God is not something incidental to God; it is part of his very nature. John says, "God is love" (I John 4:8). Since love is part of the very nature of God, it is eternal. Since God is love, every one that is born of God loves also. "For love is of God; and every one that loveth is begotten of God, and knoweth God" (I John 4:7). Since love is of the nature of God it must be expressed; this expression is found in Calvary. "For God so loved the world, that he gave his only begotten Son" (John 3:16). We might say that love is that attribute of God which moves him to self-communication with his creatures. "Hereby know we love, because he laid down his life for us" (I John 3:16). Jesus, speaking to the Father, says, "For thou lovedst me before the foundation of the world" (John 17:24). So the immanent love of God finds an object for its love within the Godhead itself, which also reveals the eternal quality of that love and which makes it independent of creation.

(2) SHOWS RATIONAL AND VOLUNTARY AFFECTION

God's love is not swayed to and fro by emotions and whims of nature. It is a rational affection, grounded in reason and moved by deliberate choice. It is subject to the regulation of other faculties. There is a copartnership with reason. God's love is not arbitrary and wild; it does not consist of uncontrolled emotion. If this latter were the case God could bestow his love regardless of the presence of sin in man and regardless of the fact that he himself is a righteous God. But since God's love is rational, it must be subordinated to truth and holiness. Wisdom is used in the expression of love.

(3) DESIRES THE BEST FOR ITS OBJECTS

God's love is not just amiable good will, but a love that wants to bestow the supreme good upon the object loved. Throughout the whole New Testament this is clearly seen. "For the Son of man came to seek and to save that which was lost" (Luke 19: 10). This seeking and saving was motivated by the desire to give to man the very best — redemption itself. God wants to reclaim the wandering ones and effect a reconciliation back into his presence. He wants to mold and form and enlarge man by trial and discipline and suffering into one morally pure and intellectually mature. He wants to condition man for entrance into a holy society, his eternal kingdom. He is not content with anything less than the best. This best comes to us through Christ and all that is involved in following him. Therefore God's love is benevolent, both wishing well and doing well in behalf of others.

(4) MANIFESTS ITSELF IN REGARD TO RIGHTEOUSNESS

God has expressed his love to man, but every expression of that love has due respect for the fact that God is righteous. His righteousness must never be cast aside. His love must at all times be morally conditioned. The reconciling of man back into the presence of God was truly the expression of God's love, but God did not cast off his righteousness and welcome unrighteous man, with all his sin and degradation, back into his holy fellowship. This would never do! "For what fellowship have righteousness and iniquity? or what communion hath light with darkness?" (II Cor. 6:14). So man must become righteous to have fellowship with God who is righteous. The motive of the atonement is love, but the condition surrounding that love is righteousness. Man must be received into the divine favor with due regard to all moral principles. Maintaining the integrity of God's character is even a higher principle than the giving and receiving of love; hence we say that his love must be morally conditioned.

(5) ACTS IN BEHALF OF ITS OBJECT

God's love is not static; it is dynamic. It craves expression. It is not content to be retained within the Godhead; it must flow out to man. Jeremiah says, "Jehovah appeared of old unto me, saying, Yea, I have loved thee with an everlasting love: therefore with lovingkindness have I drawn thee" (31:3). This "lovingkindness" is identified with "grace" in the New Testament. Because God loves Israel he acts with grace to draw Israel to him. This is the story in the New Testament also. Because God loves the world he gives his only Son to redeem the world. "Herein is love, not that we loved God, but that he loved us, and sent his Son to be the propitiation for our sins" (I John 4:10). "For the grace of God hath appeared, bringing salvation to all men" (Titus 2:11). Man must know God loves him; what greater way than through the cross! "Greater love hath no man than this, that a man lay down his life for his friends" (John 15:13). The redeeming activity of Christ manifested the perfection of God's love, for it was love sacrificing itself for its object. To show man his love God gave the supreme object of his love, his only Son (John 3:16). The Christ who suffered on the cross was God incarnate, which shows that the divine being can suffer. Therefore the cross shows God's suffering for fallen humanity. This does not reveal a God apart from the world, an absentee God unmoved as he looks down upon human suffering. It reveals a God with the capacity and the desire to suffer for us. It is a sympathizing love, a love suffering because of identification with another. It is the zenith of voluntary sacrifice. The permission of moral evil at the time of creation was at cost to God. This cost is seen when God "spared not his own Son" (Rom. 8:32). There can be no conception of self-sacrifice without suffering.

(6) SEEKS THE LOVE OF ITS OBJECT

God instructed Israel not to bow down to other gods or to images, for he is a jealous God (Exod. 20:5). This means that he desired all of Israel's love. "Hear, O Israel: Jehovah our God is one Jehovah: and thou shalt love Jehovah thy God with all thy heart, and with all thy soul, and with all thy might" (Deut. 6: 4, 5). This is a categorical statement of God's demand for their love and is the very passage quoted by Jesus as the great commandment, thus showing its importance in the mind of our Lord. He came to establish this love for God in the heart of mankind. All through the Old Testament the relation between God and Israel is described as that between husband and wife; when Israel goes out in idolatry and apostasy after other gods the nation is termed an adulterous one (Matt. 12:39). Thus what God desires is a mutual self-giving between himself and man, his love expressed in the atoning work of Christ and man's love expressed in undivided affection and loyalty to his Redeemer.

(7) EXPRESSES ITSELF IN VARIOUS WAYS

The supreme manner in which God has shown his love to us is in Calvary, the great atonement of our Lord. Yet his love is discerned in many other ways. Creation itself was motivated by love, for God's design in creation was a spiritual, loving relationship with his creatures. His preservation and providence are motivated by the same love that brought creation into being. These, along with his benevolent love, go out to all creatures, regardless of their moral condition. Jesus, while here on earth, showed a compassionate love to those in distress and suffering. This love was proffered to all around, regardless of their moral or social condition. God's love to the guilty is mercy. His love in redemption is grace. The former forgives; the latter transforms.

(8) INCLUDES ALL MANKIND

God's love is a universal love, going out to all races of all climes of all ages. It is true that God chose Israel out of all the nations for his supreme blessing; but he also stated, "In thee shall all the families of the earth be blessed" (Gen. 12:3). God said to Israel, "I will also give thee for a light to the Gentiles, that thou mayest be my salvation unto the end of the earth" (Isa. 49:6). Likewise, in the New Testament the love of God is to flow out through Christians unto the uttermost parts of the earth; they have been chosen for this purpose. The Great Commission is indicative of this momentous responsibility (Matt. 28:19, 20). God loves all and desires to redeem all. John 3:16 reveals this universal love. The Lord "is longsuffering to you-ward, not wishing that any should perish, but that all should come to repentance" (II Pet. 3:9). God's elective love of Christians is part of his means of expressing his love to all of the world.

In the Greek language there are three terms that can very well be translated with the English word love: *agapē*, *philos*, and *erōs*. The first two are employed by the New Testament writers, while the third is not found even once in the New Testament. The first two are also found in the Septuagint. There are three corresponding verb forms.

Agapē is the more dignified, lofty, and restrained of the two New Testament words, while *philos* is used to designate all degrees and all kinds of love. Many times the latter merely connotes liking. Sometimes it designates love for mankind. Yet, such a distinction, vague and general as it is, should not be pressed too far. Both the verb *agapaō* and the verb *phileō* are used in the Fourth Gospel for each of the following five categories: God's love for man, the Father's love for the Son, Jesus' love for men, the love of men for other men, and the love of men for Jesus. Therefore this famous writer *seems* to use the two terms as synonyms, although there is a difference of opinion among scholars on this point. It does appear that in "profane" Greek *agapaō* is colder and less intimate than *phileō*, but the New Testament writers took up the rather colorless word *agapaō* and highly enriched it. Purged of its coldness, it became deeper in meaning than *phileō*. In fact, it rose to be one of the most sublime words in the New Testament. Therefore, if the New Testament writers meant to distinguish at all between these two verbs, *agapaō* denotes reverential love, while *phileō* denotes friendship love. But again, one must proceed cautiously.

In the twenty-first chapter of John's gospel Jesus asks Peter three times if he loves him, using *agapaō* the first two times and *phileō* the third time. Peter answers with *phileō* all three times. *Agapē* is used in the famous thirteenth chapter of First Corinthians, where, in the King James Version, it is unfortunately translated with "charity." *Agapē* is also used in John 3:16 and in the extended passage on love found in I John 4:7-21. It is found many more times than *philos*, a fact that applies also to the corresponding verb forms.

4. TRUTH

God is a God of truth. By this is meant that he is the source of all knowledge and the source of all objects of knowledge. From God as the ground of truth come knowledge of himself, knowledge of all objects of knowledge, and all forms of knowing on the part of created beings. There is no standard of truth outside of God, for he is the standard. He is altruistic truth; for there is no truth beyond him, and all truth is derived from him. God's truth is that element of his nature by virtue of which his nature and his knowledge completely conform to each other.

"And this is life eternal, that they should know thee the only true God, and him whom thou didst send, even Jesus Christ" (John 17:3). "We know him that is true" (I John 5:20). The Greek word "true" used here means genuine or real, not so much the idea of "veracious." Jesus says, "I am ... the truth" (John 14: 6). The word "truth" used here means truth of being, more than truth of expression. To know the revelation of God is to know truth.

(1) GOD NOT ONLY KNOWS TRUTH, BUT IS THE TRUTH

Truth of being precedes knowledge of truth. The state of being precedes the activity. It is its ground. Truth as an active attribute is derived from truth that is inherent in being. He himself constitutes the truth that is known. Christ reveals truth; but he is not only the medium of the knowledge, for he is the object of the knowledge. Paul says to the Ephesians, "Ye did not so learn Christ" (Eph. 4:20). Does he mean about Christ? No, he means Christ himself, for Christ is the object of knowledge. "And this is life eternal, that they should know thee the only true God" (John 17:3). Is this to know intellectually? No, it is to know experientially. God's essence and intellect are in complete conformity; being is in accord with knowing.

(2) GOD'S TRUTH IS THE GROUND OF MAN'S TRUTH

All truth, whether mathematical, scientific, moral, musical, artistic, religious, astronomical, is grounded in God. It is derived from God, for he ordained it. Anything knowable by man was known first of God, yea, was ordained and came into being from God. God is ultimate truth, for from the immanent truth of the divine nature came truth as known by man. Therefore knowledge of the truth is knowledge of God.

Two and two make four; this is truth, but it is also an eternal principle inherent in the Godhead. Virtue is to be commended; vice is to be condemned. This is a principle resting in the eternal Godhead. A mathematical formula can be explained only in relation to God, for it was ordained by God. An apostle can say, "I speak the truth"; but he cannot say, "I am the truth." He is not, and never can be, the ground of truth; this prerogative lies with God alone.

(3) GOD AS TRUTH CONSTITUTES THE GROUND AND GUARANTEE OF REVELATION

Truth did not evolve due to the will of God; it is a characteristic of his being. Truth is not arbitrary; it is essential. God knows truth and wills truth, because he *is* truth. Truth makes God's will, not vice versa. Being conditions will. God wills truth; he cannot will that which is false or erroneous or self-contradictory. He cannot will that two plus two equal six, for this would be contrary to the truth.

From God's nature as truth comes veracity. God speaks only truth. What he states concerning himself, his laws, his methods, his procedures, his desires, his promises, his creation is true. This is the ground of revelation; this guarantees its veracity and is applicable to all revelation, whether that revelation be in nature or by means of Scripture.

III. WORKS OF GOD

The works of God may be divided into four categories: creation, preservation, providence, and redemption.

1. CREATION

(1) MEANING OF TERM

By creation we mean all that exists that is not God, which would include nature and man. It is the result of the free act of God by which he made, without using material existing prior to that time, the universe. It includes what can be seen and what cannot be seen in the universe. It is not just an idea of God, but this idea made objective. It is designed origination. It is creative energy becoming force. It is the beginning of time. It is the origination of that which becomes wholly dependent upon God. It is the origination of that which once did not exist, either in form or in substance (*creatio ex nihilo*). It is the production of an effect with no natural antecedent existing prior to its coming into being. It is not necessary to God; he did not have to create. He chose to create. It is an act of the personal and free will of God.

(2) BIBLICAL DOCTRINE OF CREATION

The Bible clearly states that creation is an act of God, the whole universe being due to the creative power of God. "In the beginning God created the heavens and the earth" (Gen. 1:1). With this terse and simple statement begins a description of God's work of willing and bringing the world into existence. Psalm 104 is a poetic description of God's creation of the world, as well as Job 38. "And God created man in his own image" (Gen. 1:27). Christ himself was the agent of creation. "All things were made through him; and without him was not anything made that hath been made" (John 1:3). "For in him were all things created, in the heavens and upon the earth, things visible and things invisible" (Col. 1:16).

God willed it, and the world came into existence. First there is the material universe, and then there is man. Every step is referred to God. This is not a scientific description of a scientific account. Rather, it is written from the religious viewpoint, and to try to force it to answer scientific questions from the modern angle is to do it violence. It is a religious explanation; from this point of view it does what it purports to do. The world is due to the creative act of God, and any development of that world is due to the directing hand of God. This is the true and biblical view of creation.

(3) FALSE PHILOSOPHICAL VIEWS OF THE EXISTENCE OF THE UNIVERSE

a. *Dualism theory*

This view holds that there are two self-existent principles, God and nature, and that they are distinct from each other and co-eternal with each other. They have always existed simultaneously and always will. Therefore God did not create matter; he merely used it for his ends, for it is subordinate to him. This theory arose from the difficulty of conceiving how God could create matter without the use of pre-existent material. This view is self-contradictory and multiplies the problems relative to creation.

b. *Emanation theory*

This holds to the view that the universe is of identical substance with God, being the product of successive evolutions, or emanations, from his being. This view, held by the Gnostics in the early Christian centuries, conceives of the world as made from the "overflow" of the divine being. It takes away the freedom of God and leads to pantheism.

c. *Eternal creation theory*

This regards the universe as the eternal creation of God. Creation is an act of God in eternity past. Those who hold to this view argue that creation from eternity past is necessitated by God's omnipotence, timelessness, unchangeableness, and love. They cannot explain why God should have remained idle through an eternity before beginning to create. But creation in the nature of the case is something that must be begun. Therefore creation from eternity is a contradiction in terms. The whole argument rests upon a misconception of the true meaning of eternity. Eternity is not endless time, but rather superiority to the law of time. It is no more past than it is present or future. This theory makes God create from necessity, not from a matter of choice.

d. *Spontaneous generation theory*

This holds that creation is merely a natural process still functioning today and that matter itself has the power to develop into organic forms involving life. Hence we have the term spontaneous generation, or what the biologist calls abiogenesis, the production of living things from inanimate objects. There is no evidence that abiogenesis has ever, or is, taking place; therefore this theory is contrary to all known facts. We have no instance of the production of living forms from inorganic material. This theory is none other than materialism and is rapidly passing away. It is contrary to all moral, spiritual, and religious truth, for it views the highest forms of existence as being derived from the lowest forms.

2. PRESERVATION

(1) MEANING OF TERM

If the doctrine of creation is an explanation of the existence of the universe, the doctrine of preservation is an explanation of its continuance. It is God's maintaining in existence that which he has created, and is therefore not to be confused with creation. Preservation presupposes creation, for that which is preserved must first exist. Nor is it a negative term, for it is maintained that God constantly and actively sustains the persons and forces of the universe. It is a personal and positive agency of God that operates at every moment. It is that by which all personal beings and all forces of nature continue to exist and function. All life, all growth, all activity, all movement, all thought — these are due to the immediate influence of the immanent God. This is preservation.

"Thou art Jehovah, even thou alone; thou hast made heaven, the heaven of heavens, with all their host, the earth and all things that are thereon, the seas and all that is in them, and thou preservest them all" (Neh. 9:6). "Thou preservest man and beast" (Ps. 36:6). "In him we live, and move, and have our being" (Acts 17:28). "In him all things consist" (Col. 1:17). The Greek word translated "consist" means maintain their coherence, which makes Christ the agent of preservation. The author of Hebrews talks about Christ's "upholding all things by the word of his power" (1:3). Jesus must have been referring to preservation when he said, "My Father worketh even until now, and I work" (John 5:17), for creation was finished and complete. The whole of Psalm 104 is a hymn of God's preservation.

DOCTRINES OF THE CHRISTIAN RELIGION

(2) THEORIES DENYING THE DOCTRINE OF PRESERVATION

a. *Deism*

This is the belief that God created the universe and then withdrew, leaving his self-sustaining creation to a process of self-development. It maintains that God is transcendent only, not immanent in the world, and that he not only does not preserve the world but that he has not revealed himself to man. It makes the universe a huge perpetual motion machine. It is as though God built a house, shut himself outside, locked the door, and threw away the key. Deism leads directly to atheism.

b. *Continuous creation*

This is the belief that the universe is still in the process of creation. It is the view that at each moment there is an immediate production out of non-existing material. It is right when it assumes that all force in the universe is due to will, but it is wrong when it asserts that this will is always divine will, divine will in direct activity. There is also human will, and there is also force in nature that is automatic. If God's will is the only will operative in the universe, he becomes the author of human sin. The whole theory contradicts itself. As deism leads to atheism, continuous creation leads to pantheism.

3. PROVIDENCE

(1) MEANING OF TERM

As creation is an explanation of the existence of the universe, and as preservation is an explanation of the continuance of the universe, so providence is an explanation of the progress of the universe. While preservation has to do with the maintenance of the existence of created things, providence has to do with the actual care of them. It is the control of creation toward the end God has chosen. It is God's foreseeing in connection with all the events of history. It is all-comprehending, involving the small and the great, the individual and the group, the national and the international. It involves both the heredity and the environment that influence men in their preparation to do God's bidding and motivate them to obedience. Negatively it is even preventive or permissive toward the sin of man.

God is one who "worketh all things after the counsel of his will" (Eph. 1:11). "He increaseth the nations, and he destroyeth them: He enlargeth the nations, and he leadeth them captive" (Job 12:23). "He hath put down princes from their thrones, And hath exalted them of low degree" (Luke 1:52). "The very hairs of your head are all numbered" (Matt. 10:30). "He that keepeth thee will

68

not slumber" (Ps. 121:3). "To them that love God all things work together for good" (Rom. 8:28). "My God shall supply every need of yours" (Phil. 4:19). Not only is Christ the agent of creation, and not only is he the agent of preservation; he is also the agent of providence. Paul speaks of "one Lord, Jesus Christ, through whom are all things" (I Cor. 8:6). Jesus says, "My Father worketh even until now, and I work" (John 5:17).

(2) THEORIES DENYING THE DOCTRINE OF PROVIDENCE

a. *Totalism*

This theory substitutes fate for providence, denying the freedom of self-determination. It practically makes necessity God, thus destroying the personality and freedom of God.

b. *Casualism*

This theory substitutes chance for providence, transferring the freedom of mind to nature. But is it not possible that what we call chance is really providential coincidence which we cannot comprehend, providence arranging every so-called chance for a certain purpose? Since reason demands a cause for order in the world, casualism is ruled out immediately.

c. *General providence only*

This rules out providence concerning particular events, God's arrangement of the specific and immediate occurrences, and argues merely for his contact over the movement of nations and of heavenly bodies. This is nothing but a partial deism, God's not wholly withdrawing from the universe but being active in it relative to general laws only. This seems to have been the view of most ancient heathen philosophers. We answer by saying that general contact over history and nations is impossible without contact over the smallest details found within these. Small incidents have been known to determine the course of nations and of empires.

4. REDEMPTION

The redemptive work of God is so magnanimous, so marvelous, that it cannot be discussed here in a mere subpoint of this chapter. It will be involved in all that is covered in every subsequent chapter. We merely cry out with Paul, "O the depth of the riches both of the wisdom and the knowledge of God! how unsearchable are his judgments, and his ways past tracing out!" (Rom. 11:33).

OUTLINE FOR CHAPTER THREE

   I. Humanity of Christ
      1. Fact of his humanity
        (1) Called himself man and was called man
        (2) Possessed body and soul
        (3) Was moved by the instincts and powers characterizing humanity
        (4) Underwent human development, both in body and in spirit
        (5) Died and was buried
      2. A manhood complete and perfect
        (1) Supernatural conception
        (2) Sinlessness
        (3) Moral ideal
        (4) Second Adam, beginning a new race
      3. Two denials of his true humanity
        (1) The Docetics (A.D. 70-120)
        (2) The Apollinarians (A.D. 381)
  II. Deity of Christ
      1. Fact of his deity
        (1) Pre-existence
        (2) Virgin birth
        (3) Called God in the New Testament
        (4) Inner divine consciousness
          a. Sent of the Father
          b. Revealed the Father
          c. Spoke of "my Father," not "our Father"
          d. Employed "I am" sayings
        (5) Divine powers and privileges exercised by him
          a. Forgiver of sins
          b. Recipient of all authority
          c. Only way of life
          d. Received honor and worship due only to God
          e. Displayed miraculous knowledge
        (6) Works of God performed by him
          a. Creation
          b. Preservation
          c. Resurrection of the dead
          d. Judgment of the world
        (7) Divinity attested by many witnesses
        (8) Divine terms ascribed to him
          a. Son of God
          b. Image of God
          c. Logos

        d. Son of Man
        e. Christ, or Messiah
    2. Two denials of his true deity
        (1) The Ebionites (A.D. 107)
        (2) The Arians (A.D. 325)
III.   Incarnation of Christ
    1. Union of two natures in one person
    2. Facts relative to this union
        (1) Its importance
        (2) Its inscrutable nature
        (3) Its necessity
    3. Two denials of his true incarnation
        (1) The Nestorians (A.D. 431)
        (2) The Eutychians (A.D. 451)
IV.   Two States of Christ
    1. Humiliation
    2. Exaltation
 V.   Two Aspects of Christ
    1. Saviour
    2. Lord
VI.   Three Offices of Christ
    1. Prophetic
    2. Priestly
    3. Kingly

CHAPTER THREE

CHRIST, THE SON OF GOD

OF EXTREME IMPORTANCE THEOLOGICALLY IS THE PERSON OF CHRIST. Who was he? From where did he come? In the chapter on revelation we found that he not only *brought* a revelation of God, he *was* the revelation. Yet in that revelation he revealed himself. What was revealed we shall now discern, and what we discern is called Christology.

I. HUMANITY OF CHRIST

During his sojourn here upon earth Jesus was fully human, genuinely human. He was one with mankind, for he identified himself completely with sinful man.

1. FACT OF HIS HUMANITY

(1) CALLED HIMSELF MAN AND WAS CALLED MAN

Jesus said to the Jews, "But now ye seek to kill me, a man that hath told you the truth, which I heard from God" (John 8:40). In his great Pentecostal sermon Peter speaks of "Jesus of Nazareth, a man approved of God unto you" (Acts 2:22). Paul in his Epistle to the Romans speaks of "the one man, Jesus Christ" (5:15). Paul discloses to Timothy that our Mediator is "himself man, Christ Jesus" (I Tim. 2:5). Luke's genealogy in the third chapter gives the natural descent of Christ from Adam. He is of the line of David and of the stock of Israel.

(2) POSSESSED BODY AND SOUL

Just prior to the cross Jesus exclaimed, "My soul is exceeding sorrowful" (Matt. 26:38). Just prior to this he instituted the ordinance of the Lord's Supper, at which time he spoke of his body and of his blood (Matt. 26:26, 28). John tells us that at the death of Lazarus "he groaned in the spirit" (John 11:33).

(3) WAS MOVED BY THE INSTINCTS AND POWERS CHARACTERIZING HUMANITY

Jesus became hungry, thirsty, weary. He was moved by anger. He slept. He loved. He showed compassion. The Bible tells us that at the temptations in the wilderness "he afterward hungered" (Matt. 4:2). While in Samaria "Jesus therefore, being wearied with his journey, sat thus by the well" (John 4:6). Jesus slept while in a boat with his apostles (Matt. 8:24). Mark tells us that Jesus "looked round about on them with anger, being grieved at the hardening of their heart" (3:5).

(4) UNDERWENT HUMAN DEVELOPMENT, BOTH IN BODY AND IN SPIRIT

Luke's gospel reveals much of this growth and development. "And the child grew, and waxed strong, filled with wisdom: and the grace of God was upon him" (Luke 2:40). This one verse is about all we have of the first twelve years of his earthly life. "And Jesus advanced in wisdom and stature, and in favor with God and men" (Luke 2:52). This is about all we know of the next eighteen years of his life; yet it is plainly discerned that he grew physically, intellectually, religiously, and socially — a fourfold development of a well-rounded personality. The writer of the book of Hebrews says that he "learned obedience by the things which he suffered" (5:8). As a little baby in Bethlehem he had to be cared for as any other small infant. He grew up in a small town, probably learning the carpenter's trade. As a youth he was not making crosses, as certain artists have depicted him; he made yokes and plows in Joseph's shop.

(5) DIED AND WAS BURIED

Jesus "bowed his head, and gave up his spirit" (John 19:30). Mark says that Jesus "gave up the ghost" (15:37). Luke says the very same thing. The Greek word used by both of these writers means, literally, breathed out, which is better translated, breathed his last, or expired. When a spear was cast into his side, both blood and water issued forth (John 19:34). Some interpret this statement to be proof that Jesus died of a broken heart. The main point is that he died and was buried. Part of the identification of himself with flesh is that he would die, that his body would cease to function.

2. A MANHOOD COMPLETE AND PERFECT

Although Jesus was fully human, possessing manhood in every sense of the term, it was ideal manhood, perfect in every detail. It was a distinctive manhood, outstanding and unique. This is manifested by means of various factors.

(1) SUPERNATURAL CONCEPTION

Jesus was supernaturally conceived, being born of a virgin. The angel said to Mary, "The Holy Spirit shall come upon thee, and the power of the Most High shall overshadow thee" (Luke 1:35). Conception took place through the agency of the Holy Spirit; there was no earthly father. The births of Isaac and of John the Baptist were miraculous in that both were born of women who had been barren all their lives and who were, at the time of giving birth, well beyond the age of childbearing. But Jesus' birth was more miraculous yet, being of a virgin.

(2) SINLESSNESS

Though genuinely human Jesus' life was free from actual sin. He went to the temple often, but he never offered sacrifices. He prayed, but he never prayed for forgiveness. He told us to pray to the Father, "Forgive us our debts," but he never said, "Father, forgive *me*." He informed us that we must be born anew, but he revealed no need of such on his own part. He challenged the Jews, "Which of you convicteth me of sin?" (John 8:46). He manifested anger; but it was not selfish and vindictive. It was a righteous anger against perverted religion and blatant hypocrisy. There was no personal experience of sin, just personal and complete resistance to it. Thus he was fitted to deliver us from sin. Besides these activities and implications of our Lord himself that show his sinlessness there are categorical attestations of his sinless character. "Him who knew no sin he made to be sin on our behalf" (II Cor. 5:21). The author of Hebrews informs us that Christ is "one that hath been in all points tempted like as we are, yet without sin" (4:15). He also informs us that he is "holy, guileless, undefiled, separated from sinners" (7:26). Peter says that "Christ also suffered for sins once, the righteous for the unrighteous, that he might bring us to God" (I Pet. 3:18). The fact of Christ's sinlessness runs throughout the New Testament.

"No miracle of Christ equals the miracle of His sinless life. To be holy in all thought and feeling; never to fail in duty to others, never to transgress the law of perfect love to God or man, never to exceed or to come short — this is a condition outstripping the power of imagination and almost of belief. Here is a casement opening on a Diviner world."[1]

(3) MORAL IDEAL

Yet the term sinless is negative in meaning; it is the absence of sin, taint, or defilement. It presents the negative viewpoint only, not a positive one. When we say that Jesus presented the moral ideal, the perfect example, we have the positive viewpoint. In him was seen not only the absence of the unrighteous but the presence of the righteous. Paul's contrast of the first Adam with the second Adam (Christ) shows us that in the second Adam was realized

[1] H. R. Mackintosh, *The Doctrine of the Person of Christ*, p. 403.

the full concept of humanity not realized in the first. It was the Father's wish "that in all things he might have the preëminence" (Col. 1:18). Peter tells his readers that Christ "suffered for you, leaving you an example, that ye should follow his steps" (I Pet. 2:21). He possessed not only passive innocence but absolute holiness. He was not only free from sin but triumphant over temptation. He constitutes the moral pattern which God intends man to realize. He is the perfect man, for he is free from all the limitations that make man narrow, provincial, or isolated.

(4) SECOND ADAM, BEGINNING A NEW RACE

He is the spiritual head of a new race, giving new life to fallen man. The first Adam was the source of physical life; the second Adam of spiritual life. The first Adam was the source of corruption; the second Adam of holiness. Over against the fallen and sinful race is the new race created by Christ. Therefore, in a sense, his humanity was germinal, capable of being communicated to all in whom he dwells.

3. TWO DENIALS OF HIS TRUE HUMANITY

(1) THE DOCETICS (A.D. 70-120)

The Docetics denied that Christ had a human body; he just seemed to have a real body. The Greek term for "it seems" is *dokei;* hence the name Docetics, the "it-seems" people. They were those entering Christianity with a background of Gnostic philosophy, who believed that all matter, including flesh, is inherently evil. Therefore Christ could not have come in real flesh, for this would have contaminated him. Therefore he was all divine and not human, which was a veritable denial of a fleshly existence. It is a blow against the Docetics (or Docetic Gnostics) that John is delivering when he exclaims, "And the Word became flesh, and dwelt among us" (John 1:14). Docetic tendencies are seen cropping up in theology even today.

D. M. Baillie rejoices over what he calls "the end of docetism." He states, "It may safely be said that practically all schools of theological thought today take the full humanity of our Lord more seriously than has ever been done before by Christian theologians." The church "was continually haunted by a docetism which made His human nature very different from ours and indeed largely explained it away as a matter of simulation or 'seeming' rather than reality. Theologians shrank from admitting human growth, human ignorance, human mutability, human struggle and temptation, into their conception of the Incarnate Life, and treated it as simply a divine life lived in a human body (and sometimes even this was conceived as essentially different from our bodies) rather than a truly human life lived under the psychical conditions of humanity. The cruder forms of docetism were fairly soon left behind, but in its more subtle forms the danger continued in varying degrees to dog the steps of theology right through the ages until modern times.... But now the belief in the full humanity of Christ has come into its own."[2] This may all be true, but it is maintained that even today tendencies, or proclivities, toward Docetism emerge both in theology and from the pulpit.

(2) THE APOLLINARIANS (A.D. 381)

The Apollinarians denied that Christ had a human mind or spirit, thus also violating his real manhood. He had a human body and soul, however. The divine Logos took the place of the mind or spirit. Much of this erroneous thinking was due to the influence of Plato's trichotomy of human nature.

Apollinaris became preoccupied with the words: "And the Word became flesh" (John 1:14). "He sought to understand the unity of the person and argued on the basis of the Eternal Logos who became truly human. But this Incarnation is to him very puzzling. The most troublesome question to him is how to understand the unity of the person. Can two beings be united into one being? To solve this intellectual difficulty Apollinaris began to teach that under no circumstances could the divine Logos have united himself with a complete human being since such a union could result only in a third kind of being. Had the Logos assumed a complete human nature, he would have adopted also human variability and human sin. Since it is certain that Jesus Christ is immutable, it is by that token impossible that he united himself with a variable human spirit. A genuine union is possible only when the Logos, as the principle of self-consciousness and self-determination, takes the place of, instead of assuming, the human spirit."[3] Over against such a false assumption as this the Council of Constantinople in A.D. 381 avowed the completeness of Christ's human nature.

II. DEITY OF CHRIST

Just as Christ was genuinely human, so he was also genuinely divine. He was God, for it was intended "that in him should all the fulness dwell" (Col. 1:19), the fulness of divinity, the fulness of the Godhead. This deity of Christ can be discerned from many directions in the New Testament.

2 D. M. Baillie, *God Was In Christ*, p. 11.
3 G. C. Berkouwer, *The Person of Christ*, p. 64.

1. FACT OF HIS DEITY

(1) PRE-EXISTENCE

Jesus pre-existed in heaven before his descent to earth in the form of man. His birth in Bethlehem was not his beginning; it was merely his advent into flesh. There was no time in the dim recesses of eternity past that he did not exist.

This pre-existence appears repeatedly in the Fourth Gospel. "In the beginning was the Word, and the Word was with God, and the Word was God. The same was in the beginning with God" (John 1:1, 2). John the Baptist avowed of him, "This was he of whom I said, He that cometh after me is become before me: for he was before me" (John 1:15). Jesus told the Jews, "Before Abraham was born, I am" (John 8:58). Jesus prayed, "And now, Father, glorify thou me with thine own self with the glory which I had with thee before the world was" (John 17:5). Paul expresses the same thing in Philippians 2:5-11.

This pre-existence was a reality, not a phantasy. Some have taught that it was an ideal pre-existence, that the Son pre-existed only as an idea in the mind of God, which idea came into fruition the moment Jesus was born on earth. This heretical belief is voiced by theologians of the present day, although it is found in the past also. G. C. Berkouwer rightly avows, "Sidetrack the confession of pre-existence and the whole message becomes meaningless. A century ago Scholten tried to explain pre-existence in the sense of an ideal foreknowledge of God which from eternity enclosed the Messiah. When Scholten bade adieu to the confession of the church his rationalism led him to say: 'Herewith collapses the unreformed conception of a Son of God who left heaven and laid aside his glory.' The pre-existence of Christ is changed over into a pre-existence of the Messiah in the mind of God, in order thus to evade the divine event of which the apostles spoke in prayerful adoration: God revealed in the flesh. The Word became flesh."[4] Hans H. Wendt, a German theologian of the latter part of the nineteenth century, is a good example of one advocating an ideal pre-existence for the Son of God. He has stated in one of his works, "It is certainly a highly idealistic mode of view and of speech when Jesus designates His ideal existence for God ... simply as existence, as if it were real existence."[5] But the New Testament does not teach an ideal pre-existence, for it talks in unmistakable terms. It states that he was in the "form of God," but he did not look upon this as something "to be grasped." Instead, he "emptied himself" of this divine and heavenly glory

4 *Ibid.*, pp. 182-3.
5 Hans Wendt, *The Teaching of Jesus,* II, 176.

(Phil. 2:5-7). These terms discount a merely ideal pre-existence. They speak of a real personal being.

(2) VIRGIN BIRTH

The virgin birth is discussed here as well as under his humanity, since it is related to both. The gospels of Matthew and Luke are the only two that proclaim this important doctrine. Mark begins his gospel with the ministry of Jesus; therefore he says nothing of his origin. John writes late, knowing that his readers already possess the virgin birth account in their gospel manuscripts of Matthew and Luke. Therefore he does not mention it, telling of the pre-existence of Jesus instead. Now we see that birth by a virgin, who has conceived through the Holy Spirit, was merely the means whereby the Son made his descent from heaven into human flesh. Now is the reason for the virgin birth perfectly apparent. The one who had lain from eternity on the bosom of his heavenly Father was to lie on the bosom of an earthly mother. "Joseph, thou son of David, fear not to take unto thee Mary thy wife: for that which is conceived in her is of the Holy Spirit" (Matt. 1:20). Thus the angel addressed Joseph prior to the miraculous birth of our Lord.

(3) CALLED GOD IN THE NEW TESTAMENT

"In the beginning was the Word, and the Word was with God, and the Word was God" (John 1:1). Thomas exclaims, "My Lord and my God" (John 20:28), which exclamation was un-rebuked by Jesus. Paul talks of the "appearing of the glory of the great God and our Saviour Jesus Christ" (Titus 2:13).

(4) INNER DIVINE CONSCIOUSNESS

Some writers term this his messianic consciousness. It is the fact that he knew himself to be the Redeemer of fallen man, God's plenipotentiary come to earth to save and to rescue. This is first seen at the age of twelve as he discusses spiritual things with the great teachers in the temple. "Knew ye not that I must be in my Father's house?" (Luke 2:49). The Greek literally says, "in the things of my Father," meaning about my Father's business.

a. Sent of the Father

Constantly through John's gospel we find the phrase "the one sending me," which phrase is used of the Father in heaven. "I seek not mine own will, but the will of him that sent me" (John 5:30). "And the Father that sent me, he hath borne witness of me" (John 5:37).

b. Revealed the Father

Jesus was the perfect revelation of the Father, which is why Philip's request that he show them the Father is superfluous. "Have I been so long time with you, and dost thou not know me, Philip? he that hath seen me hath seen the Father" (John 14:9). "No man hath seen God at any time; the only begotten Son, who is in the bosom of the Father, he hath declared him" (John 1:18). We are told that no one knows the Father "save the Son, and he to whomsoever the Son willeth to reveal him" (Matt. 11:27).

c. Spoke of "my Father," not "our Father"

Jesus never says "our Father"; it is always "my Father," thus showing a unique relationship sustained with the Father in heaven, not shared even by redeemed creatures. He is truly the Son of the Father in a unique sense, in a way shared by no other. He is the "one-of-a-kind" Son. (It is true that Jesus uses the phrase "our Father" in the model prayer for the disciples, but here he is putting words in their mouths and is not using the phrase relative to himself.) Calling God his Father shows divine consciousness.

d. Employed "I am" sayings

There are many of these sayings in the Gospel of John, all of which reveal a divine consciousness of his person, origin, and work. The most profound is that of John 8:58: "Before Abraham was born, I am," a definite application of the name "I AM" of the eternal God as found in Exodus 3:14. Here God tells Moses that "I AM THAT I AM" sends him to redeem his people. Jesus uses the same phrase "I am" for himself. Other "I am" sayings are as follows. "I am the resurrection, and the life" (John 11:25). "I am the way, and the truth, and the life" (John 14:6). "I am the living bread which came down out of heaven" (John 6:51). "I am the true vine" (John 15:1). "I am the door of the sheep" (John 10:7). "I am the good shepherd" (John 10:11). All of these statements categorically reveal an inner divine consciousness.

(5) DIVINE POWERS AND PRIVILEGES EXERCISED BY HIM

Jesus performed acts and claimed authorities that relate only to divinity.

a. Forgiver of sins

Jesus was accused of blasphemy by the Jews because he claimed to forgive sins, an act which, they said, could be performed only by God. But he was God in the flesh, and so could forgive in the full sense of the word. "But that ye may know that the Son of man hath authority on earth to forgive sins (then saith he to the sick of the palsy), Arise, and take up thy bed, and go unto thy house" (Matt. 9:6). His miracles would attest to this authority in forgiveness.

b. *Recipient of all authority*

"All authority hath been given unto me in heaven and on earth" (Matt. 28:18). This is a sweeping statement, rich in divine prerogatives. It is the basis of the Great Commission, which follows it immediately.

c. *Only way of life*

He is the only way of eternal life, the only means of redemption. "He that believeth on the Son hath eternal life; but he that obeyeth not the Son shall not see life, but the wrath of God abideth on him" (John 3:36). "I am the way, and the truth, and the life: no one cometh unto the Father, but by me" (John 14:6). "Neither is there any other name under heaven, that is given among men, wherein we must be saved" (Acts 4:12). This last statement was part of Peter's defense before the Jewish Sanhedrin after his arrest for healing the lame man as he and John entered the temple. Jesus says, "I am the door of the sheep" (John 10:7). Since a sheepfold of that day had only one door, Jesus implies that he is the only means of entrance into heaven.

d. *Received honor and worship due only to God*

It is the desire of God "that all may honor the Son, even as they honor the Father" (John 5:23). And Stephen, as they stoned him, cried out to Jesus, "Lord Jesus, receive my spirit" (Acts 7:59), thereby according to Jesus the honor due to God. Paul distinctly states the means of salvation: "Because if thou shalt confess with thy mouth Jesus as Lord, and shalt believe in thy heart that God raised him from the dead, thou shalt be saved" (Rom. 10:9). It is God's desire that all the angels should worship him. "And let all the angels of God worship him" (Heb. 1:6). It is Paul's view that sometime in the exaltation of Christ "every knee should bow . . . and that every tongue should confess that Jesus Christ is Lord" (Phil. 2:10, 11). "Worthy is the Lamb that hath been slain to receive the power, and riches, and wisdom, and might, and honor, and glory, and blessing" (Rev. 5:12). All these attestations signify deity in the fullest sense.

e. *Displayed miraculous knowledge*

He recognized Nathanael while he was under the fig tree (John 1:47-50). He knew all about the life of the woman of Samaria (John 4:17-19, 39). He knew what the mind of each man contained. "He needed not that any one should bear witness concerning man; for he himself knew what was in man" (John 2:25). He knew of a miraculous catch of fish to be made (Luke 5:6-9). He knew of the colt of an ass, upon which he was to ride royally into Jerusalem (Matt. 21:2), and where that colt was tied. He foresaw the fall of Jerusalem (Matt. 24:2), and not only a cross for him but one for Peter (John 21:18, 19).

(6) WORKS OF GOD PERFORMED BY HIM

a. *Creation*

"All things were made through him; and without him was not anything made that hath been made" (John 1:3). Paul makes the same statement in Colossians 1:16, that Jesus is the agent of creation. But he not only declares that things were made through him; they were also made *unto* him. He is not only the means of creation; he is the end of creation.

b. *Preservation*

All things hold together through him. The writer of Hebrews states that he is "upholding all things by the word of his power" (1:3). And Paul states that "in him all things consist" (Col. 1:17). The Greek portrays "hold together" more than "consists."

c. *Resurrection of the dead*

Only God raises the dead, for he alone gives life. Christ himself will raise the dead, a divine work. "The hour cometh, in which all that are in the tombs shall hear his voice, and shall come forth; they that have done good, unto the resurrection of life; and they that have done evil, unto the resurrection of judgment" (John 5:28, 29).

d. *Judgment of the world*

All authority as judge of mankind has been delegated to the Son. "For neither doth the Father judge any man, but he hath given all judgment unto the Son" (John 5:22). "And he gave him authority to execute judgment, because he is a son of man" (John 5:27). Men will rise and fall on judgment day by what they have done with Jesus. Christ shall one day "sit on the throne of his glory: and before him shall be gathered all the nations" (Matt. 25:31, 32).

(7) DIVINITY ATTESTED BY MANY WITNESSES

The Gospel of John very distinctly lists eight witnesses to the deity of Christ. These are as follows: John the Baptist: "And I have seen, and have borne witness that this is the Son of God" (1:34); the works of Christ: "The very works that I do bear witness of me, that the Father hath sent me" (5:36); the Father: "And the Father that sent me, he hath borne witness of me" (5:37); the Hebrew Scriptures: "Ye search the scriptures, because ye think that in them ye have eternal life; and these are they which bear witness of me" (5:39); Christ himself: "Even if I bear witness of myself, my witness is true; for I know whence I came, and whither I go" (8:14); the Holy Spirit: "But when the Comforter is come, whom I will send unto you from the Father, even the Spirit of truth, which proceedeth from the Father, he shall bear witness of me" (15:26); the believers: "And ye also bear witness, because ye have been with me from the beginning" (15:27); the writer of the gospel: "And he that hath seen hath borne witness, and his witness is true: and he knoweth that he saith true, that ye also may believe" (19:35).

The writer of this profound gospel brings together what can almost be termed a "great cloud of witnesses" to the divine sonship. From prologue to epilogue these witnesses are brought forward — and with one supreme motive: the proclamation that Jesus of Nazareth is the Son of God. There is no doubt that the testimony of these witnesses presents a great weight in the value-judgment John is endeavoring to set forth. Allan Barr asserts, "Yet we find in the Fourth Gospel the simple principle of corroboration transferred to testimony of this kind. Such testimony is indeed impressive and convincing if we get enough of it, and get it from the right people; and one of the most impressive things in the Fourth Gospel is the accumulated testimony adduced for the greatest of Christian value-judgments, the supernatural endowment and Divine Sonship of Jesus."[6]

(8) DIVINE TERMS ASCRIBED TO HIM

a. *Son of God*

Repeatedly throughout the Scriptures Jesus is called the Son, or the Son of God, especially in the Gospel of John, the gospel of sonship par excellence. This whole gospel is a study of the relationship of the Son with the Father. The writer never uses the term sons for believers; he uses the term children for all the redeemed ones —"children of God." He reserves the term Son for

---

[6] Allan Barr, "The Factor of Testimony in the Gospels," *The Expository Times,* Vol. 49, No. 9, June 1938, p. 407.

Jesus alone, since he is Son in a unique way. He is the only Son, the unique Son; this is what John means by the Greek term translated "only begotten," used of Jesus four times in the gospel and once in First John (4:9).

The phrase "son of . . ." in the Hebrew means "having the characteristics of. . . ." Therefore the Son of God would have the characteristics of God, which Jesus possesses in the full sense of the term — the fulness of divinity. The phrase Son of God when used of Jesus for himself never connotes a mere ethical relationship to the Father, a relation which others possess or are capable of possessing. Through adoption we become sons, but Jesus is the unique and only Son in his very being. We become sons through grace, but Jesus is Son by right. We *become* sons; he is Son *eternally* — always has been and always will be. A man may become *a son;* Jesus is *the Son.*

b. *Image of God*

He is called "the image of the invisible God" (Col. 1:15). This term suggests copy or counterpart. Where Jesus is the image of God absolutely and unconditionally, man may become the image of God relatively and derivatively. Jesus is the perfect representation of all the attributes and powers of God. The term image suggests equality with God. The writer of Hebrews says he is "the very image of his substance" (1:3). He is the image of God in a way man can never be. "We may well say that Jesus is 'the living image of God.' In him the unknowable God becomes knowable; the unapproachable God becomes approachable; the invisible God becomes flesh and dwells among us, and we see full displayed his grace, his glory and his truth."[7]

c. *Logos*

This term is translated "Word." "In the beginning was the Word, and the Word was with God, and the Word was God" (John 1:1). It denotes deity in the highest sense, for it represents the reason and speech of God, the personal self-revelation of the divine essence. It is the expression, definite and ordered, of God. The Logos is the finite form taken by the infinite God.

The term had been used by the Stoics as the rational principle in the universe. Philo, the Alexandrian Jewish philosopher, had also used it, and it was employed in the Septuagint to translate the usual Hebrew term for "word." John gives this ancient term new meaning, showing that Jesus is the fulfillment of all that the people were seeking in the Logos. He uses the term to grip his

7 William Barclay, *Jesus As They Saw Him,* p. 394.

Greek and Jewish readers, then passes on to more usual names for Jesus. John does not employ it for Jesus beyond the prologue, and the Synoptics do not employ it as such at all.

d. *Son of man*

This term is taken by many writers to refer to the humanity of Jesus. It is true that Jesus uses it for himself more than any other designation, and it is also true that throughout the Old Testament it is used synonymously with the simpler term man (except in Daniel 7:13ff.) ; but the term is used by our Lord with full messianic connotation. The term refers just as much to his divinity as to his humanity. Verses such as Matthew 25:31 show this: "But when the Son of man shall come in his glory, and all the angels with him, then shall he sit on the throne of his glory." This is God's prerogative only. Jesus goes back to the one messianic use of the term Son of man in the Old Testament and repeatedly applies it to himself, filling it with the concept of himself that he wishes the world to have. Daniel 7:13ff. is the key to the term in the mind of Jesus. The term Christ, or Messiah, in the mind of the contemporary Jew is too encrusted with a false concept; so Jesus delves into the Hebrew Scriptures and secures an obscure term, filling it with the concept that he desires them to possess. This term is Son of man. A study of the word as used in the Synoptic gospels will verify its divine implications.

It is true that the term Son of man as used by Jesus is highly involved with the kingdom idea, but this kingdom to Jesus is a purely spiritual one and is not to be confused with national Israel. Therefore Jesus prefers the term Son of man to that of Christ. He does not intend to "restore the kingdom to Israel" (Acts 1:6). Jesus desires to redeem all humanity, not just a segment of it.

e. *Christ, or Messiah*

The term Christ, or Messiah, was a purely Jewish one until universalized by our Lord himself. It means anointed one, Christ coming from the Greek and Messiah coming from the Hebrew. It is the term that Jesus accepts for himself but avoids as much as possible due to the false connotations built around it in the mind of the contemporary Jew. Yet, at the same time, it is the term that has become the favorite designation for our Lord. The very term Christology is derived from it.

Kings in the Old Testament are termed anointed, but the term Messiah is never used as a title in and of itself for the coming Redeemer. There he is termed Immanuel, Wonderful, Counsellor, Mighty God, Prince of Peace, etc. It is in the interbiblical period that the term Messiah is applied to the coming One who will deliver his people, for there the messianic hope receives a great impetus. Therefore Jesus knows himself to be the Messiah of Old Testament anticipation; yet our gospels show us that he transforms greatly the popular understanding of this term. In fact, he virtually revolutionizes it in the mind of his followers.

In his teaching and preaching Jesus so altered the concept of the role of the Messiah that the cross was inevitable. "But if the New Testament hailed Jesus as the Messiah, it is evident that the Jews did not regard him as such. Indeed, they rejected him outright and did him to death. Nor is it very difficult to see why they could not accept him. He was not at all the Messiah that was expected. Although he claimed for himself that office and made use of the various messianic titles, he understood that office and used those titles in such a way as to ensure his rejection. Evidently he was a Messiah of a novel sort."[8] He made no effort to lead the struggle against Rome. He did not set himself up as ruler of an earthly kingdom of Jews. He felt it necessary to suffer and die. The Jews saw no coming of the kingdom on clouds of heaven. And he was quite the opposite to that expected by the legalistic scribes and Pharisees with their meticulous keeping of the law. Nor was he what they expected in the "prophet like unto Moses." He was the Messiah, yes, but oh, how different than was anticipated!

2. TWO DENIALS OF HIS TRUE DEITY

(1) THE EBIONITES (A.D. 107)

These held that Christ was merely a man, that he did not possess a divine nature. Just as the Docetics denied his humanity, the Ebionites denied his divinity. His relations with God were very special, and he was led mightily of the Holy Spirit; but he was not divine. Their view of the monotheism of God would not permit attributing to Christ divine qualities.

(2) THE ARIANS (A.D. 325)

The Arians came much later than the Ebionites in point of time. They held that Christ was the first and greatest of created beings. Therefore he was more than man but less than God. The Son was subordinate to the Father. With the name of Arius of Alexandria is linked the term subordinationism, an opinion of great heresy furthered today by the Jehovah's Witnesses. Arius said that since the Son had a beginning there was a time that he was not. Therefore he is not co-eternal with the Father. He maintained that the Son is like the Father but not of the same substance.

8 John Bright, *The Kingdom of God*, p. 198.

DOCTRINES OF THE CHRISTIAN RELIGION

III. INCARNATION OF CHRIST

The fact of the humanity of Christ and the fact of the divinity of Christ pose the question of the relationship of these two natures during the earthly sojourn of Jesus. This relationship involves the doctrine of the incarnation, which is a term derived from the Latin, meaning an embodiment in the flesh, and, when used theologically, that God was incarnate in Jesus Christ.

1. UNION OF TWO NATURES IN ONE PERSON

The divine and the human were united in the person of Jesus. "And the Word became flesh, and dwelt among us (and we beheld his glory, glory as of the only begotten from the Father), full of grace and truth" (John 1:14). This is perhaps the strongest passage on the incarnation found in the Bible. "God was in Christ reconciling the world unto himself" (II Cor. 5:19). Each nature was unaltered in essence and not divested in its attributes; he was fully God and fully man. Jesus was a single undivided personality in whom these two natures were united. This is the supreme paradox! It was not a union of God *and* man, nor a manifestation of God *in* man. The former would imply an imperfect union, and the latter might apply to Christ indwelling in the believer. The best phrase is the God-man.

Christ never uses the word us to refer to the two natures within him. (The only exception to this is the statement, "we speak that which we know" in John 3:11; but here he is probably including the disciples.) Yet he uses "I" and "thou" relative to the persons of the Trinity. This is true because the personality of Christ was one, though two natures were united in this one, a God-man personality. We are forbidden to divide the person or to confound the natures. After stormy Christological discussions through the ages this orthodox position was promulgated at the Council of Chalcedon, A.D. 451, and has held sway ever since. In the one person Jesus Christ there are two natures, a human and a divine, each complete, yet united in such a way that no third nature is found thereby.

2. FACTS RELATIVE TO THIS UNION

(1) ITS IMPORTANCE

This is not only the crowning fact of Christianity; it is the central problem of Christology. Here is the vertex of God's redemption of mankind. The person of Christ is the central point of Christianity; error here in doctrine will pervade every square inch of one's concept of God and of salvation. Christianity *is* the person of Christ.

(2) ITS INSCRUTABLE NATURE

It is a mystery incapable of psychological explanation. We cannot explain, for finite mind cannot comprehend. Paul talks of "the mystery of God, even Christ, in whom are all the treasures of wisdom and knowledge hidden" (Col. 2:2, 3). It was a mystery to this inspired Apostle of Tarsus, as it is to us today.

> *I know not how that Bethlehem's Babe*
> *Could in the Godhead be;*
> *I only know the Manger Child*
> *Has brought God's life to me.*
> —Harry Webb Farrington

(3) ITS NECESSITY

The incarnation is necessary to constitute Jesus Christ a proper mediator between God and man, since his twofold nature involves him with both parties, the Redeemer and the redeemed. There is the status of divinity and there is sympathy with the fallen. "Wherefore it behooved him in all things to be made like unto his brethren, that he might become a merciful and faithful high priest in things pertaining to God, to make propitiation for the sins of the people. For in that he himself hath suffered being tempted, he is able to succor them that are tempted" (Heb. 2: 17, 18). "If the idea of incarnation is to retain a secure hold of our minds, we must find its great raison d'etre in the dread problem created both for God and man by the reality of sin. Because sin had desolated humanity and man must have forgiveness if he is to live in God's sight, therefore God became man."[9] Because he is man he can make atonement for man; because he is God his atonement has infinite value. A divine-human Saviour meets all the needs for man's reconciliation.

3. TWO DENIALS OF HIS TRUE INCARNATION

(1) THE NESTORIANS (A.D. 431)

The Nestorians denied the union of the human and divine natures in Christ's person. God and man were morally related to each other in Christ. It was an alliance between God and man and not a case of the God-man personality. This led to the erroneous view of some in the early church who maintained that Jesus suffered only in his humanity but not in his deity.

(2) THE EUTYCHIANS (A.D. 451)

The Eutychians held that the two natures were merged into

[9] Mackintosh, *op. cit.*, pp. 442-3.

one nature; and, since the divine overpowered the human, only the divine nature remained, the human being absorbed into it. The Eutychians were also called Monophysites, due to this one-nature belief.

IV. TWO STATES OF CHRIST

The two states of Christ consist of humiliation and exaltation.

1. HUMILIATION

By humiliation we do not mean merely the outward trials and suffering of Christ's earthly life. Nor by humiliation do we mean the surrender of the relative divine attributes, such as omniscience, omnipotence, and omnipresence, while retaining the immanent ones of holiness, love, and truth. This has been called the Kenosis Theory, derived from the Greek word for "emptied himself" as found in Philippians 2:7. To give up divine attributes would be to give up the essence of divinity, the substance of the Godhead. For a full discussion and answer to the Kenotic Theory the student is referred to D. M. Baillie's *God Was In Christ*. Here it is maintained that this theory seems "to give us a story of a temporary theophany, in which He who formerly was God changed Himself temporarily into man, or exchanged His divinity for humanity."[10]

By humiliation is meant the surrender of the independent exercise of the divine attributes. The pre-existent Son set aside his divine glory to take the form of a servant, resigning not the possession but the independent exercise of the divine attributes. (Sometimes even the latter shines forth, as in supernatural knowledge of present conditions and future events, the miraculous manifestation of divine power, etc.) There was a voluntary submission to the guidance of the Holy Spirit and a voluntary acceptance of the temptation, suffering, and death that were necessarily entailed in the identification with the human.

The passages that depict this humiliation are as follows. "Have this mind in you, which was also in Christ Jesus: who, existing in the form of God, counted not the being on an equality with God a thing to be grasped, but emptied himself, taking the form of a servant, being made in the likeness of men; and being found in fashion as a man, he humbled himself, becoming obedient even unto death, yea, the death of the cross" (Phil. 2:5-8). "For ye know the grace of our Lord Jesus Christ, that, though he was rich, yet for your sakes he became poor, that ye through his poverty might become rich" (II Cor. 8:9). Jesus requests the Father, "Glorify thou me with thine own self with the glory which I had with thee before the world was" (John 17:5). This request

10 Baillie, *op. cit.,* pp. 94-8.

is made in the state of humiliation, that the glorious condition prior to humiliation might be restored. It might be said that the Godhead had narrowed itself down almost to the point of extinction. God laid aside that glorious form, that blazing majesty, that he might approximate and beseech the finite. The humiliation does not consist of one act but is a continuous process of self-renunciation beginning with the laying aside of heavenly glory and culminating in obedience "even unto death, yea, the death of the cross." It runs from the pouring out of glory at Bethlehem to the pouring out of life at Golgotha.

2. EXALTATION

In exaltation the independent exercise of the divine attributes is resumed, or taken up again. All limitations of his divine nature are cast aside. There is a quickening and a resurrection, thus displaying to the world the perfected man, triumphant over sin and death. There is an ascension and sitting at the right hand of God, thus proclaiming to every living being, in heaven and upon earth, Christ as the glorified God, holding dominion over all the universe and being the object of worship.

The glory that he requested in the famous high-priestly prayer has been granted. "And now, Father, glorify thou me with thine own self with the glory which I had with thee before the world was" (John 17:5). Christ has again been clothed with the pre-existent glory; he is now the glorified Christ. And, just as it was stated that humiliation did not consist of one act but was a process, so glorification, or exaltation, did not consist of one act but was a process — quickening, resurrection, ascension, being seated at the right hand of God.

It was the resurrected Christ who said unto Mary outside the empty tomb, "Touch me not; for I am not yet ascended unto the Father; but go unto my brethren, and say to them, I ascend unto my Father and your Father, and my God and your God" (John 20:17). In his Pentecostal sermon Peter proclaimed the Christ "whom God raised up, having loosed the pangs of death: because it was not possible that he should be holden of it" (Acts 2:24). "So then the Lord Jesus, after he had spoken unto them, was received up into heaven, and sat down at the right hand of God" (Mark 16:19). The reinstatement into glory has taken place.

V. TWO ASPECTS OF CHRIST

1. SAVIOUR

Christ came to earth, God incarnate, to save a lost humanity. Being spiritually bankrupt and hope bereft, man's plight was a formidable one. Christ came to redeem man from this quagmire of despair. The supreme motive of his advent to earth was to be a Saviour. The New Testament writers had experienced the salvation he offered to all mankind; others must experience it also. Therefore they wrote.

The angel says to Joseph concerning Mary, "And she shall bring forth a son; and thou shalt call his name Jesus; for it is he that shall save his people from their sins" (Matt. 1:21). The name Jesus means Saviour; so even his name suggests his supreme activity. The angel announces to the shepherds the night of his birth, "There is born to you this day in the city of David a Saviour, who is Christ the Lord" (Luke 2:11). Jesus himself clearly states the purpose of his advent. "For the Son of man came to seek and to save that which was lost" (Luke 19:10). John the Baptist views him as the Lamb of God whose supreme function is salvation from sin. He announces, "Behold, the Lamb of God, that taketh away the sin of the world!" (John 1:29).

In the book of Acts this very important function is graphically presented. Peter reveals him as the only Saviour. "And in none other is there salvation: for neither is there any other name under heaven, that is given among men, wherein we must be saved" (Acts 4:12). Peter also tells Cornelius and his household "that through his name every one that believeth on him shall receive remission of sins" (Acts 10:43). When the Philippian jailer asks Paul and Silas what to do to be saved, they reply, "Believe on the Lord Jesus, and thou shalt be saved" (Acts 16:31).

Paul's epistles are replete with passages portraying his role as Redeemer. "For I am not ashamed of the gospel: for it is the power of God unto salvation to every one that believeth; to the Jew first, and also to the Greek" (Rom. 1:16). In the fifteenth chapter of First Corinthians Paul gives a vivid picture of the gospel he preached to them, in which gospel they are saved. The keynote of this is "that Christ died for our sins according to the Scriptures" (15:3). Paul states that for one in Christ there is no condemnation, no negative judgment to be received on judgment day (Rom. 8:1). The man in Christ has been saved from sin; from both the power of sin now and the consequence of sin later.

2. LORD

When we view Jesus as Saviour we are vividly reminded of what he does for us. We are the recipients. He saves us, redeems us, purifies us, sanctifies us, regenerates us, justifies us. We receive; he bestows. When we view Jesus as Lord, however, the passive takes on an active note. Here obedience is the keynote of the relationship. Lordship entails obedience, a fulfillment of commands and statutes.

The word lord means master, and when applied to Jesus it denotes that he has a moral mastery of the life of the believer. The correlative word is slave or bondservant, which is Paul's favorite term for himself. Lord, or Kurios, and slave, or *doulos* — these are the terms borrowed from the Greco-Roman slave world to depict the spiritual relationship between Christ and the believer. Just as the slave had but one compulsion, to please and obey his master, so the Christian's supreme desire is to do the will of Christ and to obey his commands. Christ must be first in every phase of life: before business, before family, before friends, before life itself.

When Jesus fails to receive the obedience and following he could expect from his disciples, he says to them, "And why call ye me, Lord, Lord, and do not the things which I say?" (Luke 6:46). To be called Lord and then not to be obeyed is ironical. Merely calling him Lord will not insure access to heaven; obedience to his will is the fundamental requisite. "Not every one that saith unto me, Lord, Lord, shall enter into the kingdom of heaven; but he that doeth the will of my Father who is in heaven" (Matt. 7:21). An utterance such as that of Thomas, "My Lord and my God" (John 20:28), must be accompanied by rigid adherence to his precepts.

The exactitude of discipleship, the counterpart of Jesus' lordship, is clearly demonstrated in the Scriptures. "If any man would come after me, let him deny himself, and take up his cross, and follow me" (Mark 8:34). "So therefore whosoever he be of you that renounceth not all that he hath, he cannot be my disciple" (Luke 14:33). Jesus must have the supreme loyalty and the paramount love. "He that loveth father or mother more than me is not worthy of me; and he that loveth son or daughter more than me is not worthy of me. And he that doth not take his cross and follow after me, is not worthy of me" (Matt. 10:37, 38).

In the book of Acts Jesus is regarded as Lord in the full sense of the term. Peter remonstrates with the Jews, "Let all the house of Israel therefore know assuredly, that God hath made him both Lord and Christ, this Jesus whom ye crucified" (Acts 2:36). When Stephen is being stoned he cries out, "Lord Jesus, receive my spirit," and in practically the same breath, "Lord, lay not this sin to their charge" (Acts 7:59, 60).

To Paul confession of Jesus as Lord must be accompanied with sincere belief in the resurrection. "Because if thou shalt confess with thy mouth Jesus as Lord, and shalt believe in thy heart that God raised him from the dead, thou shalt be saved" (Rom. 10:9).

The resurrection confirmed his sonship and his lordship, for he is the one who was "declared to be the Son of God with power, according to the spirit of holiness, by the resurrection from the dead; even Jesus Christ our Lord" (Rom. 1:4). It is God's desire that in exalting him "every tongue should confess that Jesus Christ is Lord, to the glory of God the Father" (Phil. 2:11). The terms Lord, Lord Jesus, or Lord Jesus Christ, are so recurrent in the writings of this apostle that they are too numerous to mention. Yet one thing must be remembered: "No man can say Jesus is Lord, but in the Holy Spirit" (I Cor. 12:3). It is a matter of spiritual discernment, not physical apprehension. Then one will see that he is "the blessed and only Potentate, the King of kings, and Lord of lords" (I Tim. 6:15).

VI. THREE OFFICES OF CHRIST

Christ's offices are three in number: prophet, priest, and king. All three of these concepts are found in the Old Testament, but in Christ alone is found the ideal reality of each. As prophet he saves us from the ignorance of sin; as priest he saves us from the guilt of sin; as king he saves us from the rule of sin.

1. PROPHETIC

As prophet Jesus was the revealer of divine will, the interpreter of divine truth. So many people have the narrow conception that a prophet is one who foretells future events; this is only an incidental feature of prophecy. It may or may not occur. A prophet is a "forthteller" more than a "foreteller." He may tell of past events, present events, or future events. Jesus did just that. He told the woman of Samaria of her past life, he revealed to the unbelieving Jews that they were sons of the devil and sons of hell, and he foretold to his disciples the destruction of Jerusalem, which took place in A.D. 70. A prophet taught, and this Jesus did, in the Sermon on the Mount (Matt. 5-7). A prophet admonished, as Jesus did constantly. "Woe unto you, scribes and Pharisees, hypocrites!" (Matt. 23:15). A prophet performed miracles, as Jesus did repeatedly. A prophet revealed God in his life, his work, and his person, as did Jesus — par excellence!

Jesus called himself a prophet. "A prophet is not without honor, save in his own country, and in his own house" (Matt. 13:57). The people called him a prophet. "When therefore the people saw the sign which he did, they said, This is of a truth the prophet that cometh into the world" (John 6:14). The two on the way to Emmaus, Cleopas and his unnamed friend, called Jesus "a prophet mighty in deed and word before God and all the people" (Luke 24:19).

He depicted true prophecy (insight and expression) in a perfect manner. His work as a prophet began even in his pre-existent state. "The things which I heard from him [the Father], these speak I unto the world" (John 8:26). Yet, while here on earth, his true prophetic nature shone forth, and with a difference from the prophets preceding him. They were given a message; he was the message. They gave the word of God; he was the Word of God. They were inspired; he was the Inspirer. They spoke for God; he was God speaking. His prophecy is continuing now through his faithful proclaimers, even until the final revelation in glory. "I made known unto them thy name, and will make it known" (John 17:26).

2. PRIESTLY

The priest was one divinely appointed to function with God on behalf of man. He offered sacrifice, and he interceded. Christ fulfilled both of these requisites. God chose Israel as a priestly nation, Levi as a priestly tribe, Aaron's family as a priestly family. The high priest came from this family, until the time of *the* High Priest, Jesus Christ.

The book of Hebrews portrays Christ as our High Priest, immutable and eternal. "And they indeed have been made priests many in number, because that by death they are hindered from continuing: but he, because he abideth for ever, hath his priesthood unchangeable. Wherefore also he is able to save to the uttermost them that draw near unto God through him, seeing he ever liveth to make intercession for them. For such a high priest became us, holy, guileless, undefiled, separated from sinners, and made higher than the heavens; who needeth not daily, like those high priests, to offer up sacrifices, first for his own sins, and then for the sins of the people: for this he did once for all, when he offered up himself. For the law appointeth men high priests, having infirmity; but the word of the oath, which was after the law, appointeth a Son, perfected for evermore" (Heb. 7:23-28). He is our High Priest in heaven above, which is our holy of holies; but he is not only the High Priest, he offered himself as the sacrifice, once and for all. He is both priest and sacrifice, both offerer and victim.

As priest his work is that of priestly mediation, reconciling man, at enmity with God, back to God. Peace is made through a sacrifice. He is both the priest and the sacrifice. Here we enter into the doctrine of the atonement, which will be discussed later. The atonement may be viewed from many angles, but the prevailing language of Scripture is that it was a sacrifice. Christ was the victim, the righteous being offered for the unrighteous.

But a priest not only offers sacrifice; he also intercedes. This

Christ, as our High Priest, does for us. He can intercede for us because he knows our weaknesses. "For we have not a high priest that cannot be touched with the feeling of our infirmities; but one that hath been in all points tempted like as we are, yet without sin" (Heb. 4:15) . He never ceases to intercede for us. "Wherefore also he is able to save to the uttermost them that draw near unto God through him, seeing he ever liveth to make intercession for them" (Heb. 7:25) .

3. KINGLY

Christ was sovereign prior to his incarnation and redeeming work; he was sovereign merely because he was divine. But now, subsequent to his redeeming mission and consequent to his exaltation, he is sovereign in a more complete way. He is sovereign in virtue of the fact he is the God-man Redeemer. Because of this he is King, ruling all things and all beings in heaven and on earth. He is "the ruler of the kings of the earth" (Rev. 1:5) . Therefore he is "King of Kings and Lord of Lords" (Rev. 19: 16) . He is the one "upholding all things by the word of his power" (Heb. 1:3) . "All authority hath been given unto me in heaven and on earth" (Matt. 28:18), Jesus proclaims just prior to his ascension. A. J. Gordon: "Christ is now creation's sceptre-bearer, as he was once creation's burden-bearer."

As he rode triumphantly into Jerusalem the crowd cried out, "Blessed is the King that cometh in the name of the Lord" (Luke 19:38) . Yet his kingdom is a spiritual one, difficult as this was for the Jews to conceive. "My kingdom is not of this world," Jesus told Pilate. Then, to the query if he were a king, he replied, "Thou sayest that I am a king" (John 18:36, 37) . "Our Lord's offer of the Kingdom of God was not the offer of a political kingdom, nor did it involve national and material blessings. The Jews wanted a political king to overthrow their enemies; but Jesus refused an earthly crown (John 6:15), offering spiritual bread instead of an earthly kingdom (John 6:52-57) ."[11]

His kingdom is one of glory, where he reigns upon his throne, the omnipotent God and the omnipotent Judge. Regal splendor adorns that throne.

[11] George E. Ladd, *The Gospel of the Kingdom*, p. 109.

OUTLINE FOR CHAPTER FOUR

I. Meaning of Term Spirit
1. Use of term in Old Testament
2. Use of term in New Testament
3. Contrast of function of Spirit in the two Testaments
   (1) In Old Testament
   (2) In New Testament
4. "Holy Spirit," not "Holy Ghost"

II. Spirit Recognized as God
1. Attributes of God ascribed to him
2. Works of God performed by him
3. Called God in New Testament
4. Equal status with Father and Son

III. Spirit as Personal
1. Scriptural evidence
   (1) Terms used of personality applied to him
      a. Ekeinos
      b. Paraclete
   (2) Mentioned in immediate connection with the Father and the Son
   (3) Acts as a person
   (4) Reacts as a person to the acts of others
2. Evidence from Christian experience
   (1) Conviction
   (2) Call
   (3) Spiritual growth

IV. Spirit and Christ
1. While Christ incarnate
2. After Christ's ascension

V. Work of Spirit
1. In revelation
2. In salvation
   (1) Conviction of sin
   (2) Renewal of sinner
   (3) Assurance of salvation
   (4) Sealing of Spirit
3. In bestowing gifts
4. In imparting power for holy living
5. In teaching
6. In interceding

7. In leading churches
   (1) In establishing churches
   (2) In guiding work of churches
   (3) In leading worship of churches

8. In speaking in tongues

CHAPTER FOUR

THE SPIRIT OF GOD

THROUGHOUT THE OLD TESTAMENT AND THE NEW TESTAMENT WE read of the Spirit of God, the Spirit of Jehovah, the Holy Spirit, the Spirit of Truth, or just simply the Spirit. Who is he? What does he do?

I. MEANING OF TERM SPIRIT

The root meaning of the Hebrew word translated "spirit" and of the Greek word translated "spirit" is identical: wind, breath, air. This is seen today in our English words pneumonia, pneumatic, pneumonic, etc., all of which refer to air, wind, or breath, and which are built on the Greek word *pneuma,* or spirit. In fact the doctrine of the Holy Spirit is termed pneumatology.

1. USE OF TERM SPIRIT IN OLD TESTAMENT

The Spirit of God brooded over the face of the waters and from the waste and void came order in creation (Gen. 1:2). Thus the Spirit created. God took dust of the ground and breathed into it his Spirit, and a living soul was produced (Gen. 2:7). Then in Psalm 104 we read, concerning the beasts of land and sea, "Thou hidest thy face, they are troubled; Thou takest away their breath, they die, And return to their dust. Thou sendest forth thy Spirit, they are created; And thou renewest the face of the ground" (29, 30). Therefore we discern that the Spirit of God is the animating principle in both man and beast. His Spirit enters, they live; his Spirit withdraws, they die.

The Spirit gives physical strength, enabling Samson to prevail against a young lion. "And the Spirit of Jehovah came mightily upon him, and he rent him as he would have rent a kid" (Judg. 14:6). The Spirit gives military strength. "Then the Spirit of Jehovah came upon Jephthah" (Judg. 11:29), and he defeated the Ammonites. The Spirit gives mechanical and technical skill. "See, I have called by name Bezalel ... and I have filled him with the Spirit of God, in wisdom, and in understanding, and in knowledge, and in all manner of workmanship" (Exod. 31:2, 3). The psalmist fears the departure of the Spirit. "Take not thy holy Spirit from me" (Ps. 51:11). Through his Spirit God is present everywhere. "Whither shall I go from thy Spirit? Or whither shall I flee from thy presence?" (Ps. 139:7). The Spirit came upon Saul, and he prophesied. "And the Spirit of God came mightily upon him, and he prophesied among them" (I Sam. 10:10). The Spirit gave David regal power. "Then Samuel took the horn of oil, and anointed him in the midst of his brethren: and the Spirit of Jehovah came mightily upon David from that day forward" (I Sam. 16:13).

It is to be noted that the Spirit in the Old Testament is generally termed the Spirit of God or the Spirit of Jehovah ("the Spirit of the Lord" in the King James Version), never the Holy Spirit. This is the New Testament term used for the same person, the third person of the Trinity. It is true that "holy Spirit" is found three times in the Old Testament (Ps. 51:11; Isa. 63:10; Isa. 63:11), but in each case the word "holy" is used as an adjective describing the nature of the Spirit, not as a part of the name. In the New Testament the adjective has become part of the name itself and is therefore capitalized in the English. The article in the Greek substantiates this view.

2. USE OF TERM SPIRIT IN NEW TESTAMENT

In the New Testament we find a more complete manifestation of the Spirit of God, a manifestation centering itself in a mighty outpouring of the Spirit during the Feast of Pentecost about forty days after the resurrection of our Lord. Jesus, just prior to his ascension, had predicted this great event, saying, "Ye shall be baptized in the Holy Spirit not many days hence" (Acts 1:5). On the Day of Pentecost the Holy Spirit came as a mighty rushing wind, appearing as cloven tongues of fire. "And they were all filled with the Holy Spirit, and began to speak with other tongues, as the Spirit gave them utterance" (Acts 2:1-4). Peter preaches his great Pentecostal sermon, interpreting all the phenomena of that great day as the fulfillment of Joel's prophecy of the pouring out of God's Spirit upon all flesh (Joel 2:28ff.). He promises the gift of the Holy Spirit to all who will repent and believe. Great power comes upon the apostles, and great signs and wonders are henceforth done by them.

In the New Testament there is an indwelling of the Holy Spirit within every believer. In speaking of the Spirit Jesus declares to his disciples, "Ye know him; for he abideth with you, and shall be in you" (John 14:17). Paul prays that the Ephesians "may be strengthened with power through his Spirit in the inward man" (Eph. 3:16). The bodies of Christians are temples of the Holy Spirit. "Know ye not that ye are a temple of God, and that the Spirit of God dwelleth in you?" (I Cor. 3:16). The Spirit binds believers together into one fellowship. "For in one Spirit were we all baptized into one body, whether Jews or Greeks, whether bond or free; and were all made to drink of one Spirit" (I Cor. 12:13).

Since the Spirit bestows life, the Christian should walk accordingly. "It is the spirit that giveth life" (John 6:63). "If we live by the Spirit, by the Spirit let us also walk" (Gal. 5:25). The Spirit teaches. "But the Comforter, even the Holy Spirit, whom the Father will send in my name, he shall teach you all things, and bring to your remembrance all that I said unto you" (John 14:26). The Spirit guides. "Howbeit when he, the Spirit of truth, is come, he shall guide you into all the truth" (John 16:13).

3. Contrast of Function of Spirit in the two Testaments

In the Old Testament the Spirit works much upon nature and mostly with key individuals to produce divinely intended ends. Dealing mainly with certain individuals, his work is not so much general in character and permanent in scope but comes upon them suddenly and without explanation as an aid in the providential workings of God. His activity is highly objective in character and not so much moral or ethical.

In the New Testament the work of the Spirit is more personal and intimate. It is with every Christian rather than just with those in key positions. His work is highly subjective. It is also very ethical, as is discerned in his activity in sanctification and in the very name Holy Spirit.

4. "Holy Spirit," not "Holy Ghost"

"Holy Spirit" is the usual term for the Spirit of God as found throughout the books of the New Testament. It is unfortunate that the King James Version translates this term with "Holy Ghost." In this version wherever the Greek word for "Spirit," *pneuma,* is found by itself, it is translated with "Spirit," and rightly so. This is the case with the many times *pneuma,* or "Spirit," is found in the eighth chapter of Romans. But when the term "Holy" becomes part of the name, the very same Greek word *pneuma* is translated with "Ghost" instead of with "Spirit." Therefore what should be "the Holy Spirit" becomes "the Holy Ghost," which is not accurate. This is why all the later translations have consistently switched to "Holy Spirit," as have practically all the hymn writers as well. All books of doctrine and theology use the more familiar term "Holy Spirit." Incidentally there is a Greek term in the New Testament which should be translated "ghost"; it is found in Mark 6:49, where it is recorded that they saw Jesus walking on the water and "supposed that it was a ghost."

II. SPIRIT RECOGNIZED AS GOD

The Holy Spirit is universally recognized as divine, as truly God. The controversies that engulfed the minds of church leaders over the divinity of the second person of the Trinity do not seem to have carried over to the third person.

1. ATTRIBUTES OF GOD ASCRIBED TO HIM

He is called "the Spirit of life" (Rom. 8:2). He is called "the Spirit of truth" (John 16:13). Paul speaks of "the love of the Spirit" (Rom. 15:30). The writer of Hebrews calls him "the eternal Spirit" (9:14). He is omnipresent, for the psalmist cannot flee from him (Ps. 139:7). He is holy, for this attribute has become part of his name.

2. WORKS OF GOD PERFORMED BY HIM

The Spirit was present in the great act of creation. "And the Spirit of God moved upon the face of the waters" (Gen. 1:2). The Spirit convicts of sin. "And he, when he is come, will convict the world in respect of sin" (John 16:8). Regeneration is brought about through the Holy Spirit. Jesus tells Nicodemus he must be born of the Spirit (John 3:5). Paul also speaks of the "renewing of the Holy Spirit" (Titus 3:5). The resurrection of the body accompanies the indwelling Spirit. "But if the Spirit of him that raised up Jesus from the dead dwelleth in you, he that raised up Christ Jesus from the dead shall give life also to your mortal bodies through his Spirit that dwelleth in you" (Rom. 8:11). The casting out of demons was performed by Jesus through the aid of the Holy Spirit (Matt. 12:28).

3. CALLED GOD IN NEW TESTAMENT

Peter asks Ananias why Satan has filled his heart "to lie to the Holy Spirit," and then immediately accuses him, "Thou hast not lied unto men, but unto God" (Acts 5:3-4). Paul tells the Corinthians, "Know ye not that ye are a temple of God, and that the Spirit of God dwelleth in you?" (I Cor. 3:16). Here in one breath God and Holy Spirit are employed interchangeably. Later on, in this same epistle, he uses Spirit, Lord, and God synonymously. "Now there are diversities of gifts, but the same Spirit. And there are diversities of ministrations, and the same Lord. And there are diversities of workings, but the same God, who worketh all things in all" (I Cor. 12:4-6).

4. EQUAL STATUS WITH FATHER AND SON

In the formula for baptism the Holy Spirit is mentioned right along with the Father and the Son: "baptizing them into the name of the Father and of the Son and of the Holy Spirit" (Matt. 28:19). Paul's apostolic benediction, as found in Second Corinthians, finds all three persons mentioned in one sentence. "The grace of the Lord Jesus Christ, and the love of God, and the communion of the Holy Spirit, be with you all" (13:14). These passages show that the homage, reverence, and worship accorded the Father and the Son are also accorded the Holy Spirit. He is as truly God as are the other two persons of the Trinity.

III. SPIRIT AS PERSONAL

The Spirit of God is a person having all the marks of personality. Just as the Father is a person, and the Son is a person, so is the Spirit. As the Son is distinct from the Father, so the Spirit is distinct also. There are very few who do not see the activity of God in the activity of the Spirit, but there are those who are reluctant to recognize the Spirit as distinctly personal. Not to do so is to emerge with a binitarian concept of God rather than a trinitarian one.

1. SCRIPTURAL EVIDENCE

(1) TERMS USED OF PERSONALITY APPLIED TO HIM

a. *Ekeinos*

This is the Greek term for "that one" or "he," a masculine pronoun. This is employed in John 16:14: "He shall glorify me."

b. *Paraclete*

This Greek term can be translated Comforter, Advocate, Counselor, or Helper, and therefore implies nothing short of true personality. In fact, it is used of Christ in I John 2:1, thus confirming its personal nature. The term is a verbal adjective, meaning called to one's aid, hence a helper; but the idea of encouragement and of speaking for another is also present. G. G. Findlay observes that the Paraclete "of the old jurisprudence, in the best times of antiquity, was no hired pleader connected with his client for the occasion by his brief and his fee; he was his patron and standing counsel, the head of the order or of the clan to which both belonged, bound by the claims of honor and family association to stand by his humble dependent and to see him through when his legal standing was imperilled; he was the client's natural protector and the appointed captain of his salvation."[1] The insight furnished by such an observation should help us to gain a greater appreciation of the work of the Holy Spirit as our Paraclete, or Comforter, and therefore the very personal nature of his being.

(2) MENTIONED IN IMMEDIATE CONNECTION WITH THE FATHER AND THE SON

The Spirit is mentioned throughout the Scriptures in close con-

[1] G. G. Findlay, *Fellowship in the Life Eternal*, p. 117.

nection with the Father and the Son. Their personality implies his. Jesus says of the Holy Spirit, "He shall glorify me: for he shall take of mine, and shall declare it unto you" (John 16:14). Again, the baptismal formula, where all three names are mentioned consecutively, denotes this fact. Jesus instructs us to baptize "into the name of the Father and of the Son and of the Holy Spirit" (Matt. 28:19). Paul's benediction in II Corinthians 13:14 denotes the same thing, as well as Peter's phrase "according to the foreknowledge of God the Father, in sanctification of the Spirit, unto obedience and sprinkling of the blood of Jesus Christ" (I Pet. 1:2). If the Father and the Son are persons, then so is the Holy Spirit.

(3) ACTS AS A PERSON

We are told in the Scriptures that the Spirit knows, speaks, reveals, convicts, teaches, guides, helps, inspires, makes intercession, etc. These are all functions of a person, not an impersonal force. An impersonal force cannot think, help, or inspire. The examples on this score are numerous. "My Spirit shall not strive with man for ever" (Gen. 6:3). Jesus promises his disciples, "The Holy Spirit shall teach you in that very hour what ye ought to say" (Luke 12:12). Jesus teaches that the Holy Spirit "will convict the world in respect of sin, and of righteousness, and of judgment" (John 16:8). On the Day of Pentecost the apostles spoke with tongues "as the Spirit gave them utterance" (Acts 2:4). Relative to the encounter of the Ethiopian treasurer and Philip we read, "And the Spirit said unto Philip, Go near, and join thyself to this chariot" (Acts 8:29). The Spirit intercedes for us as we pray; for, not knowing how to pray as we ought, "the Spirit himself maketh intercession for us with groanings which cannot be uttered" (Rom. 8:26). We are also told that the Spirit gives spiritual, or charismatic, gifts to the members of the church as he wills (I Cor. 12:11). The member does not choose; the Spirit gives as he desires. This is a personal trait.

(4) REACTS AS A PERSON TO THE ACTS OF OTHERS

He can be grieved, vexed, resisted, blasphemed, etc. Jesus says, "Every sin and blasphemy shall be forgiven unto men; but the blasphemy against the Spirit shall not be forgiven" (Matt. 12:31). Paul admonishes, "And grieve not the Holy Spirit of God, in whom ye were sealed unto the day of redemption" (Eph. 4:30). Only a person can be grieved. Ananias lied to the Holy Spirit, while he and his wife Sapphira "agreed together to try the Spirit of the Lord" (Acts 5:3, 9). This could be done only to a person.

102

2. Evidence from Christian experience

Not only does Scripture tell us that the Holy Spirit is a person; this evidence comes to us unequivocally from our experience as a Christian.[2]

(1) CONVICTION

The convicting power of the Holy Spirit, felt just prior to conversion, is the act of a personal being informing us that we are lost and in need of a Saviour. There is a personal reaction between an unrighteous soul and the divine Spirit of holiness.

(2) CALL

The call of one into special service is the work of the personal Spirit of God. God's Spirit not only calls, but directs after the call. This is the work of a personal being.

(3) SPIRITUAL GROWTH

Growth in ethical living takes place through the work of the Spirit. Growth in grace, as it is usually termed, is the result of the power that comes through the indwelling Spirit of God.

IV. SPIRIT AND CHRIST

What was, and is, the relation between the Spirit of God and Christ, between the third person of the Trinity and the second? Let us look at this from two viewpoints: while Christ was here upon earth and now that he is in heaven above.

1. While Christ incarnate

From the very moment of conception on Christ was under the leadership of the Spirit. Joseph is informed concerning Mary, "That which is conceived in her is of the Holy Spirit" (Matt. 1:20). Simeon is promised of the Holy Spirit that he shall not die till he has seen the Lord's Christ (Luke 2:26). Therefore he recognizes Jesus when the latter is only forty days old, as Mary and Joseph bring him to the temple. The Spirit comes upon Jesus at his baptism, for "the Holy Spirit descended in a bodily form, as a dove, upon him" (Luke 3:22). The Spirit leads him into the wilderness to be tempted of Satan. "And Jesus, full of the Holy Spirit, returned from the Jordan, and was led in the Spirit in the wilderness during forty days, being tempted of the devil" (Luke 4:1, 2). At the completion of the temptations the Spirit

---

[2] See H. Wheeler Robinson, *The Christian Experience of the Holy Spirit*, for a fuller discussion of this phase, as well as other phases, of the doctrine of the Holy Spirit.

leads him out of the wilderness. "And Jesus returned in the power of the Spirit into Galilee" (Luke 4:14).

One of the key passages depicting the relationship between Christ and the Spirit is found in the fourth chapter of Luke. Jesus enters the synagogue at Nazareth and reads from the roll of the prophet Isaiah at the place which is now our sixty-first chapter. He reads, "The Spirit of the Lord is upon me, Because he anointed me to preach good tidings to the poor: He hath sent me to proclaim release to the captives, And recovering of sight to the blind, To set at liberty them that are bruised, To proclaim the acceptable year of the Lord" (Luke 4:18, 19). He interprets himself as the fulfillment of this poignant prophecy; therefore the Spirit anoints him for all his teaching, preaching, and healing. Another verse giving an insight into this relationship is the statement that he casts out demons "by the Spirit of God" (Matt. 12: 28).

His whole being was so under the guidance of the Spirit of God that his work was the work of God. The work of Christ was the work of God, which in turn was the work of the Spirit. We are even told in Hebrews that Jesus offered himself upon the cross "through the eternal Spirit" (9:14). And Paul states that he was raised from the dead according to the Spirit of holiness (Rom. 1:4).

2. AFTER CHRIST'S ASCENSION

During his last days upon earth Christ promises power from heaven for all the disciples, that they will be baptized with the Holy Spirit. This promise is fulfilled on the Day of Pentecost, for it could not take place till after the crucifixion, resurrection, and ascension. During the farewell discourse Jesus says, "It is expedient for you that I go away; for if I go not away, the Comforter will not come unto you; but if I go, I will send him unto you" (John 16:7). On the Day of Pentecost the Spirit comes as a mighty rushing wind, dwelling upon each one like split tongues of fire and giving to each the power to speak in tongues. Peter interprets this not only as the fulfillment of the promise of Christ but the fulfillment of the prophecy of Joel. He quotes Joel 2:28ff. to prove it; then he says of Jesus, "Being therefore by the right hand of God exalted, and having received of the Father the promise of the Holy Spirit, he hath poured forth this, which ye see and hear" (Acts 2:33). This is the baptism of the Spirit, the turning point in the activities of the first generation of Christians.

We see that the Spirit works in relation to Christ. He reveals Christ, interprets his words, makes effective his work. He does not work in and of himself; it is all for the sake of what Christ has done. If this were not true Christ could not have said while on the cross, "It is finished" (John 19:30). The Spirit does not do a new work; he makes effective in us subjectively what Christ has wrought out objectively. The Spirit does not replace Christ; he makes him real. The Holy Spirit is the divine essence breathed out and flowing out to mankind to effect the work already decided and accomplished. He has been termed the executive of the Godhead. This is why Paul can use the term Spirit of Christ interchangeably with the term Spirit of God, or, just simply, the Spirit.

V. WORK OF SPIRIT

1. IN REVELATION

The Holy Spirit plays a very important part in the revelation of God, one of completing or perfecting the idea of God. Through the Spirit we experience God as immanent in the world, thus avoiding a conception of God as transcendent only, or as apart from the world.

But not only does the revelation of the Holy Spirit show God to be immanent in the world, it shows religion to be fellowship between God and man. God is not only in the world, he is in the heart as well. Through the Holy Spirit one is made new again in Christ Jesus. Through the Holy Spirit the revelation in Christ Jesus becomes meaningful and operative. Through the Holy Spirit religion becomes subjective and personal.

Also, the Holy Spirit illumined and inspired the biblical writers of old to record faithfully and accurately that which they received in revelation. As a result the Bible, the record of the revelation, comes to us as a result of the action of God's Spirit upon those receiving God's revelation a very important work of the Holy Spirit.

2. IN SALVATION

Every phase of the process of the redemption of a human soul is accomplished through the work of the Holy Spirit. He is God immanent in the world, through whom conversion takes place.

(1) CONVICTION OF SIN

Jesus says that the Paraclete (Holy Spirit) will convict the world. "And he, when he is come, will convict the world in respect of sin, and of righteousness, and of judgment" (John 16:8). The King James Version uses the word "reprove," instead of "convict." Some versions use "convince." Neither of these is so close to the Greek as "convict." Besides, this is the term that is used in common speech when we talk about someone "being under conviction" in an evangelistic service.

The Holy Spirit makes one realize that he is in sin, that he cannot save himself, that he is under guilt, and that he needs the power of God for salvation. This is the condition of those hearing Peter's sermon on the Day of Pentecost, when "they were pricked in their heart, and said unto Peter and the rest of the apostles, Brethren, what shall we do?" (Acts 2:37). It is also the feeling of the Philippian jailer when he cries out to Paul and Silas, "Sirs, what must I do to be saved?" (Acts 16:30). This convicting takes place through the work of the Holy Spirit.

(2) RENEWAL OF SINNER

The Holy Spirit not only convicts the sinner and shows him his need for Christ; he is the one through whom regeneration takes place. Jesus said to Nicodemus, "Verily, verily, I say unto thee, Except one be born of water and the Spirit, he cannot enter into the kingdom of God" (John 3:5). Birth by the Spirit is birth from above. Paul informs us that "according to his mercy he saved us, through the washing of regeneration and renewing of the Holy Spirit" (Titus 3:5). The Holy Spirit makes effective within us that which Christ wrought objectively for us. The result is a complete renewal of the one accepting this grace of God.

(3) ASSURANCE OF SALVATION

After his work of conviction and renewal the Holy Spirit gives assurance to the redeemed one that he is now a child of God. He can sing with Fanny Crosby:

> Blessed assurance, Jesus is mine!
> Oh, what a foretaste of glory divine!
> Heir of salvation, purchase of God,
> Born of His Spirit, wash'd in His blood.

He sings this because the work of the Holy Spirit gives him that assurance; he can now say, "I know I am saved, that I am a child of God." The passage informing that the Holy Spirit provides us with this assurance is found in the book of Romans. "For as many as are led by the Spirit of God, these are sons of God. For ye received not the spirit of bondage again unto fear; but ye received the spirit of adoption, whereby we cry, Abba, Father. The Spirit himself beareth witness with our spirit, that we are children of God: and if children, then heirs; heirs of God, and joint-heirs with Christ" (8:14-17). John wrote his first epistle with this in mind, for he says, "These things have I written unto you, that ye may know that ye have eternal life, even unto you that believe on the name of the Son of God" (I John 5:13). This knowledge is derived through the Holy Spirit.

(4) SEALING OF SPIRIT

The indwelling Spirit is God's guarantee that he will raise our bodies from the dead. Through him we are sealed unto the day of redemption. "And grieve not the Holy Spirit of God, in whom ye were sealed unto the day of redemption" (Eph. 4:30). The tense of the Greek term translated "were sealed" shows that this refers to a sealing once for all, so there is no suggestion of a possible departing of the Spirit; we are sealed by the Spirit, unto the resurrection day. We have the first-fruits of the Spirit within, so we groan for the consummation day, the redemption of our bodies. "And not only so, but ourselves also, who have the first-fruits of the Spirit, even we ourselves groan within ourselves, waiting for our adoption, to wit, the redemption of our body" (Rom. 8:23).

3. IN BESTOWING GIFTS

The Spirit bestows spiritual gifts upon the members of the church as he wills. These are called charismatic gifts, so named from the Greek word for grace, *charis;* they are gifts, coming purely through the grace of God. The redeemed one does nothing to merit them; they are granted through the Spirit. "Now there are diversities of gifts, but the same Spirit" (I Cor. 12:4). The same Spirit gives different gifts to the various members. To one he gives the word of wisdom, to another the word of knowledge, to another faith, to another gifts of healing, to another workings of miracles, to another prophecy, to another discerning of spirits, to another speaking in tongues, and to another interpreting the tongues (I Cor. 12:8-10). These charismatic gifts, or enduements of power, are found subsequent to the outpouring of the Holy Spirit upon the Day of Pentecost; they constitute but one result of the baptism of the Spirit on that great day. Through these gifts the work of the kingdom has since been carried on in the world.

4. IN IMPARTING POWER FOR HOLY LIVING

This phase of work comes out in the later writings of the New Testament. Paul's concept of the Christian life is one controlled by the indwelling Spirit. We are told not to grieve the Holy Spirit by unethical and unrighteous living (Eph. 4:30). We are told to pray at all seasons in the Holy Spirit (Eph. 6:18). He says, "Walk by the Spirit, and ye shall not fulfil the lust of the flesh" (Gal. 5:16). He lists the fruits of the Spirit: love, joy, peace, longsuffering, kindness, goodness, faithfulness, meekness, self-control (Gal. 5:22, 23). Instead of being drunk with wine Christians are to be "filled with the Spirit" (Eph. 5:18). Paul states, "For if ye live after the flesh, ye must die; but if by the Spirit ye put to death the deeds of the body, ye shall live" (Rom. 8:13).

5. IN TEACHING

The Holy Spirit is our teacher, yet he does not teach in and of himself. He brings no new concepts, no new revelation. He interprets that which Christ has already revealed. Jesus says of him, "He shall teach you all things, and bring to your remembrance all that I said unto you" (John 14:26). Then later he adds, "He shall not speak from himself; but what things soever he shall hear, these shall he speak: and he shall declare unto you the things that are to come. He shall glorify me: for he shall take of mine, and shall declare it unto you" (John 16:13, 14). This is an internal work of the Holy Spirit by which the objective truth becomes subjective truth for the believer. There is no giving of new vistas of truth but the illumination of the mind of the child of God to discern the meaning of the truth already Christ-revealed.

6. IN INTERCEDING

The Holy Spirit intercedes for us in our prayer life, for we do not know how to pray as we ought. "And in like manner the Spirit also helpeth our infirmity: for we know not how to pray as we ought; but the Spirit himself maketh intercession for us with groanings which cannot be uttered; and he that searcheth the hearts knoweth what is the mind of the Spirit, because he maketh intercession for the saints according to the will of God" (Rom. 8:26, 27). It is almost like the mother who teaches the child to pray by putting words into his mouth or by suggesting objects of prayer. Thus the interceding of the Holy Spirit and the interceding of Christ are related; the one complements the other. The Holy Spirit is our Advocate on earth, by teaching us to pray; Christ is our Advocate in heaven, by securing for us a hearing of our prayers.

7. IN LEADING CHURCHES

(1) IN ESTABLISHING CHURCHES

The Holy Spirit leads in the establishment of churches by disclosing the need of a new church and by bringing together those believers who are to form the nucleus of it. A church is the product of the Holy Spirit. He leads in the conviction and regeneration of the individual, thus bringing him into the fellowship of the triune God; then he also leads in the bringing together of regenerated individuals into the fellowship of a Christian community. "For in one Spirit were we all baptized into one body, whether Jews or Greeks, whether bond or free; and were all made to drink of one Spirit. For the body is not one member, but many" (I Cor. 12:13, 14).

(2) IN GUIDING WORK OF CHURCHES

The Holy Spirit inspires and guides the churches submitting to him, which is the desire of God for every church. This was the secret of the power and evangelistic zeal of the first church at Jerusalem. "And when they had prayed, the place was shaken wherein they were gathered together; and they were all filled with the Holy Spirit, and they spake the word of God with boldness" (Acts 4:31). There is a place in every church for organization, but this organization must be imbued with fervor by the presence of the Holy Spirit. Otherwise there will be only dead formalism. Every church decision should be in conformity to the will of the Spirit, for every church vote should be cast with the desire of doing the Spirit's bidding. Every undertaking should seek the power of the Spirit.

(3) IN LEADING WORSHIP OF CHURCHES

The worship service should be conducted in a manner that is conducive to the leadership of the Holy Spirit. There must be a proper balance between warmth and dignity. "And be not drunken with wine, wherein is riot, but be filled with the Spirit; speaking one to another in psalms and hymns and spiritual songs, singing and making melody with your heart to the Lord" (Eph. 5:18, 19). The interceding power of the Spirit is available for every praying church. "And in like manner the Spirit also helpeth our infirmity: for we know not how to pray as we ought; but the Spirit himself maketh intercession for us with groanings which cannot be uttered" (Rom. 8:26). The presence of the Holy Spirit will give warmth and feeling to the worship service, where otherwise there will be only a frigid dullness. The early church, controlled and energized by the Spirit, was practically free from ritual. In fact there is very little that is ritualistic in the whole New Testament. When ritual replaces the Spirit, it has defeated its purpose. Nor, on the contrary, should a worship service be one of uncontrolled emotion, with the pretense that the Spirit is leading in the disorder that generally ensues. This is called ecstatic religion. Paul deprecates such in I Corinthians 12-14, when he shows that the ethical, with order and arrangement, is vastly superior to even the miraculous and the physical. Seek faith, hope, and love, for they surmount speaking in tongues. Unrestrained emotionalism does not constitute worship any more than rigid formality constitutes worship. God is a God of order, not of confusion (I Cor. 14:26-33).

The study of church history shows one undisputable fact. As the leadership of the Spirit is progressively rejected, there is a turning from evangelistic zeal and benevolent warmth to institutionalism and ritualism. And what is observed in this respect in the history of the church is true relative to individual churches as well. The Spirit of God is vitally needed as the directing and motivating power in each and every church today.

8. IN SPEAKING IN TONGUES

Speaking in tongues, known as glossolalia, is a phenomenon encountered in the New Testament in Acts and First Corinthians only. In I Cor. 14:2, 4, 13, 14, 19, and 27 in the King James Version the term "unknown tongues" is used to translate the Greek, but the term "unknown" is not in the original language at all. This unfortunate translation has been rectified in the American Standard Version and other later translations, where only "tongues" is used. (The term "new tongues" is found in Mark 16:17, but this verse is not in any of the old Greek manuscripts that are near the original writing, the autograph. Also, the early church writers never mention this verse.)

We read in Acts 2:4; 10:46; and 19:6, as well as in First Corinthians 12:10, that the gift of speaking in tongues is of the Holy Spirit. When the Spirit came to the one hundred and twenty disciples in the upper room at the time of the Feast of Pentecost, they immediately began to speak in "other tongues," which were understood by the large gathering of Jews from "every nation under heaven," each in his own "dialect" (Acts 2:1-13). There was no confusion, just an orderly but amazing manifestation of the endued power of the Spirit promised by Jesus prior to his return to heavenly glory. Of course, a few onlookers scoffed and charged drunkenness, but this does not constitute evidence that the phenomenon at Pentecost was like that of the disorderly condition later at the church at Corinth. On that very day at Jerusalem, after Peter's powerful sermon, three thousand believed and were baptized (2:41). The confusion of tongues at Babel (Gen. 11:9) had at last been replaced by an understanding of tongues at Zion.

What a contrast to the speaking in tongues at Corinth, where the situation tends to revert to Babel (I Cor. 14). Here tongues is quite a problem. Paul pleads with them to "let all things be done decently and in order" (I Cor. 14:40). He does not command them to cease speaking in tongues, but says there are greater gifts of the Spirit. A more excellent way is that of faith, hope, and love (I Cor. 13). Speaking in tongues without love makes one like "sounding brass, or a clanging symbol" (I Cor. 13:1). Evidently many were speaking in tongues simultaneously, with no understanding on the part of the remaining ones (I Cor. 14:2, 6, 14). Paul admonishes them to speak one at a time, and not more than two or three at any one gathering, and that there be an interpreter for the hearers. Only then will there be edification (14:26-28). If all speak at once an outsider might consider them mad (14:23).

Modern movements of glossolalia, from all appearances, resemble the picture at Corinth, not Jerusalem. They seem to be Corinthian, and not Pentecostal. The Spirit's gift of the speaking in tongues at Pentecost gave the newly born Christian movement a great impetus. It was a crucial moment, when the power of God was highly needed. But the ecstatic utterances later at Corinth served no such great purpose, but brought reproval upon the church instead. In fact, the problem of tongues was merely one of many plaguing the church at Corinth, which a quick review of First Corinthians will show. Modern glossolalia movements have a propensity to show the church today in the same light as the movement at Corinth did for the church then. In speaking of the Pentecostal glossolalia Professor F. F. Bruce states, "The Corinthian glossolalia does not seem to have been quite the same as this, to judge from Paul's deprecating description of it (I Cor. 14:23). The effect of the Pentecostal glossolalia was better understanding on the part of the hearers; this does not appear to have been so at Corinth, nor is it so in many circles where the gift of tongues is cultivated nowadays. The test as to whether this or any other form of utterance represents the Holy Spirit's activity is this: Does it edify the hearer? Does it help him to become a Christian, or to be a better Christian than he already is?"[3]

3 F. F. Bruce, *The Acts of the Apostles*, p. 82.

OUTLINE FOR CHAPTER FIVE

I. Unity of God
   1. Fundamental to both Old and New Testaments
   2. Trinity not a negation of unity
II. Scriptural Teaching
   1. Intimations in Old Testament
      (1) Plurality in the Godhead
      (2) Angel of Jehovah
      (3) Wisdom
      (4) Word
      (5) Spirit
      (6) Messianic passages
   2. Teachings from New Testament
      (1) The Father is God
      (2) The Son is God
      (3) The Holy Spirit is God
      (4) There is but one God
III. True View of Trinity
   1. Distinctiveness of the three persons
   2. Caution in use of explanatory terms
   3. Extremes in thinking to be avoided
   4. Eternal, not temporary
   5. Essential, not merely functional
   6. Plurality possible in the Godhead but not in man.
   7. Equality of the three persons
   8. Difficulty of comprehension
   9. Necessary for proper revelation of God
   10. Necessary in economy of salvation
IV. False Means of Dealing with Trinity
   1. Sabellian view (Modalistic)
   2. Arian view (Unitarian)

CHAPTER FIVE

THE TRINITY

THE WORD TRINITY IS NOT FOUND IN THE HOLY SCRIPTURES, BUT THE fact of the tripersonality of God is easily discerned. It is clearly taught, though not formally stated, in the New Testament; and intimations are found in the Old Testament. The word Trinity is of Latin derivation, meaning three in one. The knowledge of the doctrine of the Trinity comes through revelation; man may derive from reason the unity of God, only revelation could show the manifold richness of that unity. Though the Montanists first defined the doctrine of the Trinity, Tertullian (the first of the early church fathers to write in Latin) was the one who named it.

I. UNITY OF GOD

We must first secure our minds with the fact that God is one. This is called the unity of God, or the oneness of God. Monotheism is the fact that he is one being, or one essence.

1. FUNDAMENTAL TO BOTH OLD AND NEW TESTAMENTS

Both the Old Testament and the New Testament reveal God as one. "Hear, O Israel: Jehovah our God is one Jehovah: and thou shalt love Jehovah thy God with all thy heart, and with all thy soul, and with all thy might" (Deut. 6:4, 5). These words, called the Shema, became the cornerstone of Jewish theology; they were to be taught to the children from toddling days. The monotheism of Judaism, firmly fixed from the days of the exile onward, became its distinctive feature. "Unto thee it was showed, that thou mightest know that Jehovah he is God; there is none else besides him" (Deut. 4:35).

In Christianity this monotheism is just as decisive. Jesus himself quotes the Shema as found in the book of Deuteronomy, thus manifesting his complete agreement with its statement. When asked concerning the great commandment Jesus replies with these very familiar words: "The first is, Hear, O Israel: The Lord our God, the Lord is one: and thou shalt love the Lord thy God with all thy heart, and with all thy soul, and with all thy mind, and with all thy strength" (Mark 12:29, 30). Since God is one, his people owe him an undivided, unmitigated love. Therefore we see that the unity of God is fundamental to both the Old and the New Testaments.

2. TRINITY NOT A NEGATION OF UNITY

When we say that God is three in one we do not negate the unity, even though the Jew would say that we do. There is a threeness, and there is a oneness. We see that Jesus himself verified the oneness; yet the threeness is strikingly evident throughout the New Testament, for there is a distinct mentioning of each person. There is God the Father; there is God the Son; there is God the Holy Spirit. Each is truly God; yet the New Testament clearly reveals that God is one. It has been suggested that we think of God the Father as transcendent, of God the Son as incarnate, redemptive love, of God the Holy Spirit as immanent. But this does not say all. The New Testament writers spoke of that which they had experienced — something almost beyond comprehension! The God of Abraham, Isaac, and Jacob, the God of the covenant at Sinai, the God of prophetic utterance, the God of ubiquitous power — this one had visited earth, in flesh! Then, since a mighty wind at Pentecost, he had continued to be present on earth as the Holy Spirit. To go beyond this would be to enter the realm of metaphysical wanderings about the nature of God, for which the inspired writer had no time.

Manifoldness of life does not constitute a self-contradictory idea. Diversity seen in richness of nature is entirely possible, especially in regard to the nature of God. Besides, the threeness and the oneness are relative to different aspects of his being. He is three in one respect and one in another. Therefore it is perfectly possible for God to be three persons in one at one and the same time.

II. SCRIPTURAL TEACHING

1. INTIMATIONS IN OLD TESTAMENT

In the Old Testament are seen many indications of the richness of God's nature. He manifests himself in various ways to the characters found there. Therefore we employ the term Old Testament intimations, for they do not furnish a basis for an Old Testament doctrine of the Trinity. They merely contain the germ of such a doctrine, which can be detected as we look back upon the Old Testament from the New Testament point of view. God as a Trinity was present in the Old Testament age, for he has always been his present self; but he did not reveal himself as the tripersonal God until the advent of Christ with his ensuing revelation. It is the language and terminology used to designate God in the Old Testament that lead us to observe trinitarian overtones in these Hebrew Scriptures.

(1) PLURALITY IN THE GODHEAD

a. *Elohim*

This Hebrew term for God in the Old Testament, which is translated with the singular English word God, is a plural noun, normally requiring a plural Hebrew verb. There was also a singular form El, but the plural was the one constantly used in the Hebrew Scriptures. (There are two instances in the creation narrative, however, where the plural Elohim is linked with the singular verb *bara,* meaning "to create.")

b. *The "us" passages*

"Let us make man in our image, after our likeness" (Gen. 1:26). "Behold, the man is become as one of us" (Gen. 3:22). "Let us go down..." (Gen. 11:7). "Whom shall I send, and who will go for us" (Isa. 6:8). This plural pronoun displays the same idea as the plural noun Elohim.

c. *Jehovah speaks of his son*

"Thou art my son, this day have I begotten thee" (Ps. 2:7).

d. *Jehovah distinguished from his Spirit*

"And now the Lord Jehovah hath sent me, and his Spirit" (Isa. 48:16). "I will make mention of the lovingkindnesses of Jehovah.... But they rebelled, and grieved his holy Spirit" (Isa. 63:7, 10).

(2) ANGEL OF JEHOVAH

The angel of Jehovah identifies himself with Jehovah, as is easily discerned in some passages. "And the angel of Jehovah called unto him out of heaven, and said, Abraham, Abraham: and he said, Here am I.... And the angel of Jehovah called unto Abraham a second time out of heaven, and said, By myself have I sworn, saith Jehovah" (Gen. 22:11, 15, 16). The angel of Jehovah is identified with Jehovah by others. He appears to Hagar, handmaid of Sarah and mother of Ishmael, while she is fleeing from the face of Sarah. "And the angel of Jehovah said unto her, Return to thy mistress, and submit thyself under her hands.... And she called the name of Jehovah that spake unto her, Thou art a God that seeth" (Gen. 16:9, 13). Therefore it is discerned that God embodies himself in his angel to minister to his people.

(3) WISDOM

Wisdom is pictured in a manner distinct from God. "Doth not wisdom cry, And understanding put forth her voice?" (Prov. 8:1). "Jehovah possessed me in the beginning of his way, Before his works of old.... Then I was with him, as a master workman; And I was daily his delight.... And my delight was with the sons of men" (Prov. 8:22, 30, 31).

(4) WORD

The Word is pictured also in a manner distinct from God. "He sendeth his word, and healeth them" (Ps. 107:20). "So shall my word be that goeth forth out of my mouth; it shall not return unto me void, but it shall accomplish that which I please, and it shall prosper in the thing whereto I sent it" (Isa. 55:11). We must realize that for neither wisdom nor word is the idea of personality clearly developed. These are only intimations of a later development, especially as seen in Word (Logos) in the Gospel of John.

(5) SPIRIT

The Spirit of God is also depicted as distinguishable from God, yet not being apart from God. God is present in the world through his Spirit. "The Spirit of God moved upon the face of the waters" (Gen. 1:2). "The Lord Jehovah hath sent me, and his Spirit" (Isa. 48:16). "I will make mention of the lovingkindnesses of Jehovah.... But they rebelled, and grieved his holy Spirit" (Isa. 63:7, 10). God is active in his created order through his Spirit.

(6) MESSIANIC PASSAGES

The great messianic passages in the Old Testament picture a Being who is one with Jehovah and yet distinct from Jehovah. "For unto us a child is born, unto us a son is given; and the government shall be upon his shoulder: and his name shall be called Wonderful, Counsellor, Mighty God, Everlasting Father, Prince of Peace" (Isa. 9:6). "But thou, Bethlehem Ephrathah, which art little to be among the thousands of Judah, out of thee shall one come forth unto me that is to be ruler in Israel; whose goings forth are from of old, from everlasting" (Mic. 5:2). This is the passage to which the seers of Herod turned to determine the birthplace of him who was to be King of the Jews, that Herod might inform the Magi from the East. It is quoted by Matthew in his gospel. Also quoted by Matthew is the messianic passage: "Behold, a virgin shall conceive, and bear a son, and shall call his name Immanuel" (Isa. 7:14). Immanuel means God with us. All these passages show that the one to appear in regal splendor is one with Jehovah and yet distinct from Jehovah.

2. TEACHINGS FROM NEW TESTAMENT

The doctrine of the Trinity is not derived from metaphysics;

its source is scriptural. Certain basic facts are readily apparent from New Testament study.

(1) THE FATHER IS GOD

Passages here are too numerous to mention; two will suffice. John, in speaking of Christ the Son, says, "For him the Father, even God, hath sealed" (6:27). And Peter, in opening his first epistle, uses the phrase "according to the foreknowledge of God the Father" (1:2).

(2) THE SON IS GOD

"In the beginning was the Word, and the Word was with God, and the Word was God" (John 1:1). Here the Word is distinguishable from God; yet the Word is divine in nature and, therefore, *is* God. He does not say the Word is "a God"; he says the Word is of the essence of God. Thomas looks at the post-resurrection Christ and exclaims, "My Lord and my God" (John 20:28). These words, addressed directly to Christ and accepted by Christ, are an acknowledgment that Christ is God. These words do not constitute an exclamation, stated in overwrought enthusiasm, but instead they manifest Thomas' view of his Lord. They also state the overall view of John's gospel; for the opening verse of this gospel, as given above, is now the view of all the apostles. The Son *is* God.

Paul states that in Christ Jesus "dwelleth all the fulness of the Godhead bodily" (Col. 2:9). The term translated "fulness" is a very rich term in Paul's spiritual vocabulary; he is stating unambiguously that Jesus as the Son come in flesh is genuinely God. The same apostle also speaks of "the great God and our Saviour Jesus Christ" (Titus 2:13). The very faith of the early Christians was undergirded by their recognition of Christ as the Incarnate God. The whole New Testament rests on the belief that redemption is in God's hands alone. Only God can redeem a strayed and lost humanity.

(3) THE HOLY SPIRIT IS GOD

In reproving Ananias Peter speaks of lying to the Holy Spirit and of lying to God as being identical. "Why hath Satan filled thy heart to lie to the Holy Spirit?. . . thou hast not lied unto men, but unto God" (Acts 5:3, 4). We are told that the body of the believer is a temple of God, for the Holy Spirit dwells within him. "Know ye not that ye are a temple of God, and that the Spirit of God dwelleth in you?" (I Cor. 3:16). As the spirit of man is his inmost principle, or essence, so the Spirit of God is God himself, God's innermost being, or essence. It is that of God through which the Father and the Son express themselves and deal with mankind.

(4) THERE IS BUT ONE GOD

Though all three of these persons are God, there is but one God. It is not maintained that each is "a God," but that each *is* God. Each one is of the essence of God. This makes it possible for each to be God and at the same time for the unity of God to be a reality. This is tripersonal monotheism, as over against unipersonal monotheism.

III. TRUE VIEW OF TRINITY

It would be difficult to depict the doctrine of the Trinity in a definition. It is too complex for such a facile attempt at explanation; therefore several statements will be made relative to it.

1. DISTINCTIVENESS OF THE THREE PERSONS

The Father and the Son are distinct, and the Holy Spirit is in turn distinguished from each of these. "It is another that beareth witness of me ... the Father that sent me, he hath borne witness of me" (John 5:32, 37). "All things have been delivered unto me of my Father: and no one knoweth the Son, save the Father; neither doth any know the Father, save the Son, and he to whomsoever the Son willeth to reveal him" (Matt. 11:27). "I will pray the Father, and he shall give you another Comforter, that he may be with you for ever, even the Spirit of truth" (John 14:16, 17). Notice the word "another"; for Jesus had been their Paraclete and now promises them another Paraclete. He is a person, praying to a second person, to send them a third person — all distinct in personality.

Yet, at the same time there is the cognate truth that each of these persons *is*, in essence, God, and that there is only *one* God. Each distinct from the other, yet each in being God — this is the eternal verity that eludes finite comprehension. Each distinct, yet a distinctiveness without separation — this is the paradox that beclouds human understanding.

2. CAUTION IN USE OF EXPLANATORY TERMS

The terms used in describing the Trinity must be selected with care. Even the word person has its limitations, since it only approximates the truth that is meant to be portrayed. Yet it, like the word Trinity, is the best overall term at our disposal. Since it is not employed in this sense in the Scriptures, we must use it with reservation and with caution. We must not use it in an external, or generic, sense, since this would tend to stress individualism. The unity is displayed by the persons; yet the persons are limited by the unity, for they are phases of it. In the Trinity there is distinctiveness without separation. In the common use of the term personality there is generally the connotation of complete separation from all others, to the point of individuality. Yet in our conception of God there must be no separation; there must be distinctiveness, but a quasi-distinctiveness consistent with the unity of the Godhead. Even the term Godhead is a non-biblical one and must be used with caution. Yet it places emphasis on the unity, thus preventing the tendency toward any separation, of which we have been speaking. The term individuals, instead of persons, is unquestionably wrong for use, since this places too much stress on the distinction and would be to speak of Father, Son, and Spirit as we would speak of human individuals. Nor can the term cooperate be used relative to the function of the three persons, since this might imply a sitting down at a conference table till all agree on a plan, with the subsequent working out conjointly of that plan. The thought of one is the thought of the other; the will of one is the will of the other. Likewise the term councils of eternity cannot be used in discussing the relative work of the three persons; this places too much stress on a conferring with one another.

3. EXTREMES IN THINKING TO BE AVOIDED

If too much stress is placed upon the threeness, we come out with tritheism. If too much stress is placed upon the oneness, we come out with the view of Judaism, Mohammedanism, and Unitarianism. The right conception involves a threeness within the oneness; there must be a proper balance in thought. Either extreme leads to heretical tendencies, and much popular writing and speaking on the subject of the Trinity has been dangerously close to one or the other of these extremes.

4. ETERNAL, NOT MERELY TEMPORAL

God has always existed as the tripersonal, monotheistic God. There has always been a Trinity. God did not suddenly evolve as the Father, the Son, and the Spirit. He did not become such when he revealed himself so in New Testament times; he has always been such. Each person of the Trinity is, and has been, eternally that person. None was created in a point of time. No person is a temporary manifestation, passing out like an ebb-tide when his function is complete. "In the beginning was the Word" (John 1:1). Paul talks of Jesus "existing in the form of God ... being on an equality with God" (Phil. 2:6), thus implying that it has always been so. Jesus says to the Jews, "Before Abraham was born, I am" (John 8:58). We read of "the only begotten Son, who is in the bosom of the Father" (John 1:18). In these sentences the Greek verbs of being used relative to Jesus are all in the present tense, not the aorist tense. This denotes an eternal fact, expressing permanent being, something displayed in the Greek much better than in the English. Genesis 1:2 states "The Spirit of God moved," therefore existed before creation. Also, we read in Hebrews of "the eternal Spirit" (9:14). The relationship between any two persons of the Trinity is independent of time and of creation. The three eternal persons have always been and always will be; there is nothing temporal in their nature.

5. Essential, not merely functional

It is immanent, not merely economic. The persons of the Trinity are persons in essence of being, not just because they function as such. The Son is essentially the Son, and because of this he acts, or functions, as the Son. His functioning as the Son does not constitute his being such, but vice versa. The Trinity goes much deeper than activity; it is immanent in being. A Trinity which is economic only would be one of merely forms. This is not true, for the functions evolve from the essential being. The Trinity is not simply an economic division of divine activity.

6. Plurality possible in the Godhead, but not in man

We would expect God to have a more complex nature than our own. Man is a being, a self, an ego. That self can manifest itself in only one personality. God is a being so rich in nature that he can manifest himself as three personalities and yet be one in nature, and not only manifest himself as such but essentially be such. Just as man has many faculties united in one being, which become more distinct as the intelligence increases, so God has various functions, which become so distinct that they are seen to be personal. Unity characterized by interpersonal relations is not only possible within the Godhead; it is a reality there. Unity can be thought of as an abstract "one," or the absence of multiplicity, which would be to conceive of it in an exclusive manner. But it can also be framed in a concept that is inclusive, a complexity or multiplicity within unity. So it is with the tripersonal, monotheistic God of the Christian revelation.

7. Equality of the three persons

In the essence of their being, these three persons are equal. The Father is not God exclusively, for God is also Son and Holy Spirit. And the Son is not God exclusively, for there are also the Father and the Holy Spirit. The same can be said of the Holy Spirit. If the Son and the Spirit had been created by the Father at some point in time, then there might be some argument for the belief that these two are subordinate and dependent. But they were never created; they are eternal persons of the Godhead. We must remember that the terms Father, Son, and Spirit are not used with the same limitations of meaning as when applied to man. There are scriptural passages which *seem* to teach the subordination of the Son. "For I am come down from heaven, not to do mine own will, but the will of him that sent me" (John 6:38). "I do nothing of myself, but as the Father taught me, I speak these things" (John 8:28). Yet these passages apply only to the incarnate state of Christ, after he emptied himself of his glory (Phil. 2:7) and came in the limitations of the flesh. They are not statements of eternal subordination; they apply only to the incarnate state.

8. DIFFICULTY OF COMPREHENSION

This doctrine of the Trinity tends to be inscrutable because it evades finite comprehension. It is extremely difficult to explain to others. Many analogies have been devised with which to depict this tripersonality of God, but they all fail at some point or another. There is the one of ice, water, and steam. There is the one of the fountain, the stream, and the rivulet. There is the one of the cloud, the rain, and the rising mist. There is the one of color, shape, and size. There is the one of husband, father, and son. These help in downing objectors to the Trinity, but they do not begin to dissolve its mystery.

9. NECESSARY FOR PROPER REVELATION OF GOD

If there were no Trinity, Christ would not be God; therefore he could not know God absolutely and perfectly so as to reveal him as such to man. Instead of being the final and complete revelation Christ would only be bringing *a* revelation, as the prophets did in the centuries that preceded his advent. Also, if there were no Trinity the Holy Spirit would not be God, only an impersonal, invasive power. But this is not so; for as Christ is the means of external revelation, so the Holy Spirit is the means of internal revelation. If the Holy Spirit were not God he could not be the means of this subjective revelation. God is revealed only in God (Christ), and God is made real only in God (Holy Spirit).

10. NECESSARY IN ECONOMY OF SALVATION

If God were one in an absolute sense only there could be no mediation and no atonement. Only one who is God can reconcile alienated man back to God. Only one who is God can forgive. Only one who is God can pour out his blood effectively as an atonement.

DOCTRINES OF THE CHRISTIAN RELIGION

The tripersonality of God made it possible for God to be immanent through his incarnate Son and at the same time transcendent as the Father. The Holy Spirit continues the work of the immanent God subsequent to the ascension and glorification of the Son. The economy of salvation demands a Trinity. Through Christ God entered human history; through the Holy Spirit God entered human hearts. In both these "enterings" God was immanent; at the same time, and always, he was transcendent through the Father.

IV. FALSE MEANS OF DEALING WITH TRINITY

1. Sabellian view (Modalistic)

Sabellius (A.D. 250) held that the Father, Son, and Holy Spirit are simply manifestations, or revelations, of God to his creatures, which manifestations are not eternal. God is one, and this one God has shown himself in three offices, or modes. Hence this view is also called modalism. God is not tripersonal; he is unipersonal, manifesting himself in three different aspects. As the Father he creates and plans; as the Son he reveals and saves; as the Holy Spirit he regenerates, sanctifies, and leads the church.

Here we have only an economic Trinity, one of function alone. It is not an immanent Trinity, one of essence. It is not permanent, only temporary. Each mode is a temporary manifestation. The only thing of merit in this system is that it preserves the deity of Christ and the personality of the Holy Spirit.

2. Arian view (Unitarian)

Arius (A.D. 325) held that the Father is the only divine being who had no beginning, was not created. The Son and the Holy Spirit were created. The Son is the first and greatest of created beings, being called God because he is next in rank to God and because he has been endowed with divine powers. He is subordinate to the Father. One of the followers of Arius in subsequent history was Socinus, the source of the modern Unitarians. Arius insisted that Christ be worshiped, but modern Unitarians do not believe in worshiping a created being, so do not believe in worshiping Christ.

This system throws Christ and the Holy Spirit out of the Godhead. Sometimes it has regarded Christ as a man exceptionally brilliant and talented. Sometimes it has regarded him as a man supernaturally endowed, a superman, so to speak. Sometimes it has regarded him as a supernatural being but not God. But regardless of the specific view toward him, he is never conceived as God Incarnate. There is hardly anything of merit in this system.

OUTLINE FOR CHAPTER SIX

I. Biblical Psychology
  1. Four most significant terms
    (1) Spirit
      a. Inner life of man
      b. God-derived life
      c. Synonymous with new nature
    (2) Soul
      a. Life-spirit embodied in the flesh
      b. Subject of all activities
      c. Individual possessing life
    (3) Flesh
      a. Natural use of term
      b. Ethical sense of term
    (4) Heart
  2. Other biblical terminology
    (1) Mind
    (2) Body
    (3) Conscience
    (4) Will

II. Theories of Man's Nature
  1. Trichotomous
  2. Dichotomous
  3. Wholeness

III. Theories of Origin of Soul
  1. Pre-existence
  2. Creationism
  3. Traducianism

IV. Moral Nature of Man
  1. Personality
    (1) Intellectual power
    (2) Emotional power
    (3) Volitional power
  2. Power of choice

V. Spiritual Nature of Man
  1. Man created in image of God
  2. Privileges of being in image of God
    (1) Dominion over lower orders
    (2) Fellowship with God

VI. Original State of Man
  1. Man's nature not infallible

2. Man's environment conducive to happiness and growth in holiness
3. Provisions for testing man's virtue

VII. Fall of Man
    1. Scriptural account
    2. Disastrous result

CHAPTER SIX

VIEW OF MAN

THE DOCTRINE OF MAN GOES UNDER THE NAME OF ANTHROPOLOGY, from two Greek words meaning study of man. When this study is derived from the Bible it is termed biblical anthropology. The proper concept of the biblical view of man must never be underestimated, for it has been rightly stated "that one must correctly understand the biblical doctrine of man in order to understand its doctrine of sin or salvation. Much of its inadequacy and even distortion of the doctrines of sin and salvation root in the confusion of nonbiblical ideas with the biblical doctrine of man.... in the doctrine of man one stands at the crossroads for his theology. The road he chooses here determines the balance of his theology."[1]

I. BIBLICAL PSYCHOLOGY

The psychology of the Bible can be best understood through the proper conception of the biblical terms used to designate the various aspects of man's nature. There are four leading terms used in this way.

1. FOUR MOST SIGNIFICANT TERMS

(1) SPIRIT

In the Old Testament this is called *ruach,* and in the New Testament it is called *pneuma.* Spirit is the life-principle coming from God. It is the imparted power from God by which the individual lives. It is very seldom (or not at all) used to designate an individual human being. Rather, it denotes the higher aspects of the personality, the finest part of the inner being. Yet the Scriptures seem to use this term in connection with man in three different senses.

a. *Inner life of man*

Sometimes this term is used to denote man's inner life, his self-consciousness. "For who among men knoweth the things of a man, save the spirit of the man, which is in him?" (I Cor. 2:11). "Blessed are the poor in spirit: for theirs is the kingdom of heaven" (Matt. 5:3).

[1] Frank Stagg, *New Testament Theology,* p. 31.

b. God-derived life

Sometimes the term is used in the sense of life which is God-originated. This is the religious sense. "Create in me a clean heart, O God; And renew a right spirit within me" (Ps. 51:10). "With my soul have I desired thee in the night; yea, with my spirit within me will I seek thee earnestly" (Isa. 26:9).

c. Synonymous with new nature

When we come to Paul we find it synonymous with the new nature. This is the highest meaning of the term in the Scriptures. "For the mind of the flesh is death; but the mind of the Spirit is life and peace" (Rom. 8:6). "And if Christ is in you, the body is dead because of sin; but the spirit is life because of righteousness" (Rom. 8:10).

"The spirit of man is, then, the true ego, the better self, the spiritual nature in which he is most closely kindred to God. The spirit is that immaterial part of man which relates him to the eternal and imperishable world. Hence it stands over against the corruptible flesh which has no future. He who makes the sphere of the outward and sensuous his world can only reap corruption, while he who fosters the life of the spirit will reap eternal blessedness. . . . The flesh is subject to decay, but the spirit is kindred to God, and bears within itself the potency of an endless life. Hence to live or walk according to the spirit means to cultivate the higher nature and to realize the life of fellowship with God."[2]

Jesus himself gives this same contrast when he declares to Nicodemus, "That which is born of the flesh is flesh; and that which is born of the Spirit is spirit" (John 3:6), thus depicting two orders, that of nature and that of spirit. The new birth ushers one into the latter, where spiritual interests and realities become permanent.

(2) SOUL

In the Old Testament this is called *nephesh,* and in the New Testament it is called *psuchē.* By this is meant the entire living being, the living organism. If the spirit is the life-principle, soul is the life-subject. Again, as in the case with spirit, we have a term used with an ascending meaning throughout the Scriptures. There are three aspects in which it is used.

a. Life-spirit embodied in the flesh

The first aspect found in the Scriptures is simply as the life-spirit embodied in human flesh. "But if any harm follow, then

2 George B. Stevens, *The Theology of the New Testament,* p. 343.

126

thou shalt give life for life" (Exod. 21:23). The Hebrew term translated "life" here is *nephesh,* or "soul." "If I have eaten the fruits thereof without money, Or have caused the owners thereof to lose their life..." (Job 31:39). Here again the term translated "life" is *nephesh,* or "soul."

b. *Subject of all activities*

Next, it manifests the subject of all activities, even the highest activities of man. "But from thence ye shall seek Jehovah thy God, and thou shalt find him, when thou searchest after him with all thy heart and with all thy soul" (Deut. 4:29). "My soul thirsteth for God, for the living God" (Ps. 42:2).

c. *Individual possessing life*

The highest use of the term soul is to denote the individual possessing life. The soul is the subject possessing life, which is derived by means of the life-principle, *pneuma.* "And Jehovah God formed man of the dust of the ground, and breathed into his nostrils the breath of life; and man became a living soul" (Gen. 2:7). "All the souls that came with Jacob into Egypt, that came out of his loins, besides Jacob's sons' wives, all the souls were threescore and six; and the sons of Joseph, who were born to him in Egypt, were two souls: all the souls of the house of Jacob, that came into Egypt, were threescore and ten" (Gen. 46:26, 27). Thus we see that the term "soul" in the Scriptures freely connotes a person, one having appetites and passions, but one also who possesses the power of choice and the potential of growing positively in regard to moral and ethical qualities. In fact, there are places in the Old Testament where the term *nephesh* is translated "person." "And the king of Sodom said unto Abram, Give me the persons, and take the goods to thyself" (Gen. 14:21; see also Num. 31:19; 35:15, 30; Deut. 27:25; *et al.*). This is the meaning in Romans 13:1, although translated with the word "soul." "Let every soul be in subjection to the higher powers." Yet the Hebrew and Greek terms are in most instances better translated with simply "soul" or "life."

"Clearly the word 'soul' in the Bible has a much broader meaning than in current usage now. The fact that translators are often compelled to use other English words to translate the same Hebrew or Greek noun raises the question whether they should not have done so in many more instances. Nowhere in the Old Testament, as a matter of fact, is the meaning exactly what we ordinarily mean by the soul. Sometimes, to be sure, nephesh indicates something that departs at death, but in such instances the word probably has merely its original meaning 'breath.' This meaning is hard to distinguish from 'life'; as in I Kings 17:21f., where the dead child's nephesh comes back into him. Other Old Testament passages that speak of delivering the nephesh from death are naturally taken by Christian readers as referring to the future life, but in most, if not all. such cases the meaning is simply preserving a person's life."[3]

(3) FLESH

In the Old Testament this is called *basar,* and in the New Testament it is called *sarx.* This term is found in the Scriptures with two varying connotations: the natural and the ethical. The former is found in both the Old and the New Testaments. The latter is found in the Pauline epistles.

a. *Natural use of term*

Within the natural use there are fine nuances of meaning. It may be found as literally the substance of a living body, either man or beast. Therefore it includes all beings upon the face of the earth with powers of sensation. "And all flesh died that moved upon the earth, both birds, and cattle, and beasts, and every creeping thing that creepeth upon the earth, and every man" (Gen. 7:21). A little higher meaning is that of human nature as contrasted with spiritual beings, including God himself. "And Jehovah said, My Spirit shall not strive with man for ever, for that he also is flesh" (Gen. 6:3). "In God have I put my trust, I will not be afraid; What can flesh do unto me?" (Ps. 56:4). This same sense of the term is found throughout the New Testament also, with the term augmented to "flesh and blood." "Blessed art thou, Simon Bar-Jonah: for flesh and blood hath not revealed it unto thee, but my father who is in heaven" (Matt. 16:17). Paul remarks "that flesh and blood cannot inherit the kingdom of God" (I Cor. 15:50). Along with this higher meaning, and somewhat parallel with it, is the use of flesh in contrast to something higher within the individual. It designates the lower element in man's make-up, standing in contrast to the heart, the soul, or the spirit. Yet, even in this capacity, it does not stand as the despised element in man's nature, as it was so conceived in contemporary Greek thought. It was not thought of as unethical, something to be shunned or avoided. "O God, thou art my God; earnestly will I seek thee: My soul thirsteth for thee, my flesh longeth for thee, In a dry and weary land, where no water is" (Ps. 63:1). "And after my skin, even this body, is destroyed, Then without my flesh shall I see God" (Job 19:26). "Watch and pray, that ye enter not into temptation: the spirit indeed is willing, but the flesh is weak"

3 Millar Burrows, *An Outline of Biblical Theology,* p. 137.

(Matt. 26:41). Last among the uses of the term flesh on the natural side is its employment to express the relationship established by birth or marriage. "Therefore shall a man leave his father and his mother, and shall cleave unto his wife: and they shall be one flesh" (Gen. 2:24). "And Laban said to him, Surely thou art my bone and my flesh" (Gen. 29:14).

b. *Ethical sense of term*

When we come to the term flesh as used by the Apostle Paul we find an entirely different connotation. In the natural examples given above there is nothing implied in an ethical sense, for the moral idēa is never brought to mind. Yet Paul uses the term for the seat of that which in man resists conformity to God's desires and God's laws. Even in the regenerate individual it opposes the spirit. The ethical idea is strongly connoted by the word flesh when used by this great apostle. "But I say, Walk by the Spirit, and ye shall not fulfil the lust of the flesh. For the flesh lusteth against the Spirit, and the Spirit against the flesh; for these are contrary the one to the other; that ye may not do the things that ye would" (Gal. 5:16, 17). Romans 8:1-11 is Paul's extended discourse on the flesh as antithetical to the Spirit. "For they that are after the flesh mind the things of the flesh; but they that are after the Spirit the things of the Spirit. For the mind of the flesh is death; but the mind of the Spirit is life and peace: because the mind of the flesh is enmity against God; for it is not subject to the law of God, neither indeed can it be: and they that are in the flesh cannot please God" (Rom. 8:5-8). This use of the term flesh is practically synonymous with other terms the apostle uses: the old man, the law in my members, the law of sin which is in my members, the body of sin, etc.

The whole biblical view is opposed to any idea of the flesh as inherently evil; this is Greek philosophy, especially Stoicism, and is foreign to the Bible. The biblical view of the origin of evil in Genesis does not agree with this Greek idea. Adam and Eve were certainly in the flesh prior to the advent of sin. And how could one present his body "a living sacrifice" (Rom. 12:1) if flesh were inherently evil? How can one "glorify God" in his body if that body is composed of inherently evil flesh (I Cor. 6:20)? Therefore flesh, or *sarx*, is not to be identified with sin; it is not necessarily sinful. Sin and the flesh are closely related, but they are not inseparable. Some scholars, such as Baur, would maintain that they are inseparable in the thinking of Paul, but this is not true. This apostle never identifies flesh with sin, but merely maintains that sin dwells in the flesh, making it its sphere of operation.

Paul's use of the term flesh has its roots in the view of flesh, or *basar,* in the Old Testament, not in the dualism of Greek philosophy. In the natural use, as found in the Old Testament, flesh refers to man's creaturehood, his perishable nature, in contrast to God's imperishable one. Paul starts here, for this idea can actually be seen in some of his passages; but the ethical idea predominates. "The flesh is not merely weak, but is the seat of passions and impulses which easily give occasion to sinful choices and actions. In this way the ontological dualism of flesh and spirit (to be carefully distinguished from the Greek dualism) easily emerges into the ethical dualism of Paul. He looked upon the flesh in its positive aspects. He had experienced the power of its passions and the way in which it allied itself with sin and became the instrument of sinful desire. The Old Testament contrast still remained the basis of Paul's doctrine, but the contrast was sharpened and ethicized by Paul's intense realization of the power of sin. I cannot, therefore, agree with that theory which so far disregards the Old Testament basis of Paul's doctrine as to maintain that 'the flesh' is for him a name for the whole man in one aspect of his life, in contrast to spirit which designates the whole man in another aspect of it."[4] Thus states George B. Stevens, noted professor of Yale University during the latter part of the nineteenth century.

(4) HEART

In the Old Testament this is called *leb,* and in the New Testament it is called *kardia.* The term changes in meaning very little throughout the Scriptures. Due to the central position of this physical organ in the body it came into prominence in the psychology of the ancient world far in advance of the term brain. "The life is in the blood" is the thought that must never be forgotten, and the heart is the center of the distribution of that blood; therefore it constitutes the most important organ of the body. By the same token the heart came to be viewed as the seat of the personal life, the center of man's energies and feelings. It was conceived as the center of the soul, the personal organ. It was even thought of as the organ of conscience and of knowledge. In modern thought the mind is the seat of the rational and the intellectual, and the heart of the emotional and feeling. For the Hebrew all in-coming perceptions and influences are assimilated in the heart; from it issue the moral and spiritual concepts of the soul. "But the things which proceed out of the mouth come forth out of the heart; and they defile the man. For out of the heart

---

4 Stevens, *op. cit.,* p. 342.

come forth evil thoughts, murders, adulteries, fornications, thefts, false witness, railings" (Matt. 15:18, 19). Jeremiah states, "The heart is deceitful above all things, and it is exceedingly corrupt: who can know it?" (17:9). But not only is the heart the place of human depravity, it is also the seat of moral and ethical forces. It is the starting point for moral reformation. "A new heart also will I give you, and a new spirit will I put within you; and I will take away the stony heart out of your flesh, and I will give you a heart of flesh" (Ezek. 36:26).

In the Scriptures the heart is viewed as the seat of sin, thus showing the depth of human corruption and sinful nature. This corruption reigns in the heart and is manifested by acts and words. Therefore sin has tainted and made impure the very foundation and source of life, the heart, which in turn explains the blinding and enslaving power of sin and the vital change of heart that is necessary to emancipate the soul. Sin instead of God reigns in the heart; these two powers must be reversed. Genesis 8:21 reveals that in God's view "the imagination of man's heart is evil from his youth." This certainly opposes "the superficial doctrine which makes man in a moral sense an indifferent being, in whose choice it lies each moment to be either good or bad; and so this book represents sin as a principle which has penetrated to the centre, and from thence corrupts the whole circuit of life. Accordingly the human heart is characterized in Jer. 17:9 as 'deceitful...,' so that God alone...is able to fathom the depth of its perverseness.... Hence all revelation addresses itself to the heart, even the revelation of law, Deut. 6:6; for it demands love to God from the whole heart, and, starting from this centre, also from the whole soul...."[5] Thus the Old Testament, as well as the New Testament, views the heart as the seat of sin. Only God can "make manifest the counsels of the hearts" (I Cor. 4:5).

2. OTHER BIBLICAL TERMINOLOGY

Other terminology used in the Bible relative to biblical psychology consists of the following: mind, body, conscience, and will.

(1) MIND

This term is found chiefly in the New Testament, where it goes under the term *nous*. Here it is used mainly by Paul, being seldom found in the gospels and in the writings of the older apostles (exceptions: Luke 24:45; Rev. 13:18; 17:9). This shows that the gospel writers and the older apostles adhered to the Old Testament way of thinking, where the idea of *nous* was absent. But Paul em-

[5] G. F. Oehler, *Theology of the Old Testament*, pp. 153-4.

ploys the term repeatedly. In the seventh chapter of Romans he contrasts it with *sarx,* or "flesh," and in the fourteenth chapter of First Corinthians he contrasts it with *pneuma,* or "spirit." "So then I of myself with the mind, indeed, serve the law of God; but with the flesh the law of sin" (Rom. 7:25). "In the church I had rather speak five words with my understanding [*nous,* mind], that I might instruct others also, than ten thousand words in a tongue" (I Cor. 14:19). Paul seems to be referring to the inner man in general, especially as that one is renewed in Christ.

There is another Greek term for mind, *phrēn,* found in the New Testament mainly in its verb form and used by Paul also. The verb form means "to be so minded." An example of its use is in the famous passage in Philippians: "Have this mind in you, which was also in Christ Jesus" (2:5). The noun is found only in I Corinthians 14:20, and here it is in the plural. Another term for mind is *dianoia,* which is found in Mark 12:30 quoting Deuteronomy 6:5: "And thou shalt love the Lord thy God with all thy heart, and with all thy soul, and with all thy mind, and with all thy strength."

(2) BODY

The New Testament term for body is *sōma.* The Old Testament has no corresponding term meaning distinctively body but employs kindred terms, such as trunk, bones, belly, flesh. Even the New Testament combination "flesh and blood" does not occur in the Old Testament. In Job 4:19 the term "houses of clay" is employed, and in Daniel 7:15 the term "sheath" is used, a Chaldean term (translated "body" in American Standard Version).

The biblical view of the body is unlike that of Greek philosophy. While the latter views the body in a degraded sense, as the prison house of the soul, a sort of husk in which the real man is concealed until he is finally released, the former views the earthly frame as completely honorable. The body, or fleshly nature, is not at strife with the spiritual nature. "I beseech you therefore, brethren, by the mercies of God, to present your bodies a living sacrifice, holy, acceptable to God, which is your spiritual service" (Rom. 12:1). "Or know ye not that your body is a temple of the Holy Spirit. . . . glorify God therefore in your body" (I Cor. 6: 19, 20). In fact Paul states that we wait for "the redemption of our body" (Rom. 8:23). All these statements are antithetical to the Greek view. If the body were conceived in the Scriptures as inherently evil, salvation would consist of deliverance from it, rather than its change into a higher form.

The body is composed of flesh. "Metaphysically considered, the flesh is neutral; empirically considered it is sinful. Matter as such is not evil, nor is it the source of evil; but the body, as animated by a soul capable of feelings and appetites, is a source of temptation and a seat of evil. But since by a perversion of will sin entered the world, it has made the body its slave, and has subjected it to vanity and corruption."[6]

(3) CONSCIENCE

The distinctively Greek term for conscience, *suneidēsis,* is used by Paul (especially in the eighth and tenth chapters of First Corinthians) and other New Testament writers. The term conscience is corollary in its use to the term heart, both being self-judging functions of the inner man. The writer of Hebrews, in speaking of boldness to enter the holy place, admonishes, "Let us draw near with a true heart in fulness of faith, having our hearts sprinkled from an evil conscience" (10:22). If mind is the highest faculty of the soul, conscience is the highest faculty of the heart, expressing moral approval or disapproval. The height of impurity is to have both the mind and the conscience defiled. "To the pure all things are pure: but to them that are defiled and unbelieving nothing is pure; but both their mind and their conscience are defiled" (Titus 1:15). However, the conscience may be regarded as a function of the renewed spirit, or *pneuma,* in believers. "I say the truth in Christ, I lie not, my conscience bearing witness with me in the Holy Spirit..." (Rom. 9:1). The term started out with the eternal meaning of self-consciousness and evolved to that of a full ethical import, which meaning is even discerned in pagan literature and which change was brought about in no small part by the Stoics. This full ethical import is connoted by every use of the term in the New Testament. Conscience might be termed a combination of man's moral relationships together with a certain feeling in regard to them, or a combination of intellect and of sensibility in regard to that which is right and wrong. It is both discriminative and impulsive; it judges and then demands duty in respect to the decree.

(4) WILL

Will is expressed in the New Testament by the term *thelēma,* which is the term expressing the ability of the soul to choose between motives and then to direct activity according to the motive chosen. It is the ability to choose an end and the means to that end. Just as conscience and will make up what might be considered the moral nature of man, so intellect, feeling, and will constitute the human faculties of man. Each act that a man

6 Stevens, *op. cit.,* p. 347.

performs involves all three of these faculties, although that act may be so constituted that one of the three predominates. Hence we speak of an act of the will, an act of the intellect, or an act of the feeling. Robert Browning had will in mind when he made Paracelsus say, "I have subdued my life to the one purpose whereto I ordained it."

Man is responsible for all acts of his will, as well as for the will itself. The will itself, even prior to its resultant act, manifests the character of a man. "Ye have heard that it was said, Thou shalt not commit adultery: but I say unto you, that every one that looketh on a woman to lust after her hath committed adultery with her already in his heart" (Matt. 5:27, 28). Repeated acts of the will in a certain moral direction manifest one's moral disposition, whether he is a "servant of sin" or a "servant of righteousness" (Rom. 6:16, 18).

Man's freedom, however, has certain limitations. Heredity, environment, formulated disposition due to previous willing — all these tend to limit his freedom and make certain choices automatic. Therefore we might say that a large percent of man's activity is not free but predetermined. Yet this is not to uphold the deterministic theory of the will. Determinism controverts free will, stating that all of man's activities are determined by motives acting upon him, which motives he cannot alter or contradict, and therefore his every act is predetermined. This has disastrous results in regard to man's concept of God and of his relation to God. It minimizes or destroys man's attitude toward sin, guilt, need of atonement, etc. His power to initiate any action is gone. Pessimism is the order of the day. Since man is predetermined, he cannot choose between good and evil; they are merely forms of knowledge for him to acquire.

God does not will due to motives but wills due to his infinite personality. Likewise man does not will due to motives but wills due to his finite personality. Therefore all willing is traced back to God. It is essential to personality, not resultant. For man this results from being made in the image of God. Man wills because he was made to will. Man's willing reaches its apex in the redeemed state. "I can do all things in him that strengtheneth me" (Phil. 4:13). When energized by the divine will it becomes tremendous. When subordinate to the divine will it becomes ethically true.

II. THEORIES OF MAN'S NATURE

There are various theories concerning the human make-up, whether man has a threefold nature, has a twofold nature, or is essentially one in nature. Is he a trichotomous being or a dichotomous being? Or is either term an adequate one, a true one with which to express man's nature?

1. TRICHOTOMOUS

This theory maintains that man has a threefold nature, consisting of body, soul, and spirit. It is named from two Greek terms meaning in three and to cut. It must be admitted that there are passages which at first sight seem to warrant such a view, but further analysis speaks otherwise. There are places where soul (*psuchē*) and spirit (*pneuma*) are used as contrasting terms, the former representing the immaterial part of man in its superior faculties. To a certain degree this is true; but it does not warrant the trichotomous view of man's nature.

The passage that is used most often to support the trichotomous view is the following: "and may your spirit and soul and body be preserved entire" (I Thess. 5:23). But this does not suggest two distinct immaterial parts but two points of view of one immaterial part. "Spirit, soul, and body are to be preserved in the Parousia. . . . Paul is emphasizing the entirety of the preservation. The whole man is preserved, and spirit, soul, and body singly underline the inclusiveness of the conception. Man in every aspect, man in his wholeness, is to be preserved."[7] Paul's passage in First Thessalonians is used much like the passage in Mark 12:30, "Thou shalt love the Lord thy God with all thy heart, and with all thy soul, and with all thy mind, and with all thy strength." One would not think of deriving a fourfold division of human nature from this statement. The same is true for the phrase: "piercing even to the dividing of soul and spirit, of both joints and marrow" (Heb. 4:12). This does not mean the dividing of soul from spirit, but the piercing of soul and of spirit to the very depth of the spiritual nature.

Therefore the trichotomous view of man is untenable; for the *pneuma* is man's nature looking Godward and capable of receiving the Holy Spirit, while the soul is man's nature looking earthward and touching the world of the senses. Both designate the higher part of man, the former as related to the spiritual realities and the latter as related to the body.

2. DICHOTOMOUS

This theory maintains that man has a twofold nature, consisting of a material nature and an immaterial nature. He consists of body and of soul, or spirit. This theory is named from two Greek terms meaning in two and to cut. This theory seems at first glance

[7] W. David Stacey, *The Pauline View of Man*, p. 123.

to carry weight due to the Scriptures, for here there are phrases which apparently indicate two natures for man. "And Jehovah God formed man of the dust of the ground, and breathed into his nostrils the breath of life; and man became a living soul" (Gen. 2:7). In other words, God inbreathed clay, and the resulting man became a soul. There are other passages which distinguish between man's body and his soul, or spirit. "It came to pass, as her soul was departing..." (Gen. 35:18). "O Jehovah my God, I pray thee, let this child's soul come into him again" (I Kings 17:21). "The body apart from the spirit is dead" (James 2:26). Other passages seem to use soul and spirit interchangeably. "Now is my soul troubled" (John 12:27). Compare this with: "He was troubled in the spirit" (John 13:21). Body and soul, or spirit, are spoken of as composing the whole man. "Able to destroy both soul and body in hell" (Matt. 10:28). "Absent in body but present in spirit" (I Cor. 5:3). Yet the weakness of this view is that it approaches very closely to that of Greek philosophical dualism. One wonders whether or not the philosophical view virtually has been read into the Scriptures.

3. WHOLENESS

There is much evidence that the Bible writers seem to think of man in his entirety. Man is a unit and must not be severed into component parts. Any terms used to describe man were employed from a practical standpoint, with no idea of working out a systematic psychology. Even though the dichotomous theory has more weight than the trichotomous view, it as well is inadequate when viewed from the whole New Testament. "Paul's conception of personality is not dualistic.... He did not regard body and soul as separate and relatively independent entities, nor as antithetical elements."[8] Paul and the other New Testament writers were influenced by the Hebrew concept of flesh and spirit as found in the Old Testament, not by the Greek view.

The terms dichotomous and trichotomous are highly misleading when used to discuss the biblical view of man. "Despite varied terms which characterize man from different standpoints, the New Testament views man in his wholeness and sees sin as affecting man in his wholeness. The terms flesh (sarx), spirit (pneuma), body (sōma), and soul (psuchē) in the New Testament may seem to assume a dichotomous or trichotomous view of man, but actually this is not the case. Each term describes the whole man from its particular perspective. The whole man may be described as 'flesh,' or 'spirit,' or 'body,' or 'soul.' Each term is highly serviceable in the analysis of man or for emphasis of some aspect of his being,

8 *Ibid.*, p. 176.

but this never becomes a thoroughgoing dichotomy or trichotomy."[9] These distinctive terms never become absolute, as never do distinctive terms used to describe a person in current psychology, such as reason, emotion, volition, or flesh.

III. THEORIES OF ORIGIN OF SOUL

There are three theories that have prevailed through the centuries as to the origin of the individual soul, which theories are highly speculative in nature. Yet one seems to satisfy more than the other two.

1. PRE-EXISTENCE

This theory states that the soul has pre-existed in a previous state and enters the body sometime during early development. It is urged that this theory is without support in Scripture; in fact it contradicts the Mosaic account of the creation of man in the image of God. It also knocks out Paul's view of sin and death as derived from Adam. There is no explanation of inherited sensual sin. Also, if the soul were conscious and personal in this previous state would there not be some remembrance of existence during that time? Christ remembered his pre-existence. W. David Stacey asserts, "Neither is there any evidence for the pre-existence of the soul. Some of the inter-testamental writers, under the influence of Hellenism, taught the existence of the soul before birth and, in a vague way, the Rabbis made similar statements. Not so Paul. It is not merely that he fails to mention it, but his Old Testament conception of soul as the animating principle of man leaves no room for it. Where there is no body, there can be no soul, for soul is not life in the abstract, but the vital force of the body of the flesh."[10]

Some of those holding to this view of the origin of the soul are Plato, Philo, Origen, Kant, Muller. William Wordsworth must have held to this theory, as is seen in his famous ode:

> *Our birth is but a sleep and a forgetting:*
> *The Soul that rises with us, our life's Star,*
> > *Hath had elsewhere its setting,*
> > *And cometh from afar:*
> *Not in entire forgetfulness,*
> *And not in utter nakedness,*
> *But trailing clouds of glory do we come*
> *From God, who is our home:*
> *Heaven lies about us in our infancy!*

9 Stagg, *op. cit.,* pp. 24, 25.
10 Stacey, *op. cit.,* p. 124.

2. Creationism

This theory holds that the soul is an immediate creation of God, entering the body at some time during its early development, maybe even as early as conception itself. In both this theory and the previous one the body of course is produced by natural generation. This theory is an attempt to preserve the spiritual nature of the soul, in the belief that if souls are produced by natural generation there would be a tendency to conceive of them as materialistic.

Creationism also is without support in Scripture, for God's usual method of operation since the first creation is the mediate rather than the immediate method. Any Scripture used to support the theory works just as well for the mediate creation of the soul. Besides, this theory holds that the earthly father begets only the body of his child, not the higher element. But children are like their parents intellectually and spiritually as well as physically, or in bodily traits. Also, this theory rests upon the old dualism between body and soul and does not account for the tendency in all men to sin. It makes God create a pure human soul and place it in a body that will inevitably corrupt it. Or, it makes God create a soul with sinful tendencies.

Creationism was held by Aristotle, Jerome, and Pelagius. Many Reformed theologians also held to it. James P. Boyce favored this view, as is seen in his *Abstract of Systematic Theology,* pp. 163-175. It is held in modern times by Roman Catholics.

3. Traducianism

This theory holds that both soul and body are produced by natural generation, both being derived from the parents. Man begets as the whole man. We derive our whole being by the natural laws of propagation. The term traducianism is derived from the Latin *traduco,* meaning to lead or bring together.

This theory seems to accord best with Scripture, because it represents God as creating the species in Adam and then perpetuating it through secondary means. So it agrees with God's working in general through processes of nature. It best satisfies the reason. The transmission of traits of character is accounted for. The unity of the race is reckoned with by this theory, as well as the evil moral tendencies possessed by all men congenitally.

Such a theory was held by Tertullian, Augustine, and John Milton. It was the view of E. Y. Mullins and A. H. Strong, noted Baptist theologians of the past. It is the view held by the Lutheran Church today.

IV. MORAL NATURE OF MAN

Man is a moral being, equipped for right or wrong choice. As a moral being he has certain characteristics endowed upon him at creation. As we attempt to view the moral nature of man let us remember that this phase of his being is highly integrated with the spiritual and that any terms that are used are merely for the purpose of discussion. The same terms may be involved in discussing the spiritual nature of man as well.

1. PERSONALITY

At creation man was distinguished from the brute by the bestowment of personality. He knows himself to be a self among other selves and that he is not only related to his fellow men but to the world and to God. As a personal being man was endowed with these faculties of nature.

(1) INTELLECTUAL POWER

Man has a rational nature, which is his source of knowledge of all things within the sphere of his being. He can reason, can remember, can recall, and can infer. He is able to investigate, reflect, and draw conclusions. He has the power to objectify self, to stand off and view himself as a being among other beings. The brute has a certain degree of intelligence and will, but these are highly limited. The higher thought processes are not possessed by animals. The animal has neither self-consciousness nor the power of moral choice. Man has intellect, or reason, with which he can differentiate between right and wrong.

(2) EMOTIONAL POWER

Man is possessed of an emotional nature. His feelings lie deep and strong, yet at the same time are also capable of training. The animal may possess instinctive affection, the mother even dying for the young. But in man this rises to the level of rational affection, even to the point of deliberately sacrificing himself for the welfare of others. Patriotism falls into this category. Therefore we say that if man has the intellect to discern between right and wrong, he also has the sensibility to be moved by the right and the wrong. He is a sentient being.

(3) VOLITIONAL POWER

Man has a will. This factor places him upon a high level, much above that of the mere brute. He is able to set a course of activity and to pursue that course in all its details and in its wider scope. He is able to choose an end and then to choose the means of attaining that end. His power of manifesting preference is immediately followed by executive volition. Therefore we conclude by saying that man not only has intellect, or soul-knowing, and sensibility, or soul-feeling; he also has will, or soul-choosing. Every time the soul acts all three of these faculties are involved.

2. POWER OF CHOICE

Being a free moral agent, man possesses power of choice. His actions are not predetermined by external forces, nor are they undetermined in that they are due to motives formed in the past. They are determined from within, by choice, not by compulsion. His acts are those of a free being.

What limit is there to man's freedom? Some maintain that man is completely determined by his heredity and his environment, and therefore has no freedom. Others maintain that he has power to do practically as he chooses, and is therefore unlimited. Neither of these extremes fits reality. Man has freedom, but that freedom is not unlimited. It is determined to a great extent by both his hereditary background and by the conditions comprising his known world. He is neither a slave to heredity and environment, nor can he push them wholly aside as though to ignore them. Within this framework he is self-directive, but this degree of self-direction is sufficient to make man a free moral agent.

V. SPIRITUAL NATURE OF MAN

The spiritual nature of man is generally referred to in the Scriptures as either spirit or soul, as we have seen that these terms are used somewhat interchangeably. They are popular terms, not scientific. They are aspects of the one undivided spiritual life of man. Yet the term which comes vividly to mind when the spiritual nature of man is discussed is image of God.

1. MAN CREATED IN IMAGE OF GOD

The Bible speaks of man as being made in the image of God. "And God said, Let us make man in our image, after our likeness" (Gen. 1:26). Some have tried to maintain that there is some distinction between "image" and "likeness," but apparently there is none whatsoever between the two Hebrew words. They seem to be used synonymously in Scripture, as well also the two corresponding Greek terms.

What does the term image of God, or *imago Dei,* signify? Practically all scholars will agree that, regardless of what it does imply, it does not refer to the bodily form of man. God is not physical, having a body in the likeness of which man could be created. God is Spirit. In fact the body of man is in many ways analogous to that of the brute. There can be no corresponding analogy here between man and God. So this term does not refer to the physical nature of man, but rather to his spiritual nature. Man, as formed by God, had all the characteristics of a spiritual being. H. H. Rowley maintains, "Physically, then, there can be little likeness between man and God, and it is in the spiritual quality of his being that he is made in the image of God." This author further states, "This is not to ignore the oft-noted fact that in Hebrew thought man is an animated body. The Hebrew did not think of man as a spirit inhabiting a body, in the sense that the real man consisted of the spirit, while the body was but its casket. Body and spirit belonged together in the unity of personality. In the totality of his personality, therefore, man cannot be in the image of God, and that wherein he is akin to God cannot be isolated from the totality of his personality." Rowley believes that "the spiritual quality of that animated body which the Hebrew conceived man to be showed him to be made in the image of God, who nevertheless, in the totality of His Being, is very different from man. In his spiritual attainment man is quite other than God; but in that he is a spiritual being, capable of fellowship with God, and capable of reflecting something of the character of God, he has a measure of affinity with God. And this measure of affinity is God's gift to man in the act of his creation, and not something that man has achieved for himself."[11]

2. PRIVILEGES OF BEING IN IMAGE OF GOD

(1) DOMINION OVER LOWER ORDERS

One resultant of the divine image was man's dominion over the lower orders. "And let them have dominion over the fish of the sea, and over the birds of the heavens, and over the cattle, and over all the earth, and over every creeping thing that creepeth upon the earth" (Gen. 1:26). This statement immediately follows the one which declares man to be created in the image and likeness of God. Man's dominion in this respect was not a part of the image; it was an office due to the image. "Man as the image of God is set over the animal world. This does not mean that man's being in God's image only means that he rules the animal world; the latter is, in fact, the important consequence of the former: because man stands in a special relationship to God he is entrusted by God with dominion over the world."[12]

11 H. H. Rowley, *The Rediscovery of the Old Testament*, pp. 208-9.
12 Theodore C. Vriezen, *An Outline of Old Testament Theology*, p. 208.

(2) FELLOWSHIP WITH GOD

Another resultant of the divine image was man's fellowship with God. He had communion, spirit with Spirit, and walked and talked with God. He enjoyed the divine presence and teaching (Gen. 2:15-17). This was a high privilege, for which man could only be filled with wonder and awe. There was no room for pride, but much room for responsibility. "That he is in the image of God opens up to him the infinite privilege of fellowship with God, and at the same time lays upon him the sacred obligation to enjoy that fellowship, and so fulfill the purpose of his creation."[13]

VI. ORIGINAL STATE OF MAN

After God had completely finished his creation he reviewed his work and declared it to be "very good," or "good exceedingly" (Gen. 1:31). This statement followed his creation of man, the concluding phase of his great work. After every other portion of creation he merely stated that it was "good"; so he must have experienced a special pleasure on viewing this highest phase of his creative act.

1. MAN'S NATURE NOT INFALLIBLE

Man's nature was free from taint, but this condition did not include perpetual continuance. This latter factor is seen in the fall of man due to sinning against God. Therefore we say his nature was "fallible." As of necessity fallibility is of the nature of created beings, simply because they have the power of contrary choice. If, when good and evil are presented, either may be chosen, there is always the possibility of a fall.

2. MAN'S ENVIRONMENT CONDUCIVE TO HAPPINESS AND GROWTH IN HOLINESS

That man's environment was conducive in these respects is immediately discerned in the description of Eden and in the creation of Eve. The term Eden means pleasure, delight. Man's whole surroundings were productive of happiness. He lived in perfect peace with God in a paradise of unclouded harmony. Man's relationship to God seemed to be one of childlike attachment.

3. PROVISIONS FOR TESTING MAN'S VIRTUE

Man as first created was in a state of simple innocence and holiness. There was no taint in him. He was inclined to righteousness, with a holy taste for the things of God. But his holiness had not been confirmed; he could be made perfect only through successfully

---

13 Rowley, *op. cit.,* p. 209.

overcoming temptation and through complete obedience to God. Therefore God also placed in the garden "the tree of the knowledge of good and evil" (Gen. 2:9). The prohibition of not eating would test man's obedience. If he withstood temptation his virtue would be strengthened and confirmed. He had free choice, for the temptation itself did not necessitate a fall. The tree itself constituted the source of probation.

VII. FALL OF MAN

Even though the term Fall is not a biblical one it is the best at hand with which to describe this paramount tragedy of man.

1. SCRIPTURAL ACCOUNT

The narrative, found in Genesis 3:1-7, reveals an appeal by the tempter to the innocent appetites of the man and the woman, along with the implication that God was withholding their gratification. This was followed by a denial on the part of the tempter of the truthfulness of God, accompanied by a charge that God was keeping them in ignorance so as to prevent their rise to his level. The unbelief and pride, instilled in the woman, bore fruit, and she "did eat; and she gave also unto her husband with her, and he did eat" (Gen. 3:6). Man's sin was his desire for independence, the desire to shake himself free of the childlike attachment he had experienced with God. Hence the harmony between God and man was broken, and man became a sinner.

John Milton said, in *Areopagitica:* "It was from out of the rind of one apple tasted that the knowledge of good and evil, as two twins cleaving together, leaped forth into the world. And perhaps this is that doom which Adam fell into, that is to say, of knowing good by evil." Yet, to learn good by evil is Satan's way, which is to learn by the gall of experience. God's way of knowing is better, to know evil as something that is possible, to be hated and to be rejected utterly.

2. DISASTROUS RESULT

Due to his discontent to live in a close fellowship with God, man sinned. Death became the consequence of his tragic choice. "And Jehovah God said, Behold, the man is become as one of us, to know good and evil; and now, lest he put forth his hand, and take also of the tree of life, and eat, and live for ever — therefore Jehovah God sent him forth from the garden of Eden, to till the ground from whence he was taken. So he drove out the man; and he placed at the east of the garden of Eden the Cherubim, and the flame of a sword which turned every way, to keep the way of the tree of life" (Gen. 3:22-24). The Apostle Paul proclaims that "the wages of sin is death" (Rom. 6:23). After man sinned he was shut out from the tree of life, suffering death. Professor Vriezen has remarked that Genesis 2 and 3 "do not state that man is immortal but something that resembles it, namely that man was originally placed in Paradise near the tree of life, without being forbidden to eat of its fruit. In other words, Gen. ii f. states that according to the will of God, man was initially granted the possibility of eternal life by means of the fruit of the tree of life.... man was therefore deprived of the possibility of reaching the tree of life on account of the sin of disobedience or rather high-handedness, hybris. Death is the punishment of the sin of man who had originally received from God the possibility of eternal life on earth, even if he was mortal and earthly in origin."[14]

Man died spiritually with his fatal choice. His moral likeness to God was lost. His original righteousness was no more. Intellect, affections, and will became depraved and thwarted, turning inwardly toward self rather than upward toward God. All his powers became depraved, for he had become spiritually dead. His plight was truly pathetic in the extreme. He had sought to become a god, and had become a slave. He had sought independence and had lost his freedom. Once he had walked with God, seeing all things with God's perspective. Now, supremely conscious of himself, he saw all things relative to his own selfish interests. From a paramount love for God he turned to a paramount love for his own ego. Seeking status he had found only ruin.

14 Vriezen, *op. cit.*, p. 205.

OUTLINE FOR CHAPTER SEVEN

I. Nature of Sin
   1. Definition of sin
   2. Old Testament and New Testament views of sin
      (1) Old Testament view
         a. Sin as transgression of law
         b. Sin as breach of the covenant
         c. Sin as violation of righteous nature of God
         d. Old Testament terms for sin
      (2) New Testament view
         a. Sin as want of fellowship with God
         b. Sin as subjective more than objective
         c. Sin as judged with Jesus as standard
         d. Sin as unbelief
         e. Sin as revealed by the law
         f. New Testament terms for sin
   3. Sinful tendency inherited
   4. Sinful tendency universal
   5. Sins of omission and sins of commission
II. Theories for Existence of Sin
   1. Due to human body
   2. Due to finite weakness
   3. Due to selfishness
III. Consequences of Sin
   1. Depravity
      (1) Meaning of term
      (2) Total depravity
   2. Guilt
      (1) Meaning of term
      (2) Guilt and its effect
      (3) Guilt and holiness of God
      (4) Guilt and depravity
      (5) Guilt and conscience
      (6) Degrees of guilt
   3. Servitude
   4. Suffering
   5. Moral and spiritual blindness
   6. Death
IV. Salvation of Infants
   1. Evangelical view
   2. Scriptural evidence

CHAPTER SEVEN

SIN

THE "FLY IN THE OINTMENT" IN MAN'S RELATION TO GOD IS SIN. The most important element in redemption involves the eradication of sin — its presence, its power, and its consequences. Therefore a proper concept of sin must be attained prior to any discussion of the doctrine of salvation.

I. NATURE OF SIN

1. DEFINITION OF SIN

Various definitions of sin have been set forth. One is that sin is non-conformity to the moral law of God. Yet sin goes much deeper than God's law, for it goes back to our relationship with a personal God. Sin has been defined as rebellion against the will of God for one's life. Yet this does not reveal whether sin is a state, an act, or a condition. Sin has been described as selfishness. Yet much more is involved in sin than is implied in the simple term selfishness. Sin has been described as an act, disposition, or state that is morally wrong. This is true as far as it goes, but it does not take into account one's relation to God. It is more a definition of evil than of sin. Sin has been defined as a breach of relations between the sinner and God. Yet more is involved in sin than is connoted by this bare declaration.

2. OLD TESTAMENT AND NEW TESTAMENT VIEWS OF SIN

(1) OLD TESTAMENT VIEW

In the Old Testament sin is conceived in many ways. To Amos the idea of sin is unrighteousness, or injustice; for God is the righteous ruler of the universe. To Hosea the idea of sin is the alienation of the heart of the commonwealth of Israel from Jehovah; for God is a God of love. To Isaiah the idea of sin is pride and unholiness; for God is a holy God, consuming all that is unholy and impure. "In general, in all the prophets who speak of the sin of Israel, that sin is some form of ungodliness, some course of conduct, whether in worship or in life, having its source in false conceptions of Jehovah. Hosea traces all Israel's evil to this: there is no knowledge of God in the land. The prophetic statements regarding him are mostly, if not always, particular, having reference to the conditions of society around them, and to Israel the people of God; they rarely rise to the expression of general principles, and do not make abstract statements in regard to sin or its principle."[1] Since it is difficult from a study of the Old Testament to form "general principles" of sin, it will be difficult to form a systematized view of the subject. However, the following points may be considered.

a. *Sin as transgression of law*

Sin in the Old Testament consists in the transgression of the laws of Jehovah. This is true because sin violates Jehovah's will. Since in the Mosaic law God has revealed his rule of life, it is man's guide, his norm. Man has entered into relationship with God due to the covenant; the law, therefore, is not a means of being justified. It is not a code of morals to be obeyed because of strict duty, but due to God's grace. Any violation of this law is sin. The Decalogue *must* be obeyed.

b. *Sin as breach of the covenant*

God enters into a covenant with Israel, whereby they become his peculiar people. Prohibition, stipulation, and conditions are laid down by God. Violation of any of these is considered sin, some of which can be atoned for by an offering (sins of ignorance, infirmity, or inadvertence) and some of which cannot be atoned for (high-handed sins which place one outside the covenant relation). Idolatry falls into the second category.

c. *Sin as violation of the righteous nature of God*

Here sin takes on a more personal note. The standard, or norm, is not the law or the covenant but the nature of the God who gives that law and that covenant. God has shown a redemptive disposition toward man, for he created him with a moral order in view. God's righteousness is seen most vividly in his saving disposition. Any idolatry or apostasy, thus thwarting this saving purpose, is sin. Any violation of God's righteous nature is sin, for this nature has become the objective standard. God says to Amos, "Behold, I will set a plumb-line in the midst of my people Israel; I will not again pass by them any more" (Amos 7:8). God's righteousness is the plumb-line; any deviation therefrom is sin. This personal nature of sin is discerned by the psalmist as he declares, "Against thee, thee only, have I sinned, And done that which is evil in thy sight" (Ps. 51:4).

d. *Old Testament terms for sin*

Some of the rich, Old Testament terms for sin are the follow-

---

[1] A. B. Davidson, *The Theology of the Old Testament,* p. 204.

ing. *Chata'* means to miss the mark. *'Aven* means crookedness, or perverseness. *Ra'* means violence or breaking out of evil. Sin is the opposite of *tsedeq*, which initially meant linear straightness, then finally righteousness.

(2) NEW TESTAMENT VIEW

In the New Testament there is revealed a deeper concept of sin. The emphasis is not so much upon the outward acts of the soul as upon the inner disposition and state of the soul. Sin is conceived more subjectively than objectively. Jesus radically alters men's minds as to what constitutes sin.

a. *Sin as want of fellowship with God*

The ideal life is one of fellowship with God; and any lack of this fellowship, or anything that thwarts this fellowship, is sin. Jesus regards men as lost, for he "came to seek and to save that which was lost" (Luke 19:10). He is the "friend of publicans and sinners" (Matt. 11:19). All men come under the universal sway of sin, being away from God; they must be brought back to God. Heaven is the full consummation of this fellowship, where sin is no more. Hell is the supreme lack of this fellowship, where sin has reached its zenith. Sin is the principle, or settled depravity of nature, which makes death, or being lost from God, reign in the soul. "As sin reigned in death, even so might grace reign in righteousness unto eternal life through Jesus Christ our Lord" (Rom. 5:21). This is what Paul has in mind when he speaks of "the law of sin and death" and how "the law of the Spirit of life in Christ Jesus" frees us from its devastating power (Rom. 8:2).

b. *Sin as subjective more than objective*

Jesus forcefully conveys to men the idea that sin is a condition of the heart. He traces it directly to inner motives, stating that the sinful thought leading to the overt act is the real sin. The outward deed is merely the fruit of sin. Anger in the heart is tantamount to murder. "Ye have heard that it was said to them of old time, Thou shalt not kill; and whosoever shall kill shall be in danger of the judgment: but I say unto you, that every one who is angry with his brother shall be in danger of the judgment" (Matt. 5:21, 22). The impure look is tantamount to adultery. "Ye have heard that it was said, Thou shalt not commit adultery: but I say unto you, that every one that looketh on a woman to lust after her hath committed adultery with her already in his heart" (Matt. 5:27, 28). Real defilement stems from a sinful heart. "For out of the heart come forth evil thoughts, murders, adulteries, fornications, thefts, false witness, railings: these are the things which defile the man" (Matt. 15:19). Paul names this state of the soul giving rise to evil acts sin. He says, "Sin ... wrought in me ... all manner of coveting" (Rom. 7:8), and also, "I am carnal, sold under sin" (Rom. 7:14). Therefore sin is seen as involving the essential being of man, the very essence of his nature. It is not merely something eating away at this or that peripheral organ, but that which has corroded the very heart itself. Man's inner being must be cleansed and revitalized.

c. Sin as judged with Jesus as standard

The exalted purity of Jesus' own life creates the norm for judging what is sinful, and, if any sin be found, the heinousness of that sin. His life exemplifies perfect manhood void of all sin. "Him who knew no sin he made to be sin on our behalf; that we might become the righteousness of God in him" (II Cor. 5:21). He himself challenges the Jews by saying, "Which of you convicteth me of sin?" (John 8:46). He even declares that their knowledge of sin is the very result of his works and teaching. "If I had not come and spoken unto them, they had not had sin: but now they have no excuse for their sin" (John 15:22). "If I had not done among them the works which none other did, they had not had sin" (John 15:24). He is truth personified (John 14:6), and sin is the antithesis of truth. The contrast of Peter's own life with that of his Lord becomes so acute that the apostle cries out, "Depart from me; for I am a sinful man, O Lord" (Luke 5:8). Jesus' perfect manhood forms the basis for judging that which portrays any deviation from absolute holiness.

d. Sin as unbelief

Sin is summed up in the Fourth Gospel as unbelief, and by unbelief is not meant the rejection of a dogma or creed. It is the rejection of spiritual light as revealed in Christ Jesus, or the rejection of the supreme revelation as found in the person of Christ. It is an attitude of resistance to the truth and to the Spirit of God, thus producing moral and spiritual blindness. Jesus assures his disciples that the coming Holy Spirit will "convict the world in respect of sin ... because they believe not on me [Christ]" (John 16:8, 9). Acceptance or rejection of the light as found in Christ is the true basis of judgment. "He that believeth on him is not judged: he that believeth not hath been judged already, because he hath not believed on the name of the only begotten Son of God. And this is the judgment, that the light is come into the world, and men loved the darkness rather than the light" (John 3:18, 19).

Unbelief is deliberate and willful rejection of the revelation

149

brought through the Son. It is the sin of one "who hath trodden under foot the Son of God, and hath counted the blood of the covenant wherewith he was sanctified an unholy thing, and hath done despite unto the Spirit of grace" (Heb. 10:29). Unbelief is walking in darkness. "But he that hateth his brother is in the darkness, and walketh in the darkness, and knoweth not whither he goeth, because the darkness hath blinded his eyes" (I John 2:11).

e. Sin as revealed by the law

When Paul speaks of the law he usually means the Mosaic law, especially so when he uses the article. His view is that the law is preparatory, leading men to Christ. With its coming sin is revealed in its true identity, which only arouses in man a desire to experience it the more. The law as such is not bad; it is merely that human ability is unable to observe it. Mankind is unequal to all its burdensome requirements. Therefore the law offers no means of salvation, but leaves man with a deep sense of sin and guilt instead. All this is set forth in Romans 7. In Galatians 3:24 Paul terms the law a schoolmaster, or tutor, to lead men to Christ. It is the Greek term from which is derived the English word pedagogue. Since the law merely reveals his corrupt nature and his seemingly hopeless plight, Paul cries out desperately for deliverance. This he finds in the grace of God's Son. Grace, not law, is the means of overcoming sin and of securing righteousness.

The law, therefore, serves to bring sin into bold relief. Sin becomes clearly perceptible. "Here was an absolute standard of morality by which each man had to measure his life; and those who might have been content to turn a blind eye to certain ways and habits of their own, or to use the argument (which indeed is the stock-in-trade of complacent souls in every age) that while they might not be saints they were at least as good as most of their neighbors and that nothing more was necessary, were likely to be rudely shaken out of their contentment and to have that complacent argument silenced when the searchlight of the law fell across their path."[2]

f. New Testament terms for sin

By far the most common term for sin in the New Testament is *hamartia,* meaning doing wrong, and corresponding to the Old Testament term *chata'.* It is best translated sin. Another term used by Paul and the author of Hebrews is *parabasis,* or transgression. Another is *paraptōma,* or trespass. Both of these terms have strong Old Testament foundations. *Anomia* is a word meaning iniquity,

---

2 James S. Stewart, *A Man in Christ,* p. 112.

or lawlessness. *Ponēria* means evil, or wickedness. *Kakia* also means evil, or wickedness. *Adikia* means unrighteousness, or injustice, while *adikēma* denotes a crime, or misdeed. *Akatharsia* portrays uncleanness, or impurity. The term *apistia* indicates unfaithfulness, or lack of belief. *Asebeia* denotes impiety, or want of reverence. *Aselgeia* means licentiousness, or sensuality. *Echthra* shows enmity, or a hostile attitude. *Epithumia* means desire, which may be to the good or to the evil. It is used in both senses in the New Testament, but it is only in the latter sense that we are interested here.

3. SINFUL TENDENCY INHERITED

According to the Scriptures, is man a sinner by nature, biologically? Only in the sense that man naturally turns to sin is this true. Adam's sin produced the Fall, was not the result of it. His sin of self-aggrandizement, his desire to be God, his distrust of God's veracity — these produced the Fall. Adam was a sinner before the Fall, as well as after. Jesus teaches in the Sermon on the Mount that sin lies deep in the being of man, bringing forth the overt act. Adam's choice did not give to man the tendency toward sin; rather, his nature gave this to man. Like Adam, each man does not want another to be greater than he. He desires to be a god unto himself. Adam's evil and the evil of all others provide the environment in which "I was brought forth in iniquity" (Ps. 51:5). God gave to man the right of choice between good and evil. This freedom is necessary if man is to be a moral being. The freedom itself is not evil. But if there is to be the potential for good, there must at the same time be the potential for evil. Since each must be chosen, there must not be coercion into either. God gave to man the choice; man chose the evil and has been doing so ever since, which is due to his natural bent toward the evil. Adam decided to be a sinner; each man since has decided the same.

When one comes to the age of moral consciousness he finds himself so identified with evil impulses both without and within that he is dominated by them. In the child's nature are the seeds of evil tendency, coupled with the fact that he is surrounded by an environment conducive to sin. As a result he inevitably does sin. He is held responsible for his sin in spite of this inherited tendency, the inherited tendency being considered part of all that for which atonement is necessitated.

The Scriptures reveal this hereditary bent toward sin. The psalmist says, "Behold, I was brought forth in iniquity; And in sin did my mother conceive me" (51:5). Paul says that we are "by nature children of wrath" (Eph. 2:3). We have incurred God's wrath due to sin; the native disposition, resulting in sin, brought on the wrath. "Therefore, as through one man sin entered into the world, and death through sin; and so death passed unto all men, for that all sinned" (Rom. 5:12). Paul also states that "through one trespass the judgment came unto all men to condemnation" (Rom. 5:18), and that "through the one man's disobedience the many were made sinners" (Rom. 5:19).

4. SINFUL TENDENCY UNIVERSAL

Subsequent to Adam's initial transgression sin grew and developed until the corruption necessitated the virtual annihilation of the human race. The Scriptures tell us that Noah and his family alone remained. This fact of the universal sinfulness of man persists all the way through the Old Testament. In Solomon's prayer of dedication for the temple he states that "there is no man that sinneth not" (I Kings 8:46). The psalmist supplicates, "And enter not into judgment with thy servant; For in thy sight no man living is righteous" (143:2). The preacher in Ecclesiastes cries out, "Surely there is not a righteous man upon earth, that doeth good, and sinneth not" (7:20).

When Paul wishes to prove the universal sinfulness of man he quotes from seven Old Testament passages. These are found in successive order in Romans 3:10-18. They are Psalm 14:1ff.; 53:1ff.; 5:9; 140:3; 10:7; Isaiah 59:7f.; Psalm 36:1. "There is none righteous, no, not one; There is none that understandeth, There is none that seeketh after God; They have all turned aside, they are together become unprofitable; There is none that doeth good, no, not so much as one...." This is his proof that both Jews and Greeks are under sin. He states later, "For all have sinned, and fall short of the glory of God" (Rom. 3:23). All of Paul's argument in Romans 5:12ff. is based on the assumption that every man is corrupt. According to Jesus all men are under the sway of sin, for he says, "If ye, then, being evil..." (Luke 11:13). He teaches that one of the fundamental things for which we should pray is forgiveness (Matt. 6:12). "If we say that we have no sin, we deceive ourselves, and the truth is not in us," we read in I John 1:8.

Along with these explicit statements that all men are sinful there is an implication in many passages denoting a universal need for atonement and regeneration. "For God so loved the world, that he gave his only begotten Son, that whosoever believeth on him should not perish" (John 3:16). The universal sinfulness of man is also implied in the condemnation resting upon all who do not accept Christ. "He that believeth not hath been judged already, because he hath not believed on the name of the only begotten Son of God" (John 3:18).

The observation of human history depicts the same catholic

sinfulness of humanity. The best men that have ever lived confess themselves to be sinners, Paul himself claiming to head the list. It is the common judgment of mankind that there is a basic selfishness controlling every heart and causing it to sin. The presence of priesthood and sacrifice among all peoples points to the same fact. Seneca, *De Ira*, 3:26: "We are all wicked. What one blames in another he will find in his own bosom. We live among the wicked, ourselves being wicked." Isaiah discovers himself to be a man of unclean lips living among a people of unclean lips (6:5).

5. SINS OF OMISSION AND SINS OF COMMISSION

Most people conceive of sin from the negative standpoint only, not from the positive. Sin to them consists merely in the violation of a prohibition of God. God commands, "Thou shalt not kill," or "Thou shalt not steal" (Exod. 20:13, 15). To do so is sin, and rightly so! It is direct disobedience of a divine injunction. But many times to omit is just as sinful; simply to do nothing is direct rebellion against God. The children of Israel asked Samuel at a certain time to pray for them, to which he replied, "Far be it from me that I should sin against Jehovah in ceasing to pray for you" (I Sam. 12:23). Not to pray for them would have been a sin of great reality. The New Testament presents the same teaching. "Then shall he answer them, saying, Verily I say unto you, Inasmuch as ye did it not unto one of these least, ye did it not unto me. And these shall go away into eternal punishment" (Matt. 25:45, 46). The sin of these people, for which they received eternal punishment, was simply doing nothing. "But whoso hath the world's goods, and beholdeth his brother in need, and shutteth up his compassion from him, how doth the love of God abide in him?" (I John 3:17). "If a brother or sister be naked and in lack of daily food, and one of you say unto them, Go in peace, be ye warmed and filled; and yet ye give them not the things needful to the body; what doth it profit?" (Jas. 2:15, 16). One of the strongest statements relative to the idea of sins of omission is found in this same epistle of James. "To him therefore that knoweth to do good, and doeth it not, to him it is sin" (4:17). To miss the opportunity of service is merely sin viewed from another angle.

Jesus' commands are mostly positive in nature. He says, "Go . . . do . . . teach . . . pray . . . make disciples . . . baptize . . . follow me . . . love . . . feed the hungry . . . clothe the naked . . . preach . . . visit the sick . . . make peace . . . go the second mile." Very seldom does he declare such a prohibition as "Judge not, that ye be not judged" (Matt. 7:1). Therefore to obey Jesus demands a positive commitment, one of activity. Not to engage in such is sin, the sin of omission.

II. THEORIES FOR EXISTENCE OF SIN

What is the origin of sin? This is the question asked by many people. From whence did it raise its ugly head? Would a righteous God create sin? Three theories will be explained, the first two of which are more excuses for sin (though not thought as such by those who expounded them), than theories for the existence of sin.[3]

1. DUE TO HUMAN BODY

This theory views sin as sensuousness, being the natural result of man's sensuous nature. The soul's connection with a physical organism brings dire consequences. The flesh opposes the spirit, resulting in sin. Therefore sin springs from the low grounds of human nature. Schleiermacher is an exponent of this view.

In answering this theory the fact that it involves the old assumption of the inherent evil nature of matter must be brought out. That the body is inherently evil is the erroneous view of certain Greek philosophies, especially Stoicism. It is the old dualism between the spirit and the flesh. This theory also implies that God, since he created the human body, is the originator of human sin. But God made the body pure, meaning for it to be the servant of the spirit. The blame must not be placed upon the senses, but upon the spirit that uses the senses in an evil manner. To make God the author of sin is blasphemy. This theory is merely another example of the old fallacy of identifying the moral with the physical. It also is erroneous in the fact that it places more emphasis upon the sensual sins than upon the self-exalting sins of avarice, greed, malice, hate, envy, selfishness, pride, etc. It emphasizes self-degrading sins more than self-exalting sins.

2. DUE TO FINITE WEAKNESS

This theory depicts sin as the result of the limitation of a finite being. Sin is due to an imperfect development, for as man becomes educated and progresses morally his sin becomes less and less. Therefore sin is relatively evil, not absolutely. It may be viewed as the blundering of an inexperienced individual. Discipline and training diminish it. It is like the ignorance of one who gets burned because he does not know the properties of heat and of fire. Leibnitz is an exponent of this view.

[3] See James Orr, *God's Image in Man*, pp. 197-246, for a discussion of the origin and nature of sin.

The objection to this theory is that sin is identified with weakness and right identified with might. Since sin is a necessary part of finiteness, and since creatures can never be infinite, sin must always exist in the human soul. This theory is contrary to the known facts, for not all sins are of the negative variety — due to weakness and ignorance. There are positive sins also — willful choice of evil and conscious transgression of God's laws. Increased knowledge of sin does not give one power over sin. Knowledge of sin due to the advent of the law still left Paul enslaved; so he says in Romans 7. In fact, his desire for transgression of that sin increased. He used as his example for this unusual observation the command against covetousness. Experience shows that repeated acts of transgression place one deeper and deeper in sin, the heart becoming increasingly hard. Sin is not simply a weakness, it is a power. Satan is a perfect example of the error of thinking in this theory, for he is the epitome of godless intellect and powerful cunning. Judas is another example, for his sin was not one of ignorance or infirmity.

Such a theory denies human responsibility by placing the blame for sin not upon the creature but upon the one who created the creature. It makes God the author of sin, a blasphemy of the worst sort. Like the previous theory it is an excuse for sin rather than a theory for its existence.

3. DUE TO SELFISHNESS

This theory states that the essence of sin is selfishness; and the term selfishness is not used here in the parlance of the street: that of love for self counteracting a tendency for benevolence. By selfishness is meant the choice of self instead of God as the supreme end. Since love to God is the acme of all virtue, love of self must be the essence of all sin. Therefore sin is the result of the choice of free, intelligent beings.

All varieties of sin can be shown ultimately to have their root in selfishness. Murder is committed because of a selfish aim. Men steal because of selfishness. Men envy because other selves have arisen higher than their own selves. Adultery is committed because the passions of the self must be satiated. The self is the supreme end; therefore all sin is an endeavor to please or satisfy the self. Augustine and Aquinas held that the essence of sin is pride, while Luther and Calvin held it to be unbelief. But it is maintained that selfishness is the root sin, for both pride and unbelief can be thrown back to selfishness. Paul, prior to his conversion, loved and worked for "righteousness"; but it was a "righteousness" that would result from his own will and achievement, thus bringing honor to himself. It was a case of the ego above God.

This view seems in total accord with Scripture. The law demands complete love to God. "Thou shalt love Jehovah thy God with all thy heart, and with all thy soul, and with all thy might" (Deut. 6:5). Such a demand automatically excludes the self. Jesus calls this the greatest of commandments, adding as second the requirement of love toward neighbor. The Christian is one who has ceased to live for self. Paul is in complete accord with such. "For to me to live is Christ, and to die is gain" (Phil. 1:21). "I have been crucified with Christ; and it is no longer I that live, but Christ liveth in me" (Gal. 2:20). The Christian is one who lives a Christocentric life rather than an egocentric life, for self has been eradicated. The prodigal son left for a far country because of selfishness. The rich young ruler turned away sorrowfully because of selfishness. The priest and the Levite passed by on the other side because of selfishness.

III. CONSEQUENCES OF SIN

What are the results of sin, the consequences of sin? What issues from its very presence? These factors may be summed up.

1. DEPRAVITY

(1) MEANING OF TERM

By this term is meant the possession of a corrupt and degrading nature. It is a distinct bias toward evil resulting in man's certainty to sin. Depravity is both negative and positive; it is the absence of moral likeness to God and the presence of powerful tendencies toward sin.

Theoretically it is possible for man not to sin; otherwise the possibility of good and the possibility of evil would not exist. The very fact that God holds a man guilty for his sin shows that it is possible for man not to sin. Yet, at the same time, man has — does — and will continue to sin. He finds himself unable to resist the pull of temptation, unable to give himself completely to the good. What he wills to do, he cannot; and what he wills not to do, he does. Paul propounds this captivity to sin exceedingly well in Romans 7. He says, "I am carnal, sold under sin" (14), and "For I know that in me, that is, in my flesh, dwelleth no good thing: for to will is present with me, but to do that which is good is not. For the good which I would I do not: but the evil which I would not, that I practise" (18, 19). Man cannot escape sin.

(2) TOTAL DEPRAVITY

It is immediately asked whether this depravity is partial or total in nature. The Scriptures teach that it is total. Yet the term total depravity needs to be defined, lest it be misinterpreted. It denotes that all of man's nature has been corrupted by sin. It does not mean that he has gone as deep in sin as he can possibly go, that he is as bad as he can be. It does not mean that men are equally bad, that all have been corrupted to the same degree. It does not mean that human nature is destitute of all moral good, that man is bereft of any goodness. It merely maintains that all parts of his unregenerate nature are controlled and dominated by sin, and that he is incapable of extricating himself without the grace of God. In fact, without this divine grace man becomes worse and worse, sinking deeper and deeper in sin.

Much of the error concerning total depravity lies in the fact that men have had their eyes on the extent or quantity of sin rather than on the nature of sin. It was thought that the factor making sin deadly is the degree to which man is affected by it; the lower he goes in it the more deadly its power. This is to miss the point. Sin is deadly because of its nature. Any and all sin separates from God and introduces rebellion into his universe. It is antipodal to the nature of God as holy and is directly opposite to his will. This is what makes sin deadly, rather than its quantity or its heinousness.

2. GUILT

(1) MEANING OF TERM

Guilt is the self-condemnation of man based on God's disapproval of his sin. It is the ill-desert of the sinner because of his sin. It is the consciousness that he deserves to be punished because of his transgression of God's moral law. The personal relationship must always be kept in mind. Sin is man's personal opposition to God. Therefore guilt does not result from the transgression of abstract law, but results from the fact that a relationship has been marred.

(2) GUILT AND ITS EFFECT

When man feels guilty because of sin there is a desire to hide the sense of ill-desert and to cover up his responsibility for that sin. The attempt to cover up guilt is an evidence of its very presence. And alongside of the attempt to cover up guilt is the endeavor to implicate others in it too. Both of these phases of guilt are seen in the picture of Saul and the Amalekites. Saul is told to destroy utterly all the Amalekites, along with even their flocks and herds. He does not fully obey, but spares Agag the king, plus the best of the sheep, oxen, fatlings, and lambs — all of value. When he returns home the first thing he says to Samuel reveals his guilt. "Blessed be thou of Jehovah: I have performed the commandment of Jehovah" (I Sam. 15:13). Had he really obeyed God there would have been no reason for such a remark. Then later he says that "the people spared the best of the sheep and of the oxen, to sacrifice unto Jehovah thy God" (15:15). The people must be drawn into the guilt also. Adam and Eve immediately hide themselves because of their guilt; and, when detected, Adam endeavors to place the blame upon Eve. "The woman whom thou gavest to be with me, she gave me of the tree, and I did eat" (Gen. 3:12). Jonah also endeavors to run away from God because of his guilt.

(3) GUILT AND HOLINESS OF GOD

Guilt is in direct contrast to the holiness of God. Man is ill-deserving because he has violated the divine holiness. The distinction between himself as sinful and God as holy results in guilt. The blackness of his sin and the spotless purity of God are strikingly contrasted. The sixth chapter of Isaiah reveals this truth, for when the prophet sees God high and lifted up, the exalted and holy one of Israel, he sees himself as a man of unclean lips living among a people of unclean lips. The deep sense of guilt found in the Hebrew religion is due to the strikingly holy character of the God of Abraham, Isaac, and Jacob.

This holiness of God must react against sin, which reaction is what the Scriptures term "the wrath of God" (Rom. 1:18). God's condemnatory righteousness stands over against the sinner, making him fearful. Guilt is the relation of the sinner to that righteousness. Guilt might be viewed as standing in the same relation to sin as the burnt spot is in relation to the fire which caused it. Delitzsch: "The blush of shame is the evening red after the sun of original righteousness has gone down."

(4) GUILT AND DEPRAVITY

Though distinctly different both guilt and depravity are the results of sin. Guilt may be viewed as the objective result of sin, while depravity is the subjective result of sin. Every sin is an offense against God, opposing God and bringing forth his wrath, needing to be expiated by either punishment or atonement. Therefore sin, as opposing God's holy will, manifests itself as guilt; while it also stands in opposition to his divine purity and is known as depravity. The former is ill-desert; the latter is pollution. The human nature of Christ had the guilt but not the depravity. Since he himself was sinless he had no depravity; but since he identified himself with sinful humanity and took their sin, he also took their guilt. "Him who knew no sin he made to be sin on our behalf; that we might become the righteousness of God in him" (II Cor. 5:21). It must have been the feeling of being laden with guilt that made Jesus exclaim as he pressed toward the cross, "I have a baptism to be baptized with; and how am I straitened till it be accomplished!" (Luke 12:50).

(5) GUILT AND CONSCIENCE

Since guilt is the objective result of sin it must not be mistaken for the subjective consciousness of that guilt. "And if any one sin, and do any of the things which Jehovah hath commanded not to be done; though he knew it not, yet is he guilty, and shall bear his iniquity" (Lev. 5:17). Here there is no consciousness of sin, yet the guilt is present. "If we say we have no sin, we deceive ourselves, and the truth is not in us" (I John 1:8). Conscience is the God-ordained means for manifesting to man his ill-desert, or guilt. But this conscience is not an accurate measure of guilt; it may register partially or not at all. "Because if our heart condemn us, God is greater than our heart, and knoweth all things" (I John 3:20). God knows accurately the guilt, whether man does or not.

It is a known fact that the deeper a man goes into sin the more diminished is the sensitiveness to moral judgment. So the guilt may be great though the consciousness of it may be minute. When Paul paints for the Ephesian Christians a picture of their prior unsaved condition he describes them as "darkened in their understanding...being past feeling" (Eph. 4:18, 19). The psalmist cries out, "Who can discern his errors? Clear thou me from hidden faults" (19:12). Yet, on the other hand, the greater the progress in holiness the more the depth of the sensitiveness to sinfulness.

(6) DEGREES OF GUILT

All through the Scriptures there is the recognition of various degrees of guilt, depending upon the various kinds of sin. The Old Testament demanded of Israel many kinds of sacrifices, implying various degrees of guilt. There were sins of ignorance and there were high-handed sins, or sins of inadvertence and sins of purpose. The former were involuntary and done through human ignorance or passion; the latter were voluntary and done in a spirit of rebellion against the ordinance of Jehovah. Only the former could be atoned for by sacrifice and offering; the latter placed one outside the covenant relation, outside the sphere in which Jehovah was gracious. Idolatry came in this latter category.

In the New Testament this same idea is prevalent, Jesus himself teaching the principle. He says that the scribes "who devour widows' houses, and for a pretence make long prayers...shall receive greater condemnation" (Luke 20:45-47) The same teaching is found in the parable of the two servants, one knowing his master's will and not doing it and the other not knowing his master's will and likewise not obeying it. The latter shall receive fewer stripes than the former (Luke 12:47, 48). Those cities that heard Christ and rejected him, such as Chorazin, Bethsaida, and Capernaum, shall be in greater guilt than even the extremely wicked cities of Tyre, Sidon, and Sodom that were not fortunate enough to hear him. It shall be "more tolerable" in the day of judgment for those who have never heard than for those who hear and do not accept him (Matt. 11:20-24). Jesus, speaking of Judas, says unto Pilate, "He that delivered me unto thee hath greater sin" (John 19:11). Therefore Jesus regards some sins as bringing more guilt than others, and therefore necessitating greater condemnation. Guilt seems to be measured by the degree of enlightenment, or knowledge, that one possesses. Therefore genius, talent, and privilege increase responsibility. The fact that Jesus mentions an unforgivable sin, the sin against the Holy Spirit, displays the identical principle of degree of guilt. However, the Roman Catholic distinction between venial sins and mortal sins is without scriptural support.

3. SERVITUDE

Sin enslaves. Jesus informs the Jews, "Every one that committeth sin is the bondservant of sin.... If therefore the Son shall make you free, ye shall be free indeed" (John 8:34-36). Not only does sin enslave; Jesus is the only one who can emancipate from that slavery. He is the only means of spiritual freedom. In the sixth chapter of Romans Paul makes clear that a man is either the servant of sin or the servant of righteousness. "Know ye not, that to whom ye present yourselves as servants unto obedience, his servants ye are whom ye obey; whether of sin unto death, or of obedience unto righteousness? But thanks be to God, that, whereas ye were servants of sin ... ye became servants of righteousness" (6:16-18). "But now being made free from sin and become servants to God, ye have your fruit unto sanctification, and the end eternal life" (6:22).

In the seventh chapter of Romans Paul gives a psychological account of his effort to free himself from the slavery of sin and of his inability to do so. He says that he was alive without the law; then the law appears and reveals to him sin. Seeing himself to be the victim of sin, he recognizes that he is spiritually dead. Yet the law is unable to free him, for he cannot live up to its demands. In his helplessness he cries out to God, finding his deliverance only in Christ.

4. SUFFERING

Sin brings suffering, both for the sinner and for others along with him. Much of human suffering in the world is directly due to man's sin. This is the story from the very expulsion of the first pair from the garden. Before being cast out man worked, tending the garden, but after being driven forth he was to work by the sweat of his face — strenuously and with obstacles. God said to Adam, "Cursed is the ground for thy sake; in toil shalt thou eat of it all the days of thy life; thorns also and thistles shall it bring forth to thee; and thou shalt eat the herb of the field; in the sweat of thy face shalt thou eat bread, till thou return unto the ground..." (Gen. 3:17-19). Burdensome labor became a part of the suffering due to sin. The term "thorns... and thistles" is a broad one, representing natural evil and adversity in general. This would include cyclones, floods, tornadoes, disease, earthquakes, erosion, droughts, volcanoes, and so forth.

So all sin produces suffering, either upon this earth, or in the next life, or both. Even though the suffering is accounted for vicariously, still someone suffers. The two outside crosses represent suffering due to sin directly; the middle cross represents suffering due to sin substitutionally. Those who do not accept Christ's substitutional suffering must bear their own penalty.

5. MORAL AND SPIRITUAL BLINDNESS

Man apart from God is spiritually blind, being in moral degradation. This is so because God is light and the source of man's light. Jesus says, "I am the light of the world: he that followeth me shall not walk in the darkness, but shall have the light of life" (John 8:12). Paul prays that the Ephesians may have the eyes of their heart enlightened (1:18). Man in rebellion against God goes deeper and deeper in degradation and blindness. Paul explains this in Romans 1:18ff. God disclosed himself in his visible creation, but men did not receive this revelation. Instead they went lower and lower in sin. Three times Paul says that God gave them up (1:24, 26, 28). Thus moral and spiritual blindness is a part of God's wrath visited upon man because of rebellion against his will. From this defiance-created stand man cannot free himself without divine help.

Man cannot build a moral system apart from God, for any ethical system must be grounded in the presence and in the nature of God. God must constitute the motivating force and the religious dynamic that sustains and impels the system, for man apart from God becomes more immoral all the time. We are reminded that "Sin destroys the fine balance of man's nature — dust of the

161

earth, God-breathed; man now swings back and forth between life on the brute level and life on the god level. In either direction he perverts what he ought to be, and so perverts all his efforts and so perverts his social relationships in this constant and abortive effort to be what he is not. In all these areas he is now in rebellion against his Maker and is at the same time at war with himself and with his neighbor."[4]

6. DEATH

According to the Scriptures the chief penalty of sin is death. God said to Adam, concerning the tree of the knowledge of good and evil, "In the day that thou eatest thereof thou shalt surely die" (Gen. 2:17). "Therefore, as through one man sin entered into the world, and death through sin; and so death passed unto all men, for that all sinned" (Rom. 5:12). Paul also states that "sin reigned in death" (Rom. 5:21) and that "the wages of sin is death" (Rom. 6:23). He reminds the Ephesian Christians, "And you did he make alive, when ye were dead through your trespasses and sins" (2:1). John says, "We know that we have passed out of death unto life, because we love the brethren. He that loveth not abideth in death" (I John 3:14). This death is moral and spiritual ruin, which only a God-given redemption can rectify. Man is a miserable creature indeed! "He is a being who has missed his mark — who has turned aside from the end of his creation, and is in revolt from, and active rebellion against, his Creator. For this reason he has come under condemnation. A judgment of God . . . rests upon him which he is powerless of himself to remove. His actual spiritual condition is described in the darkest colours. Forgetful of his Maker, he is unholy, prone to evil, the subject of sinful affections, following vanity, fulfilling the desires of the flesh and of the mind. He is not only morally impure, but is in bondage to sin, and again is impotent to deliver himself from its rule."[5]

IV. SALVATION OF INFANTS

1. EVANGELICAL VIEW

What is the status of infants who die before reaching the age of accountability? Are they saved? Are they in the kingdom? There is very little direct teaching on this score in the Scriptures. They do not speak categorically, but they heavily imply that an infant who dies is saved. The whole tenor of the New Testament points toward this view. Since infants cannot repent, or believe, or perform works that are good or bad, we do not understand how the

4 Addison H. Leitch, *Interpreting Basic Theology*, p. 61.
5 Orr, *op. cit.*, pp. 264-5.

grace of God in Christ operates for their benefit. Yet we know that Christ provided for them and that his redeeming power is effective in them. They are changed with regard to their natural bias toward evil. We do not understand just how the Spirit of God effects this, but it is true. This phenomenon may involve as much as one-fourth of the entire human race.

2. SCRIPTURAL EVIDENCE

The general view of God's character as found in the Scriptures, plus the weight of a few pertinent statements, leads us to this view. Some of these scriptural passages are in the eighteenth and nineteenth chapters of Matthew. "Except ye turn, and become as little children, ye shall in no wise enter into the kingdom of heaven. Whosoever therefore shall humble himself as this little child, the same is the greatest in the kingdom of heaven" (18:3, 4). "See that ye despise not one of these little ones: for I say unto you, that in heaven their angels do always behold the face of my Father who is in heaven" (18:10). Immediately after the parable of the lost sheep Jesus states, "Even so it is not the will of your Father who is in heaven, that one of these little ones should perish" (18:14). "Then there were brought unto him little children, that he should lay his hands on them, and pray: and the disciples rebuked them. But Jesus said, Suffer the little children, and forbid them not, to come unto me: for to such belongeth the kingdom of heaven" (19:13, 14). He seems to maintain that the kingdom is the present possession of little ones.

Therefore we are justified in holding the view that little children dying in infancy are saved, which is the opinion adhered to by virtually all evangelical theologians. The Roman Catholics relegate all children not christened by a recognized priest to limbo, the limbo for children. (See the chapter on eschatology for an explanation of limbo.) This is completely unscriptural, for little ones are saved in the full sense of the term. "Up to the point of positive identification of one's self with right or wrong, there is only the potentiality of moral life. In the case of the child, that potentiality is evil except for the positive influence of the grace of God in redeeming from this evil potentiality or the life of transgression that grows out of it. So far as the bent of the child's nature and the social influences of the world order are concerned, these are toward evil. To save the child from this evil inheritance requires the grace of God, which transcends nature and the world order."[6]

6 W. T. Conner, *Christian Doctrines*, p. 144.

OUTLINE FOR CHAPTER EIGHT

I. Preliminary Thoughts on the Atonement

II. Historical Theories of the Atonement
   1. The theories stated
      (1) The ransom-to-Satan theory
      (2) The divine honor theory
      (3) The example theory
      (4) The governmental theory
      (5) The gradually extirpated depravity theory
      (6) The moral influence theory
      (7) The Christus Victor theory
      (8) The sacrificial theory
   2. The inadequacy of these theories

III. The Nature of the Atonement
   1. Love the motive
   2. Redemption of man the end
      (1) From the ruin of sin
      (2) To an ideal of righteousness
      (3) As part of a holy church and a holy kingdom
   3. Christ the means
      (1) Identity with human race
      (2) Life of obedience
      (3) State of sinlessness
      (4) Subjection to law of sin and death
      (5) Endurance of wrath of God
      (6) Expiation for sin
      (7) Substitute for man
      (8) Consummation of all sacrifices
   4. Nature of God and sin of man the necessity
      (1) Nature of God
      (2) Sin of man
   5. Non-limiting the extent

IV. The Resurrection of Christ
   1. The reality
      (1) Scriptural evidence
      (2) False theories
         a. The swoon theory
         b. The spirit theory
         c. The vision theory
         d. The mistake theory
         e. The fraud theory

164

2. The significance
    (1) Witness of his deity
    (2) Consummation of Calvary
    (3) Guarantee of our resurrection
    (4) Assurance of triumph of the kingdom
    (5) Prominent in early preaching

V. The Intercession of Christ
    1. The reality
    2. The place
    3. The benefits
        (1) Assures forgiveness
        (2) Gives boldness to approach God in prayer
        (3) Guarantees permanent standing before God

CHAPTER EIGHT

THE ATONING WORK OF CHRIST

I. PRELIMINARY THOUGHTS ON THE ATONEMENT

THE ATONEMENT HAS TO DO WITH THAT SAVING WORK OF CHRIST which he accomplishes through his sufferings and death. This is central in the teachings of the New Testament, as well as being the core of the gospel itself. Not only that, it is a basic element in the Christian experience of all believers.

Various figures of speech are used by the New Testament writers to express the idea of the atonement. When one of these is pulled off by itself and built up into a theological theory or system, an inadequate or one-sided view is attained. No one term is sufficient in and of itself for such a treatment. Sometimes Christ's death is called an expiation, sometimes a reconciliation, sometimes a redemption, and sometimes a ransom. It is also described as securing remission of sins and as the purchase price for man's deliverance from the bondage of sin. In his death Christ is thought of as becoming a curse for us. He himself terms his death a cup and a baptism. He is also shown as offering his body for sin, and as offering himself a sacrifice once and for all. All of these terms refer to his death; each presents some new facet of the atonement.

Peter's great confession at Caesarea Philippi seems to be a fulcrum upon which the teaching of Jesus is pivoted. It is a turning point in the emphasis of our Lord. At this point in his ministry he says unto the disciples, "Who do men say that the Son of man is?" After he receives an answer to his query he in turn asks, "But who say ye that I am?", to which Peter replies, "Thou are the Christ, the Son of the living God." Then Matthew informs us, "From that time began Jesus to show unto his disciples, that he must go unto Jerusalem, and suffer many things of the elders and chief priests and scribes, and be killed, and the third day be raised up" (Matt. 16:13-21). From this point on he places great emphasis upon his suffering and death, for he must teach them what kind of a Messiah he is meant to be, namely, a suffering one. Prior to this time his teaching has been general and to the multitudes, only speaking of his death in hidden, or cryptic, sayings, as for instance the sign of Jonah (Matt. 12:38-40). Now his teaching must be mainly to the apostles in order to prepare them to take his place. So Jesus' statement relative to his coming death is found not only in Matthew 16:21 but also in 17:22, 23 and in 20:17-19. All this is but a fulfillment of the Suffering-Servant passage found in Isaiah 52:13-53:12.

The main theological bearing of the temptations in the wilderness is the enticement to turn aside from the cross and to take an easy way out in man's redemption. This he settles early in his ministry in that very desolate place. When he foretells at Caesarea Philippi his crucifixion, Peter rebukes him, implying that such drastic action will not be necessary. This is virtually the same temptation with which he has been confronted in the wilderness, so he addresses Peter with the name Satan. Again in Gethsemane on the eve of Golgotha he is confronted with the temptation to assume the easy way out. The conflict is so intense that Luke tells us, "And being in an agony he prayed more earnestly; and his sweat became as it were great drops of blood falling down upon the ground" (22:44). Yet he marches triumphantly from the garden to the cross. On that cross he exclaims, "It is finished," a more exact translation of the Greek being "It is paid off" (John 19:30).

"The Son of man must suffer and be killed and rise again." He must be a suffering Messiah, for an atonement must be made. In speaking of the Caesarea Philippi experience C. H. Dodd reminds us, "That it was only now that Jesus Himself had formed this conception of His mission and destiny is unlikely. The story of the Temptation suggests that before His ministry began He had faced alternative forms of the Messianic idea, and had rejected them; and His whole conception of the kingdom of God was such that its coming must involve the most intense conflict with evil, and the utmost renunciation, even unto death, for Him who was its bearer. But also it must involve victory in conflict and life through death. Jesus invited His followers to share with Him in the conflict and the triumph — to drink of the cup of which He drank, and to be baptized with the baptism with which He was baptized. As things turned out, they proved themselves unequal to the demand. Only after He had died and risen for them did they know the fellowship of His suffering and the power of His resurrection (cf. Phil. 3:10)."[1] When Professor Dodd speaks of "victory in conflict and life through death" he is referring to the paradox of the atoning death of our Lord. Out of apparent defeat comes victory, out of seeming frustration comes triumph, out of death comes life, out of shame comes glory, and out of loss comes gain. In speaking of the cross Jesus announces, "The hour is come, that the Son of man should be glorified" (John 12:23); the most ignominious of deaths, the cross, is to be the means of glorification for

[1] C. H. Dodd, "The Life and Teaching of Jesus Christ," *A Companion to the Bible*, ed. T. W. Manson, p. 384.

the Son. Likewise, Jesus is not only the high priest; he is the sacrifice as well. The priesthood of Christ, as has been seen, is one of his three offices; yet he himself is the one offered up. "And every priest indeed standeth day by day ministering and offering oftentimes the same sacrifices, the which can never take away sins: but he, when he had offered one sacrifice for sins for ever, sat down on the right hand of God" (Heb. 10:11, 12). By offering up his body he makes at-one-ment between God and the sinner. The term atonement is found in only one place in the King James Version of the New Testament: Romans 5:11. And here it translates the same Greek word that has been translated "reconciliation" or "reconciling" in all other incidents. Paul's doctrine of reconciliation is his doctrine of atonement.

The Scriptures are replete with the fact that Christ must die to atone for man's sin. In the Synoptics there are some classic statements made by Jesus himself. "Even as the Son of man came not to be ministered unto, but to minister, and to give his life a ransom for many" (Matt. 20:28). "I came to cast fire upon the earth; and what do I desire, if it is already kindled? But I have a baptism to be baptized with; and how am I straitened till it be accomplished!" (Luke 12:49, 50). At the institution of the Lord's Supper he informs the apostles, "For this is my blood of the covenant, which is poured out for many unto remission of sins" (Matt. 26:28).

The Fourth Gospel contains allusions to the significance of his death. John the Baptist, declaring him to be "the Lamb of God, that taketh away the sin of the world!" (1:29), probably has in mind both the paschal lamb and the lamb of the Suffering-Servant passage in the fifty-third chapter of Isaiah. "And as Moses lifted up the serpent in the wilderness, even so must the Son of man be lifted up; that whosoever believeth may in him have eternal life" (3:14, 15). This "lifted up" means lifted up on the cross, as is seen in: "And I, if I be lifted up from the earth, will draw all men unto myself. But this he said, signifying by what manner of death he should die" (12:32, 33). The idea in the bread-of-life discourse in the sixth chapter is that of giving his life for the sin of man. "I am the living bread which came down out of heaven: if any man eat of this bread, he shall live for ever: yea and the bread which I will give is my flesh, for the life of the world" (6:51).

Paul does not reveal much of the earthly life of Jesus but dwells at length upon the significance of Calvary. "But God commendeth his own love toward us, in that, while we were yet sinners, Christ died for us. Much more then, being now justified by his blood, shall we be saved from the wrath of God through him. For if, while we were enemies, we were reconciled to God through the death of his

Son, much more, being reconciled, shall we be saved by his life" (Rom. 5:8-10). "For I determined not to know anything among you, save Jesus Christ, and him crucified" (I Cor. 2:2). "For I delivered unto you first of all that which also I received: that Christ died for our sins according to the scriptures" (I Cor. 15:3). "Him who knew no sin he made to be sin on our behalf; that we might become the righteousness of God in him" (II Cor. 5:21). In Ephesians Paul states that in Christ "we have our redemption through his blood, the forgiveness of our trespasses" (1:7). He states that "Christ redeemed us from the curse of the law, having become a curse for us" (Gal. 3:13).

Peter has a classic statement in which he reveals the extreme cost of the atonement: "Knowing that ye were redeemed, not with corruptible things, with silver or gold, from your vain manner of life handed down from your fathers; but with precious blood, as of a lamb without blemish and without spot, even the blood of Christ" (I Pet. 1:18, 19). Peter states that it is Christ "who his own self bare our sins in his body upon the tree, that we, having died unto sins, might live unto righteousness" (I Pet. 2:24).

The writer of Hebrews states, "By which will we have been sanctified through the offering of the body of Jesus Christ once for all" (10:10). In First John we read, "And he is the propitiation for our sins; and not for ours only, but also for the whole world" (2:2). In Revelation we read, "Unto him that loveth us, and loosed us from our sins by his blood" (1:5). The new song that is sung before the Lamb declares, "For thou wast slain, and didst purchase unto God with thy blood men of every tribe, and tongue, and people, and nation" (Rev. 5:9).

These passages and many, many others show that it is through his death that reconciliation is made. He does something for us in his death that we cannot do for ourselves. "Apart from shedding of blood there is no remission" (Heb. 9:22). He pours out his blood, remitting sins eternally for those who accept him. This is the atonement.

II. HISTORICAL THEORIES OF THE ATONEMENT

Through the centuries many theories have arisen endeavoring to explain the relation between the death of Christ and the salvation of man. Most of these theories contain various elements of truth, but at the same time most of them are defective in that they omit certain aspects that should have been included. Some people object to any attempt to determine the meaning of the death of Christ, crying for "facts," not "meaning." They advocate the teaching and preaching of "facts." But how, it is asked, can one think of the death of Christ without at the same time attaching a meaning to that death? The interpretation of the death, based upon the content of Scripture, is the vital element after all. His death constitutes the greatest "fact" in all history, but a "fact" divorced from its significance is at the same time divorced from all value to the intelligence. And even though we may not ascertain all the meaning relative to his death, we should endeavor to search valiantly for it.

1. THE THEORIES STATED

(1) THE RANSOM-TO-SATAN THEORY

This is also called the military theory, as well as the patristic theory, since it was held by the early church fathers. It is the view that the death of Christ is a ransom paid by God to Satan to redeem fallen humanity held captive by the latter. Satan, as any captor in war, has a right to retain his captives, which can only be released by a ransom. Christ pays the ransom. This view is based exclusively on the ransom passage found in the Synoptics (Mark 10:45), thus virtually ignoring other great atonement passages. It is maintained that if Christ's death is a ransom it must be paid to someone, and God would not pay it to himself. Therefore it must be paid to Satan. Justin Martyr first expounded this view.

(2) THE DIVINE HONOR THEORY

This is also called the commercial theory and the criminal theory, being the one set forth by Anselm in the eleventh century as a substitute for the early patristic view. Therefore it is also called the Anselmic theory. The emphasis here is upon the divine honor, or majesty, of God, and the sin of man. Sin violates the honor of God; and since God is infinite, this requires infinite punishment. The honor of God requires retribution, while the love of God desires to see the guilty ones spared. This produces a conflict in divine attributes, which can only be reconciled by the voluntary sacrifice of the incarnate Son of God. Only the God-man, because of his person, can bear the intensive infinite punishment of sin. Otherwise sinful man must suffer extensively for his own sins, a suffering eternal in duration. The suffering of the Son presents to the divine majesty the exact equivalent of the deserved suffering of the elect ones, which satisfies the divine honor. But, as sinless, the Son is not due death; so his great act on Calvary furnishes him an excess of merit to be placed at the disposal of sinners (Catholic idea). This view was held in this century by the Princeton school.

Such a theory emphasizes the honor of God more than his righteous love, making the atonement an objective and formal act as over against a view that deals more with the saved-Saviour relationship. It is too abstract, dealing with honor, satisfaction, and majesty rather than the personal characteristics of love and mercy. It gives too much weight to those passages which represent the atonement under commercial analogies: payment of a debt, or ransom, and not to those which deal more with the ethical. Christ's death should be considered more from the qualitative standpoint than the quantitative; this theory considers the latter too heavily. The ransom passage in the Synoptics is emphasized in this theory as well as in the one previously discussed.

(3) THE EXAMPLE THEORY

In the sixteenth century Laelius and Faustus Socinus of Poland brought forth the example theory of the atonement, hence also called the Socinian theory. This view, held today by the Unitarians, maintains that Christ's death is that of a martyr, being a great example of loyalty to truth and thus inspiring men to moral victory. God does not need an atonement; he does not require reconciliation; and man needs only the example of Christ. There is no obstacle in God's way of pardoning; therefore repentance is all that is required of man. Sinfulness is the only barrier between man and God; so the means of reconciliation is the betterment of man's moral condition. Man can do this through his own will and reformation. Christ redeems man through his death only because his human example of faithfulness to truth and to responsibility influences man to moral betterment. Christ's example rouses humanity to imitation.

There is an element of truth in this theory; for Peter tells us, "Because Christ also suffered for you, leaving you an example, that ye should follow his steps" (I Pet. 2:21). So Christ *is* our example; but he is much more than that. He *is* a martyr to truth, but far more. This view is void of those elements in the gospel that have made it a source of power through the centuries. It ascribes transforming power to that which works for the benefit of man after the transformation takes place. It gives man the power of self-transformation, thus eliminating his need for the regenerative power of the Holy Spirit on the basis of the atoning work of Christ. Sin involves both objective guilt and subjective defilement. This theory deals with the latter and ignores the former, while the Scriptures stress mainly the former. The biblical revelation maintains that the sacrifice is offered to God in order to satisfy the divine holiness and to remove that which prevents God from forgiving the guilty. This example view warps the biblical doctrine of sin; for in the Scriptures sin is seen to produce perversion of nature, thus rendering man unable to save himself. It also makes void the necessity of the deity of Christ, for a human Christ would be able to set the example as well as a divine one.

(4) THE GOVERNMENTAL THEORY

This theory was first propounded by Hugo Grotius, a Dutch jurist, poet, historian, statesman, and theologian of the early seventeenth century, hence the name Grotian theory. He was one who dealt with doctrine more as a statesman than as a theologian. Therefore it is not surprising that this theory maintains that God's government rather than his honor, or his righteousness, is at stake. God's law has been violated by sinners; therefore some exhibition of the high estimate God places upon his law and the extreme heinousness of violating it must be shown to man before God can pardon him. This exhibition of God's regard for his law is seen in the sufferings and death of Christ. Yet Christ does not suffer the actual penalty of man's sin; God just accepts his suffering as a substitute for that penalty. It is a substitute suffering on the part of Christ, thus giving God's law a hold on the hearts of men leading them to repentance. Thus God can pardon sinners without peril to his government. The text most frequently used to support this theory is Isaiah 42:21: "It pleased Jehovah, for his righteousness' sake, to magnify the law, and make it honorable." The explanation has been added: "even when its demands are unfulfilled." This view was characteristic of New England theology in days past.

This theory, as the others, has an element of truth, for God does have regard for his law. But it substitutes this subordinate phase of the atonement for the main issue itself. It ignores the immanent holiness of God, from which law and its threatened penalties stem. Government is merely the reflection of the justice of God, which is what must be satisfied. What sinner under conviction feels that his controversy is with government? No, he feels that in his depravity and polluted condition he is at variance with the righteousness and purity of a personal God. His sin is against God himself, more than his law; and what satisfies God satisfies his law also. The atonement must be viewed in relation to that which is central in God, his righteous love, and in the reproduction of that love in the sinner. Here we have an exhibition in regard for law, rather than an execution of law itself. It makes the atonement merely a scenic representation for the purpose of requiring respect for law. Even the Socinian view of Christ's death as an example of virtue makes more sense than the Grotian view of Christ's death as an example of chastisement! But Christ's death on Calvary is no passion-play; it is a sacrifice of eternal significance.

(5) THE GRADUALLY EXTIRPATED DEPRAVITY THEORY

This theory was brought forth in the early nineteenth century by Edward Irving of London and is therefore termed the Irvingian theory. This holds that Christ in his incarnation takes on human nature in its depraved state, with all of its natural corruption and predisposition toward sin. This is human nature as it was in Adam after the Fall, not in its innocent condition before the Fall. Yet Christ, through the power of the Holy Spirit and because he is divine, keeps this nature from manifesting itself in any personal sin. Not only so, he gradually purifies it through suffering and struggle until, through his death, he removes utterly its original depravity, thus reuniting it with God. The atonement, therefore, in this theory, consists of the subjective purification of human nature in Christ's person, man being redeemed by partaking of this new humanity through faith. It is maintained that unfallen humanity does not need redemption, only fallen humanity. Therefore Jesus takes the latter and purges it of all sin. Irving often quoted Hebrews 2:10: "make the author of their salvation perfect through sufferings."

It is true that there is a new humanity in Christ in which all believers are partakers, but this view denies the great objective phase of the atonement which makes the subjective phase possible. This is purely a subjective view of the atonement. Deliverance from sin that there may be deliverance from the penalty is just the reverse of what is found in the Scriptures. Also, sin is viewed as a power of moral evil in the soul and not also as that which entails guilt and ill-desert. An inclination toward evil is not considered sin; only evil acts are considered so. Also, in this view the death of Christ works the regeneration of his sinful nature; but this is to make sin physical only, with the body the only part needing redemption. Besides all this, the Scriptures explicitly teach Christ's freedom from all taint of hereditary depravity.

(6) THE MORAL INFLUENCE THEORY

This theory was popularized by Horace Bushnell of America around the middle of the nineteenth century. It maintains that no necessity of the divine nature is met in the death of Christ, nothing in the nature of God is appeased. Instead, his death is a manifestation of the love of God, suffering in and with the sins of his people, with the aim of softening human hearts to the point of repentance. God is already reconciled, so divine justice does not have to be satisfied. Christ does not die to remove an obstacle in God's pardoning of sinners but to show men that no obstacle exists. Repentance is all that is necessary. Since the incarnation unites

Christ with sinful mankind, his death results from his sympathetic efforts for man's salvation. Bushnell used the verse, "Himself took our infirmities, and bare our diseases" (Matt. 8:17), as indicative of Christ's atoning work. This view has been held by many preachers and theologians, beginning with Origen, a very early preacher and writer. Pierre Abelard is the next in line, writing and teaching in the early 1100's. In England the advocates of this theory were Robertson, Maurice, Campbell, and Young, and in Germany, Schleiermacher and Ritschl.

The objection to this theory is that it substitutes a subordinate element of the atonement for the chief aim. It is true to a certain extent, because the sufferings of the incarnate Christ do present a moral influence upon sinners; but a suffering *with* the sinner is by no means equivalent to one *for* the sinner. Bushnell wrote a work, *Vicarious Sacrifice*, depicting this view; but the word vicarious should not be used as he used it; for this word (from *vicis*) implies substitution, which this theory denies. Also, this theory shows no proper reason for the sufferings of Christ. It is true that he suffers because of his contact with human sin, but it ignores the fact that the universe is so constituted that the consequence of sin is suffering, either directly or indirectly, for the sinner and for the innocent. This is to say that God's holiness, engrained in the moral order which he has brought forth, is ignored. This view does show God's love, but it does not satisfy his justice. It ignores the fact that Christ's blood does something for us in heaven, when presented there by our Intercessor. It seems to mix the experience of the sinner in being saved with God's method of saving.

McLeod Campbell, one of the main advocates of this theory, gives it a little different twist. He maintains that Christ is the representative penitent. Since Christ becomes one with humanity through his incarnation he shares the guilt feeling of man due to sin and actually repents for mankind, yet with all this remaining sinless himself. On the basis of this representative penitence God forgives sinners. We reply by acknowledging that there is an element of truth, but we deny the fact that Christ repents. Campbell's view does not agree with that of the other advocates of the theory.

(7) THE CHRISTUS VICTOR THEORY

A Swedish Lutheran theologian, Gustaf Aulén, wrote a book entitled *Christus Victor*, released in English in 1931. In it he presents a theory of the atonement based upon early Greek Christian thought, for he gives a reconstruction of what he calls the classic theory. Too long have theologians passed over the period from the old patristic period to that of Anselm in 1098; so therefore this man has made a great contribution to theological thought. The main text that he employs is the Pauline one, "God was in Christ reconciling the world unto himself" (II Cor. 5:19), though much of his theory goes back to the Gospel of Mark. Here we see the God-man engaging in warfare with the forces of evil, which continues from the temptation on down to the storm of opposition of the political and religious leaders, climaxing in Calvary. This military metaphor, which is the basis of his theory, views Christ's work of salvation as a battle against demons, sin, death, the devil, wrath, and the law, the last two as found in Paul. There is a dualism between God and that which opposes his will; yet Aulén maintains that this is not an ultimate dualism (as in Zoroastrianism) but a provisional one overcome in the classic theory that God is both reconciler and reconciled. "The patristic theology is dualistic, but it is not an absolute Dualism. The deliverance of man from the power of death and the devil is at the same time his deliverance from God's judgment. God is reconciled by his own act in reconciling the world to himself."[2] There is a cosmic warfare, one against a very real enemy and one involving a divine self-sacrifice, where there is triumph over evil lasting eternally. In this theory the atonement is viewed mainly in an objective manner, sin standing as an objective power between God and man. God triumphs over sin.

Aulén comes very near the true view, for Christ *is* conqueror over demons and all that opposes man's existence. In fact, the theme of a military triumph over all the hosts of darkness is one of Paul's favorite metaphors. Yet Aulén's emphasis is solely upon the God-in-Christ aspect of atonement rather than upon the God-man as atoner because of his twofold nature. There is not enough stress on his identification with sinful humanity, upon that portrayed in "Him who knew no sin he made to be sin on our behalf; that we might become the righteousness of God in him" (II Cor. 5:21). There is an overemphasis upon the part of deity in the atoner, thus implying that the humanity is not basic in the work done by the incarnate Christ. (Anselm does just the opposite, placing too much emphasis upon Christ as the human offerer of salvation.)

(8) THE SACRIFICIAL THEORY

This theory immediately brings to mind the name of an English writer and theologian, Vincent Taylor.[3] Professor Taylor believes

2 Gustaf Aulén, *Christus Victor*, p. 59.
3 See his books *Jesus and His Sacrifice* and *The Atonement in New Testament Teaching*.

that, even though much of the preaching today on the atonement is some form of Abelard's theory, this theory is inadequate. It does have an element of truth, for Christ does reveal the love of God in his life and in his death, and so moves man to trust and love him in return. But the suffering and death of Jesus are not satisfactorily taken into account; therefore the theory is inadequate to human need, especially to anyone really conscious of the power and reality of sin.

Taylor's theory calls for a return to an expiatory view of the atonement, one in which the self-offering of Jesus as a sacrifice is the central core. That Jesus' whole ministry was conducted with the conviction that his messianic service was the self-offering of himself for man is evident from a study of all his passion-sayings as found recorded in the four gospels. To this study Taylor devotes quite a bit of space in his. *Jesus and His Sacrifice*. His conclusion from this study is threefold: "In the first place, the self-offering of Jesus is His perfect obedience to the Father's will. The obedience is His own, but since He presents it as the Son of Man, it is also representative obedience; it is the obedience which men ought to offer to God, and which they would offer if they fulfilled the obligations of their sonship.... Secondly, the self-offering of Jesus is His perfect submission to the judgment of God upon sin. This is the living truth behind the long history of the successive attempts to find a penal element in the sufferings of Christ.... What is needed is the vision of a perfect submission with which man may identify himself. No offer of penal suffering as a substitute for his own will meet his need, but a submission presented by his Representative before God becomes the foundation of a new hope.... Thirdly, the self-offering of Jesus is the expression of His perfect penitence for the sins of men. This is a view with which J. M'Leod Campbell and R. C. Moberly have made us familiar.... But is sinlessness a fatal bar to the exercise of such a ministry? Can representative penitence be expressed by one 'who did no sin, neither was guile found in his mouth'?... it is actually sin in men which makes their offering imperfect; they are held back from the exercise of representative penitence because they are sinners. The bearing of this argument upon the self-offering of Christ is manifest: His sinlessness is the necessary condition of His oblation."[4] According to this threefold conclusion Taylor sees, on the part of Christ, a representative obedience, a representative submission to penal suffering, and a representative penitence. He is somewhat eclectic in his method, for his theory contains expiatory and non-expiatory elements of other theories. In fact, he admits that the sacrificial theory either

[4] Vincent Taylor, *Jesus and His Sacrifice*, pp. 306-312.

contains elements of other historical theories or can easily be harmonized with the positive elements of merit in those theories. He uses the terms "deification," "ransom," "substitution," "imputation," and "love revealed" to demonstrate his point. He believes the work of Christ for man can be considered as vicarious, representative, and sacrificial. He has absolute confidence in his theory, for he states, "The sacrificial theory of the Atonement meets the deepest spiritual needs of the individual, but always in the closest relation to a conception of reconciliation which stops at nothing short of the ideal of the world in fellowship with God."[5] Considered as a whole, this theory has much to commend it.

2. The inadequacy of these theories

It is contended that, in the main, the inadequacy of the above-mentioned theories lies in the fact that each stresses only one phase of the atoning work of Christ, thus ignoring the many other metaphors with which the New Testament depicts this very important work of our Lord. For instance, a theory may be based on respect for God's law and the restoration, but this is only one phase of the total problem. "The basic trouble with many theories of atonement is that they describe the breakdown in the personal relationship between God and man as though the secondary and derived level of law and responsibility were the total problem to be faced. The assumption behind these theories is that, once the law's demands are satisfied, atonement has by this very act been accomplished.... The meeting of the 'law's demand' is not God's whole aim in redemption. He wishes that men, by the love which he will communicate to them if they will not shut up their hearts, will mature into the new status of sons. It is the picture of deeply personal ties and family intimacy between God and men, not the picture of broken law, that must be the controlling image for theories of the atonement."[6] And the same statement that is thus made relative to the atonement and God's law, or government, could be made relative to the atonement and God's honor. It would also apply to the cross as an example, or as an influence for ethical living. It would also apply to debt and payment, and to victory in battle. Therefore it is quite obvious that each theory possesses an element of truth; yet this element becomes distorted when it is offered as the exclusive theory, neatly tied up with the theologian's trade name on it. There is no desire for insight into the views of others, not to mention the many other New Testament metaphors used by the inspired biblical writers themselves.

5 Vincent Taylor, *The Atonement in New Testament Teaching*, pp. 173-209.
6 William J. Wolf, *No Cross, No Crown*, pp. 188-9.

Some theories stress the "objective" side of the atonement, the great act on the part of God that gives man a new heavenly status, while others stress the "subjective" side of the atonement, the producing of a holy and reformed person capable of fellowship with a God free from impurity and taint. Either extreme is inadequate and misleading, for the atonement involves both elements. "The attempt to mediate between the so-called 'objective' theories on the one hand and the so-called 'subjective' theories on the other is not simply a device to secure theological harmony. It is an imperative for anyone who takes seriously the New Testament teaching on salvation and atonement. It is also an act of contrition that such a radical and sterile antithesis should even have established itself in Christian tradition."[7] What Professor Wolf maintains here is equally advocated by Professor D. M. Baillie. "Is it an 'objective' reality, something done by Christ, something ordained and accepted by God, in expiation of human sin, quite apart from our knowledge of it and its effect upon us? Or is it a subjective process, a reconciling of us to God through a persuasion in our hearts that there is no obstacle, a realizing of His eternal love? Surely these two aspects cannot be separated at all, though the attempt has often been made to classify atonement-theories in that way. In theological argument on this subject we are apt to forget that we are dealing with a realm of personal relationships and nothing else."[8] The atonement is both "objective" and "subjective" in nature, and to make it exclusively one is to distort it. This is maintained biblically by the Apostle Paul when he enjoins the Philippian Christians to "work out your own salvation with fear and trembling; for it is God who worketh in you both to will and to work, for his good pleasure" (2:12, 13).

III. THE NATURE OF THE ATONEMENT

Any doctrine of the atoning work of Christ must be rooted in a total understanding of the nature of God. Therefore nothing less than the doctrine of the Trinity is involved. The entire depth of the New Testament event of redemption must be sounded. More is required than a mere balancing of the love of God over against the justice of God. The personal element must not be lost in a bare objectivity, and the expiatory element must not be swallowed up in an exclusive subjectivity. One must not stop short of the magnitude of New Testament salvation. "Strictly speaking, there is no Atonement apart from the whole process by which sinners are reconciled to God; and this includes the passion of God expressed in the Cross, the life and death of Christ Himself,

---

7 *Ibid.*, p. 206.
8 D. M. Baillie, *God Was In Christ*, pp. 197-8.

and the relation of men to Him and His atoning work. All this, and nothing less, is the Atonement."[9]

1. LOVE THE MOTIVE

Back of the cross stands the love of God, which is the motivating power of this great redeeming act. "For God so loved the world, that he gave his only begotten Son, that whosoever believeth on him should not perish, but have eternal life" (John 3:16). "Herein was the love of God manifested in us, that God hath sent his only begotten Son into the world that we might live through him. Herein is love, not that we loved God, but that he loved us, and sent his Son to be the propitiation for our sins" (I John 4:9, 10). Paul speaks similarly. "But God commendeth his own love toward us, in that, while we were yet sinners, Christ died for us" (Rom. 5:8). The work of the atonement is, in its entirety, the expression of the love of God. It is love that prompts the Father to send the Son. It is love that motivates the Son to give himself completely in sacrificial death. It is love that sends the Holy Spirit after the resurrection and the ascension to lead men to respond to God's gracious gift. The Father sends because of love, the Son manifests the love, the Holy Spirit is sent that the love might be poured out into our hearts. Each person of the Trinity is involved in expressing the love of the atonement.

God created with the motive of love, having in mind a loving relationship between himself and his created ones. But man rebelled and thwarted that gracious purpose, turning inward toward self or outward toward that which is paltry and petty. Thus alienation ensued. Yet God never ceases to love his rebellious creation, but of necessity is forced to express that love in the form of discipline, much as a parent might express himself toward a wayward child in wrathful indignation. God loves both the unsaved and the saved; each is surrounded by his magnanimous love. Paul expresses such a thought when he states that God proves his love in that while we are in an unlovely, ungracious condition Christ loves us and dies for us (Rom. 5:8). Never should the doctrine of the atonement be presented as picturing the Father as the embodiment of justice and the Son the embodiment of love, with the death of the Son turning the Father back toward a loving disposition in regard to wayward man. The love of Christ on Calvary is the love of the Father that sends Christ in the first place. Never does one person of the Trinity work in a manner opposite to that of another person of the Trinity. The work of one is the work of the other; the will of one is the will of the other. The very wrath of God itself is not antithetical to his love but

9 Vincent Taylor, *Jesus and His Sacrifice*, p. 304.

is an expression of it. Our own wrath, as well as our love, is corrupted by sin, the former probably more than the latter. Our wrath is often our displeasure at not having our way, while our love is corrupted with ulterior motives, such as self-interest and indulgence. God's wrath and love are not so corrupted, for his wrath expresses his love toward man. God hates sin and wills against any expression of it; therefore he sets himself in wrath or antagonism against the sinner. This very wrath is shown by the love of Calvary. The divine punishments of God for sin are not irate expressions of vindictive anger, but expressions of his utter disgust toward sin. God takes these punishments upon himself by means of the cross. Therefore his wrath does not destroy the sinner but endeavors to win the sinner away from his sin.

The death of Christ is the love of God in action, love stooping to redeem fallen man from his plight of depravity. It is God's pledge to a ruined and spiritually bankrupt race. It is love going to the extreme of suffering to cancel the alienation of a rebellious mankind.

2. REDEMPTION OF MAN THE END

The end of the atonement can hardly be stated succinctly. Karl Barth's statement is elucidating: "To what end? So that His creature may go out freely, so that the burden which it has laid upon itself may be borne, borne away. The creature itself must have gone to pieces, but God does not want that; He wants it to be saved."[10] But what is involved in this "to be saved"? There are various aspects to be considered.

(1) FROM THE RUIN OF SIN

The penitent one is forgiven and his sins remitted. When John the Baptist sees Jesus approaching, he says, "Behold, the Lamb of God, that taketh away the sin of the world!" (John 1:29). Jesus, in speaking of the cup, says, "For this is my blood of the covenant, which is poured out for many unto remission of sins" (Matt. 26:28). In the epistles the examples of this thought are legion. Paul rejoices in what is received through Christ, "in whom we have our redemption through his blood, the forgiveness of our trespasses, according to the riches of his grace" (Eph. 1:7). Peter reminds us of the extreme cost of this redemption from sin: "knowing that ye were redeemed, not with corruptible things, with silver or gold, from your vain manner of life handed down from your fathers, but with precious blood, as of a lamb without blemish and without spot, even the blood of Christ" (I Pet. 1:18, 19).

10 Karl Barth, *Dogmatics in Outline*, p. 16.

Redemption from sin has a threefold note: past, present, and future. There is deliverance from the guilt of sin, so that the child of God is free from the bondage of his past. There is deliverance from the power of sin, so that its enslaving shackles are cast off in present living. The old man has been crucified with Christ, "that the body of sin might be done away, that so we should no longer be in bondage to sin" (Rom. 6:6). Paul also enjoins, "Let not sin therefore reign in your mortal body, that ye should obey the lusts thereof" (Rom. 6:12). And there is deliverance from the condemnation of sin, so that the redeemed has nothing to fear on the day of judgment. "There is therefore now no condemnation to them that are in Christ Jesus" (Rom. 8:1).

(2) TO AN IDEAL OF RIGHTEOUSNESS

A holy character leading to holy living becomes the order of the redeemed life. The purpose of Christ is "that we should be holy and without blemish before him in love" (Eph. 1:4). The aim of our Lord is that, "denying ungodliness and worldly lusts, we should live soberly and righteously and godly in this present world" (Titus 2:12). We are redeemed by grace for a purpose: "For we are his workmanship, created in Christ Jesus for good works, which God afore prepared that we should walk in them" (Eph. 2:10). Jesus as the perfect man furnishes this ideal of righteousness. That which was lost in Eden is regained through Golgotha, and the redeemed one becomes a holy child of God.

(3) AS PART OF A HOLY CHURCH AND A HOLY KINGDOM

Man's redemption involves his becoming a member of the body of Christ. God's purpose is "to the intent that now unto the principalities and the powers in the heavenly places might be made known through the church the manifold wisdom of God" (Eph. 3:10). Christ's very death is a self-giving for the church. "Husbands, love your wives, even as Christ also loved the church, and gave himself up for it; that he might sanctify it, having cleansed it by the washing of water with the word, that he might present the church to himself a glorious church, not having spot or wrinkle or any such thing; but that it should be holy and without blemish" (Eph. 5:25-27). Through Christ's death man becomes part of a holy priesthood. "Unto him that loveth us, and loosed us from our sins by his blood; and he made us to be a kingdom, to be priests unto his God and Father" (Rev. 1:5, 6). Not only redeemed and holy individuals, but these holy individuals comprising a holy society, so that Paul can exclaim, "Christ in you [plural], the hope of glory" (Col. 1:27) — this is the ultimate end of the atonement. "This is why an analysis of atonement must lead at once into a consideration of life in the Holy Spirit, of the Church as the atoning body of Christ, and the sacraments as the means by which men are incorporated into Christ and then nourished there in the communion of his body and blood. This is why the explanation of atonement must be intimately related to the hope of Christ's return and the redemption of history."[11]

3. CHRIST THE MEANS

The means of the atonement is Christ, the unique Son of the Father, the second person of the Trinity. Though his death is the culminating event in the great atoning action, there is also much more involved, without which his sacrificial death would not be efficacious in redeeming power.

(1) IDENTITY WITH HUMAN RACE

That Christ identifies himself with sinful humanity is found throughout the Scriptures, for the incarnation is the means whereby God enters into saving relations with mankind. "But when the fulness of time came, God sent forth his Son, born of a woman, born under the law, that he might redeem them that were under the law, that we might receive the adoption of sons" (Gal. 4:4, 5). A classic passage is found in the book of Hebrews. "Since then the children are sharers in flesh and blood, he also himself in like manner partook of the same; that through death he might bring to nought him that had the power of death, that is, the devil; and might deliver all them who through fear of death were all their lifetime subject to bondage. . . . Wherefore it behooved him in all things to be made like unto his brethren, that he might become a merciful and faithful high priest in things pertaining to God, to make propitiation for the sins of the people" (2:14-17; see also John 1:1-18; Phil. 2:5-11; and Col. 1:14-20).

The true manhood of Jesus is essentially basic to the proper concept of the atonement. "All true Christian ideas in regard to atonement may be viewed as aspects of Jesus' self-identification with the sinful. If then he who lived and died for men had himself been man only in seeming, or in part, no expiation were after all made in our name; for only He can act with God for man who speaks from man's side. It is as Christ became our fellow, moving in a true manhood through obedience, conflict, and death, that He entered into our condition fully and availed in our behalf to receive from God's hand the suffering in which is

11 Wolf, *op. cit.*, p. 203.

expressed the Divine judgment upon sin. Jesus' manhood is the corner-stone of reconciliation."[12]

It is maintained that this unity with the race has a backward and a forward look. It looks back to Christ's original relation to mankind, for man was made in his image. He was the original creative head of the race. But there is also a forward aspect, for Christ is the new spiritual head of all the redeemed. His unity with mankind, his entering flesh, his taking human conditions — all this is that he might become the effective power in man's redemption. Man cannot of himself throw off his sin, cannot live apart from a sinful condition. There must be a power from without acting from within; this is possible only through the incarnation, through God made flesh. Being one with God and one with man Christ can act for both.

(2) LIFE OF OBEDIENCE

His incarnate life is one of perfect obedience, both up to and including his death. Paul reminds us that "he humbled himself, becoming obedient even unto death, yea, the death of the cross" (Phil. 2:8). The author of Hebrews says, "Who in the days of his flesh, having offered up prayers and supplications with strong crying and tears unto him that was able to save him from death, and having been heard for his godly fear, though he was a Son, yet learned obedience by the things which he suffered" (5:7, 8). Because he is genuinely human his obedience is a learning process brought about by his passion. His supreme desire is to obey the Father and to do his will. "I can of myself do nothing: as I hear, I judge: and my judgment is righteous; because I seek not mine own will, but the will of him that sent me" (John 5:30). His sacrificial death is his own moral act of obedience. "Then said I, Lo, I am come (In the roll of the book it is written of me) To do thy will, O God" (Heb. 10:7). His life is the answer of the Son to every requirement of the Father.

(3) STATE OF SINLESSNESS

The manhood of Jesus is an ideal that is unique in history by virtue of his sinlessness. There are two categorical scriptural accounts of his absolute freedom from taint. "For we have not a high priest that cannot be touched with the feeling of our infirmities; but one that hath been in all points tempted like as we are, yet without sin" (Heb. 4:15). "Him who knew no sin he made to be sin on our behalf; that we might become the righteousness of God in him" (II Cor. 5:21). Besides these two explicit state-

---

12 H. R. Mackintosh, *The Doctrine of the Person of Jesus Christ*, p. 405.

ments of his sinless character there are others that imply the same. He says to the Jews around him, "Which of you convicteth me of sin?" (John 8:46). Also, his very forgiving of sin manifests his own sinlessness. "And Jesus seeing their faith saith unto the sick of the palsy, Son, thy sins are forgiven" (Mark 2:5). He affirms that his blood is poured out for the remission of sins (Matt. 26:28).

"Only a sinless person can guarantee the Divine pardon of sin. If redemption is to be achieved, the Redeemer must stand free of moral evil. As the source of victorious spiritual energy, He must Himself be in utter oneness with the will of God. The perfect moral health, the unstained conscience, to which He is slowly raising others, must be present absolutely in His own life. If He shed His blood for the remission of sins, it is because He is without spot or blemish. Like to His brethren in all else, He is unlike them here. Yet it is no paradox to say that such unlikeness makes His kinship perfect; for sin had made Him not more a man, but less. Sin dehumanises, and by its entrance the perfection of His vital sympathy would have been irrecoverably lost."[13]

(4) SUBJECTION TO LAW OF SIN AND DEATH

There is a definite connection between sin and death. "The wages of sin is death" (Rom. 6:23). Death follows sin as its penalty, an eternal law decreed so by God himself. This sin-death principle is operative throughout the human race, holding its powerful sway over all mankind. Man has no means within himself to break such power; yet this force must be annulled if he is to be redeemed.

Paul tells us, "Him who knew no sin he made to be sin on our behalf; that we might become the righteousness of God in him" (II Cor. 5:21). Peter speaks of Christ when he says, "Who his own self bare our sins in his body upon the tree, that we, having died unto sins, might live unto righteousness" (I Pet. 2:24). By identifying himself with sinful humanity, even though he himself is sinless, he comes under the burden of man's sin and is subject to the sin-death decree. He is willing to enter the sphere of operation of that principle that he might break its power in fallen man; this he can do because he is the God-man, bringing power from without belonging to an all-powerful, transcendent God. But, as of necessity, he himself is crushed, suffering humiliation and death. Man, then, by faith in the God-man and the atoning power of his death, is himself freed from the law of sin and death. The sin-death principle is overcome by the obedience-life principle operative in Christ; and Paul can now say, "For the

13 *Ibid.*, p. 401.

184

law of the Spirit of life in Christ Jesus made me free from the law of sin and of death. For what the law could not do, in that it was weak through the flesh, God, sending his own Son in the likeness of sinful flesh and for sin, condemned sin in the flesh" (Rom. 8:2, 3). The law of the spirit of life in Christ overcomes the law of sin and of death operative in fallen man.

(5) ENDURANCE OF WRATH OF GOD

It is imperative that we realize that the wrath of God is not angry, vindictive passion. It is not enraged hatred. It is God's resistance and reaction toward sin, expressing itself in penalty. The wrath of God is not poured out upon Christ at Calvary as against a personal sinner; for he endures the wrath of God only in that he permits, by his partaking of the flesh of humanity, the sin-death principle to operate in him. The wrath of God lies upon sinful man because of his iniquity. By entering into the condition of humanity Christ can endure death, the expression of God's wrath and penalty against man for his sin.

It is true that the wrath of God may be considered as the expression of his love. The personal assertion of the will of God against sin is his wrath against the sinner, which wrath is expressed by the love poured out at Golgotha. In fact, it has been maintained that it would be better to speak of "God's wrathful love" than "God's wrath." God's love is the supreme attribute, the one from which all others, including his wrath, must be interpreted.

(6) EXPIATION FOR SIN

Christ's death is an expiation in that he endures the righteous judgment of God upon man's sin. He exhausts God's judgment against sin, and therefore obliterates death, in his own victorious death and resurrection. He removes the wrath of God against man for his sin. His expiation does not turn God's love back toward fallen humanity, for it has always been there; it merely makes possible God's exercise of that love toward man, yet within the bounds of God's holiness and his antagonism toward sin. God's righteous wrath against sin is satisfied, so that God's mercy may go out to the sinner.

The Greek term *hilasmos*, as found in I John 2:2 and 4:10, and the term *hilastērion*, as found in Romans 3:25 and in Hebrews 2:17, is translated with "propitiation" in the King James Version and in the American Standard Version. (The verb form of the term, and not the noun, is found in the Hebrew passage.) This is not a good English word to use; "expiation" would be much better, since it is used in the Revised Standard Version and many others. These four verses as used in the American Standard will illustrate. Paul speaks of the redemption that is in Christ, "whom God set forth to be a propitiation, through faith, in his blood" (Rom. 3:25). The writer of Hebrews, presenting Christ as our high priest, says, "Wherefore it behooved him in all things to be made like unto his brethren, that he might become a merciful and faithful high priest in things pertaining to God, to make propitiation for the sins of the people" (2:17). John shows the universality of this great work of Jesus. "And he is the propitiation for our sins, and not for ours only, but also for the whole world" (I John 2:2). He also states, "Herein is love, not that we loved God, but that he loved us, and sent his Son to be the propitiation for our sins" (I John 4:10). It would have been nearer the meaning of the Greek to have used "expiation" in each of these cases. (Hebrews 9:5 contains the word *hilastērion*, but here it should be translated "mercy seat," as it is in most translations.)

The Greek verb from which *hilasmos* is derived is used in pagan Greek, meaning to placate, to pacify, or to propitiate some offended person, especially a pagan deity. Judging from this alone, the best English translation for *hilasmos* would be "propitiation," for to "propitiate" means to make favorably inclined, to appease, or to conciliate. But this Greek verb has another meaning besides that of rendering favorable, a meaning much rarer among pagan writers. This meaning is to perform an act whereby defilement is removed, a defilement either ritual or moral, which is to expiate. To "expiate" is to atone for, to make amends for, to make reparation for, and this is exactly the meaning attached to both *hilasmos* and *hilastērion* as used by the New Testament writers. Therefore "expiation" is much preferred to "propitiation" for the translation of these two Greek terms. It is disappointing to find the American Standard Version still holding to "propitiation." Vincent Taylor goes so far as to say that we may yet find a word even more appropriate than "expiation" with which to depict this important idea. " 'Propitiation' is certainly a word with which we may well dispense, and it may be that we shall find an equivalent for 'expiation' which will preserve the Old Testament ideas it has to serve."[14]

In their famous commentary on Romans William Sanday and A. C. Headlam summarize the word *hilastērion* wisely when they affirm, "We believe that the Holy Spirit spoke through these writers, and that it was His Will that we should use this word. But it is a word which we must leave it to him to interpret. We drop our plummet into the depth, but the line attached to it is too short, and it does not touch the bottom. The awful processes

---

[14] Vincent Taylor, *The Atonement in New Testament Teaching*, p. 205.

of the Divine Mind we cannot fathom. Sufficient for us to know that through the virtue of the One Sacrifice our sacrifices are accepted, that the barrier which Sin places between us and God is removed, and that there is a sprinkling which makes us free to approach the throne of grace."[15]

(7) SUBSTITUTE FOR MAN

The dominant word used relative to Christ's becoming our substitute is the Greek preposition *huper*, which means in behalf of. Christ dies in behalf of sinful man, the sinless dying for the sinful. We can think of him as our representative, for he is that; but he is more than that, for his death is vicarious. He is our substitute, doing for us what we cannot do for ourselves. The sinful cannot atone for the sinful. The victim of the sin-death principle, man in his sin, is unable to break that principle. But Christ is able, and much more. Therefore substitution is one of the main roles in the atonement for man's sin.

This New Testament teaching finds its background in the soil of the Old Testament. Upon the scapegoat on the Day of Atonement are laid all the sins of the people; the goat is then expelled to the remote wilderness. On this same day the blood of the sacrifice sprinkled in the holy of holies makes expiation for the sins of Israel. Yet the fifty-third chapter of Isaiah presents most vividly this idea of substitution; for here there is pictured, hundreds of years before Christ's arrival on earth, the account of his substitutionary atonement. "Surely he hath borne our griefs, and carried our sorrows; yet we did esteem him stricken, smitten of God, and afflicted. But he was wounded for our transgressions, he was bruised for our iniquities; the chastisement of our peace was upon him; and with his stripes we are healed. All we like sheep have gone astray; we have turned every one to his own way; and Jehovah hath laid on him the iniquity of us all" (4-6). "... yet he bare the sin of many, and made intercession for the transgressors" (12).

The New Testament writers view the substitution of Christ as a fulfillment of this Old Testament truth. Paul declares "that Christ died for our sins according to the scriptures" (I Cor. 15:3). He also states, "Him who knew no sin he made to be sin on our behalf; that we might become the righteousness of God in him" (II Cor. 5:21). "For while we were yet weak, in due season Christ died for the ungodly" (Rom. 5:6). "But God commendeth his own love toward us, in that, while we were yet sinners, Christ died for us" (Rom. 5:8). "Christ also suffered for sins once, the righteous for the unrighteous, that he might bring us to God" (I Pet.

15 William Sanday and A. C. Headlam, *Commentary on the Epistle to the Romans*, "The International Critical Commentary," ed. C. A. Briggs, p. 94.

3:18). In each passage the Greek preposition *huper*, meaning in behalf of, is employed.

A certain question is appropriately asked, and correctly answered, concerning Christ's sufferings. "How can these sufferings be contemplated as a substitute for punishment? Because, being the consequence of sin, they were voluntarily borne by the sinless Christ as a solemn testimony, out of his own bitter experience, to the hatefulness of sin and the justice of God's appointment that misery and suffering shall follow it as its deserved penalty. Christ honored and vindicated this divine appointment by taking upon himself sufferings which belong in God's order to sin, thus upholding the justice of that divine order. Christ had entered through the vicariousness of infinite love into man's case. Man was under the penal consequences of sin. Christ comes under these, both by becoming the object of sinful treatment, and by the intense realization in his own spirit of sin's guilt; and he attests, by the severity of his sufferings, vicariously borne, the righteousness of God's hostility to sin."[16]

(8) CONSUMMATION OF ALL SACRIFICES

Christ's death is a sacrifice, which fact is expressed time and again in the Scriptures. It is a sin-offering for all transgressors. This, too, has its roots in the Old Testament, not only in the sacrificial system itself but in the sin-offering depicted in Isaiah 53. "Jehovah hath laid on him the iniquity of us all . . . . as a lamb that is led to the slaughter . . . . he was cut off out of the land of the living for the transgression of my people to whom the stroke was due . . . . when thou shalt make his soul an offering for sin . . . . and he shall bear their iniquities . . . . he poured out his soul unto death, and was numbered with the transgressors: yet he bare the sin of many, and made intercession for the transgressors" (Isa. 53:6-12). Jesus fulfills this completely. John the Baptist is alluding to this concept when he proclaims of Jesus, "Behold, the Lamb of God, that taketh away the sin of the world!" (John 1:29). The Greek word translated "taketh away" means to take away by bearing. Jesus himself declares of the cup in the Lord's Supper, "This is my blood of the covenant, which is poured out for many unto remission of sins" (Matt. 26:28). It should be noticed that the term "poured out" is used, which is an exact translation of the Greek term lying behind it. The King James here translates with "shed," but this is much too mild a term. One can shed his blood without giving his life, but one cannot pour out his blood without doing so. Besides, the Greek says "poured out," not "shed." Even the term blood must

16 George B. Stevens, *The Pauline Theology*, p. 249.

not be viewed in isolation; it is the "blood of the covenant" that is "poured out" in sacrifice. Here also, the King James unfortunately translates with "testament" rather than with "covenant," the latter being a more exact rendering of the Greek. "The term 'blood' does not simply indicate a violent death; its association with the idea of a 'covenant' in all the variant forms in which this saying appears fixes its meaning as blood poured out in sacrifice, and this interpretation is confirmed by the words 'which is shed for many.' Whatever explanation of the death of Jesus we may give today, there can be no doubt at all that Jesus Himself understood its meaning in terms of sacrifice."[17]

Paul states that in Jesus "our passover also hath been sacrificed, even Christ" (I Cor. 5:7). He also affirms that Christ "gave himself up for us, an offering and a sacrifice to God for an odor of a sweet smell" (Eph. 5:2). In First Peter we read that we are "redeemed ... with precious blood, as of a lamb without blemish and without spot, even the blood of Christ" (1:18, 19).

Yet it is the book of Hebrews which not only depicts this sacrifice but shows that it is the consummation of all sacrifices. Christ once and for all offers himself up, thus fulfilling in this one act the entire Mosaic sacrificial system. Under this system sacrifices are offered continually, year by year. "But in those sacrifices there is a remembrance made of sins year by year. For it is impossible that ·the blood of bulls and goats should take away sins .... we have been sanctified through the offering of the body of Jesus Christ once for all .... but he, when he had offered one sacrifice for sins for ever, sat down on the right hand of God. ... For by one offering he hath perfected for ever them that are sanctified. ... Now where remission of these is, there is no more offering for sin" (Heb. 10:3-18). What the blood of bulls and goats cannot do the blood of Christ poured out at Calvary accomplishes for all ages, once and for all.

> *I know not how that Calvary's Cross*
> *A world from sin could free;*
> *I only know its matchless love*
> *Has brought God's love to me.*
> — Harry Webb Farrington

4. NATURE OF GOD AND SIN OF MAN THE NECESSITY

It is necessary that Christ should suffer death in order to redeem sinners. His death is the means to a definite end. But, does this necessity lie in God or in man? It rests in both God and man.

[17] Vincent Taylor, *Jesus and His Sacrifice*, p. 74.

DOCTRINES OF THE CHRISTIAN RELIGION

(1) NATURE OF GOD

The atonement has its source in the divine nature itself, for this is the spring and source of atoning love. God's honor and God's government and God's law are maintained and satisfied by the atonement, but these are merely outward expressions of his nature and character, not the very inner being itself. God is righteous love; therefore the atonement must be the expression of such love. Now the moral order of the universe, in which man was constituted a free moral agent in the image of God, is the expression of God's inner nature. The law of sin and death is the negative side of this moral order, likewise coming from God's inner nature. Therefore the moment sin made its entrance the necessity of the atonement came into being. God's love must be expressed by redeeming man from the sin-death principle.

William Wolf asserts "that in some situations in which men are not directly responsible for what has happened they yet feel implicated to the degree that they take remedial action. May there not be here a pointer to the 'necessity' of the Cross? God felt implicated in the human ills of suffering, death, and sin, and if we may reverently put it, felt the need to take remedial action." He further adds, "While we may not assert that God was responsible for man's fall, it need not be denied us to think that God felt implicated in the ruinous consequences of man's sin. He therefore took remedial action by involving himself in the suffering and death of man and by taking the consequences of human sin upon himself."[18]

This in turn demands a Redeemer who is both God and man, the perfect moral ideal, free from sin, and yet at the same time subject to the law of sin and death operative in the moral order of man's existence. He must enter God's created order to emancipate man from his enthrallment, which he can do by virtue of his dual nature.

(2) SIN OF MAN

The atonement is necessary to produce in the sinner adequate impetus toward repentance. At Calvary sin is revealed in all its heinousness and destructiveness. God's utter disgust toward sin is plainly discerned, and its terrible price is apparent to all. Here the sinner understands the true nature of sin for the first time and comes into a penitent spirit. He sees to what extent God is willing to purchase his redemption and effect his forgiveness. The cost to God is as great as the supply of forgiveness to man is copious. "He that spared not his own Son, but delivered him up

18 Wolf, *op. cit.*, pp. 200-1.

for us all, how shall he not also with him freely give us all things?" (Rom. 8:32).

Yet this is not all, for the atonement becomes for man the means of justification. He is declared and made righteous by virtue of his faith in God's method of dealing with his sin and utter spiritual defeat. Atonement is the means of his passing from alienation to blessed sonship. It is his means of a new heavenly status, for God reckons his faith in Christ unto him for the righteousness he could not effect within himself. This faith element in justification saves it from base legalism and makes it vital. Man now has a filial consciousness and an assurance of forgiveness, for he has a new standing with God.

Therefore the atonement is necessary in man's regard, for it produces a powerful dynamic for the ethical in his experience with God. It gives him assurance of salvation. It instills in him the cross-principle of the spiritual life. It gives him a new standing with God and frees him from condemnation and guilt. It makes expiation for the sin that has his soul enthralled.

5. NON-LIMITING THE EXTENT

The atoning act of Christ is proffered to the full sweep of humanity. His identification with mankind by entering flesh makes Calvary the offering of life to everyone. The Scriptures give abundant evidence of this unlimited purpose of the atonement. John 3:16 says that "God so loved the world" that he gave his Son. In I John 2:2 we read that "he is the propitiation for our sins, and not for ours only, but also for the whole world." The writer to the Hebrews declares "that by the grace of God he should taste of death for every man" (2:9). The writer of Second Peter, in speaking of false teachers who are doomed for destruction, says that they bring in "destructive heresies, denying even the Master that bought them" (2:1). Even though lost and doomed, Christ's death includes them in its original intent. "For the grace of God hath appeared, bringing salvation to all men," Paul states in Titus 2:11. "He that spared not his own Son, but delivered him up for us all, how shall he not also with him freely give us all things?" (Rom. 8:32). The phrase "for us all" is very indicative.

This view of the extent of the atonement might be termed the general view, which says that the atonement itself is general, or that Christ dies for all men, but that it is effective only for those who exercise faith.

There are two untenable views of the extent of the atonement that should be mentioned. One is the universal view, that the atonement secures the salvation of all men regardless of belief. All men will automatically be saved due to Christ's death on Calvary.

But the Scriptures specifically say that salvation is confined to those who believe and that all men are not believers. Along with this scriptural evidence go dire threats from God for all who die in their sins. The other untenable view is the limited view, that Christ's death is for some, who believe and are saved, while it is not for others, who do not believe and are not saved. In other words, Christ's death is for those predestined to salvation and not for those predestined to reprobation. It is limited in scope to certain ones. Yet the Scriptures specifically say that Christ's atonement is meant for all men, thus revealing no limitation whatsoever to the possible efficacy of Calvary.

IV. THE RESURRECTION OF CHRIST

1. THE REALITY

(1) SCRIPTURAL EVIDENCE

On the morning of the third day some women proceed to the tomb and find that it is empty, an angel announcing that Jesus has arisen (Matt. 28:1-8). From that moment Jesus appears at various times to his disciples. He appears to Mary Magdalene without the tomb (John 20:19ff.). He appears to some other women (Matt. 28:9, 10). He appears to Cleopas and an unnamed disciple on the way to Emmaus (Luke 24:13-32). He appears to Simon Peter (Luke 24:33-35). He also manifests himself to the apostles, Thomas being absent (Luke 24:36-43). Later he appears to all the apostles, Thomas being present (John 20:26-29). Then he appears to seven of the apostles by the Sea of Galilee (John 21). There is an appearance to about five hundred on a mountain in Galilee, at which time the Great Commission is given (Matt. 28:16-20). Then there is a manifestation to James, his half-brother (I Cor. 15:7). At another appearance to the disciples he issues the Great Commission and is received up out of their sight (Luke 24:44-53). Paul places his own vision of Christ parallel with these, which tends to make us believe he classed it as an objective appearance, not just a subjective phenomenon.

Jesus foretells his own resurrection. "From that time began Jesus to show unto his disciples, that he must go unto Jerusalem, and suffer many things of the elders and chief priests and scribes, and be killed, and the third day be raised up" (Matt. 16:21). There are three other concrete, recorded statements of our Lord following this one depicting his coming resurrection (Matt. 17:9; 17:22, 23; 20:18, 19). Four times are recorded by the gospel writers ... yet the disciples do not expect him to be raised up from the dead! When Mary Magdalene and other women tell the disciples that Jesus has arisen, "these words appeared in their sight as idle talk; and they disbelieved them" (Luke 24:11). Thomas doubts that his Lord has risen (John 20:24, 25). The two on the way to Emmaus express a tinge of disbelief (Luke 24: 21-27). Some even doubt as late as the giving of the Great Commission (Matt. 28:17). The disciples are in great despair while Jesus is in the tomb, these hours being black ones indeed; therefore they will believe only if presented with overwhelming evidence. This evidence is actually presented (Acts 1:3). They see Jesus, hear him, touch him, converse with him. They even record what he teaches during this period. Not only so, this belief in his resurrection fortifies them tremendously. It produces in them a great change, for they are transformed from a small group of discouraged disciples into a band of aggressive and zealous proclaimers of the gospel. Nothing but a genuine return of Jesus from the grave could produce such a transformation. His coming forth from Joseph's sepulchre is demonstrated by factual evidence as conclusive as that supporting any other recorded event of ancient history.

(2) FALSE THEORIES

There are several false explanations relative to the resurrection stories of Christ, explanations which attempt to account for the resurrection tradition on rationalistic grounds, rather than on the factual evidence of Christ's appearances. All of these theories fail miserably.

a. *The swoon theory*

Strauss propounded this view, which maintains that Jesus did not really die, and that the coldness of the tomb, plus the spices, revived him. The reply to such a view points to the issuing of blood and water from the body of Jesus while on the cross (John 19:34) and to the statement of his death made by the centurion to Pilate (Mark 15:44, 45). Besides, according to this theory how does one account for the rolling away of the stone and the appearance of the angel?

b. *The spirit theory*

This theory, propounded by Keim, states that Jesus really died and that only his spirit returned from the grave. His spirit gave the disciples a confirmation of his continued life, much as a telegram from heaven. The reply to this theory consists of the fact that his body did arise from the tomb, for the tomb was empty and the linen grave cloths were lying in an orderly fashion (John 20:6, 7). Jesus himself denied being a bodiless spirit when he asserted, "A spirit hath not flesh and bones, as ye behold me having" (Luke 24:39). Peter preached that his flesh did not see corruption (Acts 2:31).

c. The vision theory

The vision theory was put forth by Renan, who believed that Jesus died and that there were no objective appearances at all. All the various appearances were subjective, Mary Magdalene having a subjective hallucination. The subjective vision of Mary spread, as though contagious. The Jews expected Jesus to work miracles and to rise from the dead; so the subjective visions included what they expected. The reply to this theory contains the fact that the disciples did not expect Jesus' resurrection. The remarks of Thomas and of the two on the road to Emmaus demonstrate such, as well as the fact that the women went to the tomb to embalm a dead body, not to see a risen Saviour. Subjective visions do not transform human lives, while the resurrection changed the apostles from dejected souls to courageous crusaders.

d. The mistake theory

Those who hold to this view believe that the women made a mistake, going to an old deserted tomb. Thinking it to be the burial place of Jesus, they hurried away to circulate the report that he had risen from the dead. We reply by saying that people do not so easily forget a place written so indelibly on their minds, for Matthew tells us that the women were there when he was buried. Luke says, "And the women, who had come with him out of Galilee, followed after, and beheld the tomb, and how his body was laid" (23:55). There is not even a parallel case of this preposterous theory in all history.

e. The fraud theory

Those who hold to this view maintain that Jesus' disciples stole into the tomb at night, took the body and hid it, and then circulated the report that he had risen from the dead. It is true that the guards who watched the tomb, on reporting to the Jewish authorities that it was empty, were told to say that the disciples stole the body "while we slept." How would they have known all this if they were asleep? And the disciples were not trying to prove anything, as is seen from the fact that they were reluctant to believe that he had risen. Besides, this view makes thieves and liars of the disciples, thus reflecting on their character. And would they not have been detected by the guards if they had even tried to take the body?

2. THE SIGNIFICANCE

The resurrection is the most significant of all miracles. It is the miracle of miracles, for so much depends upon it.

(1) WITNESS OF HIS DEITY

Paul says Jesus "was declared to be the Son of God with power, according to the spirit of holiness, by the resurrection from the dead" (Rom. 1:4). This great act proves to the minds of his followers that he is the Christ, the Son of God, the one who has come with all power and authority to deliver them. It brings meaning to Jesus' own statement: "I am the resurrection" (John 11:25), for it fills such a claim with divine power.

(2) CONSUMMATION OF CALVARY

The open tomb is complementary to Golgotha. The resurrection does not rectify a mistake made at Calvary, for on the cross Christ reigns. There the debt is paid, the ransom discharged, the expiation made, and the Son glorified. "It is finished" is the cry of victory. The resurrection triumphantly brings to fruition that which is accomplished at Calvary, which is what Paul has in mind when he declares that Jesus "was delivered up for our trespasses, and was raised for our justification" (Rom. 4:25). Even our justification is made complete through the resurrection of Christ. Without the resurrection Calvary would not be efficacious in atoning for sin. Paul reminds us in First Corinthians that "if Christ hath not been raised, your faith is vain; ye are yet in your sins" (15:17). Some writers even speak of these two great episodes in the earthly sojourn of our Lord as the cross-resurrection event, thus displaying the vital connection between them.

(3) GUARANTEE OF OUR RESURRECTION

Because Jesus arose we who have accepted his great atoning work will arise also. His resurrection guarantees to us life beyond the grave. The Christian does not speculate as to his eternal status, for the resurrection places him over into the realm of fact. "If we have become united with him in the likeness of his death, we shall be also in the likeness of his resurrection. . . . But if we died with Christ, we believe that we shall also live with him; knowing that Christ being raised from the dead dieth no more; death hath no more dominion over him" (Rom. 6:5-9). Paul again alludes to the same thought in the eighth chapter of Romans: "But if the Spirit of him that raised up Jesus from the dead dwelleth in you, he that raised up Christ Jesus from the dead shall give life also to your mortal bodies through his Spirit that dwelleth in you" (8:11).

The fifteenth chapter of First Corinthians teaches the identical truth. All who live in fellowship with Christ enter into a more glorious and abundant life beyond death.

> *I know not how that Joseph's tomb*
> *Could solve death's mystery;*
> *I only know a living Christ,*
> *Our immortality.*
> — Harry Webb Farrington

(4) ASSURANCE OF TRIUMPH OF THE KINGDOM

The resurrected Christ, the one who has ascended to the right hand of the Father and who reigns there all-powerfully, is all the guarantee the Christian needs of the triumph of the kingdom of God. As the glorified Christ he is extending his kingdom through the church and will bring it to a glorious fulfillment some day. The book of Revelation very graphically depicts this final triumph of the kingdom, with the exalted Christ occupying the pivotal position in the coming consummation. He is the one in the midst of the seven golden lampstands (1:13) holding the seven stars in his right hand (1:16), the one who was dead but is alive forevermore (1:18). The Lamb is in the midst of thousands of angels and of created beings who proclaim in song that he is worthy of all power, riches, wisdom, blessings, honor, and glory (5:8-14). After much turmoil the Lamb brings in the consummation, with the New Jerusalem coming down out of heaven from God (21:1, 2) and with death and Hades cast into the lake of fire (20:14). The rule of God is now universally complete. This book, written in a time of persecution, brought comfort and encouragement to those in great tribulation.

(5) PROMINENT IN EARLY PREACHING

The resurrection of Christ holds a very prominent place in the preaching of the apostles. In fact, every New Testament sermon ascribed to any of the apostles places emphasis on the resurrection. When they preach they proclaim Jesus as risen from the dead. This centrality of Jesus' resurrection in the preaching of the apostles is the theme of C. H. Dodd's book *The Apostolic Preaching in Its Development*. This eminent writer has minutely examined all the New Testament sermons of the apostles and has shown that the resurrection of Christ is the climax of each one. Peter's sermon on the Day of Pentecost is exemplary: "This Jesus did God raise up, whereof we all are witnesses" (Acts 2:32). The power of the apostolic preaching lay in the constant reference to the cross and the empty tomb.

V. THE INTERCESSION OF CHRIST

1. THE REALITY

The intercession of Christ is part of his priestly work, a work that does not cease with the cross but continues forever. As the cross may be thought of as the first priestly work of Christ, his intercession may be thought of as his second priestly work. John, Paul, and the author of Hebrews speak of this eternal activity of our Lord. Though earthly priests may die, he, the eternal High Priest, lives forever, never ceasing to intercede for his own. In contrast to earthly priests, "he, because he abideth for ever, hath his priesthood unchangeable. Wherefore also he is able to save to the uttermost them that draw near unto God through him, seeing he ever liveth to make intercession for them" (Heb. 7:24, 25). Though the arms of Moses tire when held out in intercession for the Hebrews as they fight the Amalekites, to the point that Aaron and Hur set him upon a rock and hold up his hands till sunset, the hands of our great Intercessor never tire but are constantly held out in supplication for us . . . and not until sunset but until God's great denouement itself!

This intercession is not to be conceived as external, or as spoken prayer, but as a continuing activity carrying out his redemptive work. It is the continuous influence of his great sacrifice, making it efficacious for all believers. It is that work of Christ whereby he pronounces the true priestly blessing, or benediction, upon his own. "If any man sin, we have an Advocate with the Father, Jesus Christ the righteous" (I John 2:1). "It is Jesus Christ that died, yea rather, that was raised from the dead, who is at the right hand of God, who also maketh intercession for us" (Rom. 8:34).

2. THE PLACE

Christ interceded for us while here upon earth just as he does now in heaven. As for the earthly intercession, he tells Peter, "Simon, Simon, behold, Satan asked to have you, that he might sift you as wheat; but I made supplication for thee, that thy faith fail not" (Luke 22:31, 32). Even at the cross he prays for the ones crucifying him, "Father, forgive them; for they know not what they do" (Luke 23:34). And in the great high-priestly prayer just prior to the cross he says, "I pray for them; I pray not for the world, but for those whom thou hast given me" (John 17:9).

But even now our Saviour intercedes in heavenly glory. In contrast to the earthly high priest who went into the holy of holies only on the Day of Atonement, once a year, our High Priest intercedes in the celestial holy of holies, not just once a year, but eternally. "For Christ entered not into a holy place made with hands, like in pattern to the true; but into heaven itself, now to appear before the face of God for us" (Heb. 9:24). "Having then a great high priest, who hath passed through the heavens, Jesus the Son of God, let us hold fast our confession. For we have not a high priest that cannot be touched with the feeling of our infirmities; but one that hath been in all points tempted like as we are, yet without sin" (Heb. 4:14, 15).

This intercession of Christ is related to the intercession of the Holy Spirit. As the latter is our Advocate on earth teaching us how to pray, the former is our Advocate in heaven guaranteeing an answer to our prayers. "The Spirit also helpeth our infirmity: for we know not how to pray as we ought; but the Spirit himself maketh intercession for us with groanings which cannot be uttered" (Rom. 8:26). The very impulse to prayer in our hearts shows that Christ is urging our claims in heaven.

3. THE BENEFITS

(1) ASSURES FORGIVENESS

The intercession of Christ for our sins assures divine forgiveness. Sin constitutes the necessity for Christ's work as our Advocate. The word advocate is derived from two Latin words meaning one who speaks for another. Christ intercedes for us with the Father in case we sin, which he can do because of his whole atoning work and in virtue of our acceptance of him. Christ prayed for Peter while here upon earth, that Satan have no power over him; he now prays for us in heaven above. The latter is no more difficult of conception than the former; the only difference is that in the former he was incarnate, while in the latter he is in the sovereignty of one who has achieved eternal redemption for his own.

All this is to state "that the divine sin-bearing, the atoning work, which appeared in history once for all on Calvary, goes on ever since in the heavenly sphere. . . . That work on Calvary was indeed a finished work, a perfect sacrifice made once for all on earth. Yet it was the beginning of a priesthood which goes on forever in the unseen realm, in heaven, in the Holy Place beyond the Veil, into which our High Priest entered through death, and where he ever liveth to make intercession for us, being continually 'touched with the feeling of our infirmities.' "[19]

Since Christ is continually making intercession for us in heaven we may make the mistake of thinking of the Father as harsh and exacting, almost to the point of being inaccessible, unwilling to forgive unless someone else speaks in our behalf. This is far from

[19] Baillie, *op. cit.,* pp. 194-5.

true; for the necessity of the intercession lies not in an unwillingness of the Father to show mercy but in the moral order he has created and in the sinfulness of man as set over and against the holiness of God. Christ as our High Priest is able to remove this difficulty, for he is a High Priest appointed of God (Heb. 5:1ff.). Therefore it is not that the Father is unwilling while Christ is willing; else why would he have been appointed as an Advocate? The Father is equally accessible as Christ, for he is accessible in Christ.

(2) GIVES BOLDNESS TO APPROACH GOD IN PRAYER

The intercession of Christ also gives us boldness as we approach God in prayer. "Having then a great high priest, who hath passed through the heavens, Jesus the Son of God, let us hold fast our confession. For we have not a high priest that cannot be touched with the feeling of our infirmities; but one that hath been in all points tempted like as we are, yet without sin. Let us therefore draw near with boldness unto the throne of grace, that we may receive mercy, and may find grace to help us in time of need" (Heb. 4:14-16). We dare approach God's throne boldly, knowing we have there a Mediator. We have assurance that we will find mercy in time of need and grace in time of adversity, for there pleads for us one who can understand our infirmities and our weaknesses.

(3) GUARANTEES PERMANENT STANDING BEFORE GOD

The intercession of Christ also guarantees our permanent standing before God. We will not lose our status with him even though we sin. "And if any man sin, we have an Advocate with the Father" (I John 2:1). John says that his purpose in writing is that we may not sin; but if by chance we do, we have One to plead our cause. The saved-Saviour relationship will not be destroyed. "Wherefore also he is able to save to the uttermost them that draw near unto God through him, seeing he ever liveth to make intercession for them" (Heb. 7:25). Salvation to the uttermost would be permanent in character, for a constant intercession would guarantee such. We have an abiding High Priest of whom we can say:

> *He pleads His passion on the tree,*
> *He shows Himself to God for me.*

OUTLINE FOR CHAPTER NINE

I. Preliminary Thoughts
1. God takes the initiative in salvation
2. God acts with a purpose in election
3. Danger of a one-sided view of God
4. Atonement not limited, but general

II. God's Purpose for Mankind
1. Discerned in Old Testament
2. Discerned in New Testament
    (1) In incarnation and atonement of Christ
    (2) In history and teaching of early church

III. God's Purpose for the Individual
1. God foresees the faith of the believer
2. God elects, but does not abrogate man's freedom
    (1) Treats man as moral, spiritual, and personal
    (2) Deals with man through a system of means
    (3) Appeals to man through the Holy Spirit
3. God elects to salvation only, not to damnation
4. God elects for service, not due to merit
5. God seeks the salvation of as many as possible
6. Two inscrutable realities in regard to election
    (1) Reconciling of sovereignty of God with freedom of man
    (2) Assigning a reason for God's use of election in saving man

IV. Misunderstandings Concerning Election
1. Election makes God partial
2. Election makes God arbitrary
3. Election is unjust to the unsaved
4. Election destroys human freedom
5. Election discourages effort in winning the lost
6. Election tends toward immorality
7. Election tends toward pride

CHAPTER NINE

ELECTION

I. PRELIMINARY THOUGHTS

1. GOD TAKES THE INITIATIVE IN SALVATION

THE DOCTRINE TERMED ELECTION IS NONE OTHER THAN GOD'S initiative in salvation, or God's sovereignty in relation to man's redemption. God initiates the whole process in the reconciliation of the highest being in his created order. Motive, method, and end all stem from him. What is expressed relative to creation, "In the beginning God..." (Gen. 1:1), is true also in regard to redemption. It is also true relative to revelation, for here also God takes the initiative. God reveals himself to man, for man cannot "discover" God. God is one who deals with man and his whole created order through his great acts, and he always takes the initiative in these acts. God is a God of priority.

Jesus says, "No man can come to me, except the Father that sent me draw him" (John 6:44). If a man repents of his sins and expresses faith in Christ he does so because God leads him to do thus. God moves man to turn from sin to him; man does not move himself. God not only sends Christ as a means of reconciliation; he also sends the Holy Spirit to make that means efficacious. And he also gives man the necessary qualifications to accept that means; for man's whole being — mind, heart, and will — is involved in the response to God's gracious act. All of this is in accord with the idea of salvation by grace instead of works, for grace as the basis of God's salvation necessarily involves his initiative. "So then it is not of him that willeth, nor of him that runneth, but of God that hath mercy" (Rom. 9:16). Paul also says, "Even so then at this present time also there is a remnant according to the election of grace" (Rom. 11:5).

The tenor of the whole gamut of biblical truth is that God initiates salvation. The zenith of all God's work is salvation. He sends Christ to make redemption possible. Then, through various agencies, he brings about the turning from sin, or repentance, and the turning to God, or faith. God induces the very faith whereby his grace can be accepted. In the full sense of the term he seeks the sinner. When Jesus speaks of the true worshiper, he adds, "For such doth the Father seek to be his worshippers" (John 4:23). God pleads and entreats rebellious man to come to him. Jesus' advent to earth is to fulfill this seeking. "For the Son of man came to seek and to save that which was lost" (Luke 19:10). Paul speaks of God "calling" men, evidently denoting by this term what Jesus means by the term "drawing." "And we know that to them that love God all things work together for good, even to them that are called according to his purpose" (Rom. 8:28).

2. GOD ACTS WITH A PURPOSE IN ELECTION

God's plan for man is eternal, and all that he does is in conformity with that eternal plan. He does not suddenly and arbitrarily decide to work for man's good, or for man's salvation. Whatever he does he does because he purposes to do it, so that our salvation is no mere chance or accident. God through the ages has planned the very best for his people, all to be worked out as an expression of his grace. It is God "who saved us, and called us with a holy calling, not according to our works, but according to his own purpose and grace, which was given us in Christ Jesus before times eternal, but hath now been manifested by the appearing of our Saviour Christ Jesus" (II Tim. 1:9, 10). There is nothing arbitrary, ungracious, or unloving in God's dealings with man, for such would controvert his righteous nature. All the good that comes into men's lives, of which salvation is supreme, is a result of the gracious purpose of God through the ages.

3. DANGER OF A ONE-SIDED VIEW OF GOD

In viewing the doctrine of election there is the ever-present danger of emphasizing one or two aspects of God's divine nature to the practical exclusion of many other traits of his manifold character. When God's will, infinite power, and omniscience are highly stressed, and his love, mercy, grace, and righteousness are minimized, there is the resultant danger of deriving a concept of God approaching that of an arbitrary despot rather than a forgiving, seeking God who desires the best for his creatures. It is the error of conceiving of the sovereignty of God as a function of his "good pleasure," rather than in terms of an eternal purpose desiring the good of all. This is the abstract, or philosophical, method, rather than the biblical one. Our conception of God must be that as revealed by our Lord, the infinite God rich in moral and spiritual attributes.

4. ATONEMENT NOT LIMITED, BUT GENERAL

When such a one-sided view of God is fostered relative to one's concept of God's purpose in salvation bizarre results are obtained, one of which is the view of a limited atonement. When it is maintained that God has foreordained some men to eternal life and at the same time other men to eternal death, the view is necessarily held that Christ died for some but not for others. A. H. Strong, in speaking of the atonement, asserts, "The Scriptures represent the atonement as having been made for all men, and as sufficient for the salvation of all. Not the *atonement* therefore is limited, but the application of the atonement through the work of the Holy Spirit."[1] It is J. M. Whiton, in *The Outlook* (Sept. 25, 1897), who reveals, "It was Samuel Hopkins of Rhode Island (1721-1803) who first declared that Christ had made atonement for all men, not for the elect part alone, as Calvinists affirmed."

Some passages that show that Christ's death is for all men are the following. Peter talks of false prophets and false teachers as those "denying even the Master that bought them, bringing upon themselves swift destruction" (II Pet. 2:1). John says that Christ is the expiation "for our sins; and not for ours only, but also for the whole world" (I John 2:2). Paul affirms that there is "one mediator also between God and men, himself man, Christ Jesus, who gave himself a ransom for all" (I Tim. 2:5, 6). He also states, "For the grace of God hath appeared, bringing salvation to all men" (Titus 2:11).

II. GOD'S PURPOSE FOR MANKIND

God's purpose concerns not only the individual man but all mankind. Both the Hebrew and Greek languages have different terms for these two concepts. In the Hebrew *ish* means a man and *adam* mankind, while in the Greek *anēr* means a man and *anthrōpos* mankind. The English term man must cover both of these concepts, thus tending toward confusion. We shall now consider God's purpose in regard to mankind.

1. DISCERNED IN OLD TESTAMENT

From the beginning God's purpose has been world-wide in scope. It is true that he narrows down to certain choices in the history of mankind, but these choices are always means to a larger end and not ends in themselves.

As soon as man sins and is cast from the garden there is offered to him a ray of hope, enigmatic as it is. This promise is found in God's remarks to the serpent, that the seed of the woman will bruise his head (Gen. 3:15). Then there is a narrowing to the line of Seth as over against the line of Cain, for of the former it is said, "Then began men to call upon the name of Jehovah" (Gen. 4:26). The next selection is that of Noah and his family as the channel through which God's blessings will flow (Gen. 6:8). From

---

[1] A. H. Strong, *Systematic Theology*, p. 771.

Noah's three sons Shem is chosen, and from the Shemites Abraham is selected (Gen. 12:1).

God's remark to Abraham discloses his proposed will toward mankind: "I will make of thee a great nation, and I will bless thee, and make thy name great; and be thou a blessing: and I will bless them that bless thee, and him that curseth thee will I curse: *and in thee shall all the families of the earth be blessed*" (Gen. 12: 2, 3). This very promise, in almost identical words, is presented to the great patriarch repeatedly, thus showing the world-wide purpose in his selection.

Then from Abraham's sons Isaac is chosen, and from Isaac's two sons Jacob is selected. All the descendants of Abraham through Isaac and Jacob, known as Hebrews, constitute the nation through which God will reveal himself and bless mankind. "The patriarchal claim illustrates the principle of corporate personality. The nation is not only represented by, but summed up in its ancestors. To call Abraham is to call the race that springs from him. . . . God deals with the race through its ancestors, and the time element falls into the background in comparison with the real content, the election of Israel to a great destiny."[2]

Thus the Hebrews, or the nation of Israel, become God's elect, the ones through whom he is to bestow his favor upon the world. Ezekiel says, "Thus saith the Lord Jehovah: In the day when I chose Israel, and sware unto the seed of the house of Jacob..." (20:5). The psalmist declares, "O ye seed of Abraham his servant, Ye children of Jacob, his chosen ones" (105:6). Another prophet writes, "But thou, Israel, my servant, Jacob whom I have chosen..." (Isa. 41:8). The universal sweep of Israel's call is plainly discerned in further writings of this great prophet of God: "I will also give thee for a light to the Gentiles, that thou mayest be my salvation unto the end of the earth" (49:6), and, "For, behold, darkness shall cover the earth, and gross darkness the peoples; but Jehovah will arise upon thee, and his glory shall be seen upon thee. And nations shall come to thy light, and kings to the brightness of thy rising" (60:2, 3). God ordains Israel to be *exclusive* in order to accomplish an *all-inclusive* purpose; but pride, self-righteousness, spiritual blindness, and a pharisaical spirit prove her undoing. Her great spiritual truths are never passed on. "The great sin of the Jewish nation is that they have narrowed the mercy of God and have fallen into thinking that the blessings of heaven are pledged to them and terminate upon them, instead of seeing them as a gift intrusted to them to be passed on to others. The current particularism against which Paul contended, sprang out of a narrow

2 H. Wheeler Robinson, *Inspiration and Revelation in the Old Testament*, p. 151.

conception of Israel's election as an arbitrary preference for the Jewish people, for their own sake — a divine partiality in the government of the world. Against this view Paul's whole doctrine is a protest."[3]

2. Discerned in New Testament

(1) In Incarnation and Atonement of Christ

The great redeeming activity of our Lord brings this world-wide purpose of God strikingly to the front. His very coming is that he might become identified with flesh, the flesh of all men, not just with that of the Hebrews of the first century A.D. Even the aged Simeon, meeting the baby Jesus brought to the temple at the age of forty days, sings, "Now lettest thou thy servant depart, Lord, According to thy word, in peace; For mine eyes have seen thy salvation, Which thou hast prepared before the face of all peoples; A light for revelation to the Gentiles, And the glory of thy people Israel" (Luke 2:29-32). We have seen that his atonement is for all men. The Great Commission is all-inclusive, comprising "all the nations" (Matt. 28:19, 20). The conception of the kingdom as taught by our Lord is that of a universal one. Though begun in minuteness it shall grow to great proportions (Matt. 13:31, 32). Many people shall come from all directions and sit down with Abraham, Isaac, and Jacob in the kingdom, while the sons of the kingdom shall be cast out (Matt. 8:11, 12). Those coming from all directions are Gentiles, while those being cast out are Jews that are either not among the faithful remnant, which includes Abraham, Isaac, and Jacob, or who have not, since the time of Christ and the advent of his kingdom, accepted him.

(2) In History and Teaching of Early Church

The history and teaching of the early church also depict God's world-wide purpose. Acts shows the struggle ensuing when some try to interpret the gospel in terms of Judaism. But the Judaizers are quelled by those who possess a world-wide vision, such as the Apostle Paul. The spread of the gospel among the Gentiles is clearly seen in page after page. The man of Macedonia beseeching help in virgin territory is exemplary of the call coming from a world hungry for the gospel, while Paul and his journeys signalize the universal sweep of the good news of the kingdom. The mystery hid from the ages and now made known through Christ is that the gospel is for Gentile as well as Jew; for the Gentiles are "fellow-heirs, and fellow-members of the body, and fellow-partakers of the promise in Christ Jesus through the gospel"

3 George B. Stevens, *The Theology of the New Testament*, p. 380.

(Eph. 3:4-13). Paul's going to the Gentile world is the result of a special call from God (Acts 13:1ff.). He is to be a "chosen vessel" unto God to bear his name "before the Gentiles and kings, and the children of Israel" (Acts 9:15). The book of Revelation completes this universal picture of the kingdom; for we see great multitudes redeemed through the blood of Christ singing praises to God around the throne, multitudes coming from every nation and tribe and people and tongue (7:9ff.). There is a complete and final triumph of this all-embracing kingdom as the New Jerusalem comes down from God to man (21:1ff.).

III. GOD'S PURPOSE FOR THE INDIVIDUAL

It can readily be seen that God's dealings with individual men can best be understood only in the context of his larger plan for the whole world. We also see that what at first sight might seem to be arbitrary or capricious in God's dealings with men is really to the contrary, for he has in mind a most gracious purpose for all mankind. When God saves an individual, he saves because he intends to do so; he wants his gracious design to unfold before the world.

1. GOD FORESEES THE FAITH OF THE BELIEVER

When does God choose, or elect? He does not choose after man chooses, for that would make man superior to God. Nor does he choose along with man, for that would make God dependent upon man. He must choose before man chooses, which makes God sovereign. So God chooses man prior to man's choosing God. In fact, God did his electing before the very dawn of history, for "he chose us in him before the foundation of the world" (Eph. 1:4). Paul also tells us that it is God "who saved us, and called us with a holy calling, not according to our works, but according to his own purpose and grace, which was given us in Christ Jesus before times eternal" (II Tim. 1:9). So God does not choose men because of their good works, but because of their faith. Therefore he must foresee their faith. And not only does he foresee their faith; the good works that are to follow the faith are in view also. "Ye did not choose me, but I chose you, and appointed you, that ye should go and bear fruit, and that your fruit should abide: that whatsoever ye shall ask of the Father in my name, he may give it you" (John 15:16). Not only does the scope of election include the good works to follow the faith; it includes the power of prayer expressing that faith.

Each person enters into life or condemnation by his response to the gospel; yet that response is dependent upon God rather than upon man. Jesus says, "All that which the Father giveth me shall come unto me; and him that cometh to me I will in no wise cast out" (John 6:37). "No man can come to me, except the Father that sent me draw him: and I will raise him up in the last day" (John 6:44). Relative to the preaching of Paul and Barnabas the book of Acts reads, "As many as were ordained to eternal life believed" (13:48). God evidently foresees this response, this belief.

2. GOD ELECTS, BUT DOES NOT ABROGATE MAN'S FREEDOM

Man's right of choice, bestowed upon him at creation, is not annulled by the functioning of God's sovereignty. The will of man is not in the least coerced when God acts supremely and in accordance with divine prerogative. It is not right to declare that God's grace is "irresistible," as one might speak of a physical force. It *is* true that man could not make the choice without the aid of God's grace, but at the same time man himself does the choosing. This is true of the very vital act of choosing Christ as Saviour; for here, as in lesser decisions, man is free to choose.

In dealing with this significant theological problem of the relation between freedom and predestination Millar Burrows portrays the difficulty of making categorical assertions. "The language of passages dealing at all with the subject is often ambiguous, and it is not always clear whether groups or individuals are in view. No explanation of the relation between foreknowledge and predestination is given. Only Paul and the fourth evangelist have clear statements of predestination, though it often seems to be implied elsewhere, especially in the latest books of the New Testament. All the writers consistently assume freedom and responsibility in any case. The primary, constant appeal to repentance and faith and the frequent references to judgment presuppose freedom of choice and action."[4]

(1) TREATS MAN AS MORAL, SPIRITUAL, AND PERSONAL

God works in a moral, spiritual, and personal way as he deals with man relative to salvation. Man is assumed to have a mind. Paul says, "Knowing therefore the fear of the Lord, we persuade men" (II Cor. 5:11). Man also is assumed to have a conscience, for the gospel appeals to the moral consciousness of man. In continuing the preceding statement Paul says, "But we are made manifest unto God; and I hope that we are made manifest also in your consciences" (II Cor. 5:11). Again, the gospel appeals to the emotions of man: hope, love, godly sorrow. "For in hope were we saved" (Rom. 8:24). "But now abideth faith, hope, love, these three; and the greatest of these is love" (I Cor. 13:13). "For godly sorrow

---

4 Millar Burrows, *An Outline of Biblical Theology*, p. 231.

worketh repentance unto salvation, a repentance which bringeth no regret: but the sorrow of the world worketh death" (II Cor. 7: 10). Again, man has will, for the gospel appeals to that faculty also. Jesus disappointedly informs the Jews, "And ye will not come to me, that ye may have life" (John 5:40). Therefore we see that God's electing grace deals with man as a moral force persuading him, rather than a blunt physical force coercing him. The force becomes effective as man responds to it, and not until then. In fact, it becomes supremely grace when man does respond to it.

(2) DEALS WITH MAN THROUGH A SYSTEM OF MEANS

Since man is a moral, spiritual, and personal being God deals with him by means of certain agencies. Among these are the church, the ordinances, the lives of Christians, the Bible, and Christian ministers. All such means are commensurate with the truth that God's method is always moral, spiritual, and personal. It is not a church granting or withholding salvation at will, but it is God's agency for extending the kingdom. It is not a system of sacraments possessing magical powers, but ordinances symbolizing great spiritual truths. It is not a priesthood mediating grace to those obedient to the dogmas of the church, but proclaimers of the blessings of salvation to those who believe. God's electing grace always acts through such means to effect man's salvation.

(3) APPEALS TO MAN THROUGH THE HOLY SPIRIT

Since man is moral, spiritual, and personal, God appeals to him in just such a manner through his Holy Spirit. The Spirit convicts, or convinces, one that he is lost and in need of a Saviour. He convicts of sin, of righteousness, and of judgment (John 16: 8-11), appealing thus to the intellect, the emotions, and the will. There is a moral, spiritual, and personal conquest of the soul, which results in the further teaching, leading, and guiding of the Spirit (John 16:7ff.). "Howbeit when he, the Spirit of truth, is come, he shall guide you into all the truth: for he shall not speak from himself; but what things soever he shall hear, these shall he speak: and he shall declare unto you the things that are to come. He shall glorify me: for he shall take of mine, and shall declare it unto you" (John 16:13, 14).

3. GOD ELECTS TO SALVATION ONLY, NOT TO DAMNATION

Some would say that God has elected some to salvation and some to reprobation, which is nothing more than double-edged, or Calvinistic, predestination. But the New Testament never states that some are elected to be lost. It says that God purposes, or wills, that men be saved, but never that he wills that they be lost. On the contrary, we read in Second Peter that God is longsuffering, "not wishing that any should perish, but that all should come to repentance" (3:9). To say that God wills some to damnation would be to run counter to such a clear and precise statement as we find in this New Testament document. Men may perish, and will perish; but this is not what God wills. The tragic failure of some not to be saved is due both to the failure of Christians to witness to the saving grace of Christ and to the failure of the lost to respond. In the New Testament there is a doctrine of election, but there is no doctrine of non-election. Man is free to choose, and God will not deprive him of that freedom. Man has that freedom because God initially gave it to him, which brings us back around to God's initiative in all his acts, whatever those acts may be.

The Greek term *proorizō,* which is used four times in the New Testament relative to man's salvation, is translated "I predestinate" in the King James Version and "I foreordain" in the American Standard Version. By this term Paul does not mean that God has taken away man's right of choice and has predetermined his salvation, much as we might use the term fate. Paul's whole life, work, and attitude toward fallen humanity show otherwise. In speaking of his fellow Israelites, for whom he yearns, he states, "Brethren, my heart's desire and my supplication to God is for them, that they may be saved" (Rom. 10:1). Why would he desire this if their destiny has already been cast? Paul's very zealous effort to witness to every lost person shows that he does not think that God would bypass man's right to choose, and therefore "fix" the matter of a man's salvation. And why should we read in Second Peter, "Wherefore, brethren, give the more diligence to make your calling and election sure" (1:10), if that calling and election were already predetermined? Would not this phase of man's life be already settled and beyond alteration? What these passages really say is that God has purposed that men be saved, and that this is not coincidental or capricious. God chose us in Christ "before the foundation of the world, that we should be holy and without blemish before him in love" (Eph. 1:4). So we return to a previous thought, that election is that which God purposes, or plans, for the ages. It has to do with God's purpose for mankind, redemption, and not man's response to that purpose; and God's purpose is certainly not always performed by man. Here is the crux of much of the false thinking relative to the doctrine of election.

4. GOD ELECTS FOR SERVICE, NOT DUE TO MERIT

The motivating factor of electing grace is not, and never has been, merit on man's part. Redemption is not of works, for then man would glory (Eph. 2:9). "By the works of the law shall no flesh be justified in his sight" (Rom. 3:20). "Now to him that worketh, the reward is not reckoned as of grace, but as of debt" (Rom. 4:4). So God does not grant salvation due to any moral worth of man, self-achieved. On the contrary, man is elected to serve. We have seen that Abraham was so elected. "And the scripture, foreseeing that God would justify the Gentiles by faith, preached the gospel beforehand unto Abraham, saying, In thee shall all the nations be blessed" (Gal. 3:8). The nation of Israel is endowed with this same responsibility, a fact clearly expounded by the later prophets. Is it not with the faithful remnant that God will teach all nations? "But ye shall be named the priests of Jehovah; men shall call you the ministers of our God" (Isa. 61:6). "It is too light a thing that thou shouldest be my servant to raise up the tribes of Jacob, and to restore the preserved of Israel: I will also give thee for a light to the Gentiles, that thou mayest be my salvation unto the end of the earth" (Isa. 49:6). Both Gentiles and Jews will be saved through Israel's ministry (Isa. 49:5-13). The Apostle Paul is selected for service and for suffering. "Go thy way: for he is a chosen vessel unto me, to bear my name before the Gentiles and kings, and the children of Israel; for I will show him how many things he must suffer for my name's sake" (Acts 9:15, 16). Jesus discloses to his disciples, "Ye did not choose me, but I chose you, and appointed you, that ye should go and bear fruit, and that your fruit should abide" (John 15:16). He commissions his disciples to be witnesses unto the uttermost part of the earth (Acts 1:8), all of which will be possible when they have received the power that he will send.

Therefore a cold, abstract, arbitrary view of election leads to bizarre concepts. Professor Mullins is right when he avows, "Election is not to be thought of as a bare choice of so many human units by God's action independently of man's free choice and the human means employed. God elects men to respond freely. He elects men to preach persuasively and to witness convincingly. He elects to reach men through their native faculties and through the church, through evangelism and education and missionary endeavor."[5] Electing grace is not the mere selecting of a human soul here and there as a brand from the burning. It is a rich and glorious something, for it is God's manifold dealings with all human society through human agents and instrumentalities. It involves whole series of social relationships and moral powers. It is the electing of one that he may be the means of electing another, that that one in turn may be instrumental in electing another, and so forth. And when one, through desire, prayer, witnessing, and effort, is used

[5] Edgar Y. Mullins, *The Christian Religion in Its Doctrinal Expression*, p. 347.

in the electing of a second, he himself is spiritually enriched, all of which is a very essential part of his complete salvation.

5. GOD SEEKS THE SALVATION OF AS MANY AS POSSIBLE

Regardless of what concept one has of electing grace there must always be the cognate truth that God desires the redemption of the maximum number. Some men look at election with the view that God desires to save as few as possible; this is not so, for the whole Bible advocates the opposite view. In fact it appears that God is desirous of saving as rapidly as conditions will permit, conditions involving sin and man's freedom.

What are the biblical facts substantiating such a view? God says that he will bless Abraham and his seed and that the nations of the world will be blessed through him. "And in thee shall all the families of the earth be blessed" (Gen. 12:3). Then he places him in a land located at the crossroads of the nations, a land from which the Jews later are to be dispersed in all directions. Yet this nation carries with it the synagogue, to become the nucleus for the spread of the gospel to the Gentile world. Add to this the unity of the Roman Empire at the time of Christ, with its durable roads and frequented seaways. Then to this add the universality of the Greek language, destined to become the common medium for disseminating the truth of the gospel to all realms. This Greek of the first century A.D. is called Koiné Greek, which means "common" Greek. The Apostle Paul preaches throughout Asia Minor, Greece, and Rome in this language, proclaiming to Gentile and Jew alike a doctrine of justification by faith apart from works of the law. He arrays himself rigorously against a Jewish exclusiveness that would make Christianity merely a sect of Judaism. Not only does he accomplish this by his victory at the great Jerusalem Controversy (Acts 15 and Gal. 2) but also by a constant opposition to the Judaizers wherever he finds them. The faith he plants in Europe, though to bog down later in a preponderous ecclesiasticism, is eventually to liberate itself in a vast and conquering missionary endeavor. Even the present day witnesses an enlargement of this missionary horizon. Thus we see that God's electing grace has always maintained an ever-widening attitude, rather than a narrowing one. God, desiring to bless as many people as possible with as many blessings as possible, is always motivated by a love seeking to overcome the limitations that necessarily evolve from the moral order. God seeks the redemption of the greatest possible number.

6. TWO INSCRUTABLE REALITIES IN REGARD TO ELECTION

There are two facts relative to the doctrine of election that are unfathomable.

DOCTRINES OF THE CHRISTIAN RELIGION

(1) RECONCILING OF SOVEREIGNTY OF GOD WITH FREEDOM OF MAN

The sovereignty of God and the freedom of man are two factors which simply cannot be reconciled in finite thought. Here we are dealing with ultimate philosophical concepts. We see God's sovereignty as an ultimate reality, but to view it apart from man's moral freedom of choice is a dangerous thing. We may view man's freedom in this same abstract way, but this also is a process filled with theological pitfalls. As a matter of fact, the idea of the absoluteness of God and the idea of man's freedom are found parallel throughout the Scriptures, and this with no apparent sense of contradiction on the part of the writers. Since man is God's creation, his being and power are grounded in God and his will, and man's freedom rests in the almightiness of God rather than being antithetical to it.

(2) ASSIGNING A REASON FOR GOD'S USE OF ELECTION IN SAVING MEN

The second factor that defies human comprehension is that of the reason God chose the method of election in saving man. This also is inscrutable, at least as far as full realization is concerned. Yet there are certain things that shed a little light. We must consider that God is self-limited; that is, he has imposed upon himself limitations due to the moral order of his universe. He is limited by human freedom and will not coerce man in any way. He made man free to choose. To impose his own will upon this choice would be to negate the freedom of man, which in turn would be to destroy man's personality and make him nonmoral. God must save man in some manner that will at the same time leave man free.

But God is also limited by human sin. Sin enslaves man, giving the will an inevitable bias toward choosing evil. "The mind of the flesh is enmity against God; for it is not subject to the law of God, neither indeed can it be" (Rom. 8:7). This inevitability leads to the rejection of the gospel unless aided by God's grace in Christ Jesus. But since man is free, and since he will inevitably reject the gospel unless aided by God's grace, no one can be saved. All will of necessity perish. However, if God interposes, will there not be some form of election? Yes, and this is exactly what he does. Yet at the same time he must minimize his action so as not to coerce man's will and act as sheer force or despotic power. In his electing grace he must deal with man in a moral, spiritual, and personal way, and this way is of necessity a gradual one. The new birth is instantaneous and does start the process, but man's character evolves therefrom by slow degree. God works through human agents to secure the desired product. God interposes just enough to secure this final result in the moral, spiritual, and personal process.

IV. MISUNDERSTANDINGS CONCERNING ELECTION

It is customary in some books on doctrine to treat what are called "objections to the doctrine of election." When these are read, and then viewed in the light of the teaching of the New Testament, they are discerned to be objections to double-edged, or Calvinistic, predestination. When so considered, most, if not all, of these objections are legitimate. So the crux of the misunderstanding lies in the failure to differentiate between double-edged predestination and true biblical election. The following list of objections, with comments, will suffice to illustrate.

1. ELECTION MAKES GOD PARTIAL

It is objected that the doctrine of election makes God a respecter of persons, partial to one man over another man. This is certainly true of double-edged predestination, but not of the biblical doctrine as seen in the light of the whole New Testament. Election is God's method whereby he realizes his wonderful purpose for all mankind. In fact, Peter, in his sermon to Cornelius and his household in Caesarea, says, "Of a truth I perceive that God is no respecter of persons" (Acts 10:34). When the New Testament clearly states that God does not wish that any should perish, but that all should repent and find salvation (II Pet. 3:9), how could anyone think of God as acting in a partial manner? In the true doctrine of election God is not partial.

2. ELECTION MAKES GOD ARBITRARY

It is true that double-edged predestination makes God appear arbitrary, as wielding unlimited power in a despotic and tyrannical manner. But not so the true doctrine; for here we see a holy and all-wise God, exercising his righteous and sovereign will in a manner that will best benefit mankind. Any inscrutability on the part of man tends to make God appear as arbitrary; but the lack of knowledge and understanding on man's part should not alter his faith in the goodness and righteousness of God. God is not only free to choose; he has reasons for his choices, and these reasons are grounded in him alone, not in man. "We must remember that God's *sovereignty* is the sovereignty of *God* — the infinitely wise, holy and loving God, in whose hands the destinies of men can be left more safely than in the hands of the wisest, most just, and most kind of his creatures. We must believe in the grace of sovereignty as well as the sovereignty of grace."[6]

6 Strong, *op. cit.*, p. 787.

3. Election is unjust to the unsaved

This would certainly be true of Calvinistic predestination, but not so of the New Testament teachings. Though God is to be praised for the saving of the elect, he is not to be charged with the condemnation of the lost; for God desires the salvation of all peoples. "For God so loved the world, that he gave his only begotten Son, that whosoever believeth on him should not perish, but have eternal life" (John 3:16). "He that spared not his own Son, but delivered him up for us all, how shall he not also with him freely give us all things?" (Rom. 8:32). God does not wish that any should perish (II Pet. 3:9). God offers pardon to all men through the atoning death of his Son: nothing prevents a man from being saved but his own unwillingness to accept that which is offered him.

There are limitations on God, completely self-imposed, which make it so he cannot do as he might desire. He is limited by human freedom, by unbelief, by sin — all of which are according to his own decree. God will not force anyone into redemption; he will not compel anyone to enter a moral and spiritual condition. He simply does all that he can, consistent with the personal, ethical, and spiritual order he has ordained, plus his own moral nature, to save all that he can. If the sinner persists in his own unwillingness to receive the grace God offers him, how can he complain if God does not offer him more grace? The difficulty is on his part, not upon God's part; and this difficulty is grounded in his attitude toward God.

4. Election destroys human freedom

It is maintained that the doctrine of election is inconsistent with the freedom of man, which would surely be true of any view of election that predestined one man to eternal life and the other to eternal damnation. But the true doctrine of election maintains man's God-given right in this respect. God does not save whether or not a man repents and believes; he saves only those who do so. God does all that he can, consistent with his created moral order and with his self-imposed limitations, to bring a man to repentance and belief. Through the means of the gospel and the agency of the Holy Spirit, God leads, persuades, entreats, and woos the sinner. Because of this some choose to accept the atoning work of Christ; parallel with their choosing is the giving over of the unbeliever to his tenacious will. "Wherefore God gave them up ..." (Rom. 1:24).

There are two factors to be considered: the sovereignty of God and the freedom of man. As of necessity, when we try to unite in our thinking the heavenly with the earthly, or the things of God with the things of man, a mystery inevitably ensues. This is what evolves when we dwell on the incarnation, or on prayer. "For my thoughts are not your thoughts, neither are your ways my ways, saith Jehovah. For as the heavens are higher than the earth, so are my ways higher than your ways, and my thoughts than your thoughts" (Isa. 55:8, 9).

5. ELECTION DISCOURAGES EFFORT IN WINNING THE LOST

It is said that since the matter is already fixed, one way or another, it is useless to expend any effort in evangelism. This would be true of a double-edged view, as some hold, but not of the true view. On the contrary, the doctrine of election is a stimulus to zeal in witnessing; without it all would of necessity be lost. Election produces in the one witnessing an utter dependence upon God's power. Now we understand Paul when he states, "Therefore I endure all things for the elect's sake, that they also may obtain the salvation which is in Christ Jesus with eternal glory" (II Tim. 2: 10). If the elect ones have already attained, why should Paul exert himself in their behalf? The very zeal of the Apostle Paul, who himself taught election, demonstrates the vital necessity of evangelistic effort. What greater incentive can a Christian have for a zealous attitude toward witnessing to the lost than the consciousness that God's purpose is being fulfilled in him? A man is not saved regardless of whether he hears the gospel, or repents, or believes. Instead, God produces the conditions in a man's life that bring him under the influence of the gospel, whereby God can entreat him to repent and accept his proffered grace. God does this through those already saved, the elect being the means of winning others, that these elect ones might win others, and so on.

Though many times unable to distinguish the saved from the unsaved, we are to proclaim the message of saving grace to both. Ezekiel is told of God, "And thou shalt speak my words unto them, whether they will hear, or whether they will forbear; for they are most rebellious" (Ezek. 2:7). Jesus himself says, "I thank thee, O Father, Lord of heaven and earth, that thou didst hide these things from the wise and understanding, and didst reveal them unto babes: yea, Father, for so it was well-pleasing in thy sight" (Matt. 11:25, 26). But this declaration is immediately followed by a gracious invitation to all mankind: "Come unto me, all ye that labor and are heavy laden, and I will give you rest" (11:28); for in the thinking of our Lord the sovereignty of God should not annul the persuasive effort of the redeemed to propagate the gospel.

6. ELECTION TENDS TOWARD IMMORALITY

It is maintained that, since election represents man's salvation as independent of his obedience, it would tend toward immorality. This objection is based upon scriptural ignorance, for the New Testament plainly reveals that the salvation of an individual is ordained only in connection with his regeneration, justification, and sanctification. He is a new creation, one who has died to sin and been raised to a new life in Christ. Jesus says, "If ye love me, ye will keep my commandments" (John 14:15). In I Peter 1:2 the elect are declared to be "in sanctification of the Spirit, unto obedience and sprinkling of the blood of Jesus Christ."

7. ELECTION TENDS TOWARD PRIDE

It is said that election produces the tendency toward pride in the life of the saved one. But instead of pride and self-complacency, election elicits gratitude and love. The conquered rebel can give no thanks to himself, for all thanks belong to God who chose and regenerated him. Only those who pervert the doctrine of election would countenance being proud of being among the elect ones. Paul says that we are saved by grace, and not works, "that no man should glory" (Eph. 2:8, 9). In speaking of the same thing in Romans he says, "Where then is the glorying? It is excluded" (3: 27). The real influence of election is to humble one, not to induce pride.

OUTLINE FOR CHAPTER TEN

I. Man's Response to the Atonement
1. Repentance
   (1) Scriptural teaching
      a. Conviction of sin
      b. Contrition of sin
      c. Renunciation of sin
   (2) Means of bringing men to repentance
   (3) Repentance wholly inward
   (4) Repentance a continuing factor

2. Faith
   (1) Scriptural teaching
      a. Acceptance of the truth about Christ
      b. Assent to the person of Christ
      c. Submission to the will of Christ
   (2) God, as revealed in Christ, the object of faith
   (3) Faith manifested by works
   (4) Faith the correlative of grace
   (5) Faith capable of growth
   (6) Faith and righteousness

II. God's Act of Redemption
1. Forgiveness
   (1) Scriptural teaching
      a. In the Old Testament
      b. In the New Testament
   (2) To be forgiven not exactly the same as never having sinned
      a. Scars of sin remain
      b. Greater insight into character of God
   (3) Sin removed as a barrier to fellowship with God
   (4) Not for the impenitent

2. Justification
   (1) Scriptural terminology
   (2) Meaning of the term
   (3) Ground of justification
   (4) Means of justification
   (5) Justification and forgiveness
      a. Justification a forensic term
      b. Justification once and for all

3. Adoption
   (1) Meaning of the term
   (2) Effected by faith

4. Reconciliation
   (1) Meaning of the term
   (2) God the reconciler
5. Regeneration
   (1) Meaning of the term
   (2) Scriptural teaching
   (3) Pertinent facts
      a. A moral and spiritual change
      b. Indispensable to salvation
      c. Wrought by the Holy Spirit
      d. Truth the instrumentality, not baptism
6. Sanctification
   (1) Meaning of the term
   (2) Two phases of sanctification
   (3) Erroneous views of sanctification
      a. Antinomian
      b. Perfectionist
      c. Romanist
7. Union with Christ
   (1) Explicit in New Testament
   (2) Nature of this union
      a. A mutual union
      b. A spiritual union
      c. An eternal union
      d. A faith union
      e. A heightening union

CHAPTER TEN

ENTERING THE CHRISTIAN LIFE

WHAT DOES ONE EXPERIENCE IN THE ACT OF BECOMING A CHRISTIAN? What is involved in the initiation of the Christian life? This will demand our attention in the present chapter.

I. MAN'S RESPONSE TO THE ATONEMENT

God has proffered a rich and complete salvation through the atoning act of our Saviour, but man must fulfill certain conditions, or spiritual attitudes, to make this salvation effective for himself. There are two fundamental relationships involved: the relation of man to sin and the relation of man to a saving God. Therefore both of these relationships must be altered; there must be a turning from sin, which is repentance, and there must be a turning to God in Christ, which is faith. Yet these two turnings are not mutually exclusive, for sin and God are absolutely antipodal. When one turns from sin, he automatically turns to God. One turning is not possible without the other. Therefore repentance and faith do not constitute two independent acts; they are merely the negative and positive views of the same phenomenon. If it were possible to have one to the exclusion of the other there might be an impenitent believer, or a penitent unbeliever. But this is contrary to both Christian experience and the New Testament.

A. H. Strong brings both repentance and faith together under the term conversion, which is a very good classification, since conversion comes from the Latin and means simply a turning. It is unfortunate that the term conversion has been applied to the complete process of becoming a Christian, involving both man's part and God's part. Conversion is virtually only the human aspect of this fundamental spiritual change called salvation.

"Special interest has centered in the beginning of the Christian life or in conversion, which it has been customary to regard as having both a human and a divine side. The human side is represented by repentance and faith, and the divine by justification, regeneration, and adoption. All of these are biblical terms, and they owe their theological importance in large measure to this fact, rather than to psychological analysis. In assigning faith and repentance to the human side of conversion it is not assumed that they are acts of the human will to the exclusion of the divine.

They may both be referred ultimately to the Divine Spirit. But they stand more closely related to the human will than do justification, regeneration, and adoption. Men are summoned to 'repent' and 'believe,' but they are not summoned to 'justify' and 'regenerate' themselves or to effect their own adoption. The latter are all manifestly divine acts lying beyond the reach of the human will. They may be and are conditioned by faith and repentance, but as distinct conceptions they have to do exclusively with the divine agency in conversion."[1] As is seen here, Albert C. Knudson also uses the term conversion for man's whole saving experience, but it would be more appropriate to reserve this term for only the human aspect of redemption, man's response to God's saving grace. He does use the terms "human side" and "divine side" to designate these two aspects of man's becoming a child of God; and it seems only right to do so, since we must distinguish for the sake of discussion. But even these terms, or similar ones, must be employed with caution, for ultimately everything is of God. "But all things are of God, who reconciled us to himself through Christ..." (II Cor. 5:18). Notice that Paul uses this phrase in connection with man's salvation. God takes the initiative in salvation; man merely responds, and that through repentance and faith.

1. REPENTANCE

When John the Baptist entered the area of the Jordan with his dynamic preaching, his iconoclastic admonition was: "Repent ye; for the kingdom of heaven is at hand" (Matt. 3:2). What is meant by the term "repent"?

(1) SCRIPTURAL TEACHING

The idea of repentance is conveyed in the New Testament by three Greek words. There is *metanoia*, translated "repentance," but meaning literally change of mind. There is *metanoeō,* the verb form of *metanoia,* translated "to repent." And there is *metamelomai,* translated "to repent," but with a leaning toward the idea of regret. The first is found in Matthew 3:8, 11; Luke 5:32; 15:7; Acts 5:31; and many others. The second is found in Matthew 3:2; 11:20; Mark 6:12; and many others. The third is found in only five places in the New Testament: Matthew 21:29, 32; II Corinthians 7:8 (twice in this one verse); Hebrews 7:21; Matthew 27:3 (placed separately from other Matthew references because of meaning of repenting one's self). In the American Standard Version Second Corinthians 7:8 is translated with "I regret," both times; it is "I repent" in the King James Version.

---

[1] Albert C. Knudson, *The Doctrine of Redemption,* pp. 406-7.

Thus we see that the call to repentance involves the whole spiritual and psychological being, for it is not merely an intellectual change of mind. Since man seems to be composed of three faculties — the intellectual, the emotional, and the volitional — all three are involved in his act of repenting. There must be a change of view (mind), a change of feeling (heart), and a change of purpose (will).

a. Conviction of sin

The intellectual element in repentance recognizes sin as involving guilt and defilement. "For I know my transgressions; And my sin is ever before me" (Ps. 51:3). There is a sense of helplessness due to sin. There is a simple recognition of what we are, which comes from hearing the gospel message and from the work of the Holy Spirit. The true nature of sin must be recognized. Sin is seen as *sin*, as against God, as contrary to all holiness and righteousness. Job's final words to God are: "I had heard of thee by the hearing of the ear; But now mine eye seeth thee: Wherefore I abhor myself, And repent in dust and ashes" (42:5, 6). This element in repentance is especially seen in the Greek word *metanoia*.

b. Contrition of sin

The emotional element in repentance involves sorrow for sin as against the goodness and justice of God. Sin is therefore something to be hated and detested; the love of sin must die in the heart of the sinner. This element in repentance is especially discerned in the Greek *metamelomai*, which can easily be translated "I regret."

There must be a genuine regret for sin, not that which passes easily away. It is regret of a godly sort leading to a real change, not regret lacking godly reference. Paul makes this clear in a famous passage in Second Corinthians. "I now rejoice, not that ye were made sorry, but that ye were made sorry unto repentance: for ye were made sorry after a godly sort, that ye might suffer loss by us in nothing. For godly sorrow worketh repentance unto salvation, a repentance which bringeth no regret: but the sorrow of the world worketh death" (7:9, 10). There must be a differentiation between sorrow for sin and the shame resulting on account of it, and the fear of its consequences. The former is grief because the sin is against God; the latter is discomfort because of social disapproval. A thief is sorry because he has been apprehended and must undergo punishment, but he has no regret for his sin per se. He will again pilfer as soon as his liberty is restored. To him the psalmist does not make sense: "The sacrifices of God are a broken spirit: A broken and a contrite heart, O God, thou wilt not despise" (51:17).

c. Renunciation of sin

The volitional element in repentance involves the will, the inward turning from sin to seek pardon and cleansing. There is a repudiation of sin by an act of the will, a revulsion of one's whole being against it. We agree with Paul: "We who died to sin, how shall we any longer live therein?" (Rom. 6:2). This would be a spiritual impossibility. And repentance is never complete until this repudiation takes place. The Greek term *metanoia* implies this phase of repentance, which, by the way, includes and builds upon the other two phases of meaning. "And Peter said unto them, Repent ye, and be baptized every one of you in the name of Jesus Christ unto the remission of your sins; and ye shall receive the gift of the Holy Spirit" (Acts 2:38).

Walden, in his book *The Great Meaning of Metanoia,* so emphasizes "change of mind" rather than "repentance" for the translation of the term *metanoia* that he believes that *metamelomai* alone should be translated with "repentance." He maintains, and rightly so, that the idea in *metanoia* is abandonment of sin rather than sorrow for sin; it is an act of the will rather than a state of feeling. It is repentance *from* sin, not *of* sin, nor *for* sin. Albert C. Knudson also believes that this third phase, or element, in repentance is the dominant one. "It is at bottom what the Greek word *(metanoia)* calls it, 'a change of mind.' The whole mental life is involved in it. It includes emotional and intellectual elements — and the former are often prominent — but fundamentally it is an act of will. It is a turning of one's back on the past, a repudiation of sin, and thus a necessary condition of entrance upon the Christian life."[2]

(2) MEANS OF BRINGING MEN TO REPENTANCE

God employs many means in bringing the sinner to repentance. The preaching of the gospel; the influence of holy and winsome lives; the work of the church; hymns and spiritual songs; godly parents; providential happenings, such as the death of loved ones, financial reverses, loss of health, etc. — these and other channels God uses to bring men to repentance. Man must discern the contrast between his own sinful existence and the holiness of God; only then can there be true repentance, and God may use any of the various means to bring this about. Job has a long and painful experience before he cries out to God, "I abhor myself,

2 *Ibid.,* pp. 407-8.

and repent in dust and ashes" (42:6). Paul reminds the Romans of the source of true repentance. "Or despisest thou the riches of his goodness and forbearance and longsuffering, not knowing that the goodness of God leadeth thee to repentance?" (2:4).

(3) REPENTANCE WHOLLY INWARD

In all of its aspects repentance is wholly an inward experience and is not to be confused with the outward change of life resulting from it. True repentance may be manifested by confession of sin. The publican, remote from the Pharisee, "smote his breast, saying, God, be thou merciful to me a sinner" (Luke 18:13). True repentance may be manifested by reparation for wrongs done to men. Zacchaeus is willing to restore fourfold to any man from whom he has wrongfully exacted (Luke 19:8). In the life of every penitent sinner there is always a certain change, which is termed reformation. In some lives this change may be to a considerable extent, as in the life of the Apostle Paul or in the life of a convert from Skid Row. In other lives it is meager, as in the coming to God of a small child reared in a devout Christian home. Yet the life of every convert should show at least some difference, and this outward moral change is termed reformation. W. T. Conner states, "Sometimes there may be a marked change in the habits of life without repentance. Sometimes the outward life may have been so correct, judged by the standards of social morality, that no special outward reformation was needed. So you may have reformation following repentance, or you may have repentance without reformation where it is not needed."[3] It is maintained, however, that there will be some reformation in every case, no matter how good morally may be the person who comes to God; for the term reformation includes not only a discarding of the grossly immoral but also the addition of the fine nuances leading to the ethical.

Therefore repentance and reformation should not be confused. The former is subjective and the latter is objective. Repentance is the repudiation of sin as antithetical to the godly. It is an attitude of mind against sin and not just a turning from sin as violating the holiness of God, thus leading to the repudiation of the sinful self. From this comes the fruit of repentance, for there is a scriptural differentiation between "repentance" and "fruit worthy of repentance" (Matt. 3:8).

(4) REPENTANCE A CONTINUING FACTOR

Repentance is an act that must often be repeated throughout the Christian life. It is not merely initial, taking place only when

---

3 W. T. Conner, *Christian Doctrines*, pp. 190-1.

one becomes a Christian and never happening again. It is an attitude that belongs to the whole dedicated life, of which the initial penitent spirit is but the inception. In fact, the deepest repentance does not always occur at the inceptive stage but happens later. As one grows in grace and emerges more and more from the darkness of sin his eyes become keener to its heinousness. His spiritual sensitivity becomes more acute as he lives in fellowship with a holy God. The immoral act eliciting penitence in his early Christian life engenders a deeper penitence later on. Paul reminds the Romans that all believers have died to sin (6:2), but he still exhorts them not to let sin reign in their mortal bodies (6:12). Repentance is necessary every time the Christian realizes that he has missed the mark. In fact his whole attitude is that of a penitent heart toward any possible sin, whether realized or to the contrary.

2. FAITH

(1) SCRIPTURAL TEACHING

The English word "faith" translates the Greek term *pistis,* while the verb "to believe" translates *pisteuein.* These terms are found repeatedly throughout the Scriptures, though the Gospel of John and the three Johannine epistles never use the noun form, only the verb form. John probably wants to steer clear of any static conception regarding this pivotal term; therefore he uses only the more dynamic verbals. However, the English reader can look at the two Greek terms, *pistis* and *pisteuein,* and see that basically there is no difference of meaning, that one is derived from the other. Therefore to have faith is simply to believe. Examples of the noun "faith" are found in Luke 8:48; 17:6; and Ephesians 2:8. Examples of the verb "to believe" are found in John 3:36; 5:24; and 7:38.

We have already seen that faith is the turning to God in Christ and that it is merely the correlative to repentance, the turning from sin. Again, as in repentance, faith involves the whole spiritual and psychological being — the intellectual element, the emotional element, and the volitional element. There must be a change of view (mind), a change of feeling (heart), and a change of purpose (will). Even though it is difficult to separate one of these elements from its two cognates, each of the three can probably be observed more easily in the case of faith than in the case of repentance.

a. *Acceptance of the truth about Christ*

The intellectual factor in faith is a recognition of the truth of the gospel, the verity of God's revelation. It is recognizing

God's provision for salvation in Christ and his atoning work. There is an acceptance of the historical facts and the scriptural interpretation of those facts, including man's sinfulness and utter dependence upon Christ. Yet this factor alone does not constitute saving faith, for we are told that the demons believe and shudder (Jas. 2:19). Surely the demons have not received salvation; yet the same Greek word for believe, *pisteuō*, is used in this passage as it is used elsewhere for the true child of God. Evidently the word believe is applied to the demons in only the intellectual sense.

b. *Assent to the person of Christ*

The emotional factor in faith is assent to the revelation of God's saving grace as found in Jesus Christ. Convicted of his sin and of his need for a Saviour, the penitent one finds in Christ the answer to it all. There is an awakening of the sensibilities to the power of God in Christ. In the Fourth Gospel we read, "As he spake these things, many believed on him. Jesus therefore said to those Jews that had believed him, If ye abide in my word, then are ye truly my disciples" (John 8:30, 31). It seems that the Jews, the latter group, believed *him*, but had not yet believed *on* him, which would be to make him the basis of their hope and life. They must therefore give assent to him and abide in his word.

c. *Submission to the will of Christ*

The volitional factor in faith is the subordination of one's will to the will of Christ. It is to trust in Christ as Saviour and Lord, with the surrender of one's whole being to the commands and expectations of Christ. This trust is placed in Christ as trustworthy — trustworthy in his revelation, trustworthy in his redemption, trustworthy in his offering for sin, trustworthy in his power to deliver, and trustworthy as Lord of the life.

Thus we see that true faith involves the whole being of man, man in all his faculties. To believe in Christ is to grant him one's whole being, involving mind, heart, and will. The first is *credere Deum;* the second is *credere Deo;* and the third is *credere in Deum.*

The New Testament word *pistis*, translated with the English word faith, is a rich one indeed; in fact it marks that special element in Christianity that makes it so distinctive. "The Hellenistic religious world had nothing to say about faith, and Reitzenstein's effort to show that *pistis* had a place in the mysteries fails completely: Christianity had everything to say about it. Osiris and Cybele never thought of including faith in their vocabulary: Jesus of Nazareth made it the alpha and the omega of His, and His followers saw in Him its author and perfecter. Initiation into the mysteries left faith out of sight, but baptism into Christ enthroned it. With the one, faith was nowhere; with the other, it was everywhere."[4]

(2) GOD, AS REVEALED IN CHRIST, THE OBJECT OF FAITH

Faith unites us to God. New Testament faith is not merely belief in a proposition, or the acceptance of a creed, or the assent to a dogma. It is the vital union of the soul with God, and that as he is revealed in Christ. It is belief in the saving power of God as a person, and not trust in the church as the remitting and redeeming agent. Faith is personal, the union of spirit with Spirit. It is not impersonal, the assent to an objective realm of values.

(3) FAITH MANIFESTED BY WORKS

We are not saved by works; we are saved by grace through faith. Paul, the most ardent denouncer of legalistic works, makes this clear. "We reckon therefore that a man is justified by faith apart from the works of the law" (Rom. 3:28). James says that faith apart from works is a dead faith. "Even so faith, if it have not works, is dead in itself. Yea, a man will say, Thou hast faith, and I have works: show me thy faith apart from thy works, and I by my works will show thee my faith" (2:17, 18). We are saved by our faith, not by our works; but immediately upon becoming children of God we feel compelled to express our new-found Christian joy by means of works. Paul says we are "created in Christ Jesus for good works" (Eph. 2:10). Even though this great apostle denounced works as the condition of salvation, no one more adequately proclaimed them as the consequences of it. There is no greater means whereby one may express his faith than by a willing obedience to the commands of the Saviour.

(4) FAITH THE CORRELATIVE OF GRACE

God's grace descends to man and is met by man's faith, thus issuing in salvation. "For by grace have ye been saved through faith; and that not of yourselves, it is the gift of God; not of works, that no man should glory" (Eph. 2:8, 9). To the idea of works Paul opposes the idea of faith; and to the idea of debt Paul opposes the idea of grace. The concept of Jewish legalism is that man earns his salvation through law, works, and merit; therefore salvation becomes a debt on God's side. Paul maintains

---

4 James S. Stewart, *A Man in Christ*, p. 79.

that the grace of God, or his unmerited favor, descends to man, and is met by man's faith, something that has absolutely no merit or purchasing power. Therefore faith is the means whereby man appropriates God's saving grace. Man is not saved *by* faith; nor is he saved *on account of* faith. He is saved *through* faith. It is Christ's great atoning act that saves, which man possesses for his own life through faith.

When Paul states that "we have had our access by faith into this grace wherein we stand" (Rom. 5:2), he is not only revealing the correlation of these two terms but is at the same time expressing a basic Old Testament concept. Abraham was accepted of God not on the basis of works but on the basis of faith. "For if Abraham was justified by works, he hath whereof to glory; but not toward God. For what saith the scripture? And Abraham believed God, and it was reckoned unto him for righteousness" (Rom. 4:2, 3). And all other Hebrews were saved by the same condition, for the law did not annul the promise. It was itself a gift of grace through faith. Christ reveals the conditions upon which all men are saved, both before and after his coming. It has never been works and debt but has always been faith and grace. It was never intended that men should be saved by the works of the law, nor that this should be the means of salvation in the Old Testament, whereas it is by grace in the New Testament. Man does not have the power of perfect obedience to the law; and, if he did, it would be due to God's grace. Man possesses no moral or spiritual power apart from God. Hence, the idea of an obedience which can earn or merit salvation is inconceivable.

(5) FAITH CAPABLE OF GROWTH

From man's side faith can grow, since it is composed of intellectual, emotional and volitional elements, each of which is capable of being augmented. As a work of God in man it is capable of growth, since the quickening power of the Holy Spirit can bring an increase in knowledge, sensibility, and energy. We are to seek this increase in faith by the exercise of our own power as well as in the source of all faith, God himself. The apostles themselves implore the Lord Jesus, "Increase our faith," to which Jesus replies, "If ye had faith as a grain of mustard seed, ye would say unto this sycamine tree, Be thou rooted up, and be thou planted in the sea; and it would obey you" (Luke 17:5, 6). Does not the adult Christian have more faith than he had when a child? Surely there is growth along the years. Only when we begin to believe do we feel the great need for an increase in faith. "I believe; help thou mine unbelief" (Mark 9:24); this is the cry of one who recognizes both the need of faith and the true source of faith.

(6) FAITH AND RIGHTEOUSNESS

Sometimes a false accusation is leveled at the doctrine of salvation by grace through faith, even though it is built upon the bedrock of biblical truth. It is maintained that it would encourage one to live a life of spiritual ease and of sin rather than a life of good works and of righteousness. The answer to this double objection is found in Scripture itself, for here is a vivid example of taking the part for the whole and of not basing our doctrines upon the complete revealed truth.

We answer by maintaining that it would not lead to a life of spiritual ease, an "at-ease-in-Zion" situation; for the Christian is one who has experienced the grace of God with all its saving, cleansing, and forgiving power. Now he feels drawn to work for his Redeemer; he realizes that his works should be the fruit of his salvation. We teach our children Ephesians 2:8, 9 immediately after we teach them John 3:16, wanting them to know from an early age what Martin Luther discovered so late in life. But we omit the next verse, verse ten; and Paul would emphasize highly its relation to the two preceding verses. "For we are his workmanship, created in Christ Jesus for good works, which God afore prepared that we should walk in them." We have been created in Christ, born again in Christ, made children of God through Christ, for the express purpose of performing good works. Works become the fruit of our redemption, the absence of which casts doubt upon the genuineness of our faith. "What doth it profit, my brethren, if a man say he hath faith, but have not works? can that faith save him? If a brother or sister be naked and in lack of daily food, and one of you say unto them, Go in peace, be ye warmed and filled; and yet ye give them not the things needful to the body; what doth it profit? Even so faith, if it have not works, is dead in itself" (Jas. 2:14-17). Paul and James agree completely at this point. The former states that legalistic works will not merit salvation, but that works come as a result of salvation. James underscores the latter half of this statement, saying that only the faith that issues in works is efficacious to save.

But it is also maintained that salvation by grace through faith will not lead to a life of sin. Paul probably had much to bear in this regard from the Judaizers, for he says in Romans, "Shall we continue in sin, that grace may abound? God forbid. We who died to sin, how shall we any longer live therein? Or are ye ignorant that all we who were baptized into Christ Jesus were baptized into his death? We were buried therefore with him through baptism into death: that like as Christ was raised from the dead through the glory of the Father, so we also might walk in newness of life.... Even so reckon ye also yourselves to be dead unto sin, but alive unto God in Christ Jesus" (6:1-11). A Christian is one who has died to sin to walk with Christ. How, therefore, can he be satisfied to continue in a life of sin? He has a moral guarantee, derived from his relationship with his Saviour, protecting him from such a bizarre expression of his new life in God.

II. GOD'S ACT OF REDEMPTION

It has been maintained that there is a manward and a Godward side of redemption. We have just discussed the manward side and are now ready for the Godward. Yet it must be emphasized constantly that ultimately all is of God. The response of man is possible because God willed and planned it as such. He repents and has faith because God gave him that power through creation and then drew him at the time of conversion through his Spirit. When we assign faith and repentance to the human side we are not excluding the divine. These two factors merely stand more closely to the human response than do sanctification, justification, regeneration, and such. Men are entreated to "repent" and to "believe," but never to "justify" or to "regenerate" themselves. These are divine acts lying in a sphere beyond the human will, only being conditioned by the manifestation of repentance and faith.

In discussing the following factors it must be kept in mind that these great acts of God are not consecutive, one following the other and built upon the preceding. They are merely different ways of looking at God's redeeming activity in which a soul is transformed and brought to God. They are like facets in a great diamond, none of which by itself is the diamond but all of which, in proper perspective and arrangement, constitute the gem. We might say that as far as time is concerned they all occur at the same moment, each forming an integral part of the whole divine act. One does not precede the other, nor is it complete without the other. We are merely viewing the saving act from different viewpoints.

1. FORGIVENESS

(1) SCRIPTURAL TEACHING

One of the fundamental blessings in salvation is deliverance from sin, for sin prevents fellowship with God. When sin is forgiven, a relationship can be established, a fact recognized in both the Old and New Testaments.

a. *In the Old Testament*

The Old Testament is very clear on the idea of forgiveness. Psalm 32 is one of the greatest examples of the joy of one who has experienced the forgiveness of God. The psalmist talks of the blessedness of one "whose transgression is forgiven, Whose sin is covered." God will not impute or reckon sin to that one, for there is no guile, or deceit, in his spirit. He tried to be silent and not confess his sin; but his bones wasted away, and God's hand was upon him. But when he expressed his iniquity and transgression God forgave him (1-5). Psalm 103 is very similar in thought. God is one "Who forgiveth all thine iniquities; Who healeth all thy diseases" (3). He does not deal with us according to our sins, nor reward us according to our iniquities (10). He removes our transgressions from us as far as the east is from the west (12). Psalm 51 is the greatest of the penitential psalms. It is the urgent cry of one who recognizes his sin and seeks the forgiving and cleansing hand of God. "Have mercy upon me, O God, according to thy lovingkindness: According to the multitude of thy tender mercies blot out my transgressions. Wash me thoroughly from mine iniquity, And cleanse me from my sin. For I know my transgressions; And my sin is ever before me" (1-3). He asks God to purify him with hyssop and wash him whiter than snow (7), to hide his face from his sin and to blot out his iniquities (9). God will not despise a broken and a contrite heart (17). Psalm 130 reads, "But there is forgiveness with thee, That thou mayest be feared" (4).

Jeremiah's famous passage on the future new covenant (31:31-34) lists forgiveness as one of the great blessings of that covenant. This new covenant that God will make with his people will not be like the old one, for it will be more spiritual in nature; rather than deliverance from Egypt there will be deliverance from sin. They will all know God, for he says, "I will forgive their iniquity, and their sin will I remember no more" (34).

b. *In the New Testament*

In the New Testament there is a much greater emphasis upon forgiveness, for here the new covenant has been ushered in by Christ. Jesus in the model prayer tells his disciples to pray for this significant blessing. "And forgive us our sins" (Luke 11:4). When he sees the faith of those bearing the man sick of the palsy, he says, "Son, thy sins are forgiven." Immediately he is accused of blasphemy for exercising the divine prerogative of forgiving sins, to which he replies by making the man to walk. The miracle of healing will be his evidence of authority in forgiving sin (Mark 2:3-12). The preaching of remission of sins in the name of Jesus is designated as an elemental part of the Great Commission (Luke 24:47).

Remission of sins is also basic in Peter's preaching. He announces to all the people on the Day of Pentecost, "Repent ye, and be baptized every one of you in the name of Jesus Christ unto the remission of your sins" (Acts 2:38). He proclaims to the high priest and to the council concerning Jesus, "Him did God exalt with his right hand to be a Prince and a Saviour, to give repentance to Israel, and remission of sins" (Acts 5:31). And to Cornelius and his household at Caesarea he states that the prophets witness to the fact "that through his name every one that believeth on him shall receive remission of sins" (Acts 10:43).

Paul in Ephesians remarks, "In whom [Christ] we have our redemption through his blood, the forgiveness of our trespasses" (1:7), thus linking redemption and forgiveness very closely. And in I John we find that our confession of sins is basic to our being forgiven. "If we confess our sins, he is faithful and righteous to forgive us our sins, and to cleanse us from all unrighteousness" (1:9).

In these New Testament passages the Greek terms translated "to forgive" and "forgiveness" (or "remission") are *aphiēmi* and *aphesis*. The root meaning of the verb is "to send away," and is equivalent to our term "to remit." Therefore when God forgives our sins he sends them away, metaphorically speaking, and they are known and recognized no more. When a man's sins are forgiven he is no longer held accountable for them.

(2) TO BE FORGIVEN NOT EXACTLY THE SAME AS NEVER HAVING SINNED

To forgive sin is not to make a man as though he had not sinned at all. True, there need be no fear of punishment or reparation, and the feeling of guilt that robbed life of its joy has vanished. The marred fellowship with God has been corrected. Yet there is a difference between one who has sinned and been forgiven and one who has not sinned at all. The blessedness of the forgiven is of a different hue from the blessedness of the sinless. The man with the non-reckoned iniquity is a different being from the man with a non-existent iniquity.

a. *Scars of sin remain*

The scars of sin are still apparent, though the sin itself has been erased and "taken away." Forgiveness on God's part, and even

231

on man's part, cannot completely erase from the minds of all concerned that the sin *was* there, present at one time in all its hideousness. There may even be those now suffering because of some past sin — perhaps a resultant physical malady, perhaps the stigma still hovering over the family of a onetime drunkard, perhaps the financial inconvenience and the loneliness of a family deprived of its father by a murderer now forgiven. "The man is forgiven, and now the evil he has caused in other lives is part of the world's great mass of evil, which all true men must help to bear, with God's gracious aid. It was caused by his sin. . . . We are bound to be more keenly concerned, each one, with that portion of the world's woe which our own situation presents most plainly to us; and especially with any part of it that is directly due to our own past misdeeds and that calls for active reparation."[5] God forgave David for his double sin of adultery and murder, but he shed many a tear of remorse over his iniquity. Forgiven of the consequences of his sin, yes; but that did not bring back to Uriah the life of which he had been deprived. The penitent prodigal is forgiven, but that does not erase the wasted years of a life that could have blossomed for his Saviour.

b. Greater insight into character of God

Yet there is a second, and a more positive, reason why it is not the same to have sinned and been forgiven than not to have sinned at all. The experience of the gracious act of divine forgiveness gives one an insight into the marvelous character of God that otherwise would be impossible. He knows a forgiving God, a God of mercy and of redeeming love. Conner is right when he avows, "How could a man who had never sinned understand that element in God's character that we express by the term grace? The grace of God is the most glorious element in his character according to the Christian view. This grace we know only in its redeeming work in our lives. A sinless being can never know a God of grace. The conception would have no meaning to him. Redemption in Christ, then, does not put a man back in the place of an unfallen Adam. It puts him on a new basis, gives him an insight into God's character and fellowship with God that such an unfallen man could not have."[6] Then, in turn, this divine quality of grace newly experienced will flow out through him to his fellows, the redeemed man wanting to share his grace in Christ through evangelistic and missionary means with others. This is no accident; it is God's providential plan. Life now has become redemptive.

5 D. M. Baillie, *God Was In Christ*, p. 169.
6 Conner, *op. cit.*, p. 206.

(3) SIN REMOVED AS A BARRIER TO FELLOWSHIP WITH GOD

With the forgiveness of sins the wall between God and man is removed. Sin broke the undimmed fellowship between God and man, the highest of his created order, bringing spiritual death and all its attendant evils. "Against thee, thee only, have I sinned; And done that which is evil in thy sight" (Ps. 51:4). "Your iniquities have separated between you and your God, and your sins have hid his face from you, so that he will not hear" (Isa. 59:2). But with forgiveness of sin the barrier is removed, and God's face is seen once again. Sin has been sent away, remitted, and man now walks and talks with God. There is joy in a new-found relationship; there is freedom and peace, because guilt is removed. A new light has entered the soul. Forgiveness has come through "him that loveth us, and loosed us from our sins by his blood" (Rev. 1:5); and the wall between God and man is now down. "What has happened is that the burden of sin — of sin that is ours and that cleaves to us with the warning that it will be ours forever — is lifted off, and we are drawn back in love to the Father's heart. The gates of righteousness, which seemed closed against us eternally, are set open once again. God forgives; none but God *can* forgive; and when in this creative fashion He removes the power of sin to expel us from His presence, the act is one to which the normal processes of phenomenal reality are instrumental, but no more. As such an act it involves infinitely more than cosmic relations of invariable sequence. It brings God Himself into a man's life in an immediate (yet not unmediated) way and establishes a new connection in which He and that life shall henceforth stand to one another."[7]

(4) NOT FOR THE IMPENITENT

Forgiveness is absolutely dependent upon repentance. According to the Scriptures a man becomes forgivable in God's sight only when he manifests the moral attitude that can be forgiven. This means he must have God's point of view toward sin, which must be shown through a genuine repentant spirit. For God to pronounce forgiveness upon the unrepentant would be to negate all that is essential in forgiveness and would constitute an arbitrary act on God's part rather than a spiritual transaction between God and man.

Also, as repentance is not only required at the initial point of entering the Christian life but is expected as an attitude from then on, so forgiveness is experienced repeatedly also. As often as one sins he needs to repent, and as often as he repents he feels the

---

[7] H. R. Mackintosh, *The Doctrine of the Person of Jesus Christ*, pp. 357-8.

joy of divine forgiveness. The entire Christian life is one characterized by repentance and forgiveness. Neither of these is a once-for-
all factor in Christianity.

2. JUSTIFICATION

(1) SCRIPTURAL TERMINOLOGY

The doctrine of justification, found mainly in the Pauline
epistles, is based on a metaphor drawn from the Roman law court.
Where Jesus talks mainly of forgiveness, Paul talks of justification,
the terms having much in common. Romans and Galatians make
the greatest contribution to our concept of justification.

There are five Greek words that are vitally related to the doctrine. *Dikaiōsis*, which is usually translated "justification" and
which gives the doctrine its name, is found only twice in the
New Testament, Romans 4:25 and 5:18. *Dikaioō*, the verb translated "I justify," is found many times. *Dikaios*, the adjective meaning "just," "righteous," or "upright," also occurs many times and
figures highly in the doctrine. *Dikaiosunē*, "righteousness," and
dikaiōs, "justly" or "righteously," also add meaning to the concept.
Merely a glance at these words, by even one who does not know
Greek, will reveal the fact that they all come from the same
root, *dik-*, and that justification and being righteous are quite
interrelated.

(2) MEANING OF THE TERM

The traditional view of justification is that God gives to man,
because of his acceptance of the saving grace offered in Christ
Jesus, a new standing. Justification, therefore, is God's declarative
act in which he pronounces the repentant believer, on condition
of his faith in Christ, to be righteous in God's sight, to be restored to divine favor, and to be subject no longer to the penalty
of divine law. The sinner, condemned by his sins and unable to
prevent or to erase them, and therefore to achieve righteousness
in God's sight, falls prostrate on the mercy of God. God reckons,
or imputes, his faith in Christ and his atoning act unto him for
the righteousness he could not attain through his own initiative
and strength. Man, hitherto under condemnation due to his sin,
stands acquitted. He has favorable standing with God.

It has been maintained by some that this "new status," or
"declarative" element in justification is the sum and total, that
it does not include an "efficient" element in which the sinner is
"made upright." Therefore justification is merely objective in
relation to the one being redeemed, not subjective. God *recognizes*
the believer as *dikaios* rather than *makes* him *dikaios*. And there

are certain passages in the New Testament where this meaning does shine forth and man is seen to have a new status. Paul says that "he that hath died [with Christ] is justified from sin" (Rom. 6:7). He also declares, "It is God that justifieth; who is he that condemneth?" (Rom. 8:33). The one who has been accepted as righteous by God has nothing to fear; he has been acquitted of God. But is there not also a second meaning in the idea of God's justifying man, that of making him efficiently righteous? Does not God *make* man upright as well as *recognize* him as upright? Surely the idea of new life is involved as well as new standing, for justification is a creative act of God as well as a declarative act.

The adjective *dikaios* means "righteous" (as translated in the American Standard), or "just" (as translated in the King James), or "upright." It does not mean merely to count as righteous, or to consider as righteous, even though the person it modifies may be unrighteous. It means that that person is characterized by actual uprighteousness. We read that "he that doeth righteousness is righteous, even as he [God] is righteous: he that doeth sin is of the devil" (I John 3:7, 8). The strong contrast presented in this verse shows that actual righteousness is under discussion, not just being counted righteous. The corresponding truth can be shown for the meaning of the noun *dikaiosunē,* generally translated "righteousness." This means actual uprightness, not merely imputed uprightness. "For the kingdom of God is not eating and drinking, but righteousness and peace and joy in the Holy Spirit" (Rom. 14:17). Now, if the adjective and noun of this group of words refer to actual uprightness, would not the corresponding verb mean "to make upright"? Why should the verb be more restrictive in its meaning than the adjective and noun forms from the same root? Or why should it change in meaning whatsoever? Therefore the New Testament doctrine of justification involves the double meaning of counting as righteous and as making righteous. It is both declarative and creative in meaning.[8]

(3) GROUND OF JUSTIFICATION

This marvelous justifying act of God is grounded in the atoning work of Christ, which is the heart of the whole argument presented by Paul in Romans 3:23-26. He goes to great lengths to show that all have sinned and have come short of the glory of God, therefore needing an uprightness other than they themselves can produce. But God has provided the ground for such in the expiatory work of Christ: "being justified freely by his grace through

---

8 See Ernest De Witt Burton, *The Epistle to the Galatians,* pp. 468-474, and Frank Stagg, *New Testament Theology,* pp. 95-101, for a fuller discussion of the doctrine of justification in both phases.

the redemption that is in Christ Jesus, whom God set forth to be a propitiation [expiation is a much better word], through faith, in his blood" (24, 25). God justifies freely by his grace on the condition of faith in Christ, for because of what Christ has done the way has been opened up. "But to him that worketh not, but believeth on him that justifieth the ungodly, his faith is reckoned for righteousness" (Rom. 4:5). God justifying the ungodly — what a marvel this is, and it is made possible by the blood of Christ. "Much more then, being now justified by his blood, shall we be saved from the wrath of God through him" (Rom. 5:9).

(4) MEANS OF JUSTIFICATION

Faith is the means whereby God is able to justify. This is the condition that must be fulfilled: faith on the part of the sinner in the atoning act of Christ. "Being therefore justified by faith, we have peace with God through our Lord Jesus Christ" (Rom. 5:1). Paul quotes the Old Testament as evidence of the fact that God has always justified by faith, not by works. "For if Abraham was justified by works, he hath whereof to glory; but not toward God. For what saith the scripture? And Abraham believed God; and it was reckoned unto him for righteousness" (Rom. 4:2, 3). Paul here quotes Genesis 15:6, but he also quotes Habakkuk 2:4 for the same reason: "For therein is revealed a righteousness of God from faith unto faith; as it is written, But the righteous shall live by faith" (Rom. 1:17). And in the eleventh chapter of Hebrews there is a long list of Old Testament saints all of whom lived by faith. Yet it is in Galatians 2:16, 20 that this fact is made crystal clear.

The Jews erred in that they were attempting to make salvation a works-debt arrangement rather than a faith-grace one. It was extremely hard for them to arrive at Paul's thinking in Ephesians 2:8, 9: "For by grace have ye been saved through faith; and that not of yourselves, it is the gift of God; not of works, that no man should glory." If God accepted Abraham's faith and reckoned it unto him for righteousness, would he not do the same for those accepting the pardoning grace of Calvary? To seek salvation by works would destroy the fundamental principle of the gospel; it would make unnecessary the pardoning power of Calvary. Paul takes a forensic term direct from the law court and uses it to fight Jewish legalism. "Pious Jews could only peer into a dim, mysterious future, hoping against hope that God would pronounce a sentence of acquittal at last. But it was Paul's glorious certainty that for himself, and for all who had faith in Christ, the liberating sentence had already been pronounced. What else could the peace and joy which had come to him at Damascus mean? Judaism toiled and hoped and struggled and doubted: Paul possessed. The new life surging in his heart could betoken only one. thing — God had accepted him. 'Not guilty,' had been the verdict.'"9

(5) JUSTIFICATION AND FORGIVENESS

Justification and forgiveness are two different views of the same great act of God. Paul uses the former often; the latter hardly at all. There seem to be two main differences between these metaphors.

a. *Justification a forensic term*

Justification is a legalistic term drawn from the court of Roman law used for acquitting one accused of a crime. Paul applies it in a spiritual sense for the sinner acquitted of his sins because of his faith in the atonement of Christ. The believer is not only declared upright in the sight of God, being restored to the divine favor; he is made upright as well. Forgiveness carries with it more of a personal note, for the sin that prevented personal fellowship with God has now been removed. Justification deals with sin as it brings us under the condemnation of the law; forgiveness deals with sin as it prevents fellowship with a holy God.

b. *Justification once and for all*

Justification is a once-for-all term, while forgiveness is not. Justification does not need to be repeated, having taken place initially in the Christian life and effective for all eternity. When God once declares a sinner to be acquitted, he remains so, never again to come under the condemnation of the law. Forgiveness, however, requires repetition during the entire Christian life. As often as the redeemed one sins and the fellowship is marred, he needs to repent and ask for forgiveness. And every time he turns to God with a penitent heart there is a deeper appreciation of the fellowship that was marred.

There are some, however, who would disagree with us relative to this phase of justification. Nels F. L. Ferré believes that there is not only an "act of conversion" but a "process of conversion." The latter is termed such because "man still needs to be turned from self toward God." In his "process of conversion" he places not only forgiveness and sanctification, but justification as well. He maintains, "The old theology taught that justification is instantaneous, while sanctification is gradual. It seems truer, however, that both are gradual. We are continually justified by God's

9 Stewart, *op. cit.*, pp. 249-50.

grace.... We are forgiven even as we forgive, judged even as we judge. This relation is due to the degree of man's receptivity. We do not become wholly justified until we are wholly surrendered.... We are fully justified by God's love for us but only insofar as we truly accept it."[10] It is maintained, however, that justification is completely initial and not partially progressive.

3. ADOPTION

(1) MEANING OF THE TERM

The justified man becomes aware of a new relationship, that of a son to a Father. Since he has been adopted, he is no longer an orphan. It is apparent at once that Paul has again borrowed a term from the Roman law court with which to depict this view of the glorious salvation God grants to the believer. It is the Greek term *huiothesia,* translated "adoption." "Let us think of Christ as the Son who reveals the Father, that we may know the Father's heart against which we have sinned, that we may see how sin, in making us godless, has made us orphans, and understand that the grace of God, which is at once the remission of past sin and the gift of eternal life, restores to our orphan spirits their Father and to the Father of spirits His lost children."[11]

Paul states, "For as many as are led by the Spirit of God, these are sons of God. For ye received not the spirit of bondage again unto fear; but ye received the spirit of adoption, whereby we cry, Abba, Father" (Rom. 8:14, 15). He also states that God has "foreordained us unto adoption as sons through Jesus Christ unto himself" (Eph. 1:5). "God sent forth his Son ... that we might receive the adoption of sons" (Gal. 4:4, 5). If one observes closely, he will see that Paul is not only emphasizing the work of the Spirit in connection with adoption but also the conscious possession of the Spirit by the newly created child of God. Thus, even though the term is a forensic one, it does not depict merely a legalistic transaction. The adopted child has been led from the bondage of slavish fear and legalism into glorious peace and liberty. Before adoption there is the melancholy servitude of a man with no controlling purpose, no power greater than his own reasons or desires, and faced with moral defeat. After adoption there is the consciousness of "the liberty of the glory of the children of God" (Rom. 8:21). The tone of life has become victorious; it is now life "in the Spirit." Doubt has been replaced by assurance, for the Spirit testifies within us of this adoption. As a consequence we are now "heirs of God, and joint-heirs with Christ" of all heaven's glory (Rom. 8:17, 18).

10 Nels F. L. Ferré, *The Christian Faith,* pp. 204-5.
11 John McLeod Campbell, *The Nature of the Atonement,* p. 147.

(2) EFFECTED BY FAITH

Adoption, like justification, sanctification, forgiveness, etc., is the result of the sinner's faith in God's only Son. Jesus is the only, unique Son of the Father, as we are informed in John's gospel. This is the meaning of the Greek term *monogenēs*, generally translated "only begotten," as in John 3:16. In fact this New Testament writer does not use the word son for the believer, but retains this term for Jesus only. He employs the term children for the believers, thus depicting the eternal difference between the sonship of Jesus and the sonship of redeemed sinners. The sinner places his trust in the redeeming work of the Son, God's unique Son, and then is received into the family of God as an adopted child. Yet the marvelous fact is that, even though he has entered this coveted position through adoption, he is a joint-heir of all heaven's glory right along with Jesus, the one who has eternally been "in the bosom of the Father" (John 1:18).

The Stoics had taught the universal Fatherhood of God and brotherhood of man, that men are co-substantial with God and that there is a divine spark in everyone. All one has to do is to cultivate this spark through wisdom, education, and apathy till it flames into salvation. Man merely claims a sonship already his. Not so in Christianity. Man, utterly lost and apart from God, through faith in the atoning power of Jesus is ushered back into true relation to God. He has been adopted into the family of God. The terms Father and son, as used in the Bible respecting God and man, speak of a relation that is realized only by the one who has placed his faith in the atoning work of Jesus.

It might be feasible at this point to warn the reader against any possible confusion between the terms adoption and adoptionism. Adoption is the doctrine that has just been discussed, whereby the believer is ushered into the family of God. Adoptionism is an historical heresy concerning the person of Christ, being the belief that Jesus became the Son of God at his baptism. It was found among the Ebionites, who seemed to have prepared the way for this false belief to be propounded by others later on.

4. RECONCILIATION

(1) MEANING OF THE TERM

Again, as with justification and adoption, we are dealing with one of Paul's terms. It is the word *katallagē,* normally translated "reconciliation," with its cognate verb, "to reconcile." As in adoption one is renewed in sonship, so in reconciliation one is renewed in friendship. As in justification there is the picture of the criminal before his judge, with the judge pronouncing a sentence of acquittal; so in reconciliation there is the picture of the once-estranged child before his father, with the alienation now replaced by peace. Sin causes alienation, or estrangement, between God and man; when this alienation is removed the sinner is said to be reconciled to God.

For Paul his own experience becomes the determining factor. "On the day when Jesus met him, the peace for which through bitter years of battle he had yearned in vain came to him as a sudden miraculous benediction: the man in Christ now knew himself to be right with God. And with the clearness of vision of a soul redeemed he saw that, if for him the estranging barriers had fallen, there was no reason why they should remain standing for any of the sons of men. If his own restless and distracted heart had found its perfect rest, then on that same breast of God must be rest for all the world. Reconciliation became his theme."[12] No wonder he charges the Ephesian Christians that they "no longer walk as the Gentiles also walk ... alienated from the life of God" (Eph. 4:17, 18). They have been reconciled. "And you, being in the time past alienated and enemies in your mind in your evil works, yet now hath he reconciled" (Col. 1:21, 22). The ministry of reconciliation is the all-important thing. "But all things are of God, who reconciled us to himself through Christ, and gave unto us the ministry of reconciliation; to wit, that God was in Christ reconciling the world unto himself, not reckoning unto them their trespasses, and having committed unto us the word of reconciliation. We are ambassadors therefore on behalf of Christ, as though God were entreating by us: we beseech you on behalf of Christ, be ye reconciled to God" (II Cor. 5:18-20). Paul's other great passage on this theme is found in Romans: "For if, while we were enemies, we were reconciled to God through the death of his Son, much more, being reconciled, shall we be saved by his life; and not only so, but we also rejoice in God through our Lord Jesus Christ, through whom we have now received the reconciliation" (5:10, 11). (The King James Version does not translate this last word with "reconciliation," as it does in II Corinthians 5:18, 19, but translates it with "atonement." The word "reconciliation," used consistently, would be preferable.)

(2) GOD THE RECONCILER

God is the subject of reconciliation; man is the object of reconciliation. God does the reconciling, and man is the one who is reconciled; it is the latter whose attitude is basically changed. From the preceding Pauline passages it becomes at once apparent

12 Stewart, *op. cit.*, pp. 204-5.

that there is none of the opposite idea, that God stands in need of being reconciled. Nor is there even a third idea, that it is a mutual thing, both God and man being reconciled, as would be the case due to a mutual resentment between two earthly parties. Here both parties would be reconciled, and both would do the reconciling. But not so as between God and man; for God, due to his constant love, takes the initiative, breaks into man's hostility, and throws down every barrier to an enduring and marvelous relationship. Here, as in every phase of man's becoming a child of God, God takes the initiative; man merely responds.

The view that God must be reconciled and that man takes the initiative in doing so is found in pagan creeds and pagan religions. Here man attempts to appease an angry god who is looking the other way. He endeavors to restore the favor of his god by cajoling or flattering persuasion, thus attempting to make the deity perform what he himself desires or wills, not what the deity might will. This in most cases the devotee seeks to do by weird dances, incantations, and witchcraft. The view that it is a mutual thing, both God and man being reconciled, occurs here and there in the writings of Christian theologians. W. T. Conner seems to have been inclined toward this opinion. "A question that arises in regard to reconciliation is whether man's reconciliation to God consists in the removal of man's enmity toward God, or whether it is the removal of God's displeasure toward man, or whether it is both. It is evidently both." He bases such a view upon his belief that reconciliation and justification are synonymous. In fact he places more emphasis upon the change in God than upon the change in man. "Doubtless it is meant to describe a mutual transaction, but the emphasis seems to be on the removal of God's displeasure in the non-imputation of sin."[13] J. Denney, in his *The Doctrine of Reconciliation,* also assumes the view that in a certain sense God too is reconciled. The reader is referred to James S. Stewart's *A Man in Christ,* pp. 212-221, for a strong refutation of such an outlook.

Yet, when we say that man is reconciled and not God, we are not maintaining that God's feelings toward the one being reconciled are not altered. It is true that God is *not* appeased, for he takes the initiative; yet God is affected when man, no longer a rebel, becomes one of his own. Would not this be inevitable in such personal factors as estrangement and reconciliation? Man's sin and man's rebellious nature certainly affect God; would not man's being restored to God's fellowship affect him also? This is what is taught in the three parables in the fifteenth chapter of

---

13 Conner, *op. cit.,* p. 210.

Luke: one of a lost sheep, one of a lost coin, and one of a lost son. Each parable portrays the same point: there is rejoicing in heaven when even one sinner repents and turns to God in faith. Since reconciliation is a personal thing, all persons involved are affected.

5. REGENERATION

(1) MEANING OF THE TERM

Regeneration, a term borrowed from the family, is also called the new birth, spiritual birth, and birth from above. It means begetting or generating again. "Regeneration may be defined as the change wrought by the Spirit of God, by the use of truth as a means, in which the moral disposition of the soul is renewed in the image of Christ."[14] Another definition is the following: "Regeneration is that act of God by which the governing disposition of the soul is made holy, and by which through the truth as a means, the first holy exercise of this disposition is secured."[15] It is the divine side of that which, when viewed from the human, we call conversion. It is God's turning of the repentant sinner to himself, with the sinful nature not completely eradicated but its power broken. Sin no longer dominates the life, for it has been thrust from the center to the circumference; Christ has now taken the central place and reigns within. There has been a recreating in the image of Christ.

(2) SCRIPTURAL TEACHING

Regeneration is a doctrine that is uniformly taught throughout the New Testament, being found in the Synoptics, John, Paul, and Peter. Jesus says that the pure in heart shall see God (Matt. 5:8); however, one becomes pure in heart only through God's transformation. Our Lord also says that one finds his life by losing it (Matt. 10:39), but this in turn involves the moral and spiritual renewal found only in regeneration. Yet it is the Fourth Gospel that abounds in this doctrine, with the third chapter being the classic passage. Jesus informs Nicodemus that the natural man cannot be a part of the kingdom, that a complete spiritual change is necessary. "Verily, verily, I say unto thee, Except one be born anew, he cannot see the kingdom of God" (3:3). The Greek word *anōthen,* translated "anew," could just as well have been translated "from above," thus designating not only a rebirth but depicting the source of this rebirth, God himself. "Verily, verily,

---

14 Edgar Y. Mullins, *The Christian Religion in Its Doctrinal Expression,* p. 378.
15 Augustus H. Strong, *Systematic Theology,* p. 809.

I say unto thee, Except one be born of water and the Spirit, he cannot enter into the kingdom of God" (3:5). Jesus then contrasts the natural birth with the spiritual birth. "That which is born of the flesh is flesh; and that which is born of the Spirit is spirit" (3:6). These two births are quite antithetical, each with its own resultant. In the prologue of this great gospel we find the same teaching. "But as many as received him, to them gave he the right to become children of God, even to them that believe on his name: who were born, not of blood, nor of the will of the flesh, nor of the will of man, but of God" (1:12, 13). Here we not only learn that God effects the new birth but that it is conditioned upon faith —"as many as received him."

Paul also has somewhat to say relative to the new birth. Christianity not only involves the remission of past sins, but the power to avoid their repetition. "The Christian does not desire freedom to sin; what he has been craving is freedom from sin. Salvation involves not merely exemption from the consequences of sin but deliverance from slavery to the power of sin itself." [16] There must be victory over iniquitous power in the flesh now, which involves a transformation of human nature. This transformation Paul describes by means of various metaphors, one of which is a new creation. "Wherefore if any man is in Christ, he is a new creature: the old things are passed away; behold, they are become new" (II Cor. 5:17). ("Creation" is a better translation than "creature.") Another metaphor used by Paul is the resurrected life. "And you did he make alive, when ye were dead through your trespasses and sins" (Eph. 2:1). "If then ye were raised together with Christ, seek the things that are above, where Christ is.... For ye died, and your life is hid with Christ in God" (Col. 3:1-3). "We were buried therefore with him through baptism into death; that like as Christ was raised from the dead through the glory of the Father, so we also might walk in newness of life" (Rom. 6:4). Another metaphor is that of a new man, for he exhorts "that ye put away, as concerning your former manner of life, the old man, that waxeth corrupt after the lusts of deceit; and that ye be renewed in the spirit of your mind, and put on the new man, that after God hath been created in righteousness and holiness of truth" (Eph. 4:22-24). Still another metaphor is that of being crucified with Christ. "I have been crucified with Christ; and it is no longer I that live, but Christ liveth in me" (Gal. 2:20).

The Greek word *palingenesia*, translated "regeneration," seemingly the favorite designation for this great doctrine, occurs in only one place in the New Testament as used with reference to the re-

16 Millar Burrows, *An Outline of Biblical Theology*, p. 184.

generation of the individual, Titus 3:5: "according to his mercy he saved us, through the washing of regeneration and renewing of the Holy Spirit." Peter, however, uses the verb form, "begotten again," when he speaks of our "having been begotten again, not of corruptible seed, but of incorruptible, through the word of God, which liveth and abideth" (I Pet. 1:23). He also reminds us that God "begat us again unto a living hope by the resurrection of Jesus Christ from the dead" (I Pet. 1:3).

(3) PERTINENT FACTS

From the foregoing passages certain facts are adduced relative to regeneration.

a. *A moral and spiritual change*

It is a radical change in the inmost principle of life. Notice that Jesus says to Nicodemus, "born anew"... not "altered," "reconditioned," "influenced," "reformed," "reinvigorated." There is a new beginning resulting in a new stamp of character. The very springs of action in a man are changed, so that evil is shunned instinctively and the good and pure are sought. The fundamental governing disposition is no longer the same, for God works at the very basis of character and not on the outer edge. The affections of life no longer center in self but in Christ, and love for God and fellow man becomes the dominating motive in life. The spiritual fiber is so altered that one cannot again rest in a life of sin. This is the very teaching of First John. "Whosoever is begotten of God doeth no sin, because his seed abideth in him: and he cannot sin, because he is begotten of God" (3:9). He cannot make sin his way of life; he cannot habitually sin as he formerly did. This meaning is easily discerned in the Greek, for John uses the present tense of continuous action and not the aorist tense of punctiliar action. He is not teaching sinless perfection but is talking about a habit of daily living.

b. *Indispensable to salvation*

Regeneration is absolutely necessary to salvation. Jesus tells Nicodemus not to marvel that he says, "Ye *must* be born again" (John 3:7); and this he affirms in reference to his previous statements that only the man who has experienced the new birth can see or enter the kingdom of God. Paul avows that "neither is circumcision anything, nor uncircumcision, but a new creature" (Gal. 6:15). Both Gentile and Jew must experience the new birth. Years before the advent of our Lord the prophet Jeremiah came to the realization that only God's transformation can change a man. "Can the Ethiopian change his skin, or the leopard his spots?

then may ye also do good, that are accustomed to do evil" (13:23).
Only when the moral and spiritual disposition of a man's soul is
modified by regeneration is he fit for relationship with God.
Holiness is an absolute must for one to live in a right relation to
God, to self, to others, and to holy things; and this holiness is
achieved only in regeneration.

c. Wrought by the Holy Spirit

The Spirit of God effects the new birth. "Except one be born of
water and the Spirit, he cannot enter into the kingdom of God. That
which is born of the flesh is flesh; and that which is born of the
Spirit is spirit" (John 3:5, 6). Paul declares that we are saved
"through the washing of regeneration and renewing of the Holy
Spirit" (Titus 3:5). The change that is produced is so marvelous
that only divine power is able to produce it. This is not only revealed in Scripture but is borne out in Christian experience as
well. Jesus informs Nicodemus that this new birth is "from above"
(meaning of Greek term in John 3:3 and 3:7). John categorically
states that believers are those "who were born, not of blood,
nor of the will of the flesh, nor of the will of man, but of God"
(1:13). To be "born of blood" would be by natural descent. But
the physical birth, not the spiritual, is effected in this manner. To
be "born of the will of man" would be by human nature on its
higher side. The Pelagians made this mistake years ago when they
affirmed that regeneration is solely the act of man and is identical
with self-reformation. To be "born of the will of the flesh" would
be by human nature on its lower side. Therefore we see that none
of these last three will effect the new birth. Some even maintain that
truth as a system of motives is the direct cause of regeneration,
definitely a non-biblical idea. The immediate and personal agency
of the Holy Spirit is the efficient cause of regeneration, for the
power which regenerates is none other than the power of God himself.

d. Truth the instrumentality, not baptism

When we say that the Holy Spirit is the agent of the change
effected in regeneration, we are not maintaining that the divine
Spirit does this work without any instrumentality. The means, or
instrumentality, employed is the truth of the gospel. The Spirit is
the agent; truth is the means. Peter speaks of the believer as "having been begotten again, not of corruptible seed, but of incorruptible, through the word of God, which liveth and abideth" (I
Pet. 1:23). Jesus tells his disciples, "Already ye are clean because
of the word which I have spoken unto you" (John 15:3). Paul
talks very dramatically of "the sword of the Spirit, which is the

word of God" (Eph. 6:17). The Holy Spirit does not illuminate the truth; he illuminates the mind that it might grasp the truth. As the mind of the sinner is brought into contact with the revealed Word, God completes his regenerating work.

6. SANCTIFICATION

(1) MEANING OF THE TERM

If reconciliation is something Christ accomplishes for us, sanctification is something he accomplishes in us. If justification is God declaring and making righteous, sanctification is God making holy. The Greek word *hagiasmos,* translated "sanctification," denotes the act of making holy. The verb is *hagiazō,* meaning "I sanctify," or "I hallow," or "I make holy." The adjective is *hagios,* meaning "sanctified," "hallowed," or "holy." When the adjective is used as a noun (something much more common in Greek than in English), it is translated "saint," meaning holy one, or sanctified one. A saint is one who has been sanctified, or made holy; therefore every Christian is a saint. To be holy means to be consecrated, dedicated, or set aside to God. Therefore sanctification denotes consecration or dedication to God. If this may seem to be objective in nature, there is a subjective element in sanctification also. The ethical idea is connoted by the term, for sanctification also implies that which is righteous and pure. The sanctified one possesses a power over sin that is endued by the presence of the Spirit. The sanctified one has been transferred from the domain of the flesh, with its evil impulses, to the domain of the Spirit, with Christlike impulses.

In the Old Testament things were sanctified, which meant simply that they were dedicated to the service of the Lord. This of course did not carry with it the ethical idea, for things are nonethical. Included in such a category were the tabernacle, the temple, the ark of the covenant, the vessels of the temple, the tithe, the Sabbath, etc. But when applied to God's people it connoted the ethical. Since God's being is ethically righteous, man, in order to be sanctified to his service, must be righteous also. What is said here applies to the New Testament as well as the Old, for in the former the Greek term for sanctification also expresses both the new relation to the Lord and the corresponding new character.

"And God blessed the seventh day, and hallowed it" (Gen. 2:3). "Put off thy shoes from off thy feet, for the place whereon thou standest is holy ground" (Exod. 3:5). "And Jehovah said unto Moses, Go unto the people, and sanctify them to-day and to-morrow..." (Exod. 19:10). "The sons of Amram: Aaron and Moses; and Aaron was separated, that he should sanctify the most holy things, he and his sons, for ever" (I Chron. 23:13). "And I will sanctify my great name, which hath been profaned among the nations, which ye have profaned in the midst of them; and the nations shall know that I am Jehovah, saith the Lord Jehovah, when I shall be sanctified in you before their eyes" (Ezek. 36:23). "For I am Jehovah your God: sanctify yourselves therefore, and be ye holy; for I am holy" (Lev. 11:44). These passages from the Old Testament depict the view of sanctification just explained, that both things and people are sanctified; but when people are considered, the ethical element also enters in.

In the New Testament the word sanctify carries with it both meanings: set aside to the service of God and therefore belonging to him (consecration), and also becoming holy inwardly (purity). And the idea of sanctification is present in the New Testament even where the words sanctify or sanctification are not specifically used. The whole Sermon on the Mount (Matt. 5-7) is an expression of righteousness in the kingdom, and therefore of sanctification. "Ye therefore shall be perfect, as your heavenly Father is perfect" (Matt. 5:48). When Paul asks the Roman Christians to present their bodies as a "living sacrifice" (Rom. 12:1) unto God, he is thinking of consecration, and with this he links up the fact that they are to be "transformed" in mind also. He states, "Even so reckon ye also yourselves to be dead unto sin, but alive unto God in Christ Jesus" (Rom. 6:11). The believers are to "walk by the Spirit" (Gal. 5:16, 25). They are to "put off the old man" and "put on the new man" (Col. 3:9, 10). The writer of Hebrews dwells on the idea of sanctification. "For if the blood of goats and bulls, and the ashes of a heifer sprinkling them that have been defiled, sanctify unto the cleanness of the flesh: how much more shall the blood of Christ, who through the eternal Spirit offered himself without blemish unto God, cleanse your conscience from dead works to serve the living God" (9:13, 14). "By which will we have been sanctified through the offering of the body of Jesus Christ once for all" (10:10). "For by one offering he hath perfected for ever them that are sanctified" (10:14). Paul calls the believers, in various churches to which he writes, "the saints" (Rom. 1:7; I Cor. 1:2; II Cor. 1:1; Eph. 1:1; Col. 1:2). These "saints" are the ones who have been sanctified.

(2) TWO PHASES OF SANCTIFICATION

According to the Scriptures sanctification is both positional (or initial) and progressive (or developmental). It occurs at the beginning of the Christian life, at which time one becomes a saint, or holy in nature. The English word saint translates a Greek adjective (holy) used as a noun, a very common occurrence in the Greek language. Therefore the term saint means a holy one, or one who has been sanctified or hallowed. Sanctification occurs at the same time that regeneration, justification, etc., occur, and, like these other great phases of the total picture of redemption, is effected by the faith of the believer and through the work of the Holy Spirit. Faith is the means and the Spirit of God is the agent. In this initial act one enters a new status of being set aside to the service of God and at the same time experiences the unfolding of the germ implanted in regeneration. This is positional sanctification, and is the element to which most of the scriptural passages (such as the ones already reviewed) apply.

But there is also the progressive phase of sanctification, which has to do with the developmental purification of the soul. The already redeemed soul becomes "more holy." Moral character is attained through constant struggle. We work out what God has worked in us, and we respond to what has been implanted by the Holy Spirit. Thus we see that sanctification is a continuing thing, a life process not attained in a bound. It is slow, thus leading to discouragements. It may be retarded by backsliding and negligence of the Christian life. But one is encouraged by the fact that, being now a partaker of divine strength, he has an endless panorama of growth opening before him. Therefore growth should never cease. This continuous process extends through life, being perfected only in the life to come.

The passage that most nearly depicts the progressive phase of sanctification is as follows: "And the God of peace himself sanctify you wholly; and may your spirit and soul and body be preserved entire, without blame at the coming of our Lord Jesus Christ" (I Thess. 5:23). Another pertinent passage is in Hebrews. "Follow after peace with all men, and the sanctification without which no man shall see the Lord" (12:14). This is also the idea Paul has in mind when he admonishes Timothy, "Fight the good [kalon, honorable, noble] fight of the faith" (I Tim. 6:12).

(3) ERRONEOUS VIEWS OF SANCTIFICATION

a. *Antinomian*

This view is refuted by Paul in the Roman letter. Certain men argued that Christians ought to sin, for where sin abounds grace abounds more exceedingly. Therefore the more one sins the more God's grace will abound in forgiving that sin, and abounding grace is what is desired most of all. Paul answers such abortive thinking in the sixth chapter of Romans and illustrates his refutal with three pictures: baptism, slavery, and marriage. This view illustrates the error of taking the part for the whole. It is based on the conception of salvation as a merely commercial transaction rather than a union of the soul with Christ in which there is a radical break with sin.

b. *Perfectionist*

It is held by some that the Christian can actually attain sinless perfection in this life, that he can live above sin. The scriptural passages that, on the surface, seem to teach this are as follows: "Ye therefore shall be perfect, as your heavenly Father is perfect" (Matt. 5:48). "Let us press on unto perfection" (Heb. 6:1). "And let patience have its perfect work, that ye may be perfect and entire, lacking in nothing" (Jas. 1:4). "Whosoever abideth in him sinneth not: whosoever sinneth hath not seen him, neither knoweth him" (I John 3:6). "Whosoever is begotten of God doeth no sin, because his seed abideth in him: and he cannot sin, because he is begotten of God (I John 3:9).

These passages fall into two groups: those involving the term "perfect" and those involving the term "sinneth not." The Greek word *teleios,* translated "perfect," means full grown, mature, complete; it does not connote the idea of without blemish. It denotes the fact of functionability due to maturity and does not refer to sinlessness. The Greek verb in the phrase "sinneth not," as found in I John 3:6, is in the present tense in Greek, which is that of continuous action and not punctiliar action. Therefore these verses should properly read "does not continue in sin." Besides, there are other verses in First John that completely knock out the idea of sinless perfection. "If we say that we have not sinned, we make him a liar, and his word is not in us" (1:10). "And if any man sin, we have an Advocate with the Father, Jesus Christ the righteous" (2:1). The very book of the Bible upon which the sinless perfectionist most heavily leans, First John, eliminates entirely any such theory.

Sinless perfection can never be achieved in this life. Yet at the same time this should be the goal of all Christians, regardless of the impossibility of attainment; and there should be no thought of discouragement. Also, what is called perfection is *not* perfection; it is merely some stage of the Christian life on the road to perfection. The so-called "second blessing" is often mistaken for the perfection itself, but is far from it. There ought to be many, many such blessings in the life of every Christian.

c. *Romanist*

The Roman Catholic Church, in an act termed canonization, names as a "saint" some prominent deceased person. After he has passed on to the next life the term saint is added to his name in a formal process of the church. That name is then placed on the list of saints of the Roman Church, the Canon Sanctorum. Hence we find such terminology as St. Mark, St. Matthew, St. Mary, St. Joseph, St. Anthony, *et al.* The titles to the books of the New Testament as found in the. King James Version constitute a carry-over from this Roman Catholic procedure.

This act of canonization is contrary to biblical truth. If one is not a saint in this world he cannot be made so in the next world by a decree of the church. Also, if only a relatively few, and those very prominent ones, reach sainthood, what about the vast majority of Christians? Where do they stand relative to sanctification? And what does this do to the term saint as used repeatedly by Paul in his epistles regarding Christians here on earth?

7. Union with Christ

(1) explicit in new testament

The New Testament definitely teaches a vital union of the believer with Christ which is different from God's natural and providential contact with mankind. It is a union of life in which the human spirit is interpenetrated and vitalized by the Spirit of Christ. The soul becomes one with him, while at the same time possessing its own true distinctiveness. "The relation between two individual personalities cannot be entirely analogous to that between one individual personality and Another who is not only individual personality but also Personality Itself. The relation of two good men to each other must be less close than the relation of a good man to One who is not only good but Goodness, and not only loving but Love."[17]

Jesus has in mind union with him when he declares, "I am the living bread which came down out of heaven: if any man eat of this bread, he shall live for ever" (John 6:51). "He that eateth my flesh and drinketh my blood abideth in me, and I in him" (John 6:56). "In that day ye shall know that I am in my Father, and ye in me, and I in you" (John 14:20). "Abide in me, and I in you. As the branch cannot bear fruit of itself, except it abide in the vine; so neither can ye, except ye abide in me" (John 15:4). "I in them, and thou in me, that they may be perfected into one" (John 17:23). Paul also brings forth this same teaching. "So we, who are many, are one body in Christ, and severally members one of another" (Rom. 12:5). "I have been crucified with Christ; and it is no longer I that live, but Christ liveth in me" (Gal. 2:20). Not only is the believer crucified with Christ; he is risen with him also. "If then ye were raised together with Christ, seek the things that are above" (Col. 3:1). "We were buried therefore with him

---

[17] John Baillie, *Our Knowledge of God*, pp. 238-9.

through baptism into death" (Rom. 6:4). "Wherefore if any man is in Christ, he is a new creature" (II Cor. 5:17). "I know a man in Christ . . ." (II Cor. 12:2). "I can do all things in him that strengtheneth me" (Phil. 4:13). "For to me to live is Christ" (Phil. 1:21).

(2) NATURE OF THIS UNION

a. *A mutual union*

From the above passages, and many others, it is clearly seen that the believer is in Christ and Christ in the believer. ". . . ye in me, and I in you" (John 14:20). ". . . alive unto God in Christ Jesus" (Rom. 6:11). ". . . no condemnation to them that are in Christ Jesus" (Rom. 8:1). "And if Christ is in you . . ." (Rom. 8:10). ". . . Christ liveth in me" (Gal. 2:20). It is a mutual indwelling. Paul's phrase "in Christ" seems to be the very key to his epistles, which is shown in his teaching on baptism. We are "baptized into Christ" (Gal. 3:27). Yet at the same time Christ is in the believer, which is shown in the Lord's Supper. "The bread which we break, is it not a communion of the body of Christ?" (I Cor. 10:16).

b. *A spiritual union*

This union with Christ is a spiritual one, for its source and effector is the Holy Spirit. It is a union of spirit, not of body. In fact all Paul's thinking of Christ is so bound up with his thinking of the Holy Spirit that he seems at times to use these two terms somewhat interchangeably. "But ye are not in the flesh but in the Spirit, if so be that the Spirit of God dwelleth in you. But if any man hath not the Spirit of Christ, he is none of his. And if Christ is in you, the body is dead because of sin; but the spirit is life because of righteousness" (Rom. 8:9, 10). The Holy Spirit originates this union, then maintains it.

c. *An eternal union*

The union of the believer with Christ is for eternity, all of which is according to Christ's promise. Jesus says in the Great Commission, "Lo, I am with you always, even unto the end of the world" (Matt. 28:20). And he also says, "They shall never perish, and no one shall snatch them out of my hand" (John 10:28). Paul affirms, ". . . nor height, nor depth, nor any other creature, shall be able to separate us from the love of God, which is in Christ Jesus our Lord" (Rom. 8:39). Christ's omnipresence makes it perfectly possible that he should be present in every believer, even to the point that it seems to that one that Christ is giving all his time and concern to him. Such a union knows no degree of instability.

d. *A faith union*

As in regeneration, justification, and all other viewpoints of God's great redeeming act, union with Christ is effected by the faith of the believer. "I have been crucified with Christ; and it is no longer I that live, but Christ liveth in me: and that life which I now live in the flesh I live in faith, the faith which is in the Son of God, who loved me, and gave himself up for me" (Gal. 2: 20). Paul informs the Ephesians that he is praying "that Christ may dwell in your hearts through faith" (3:17). A. M. Hunter very aptly states it: "For the act of faith initiates a faith-union between the sinner and his Saviour (Luther likened it to a wedding ring), so that he enters into the virtue of all that Christ has done for him and lives henceforth in vital communion with his living Lord."[18]

e. *A heightening union*

In the experience of union with Christ there is no absorption of the personality of the believer in a pantheistic fashion. The human personality is not impaired or destroyed, nor does it lose its distinctiveness; it is brought into bold relief. The individual powers are heightened to God's desired fruition. The very passage that might, on a superficial view, tend to teach the end of a personal identity is followed immediately by words that allay our fears. "And it is no longer I that live, but Christ liveth in me" (Gal. 2:20). The former half of the sentence is followed by a latter half where the "I" and "Thou" are completely separate in identity. Truly, when one becomes a "man in Christ" he does not cease to be himself. For the first time he "becomes himself," becomes what God intended him primarily to be. Paul's own life is the greatest example of this fact. If anyone were ever Christ-centered it was Paul. But mark the force that his God-filled life had on the lives of men, on churches, on nations! Could anyone say that the Damascus road experience blurred and swallowed up his personality? Every individual trait he possessed beamed with renewed vigor; he had at last come into possession of his true self.

---

[18] A. M. Hunter, *Introducing New Testament Theology*, p. 94.

OUTLINE FOR CHAPTER ELEVEN

I. Assurance of Salvation
  1. Varieties of Christian experience
  2. Holy Spirit and assurance
  3. Lack of assurance
     (1) Possibility of true faith without assurance
     (2) Reasons for lack of assurance
  4. Possibility of false assurance
  5. Requisites to assurance
     (1) Comprehension of basic truths in salvation
     (2) Surrender to Jesus as Lord

II. Security of Salvation
  1. Meaning of the doctrine
  2. Scriptural teaching
     (1) Explicit in certain passages
     (2) Implicit in certain biblical expressions
     (3) Inferred from other doctrines
  3. Objections to the doctrine
     (1) Violates man's freedom
     (2) Encourages immorality
     (3) Tends to spiritual indolence
     (4) Opposite taught in Scriptures
     (5) Actual examples cited

III. Prayer
  1. Varieties of prayer
  2. Purpose of prayer
  3. Scope of prayer
  4. Answer to prayer
     (1) No "unanswered" prayer
     (2) Conditions for answered prayer

IV. Mission of the Christian
  1. Exemplify Christian righteousness
  2. Ascertain and fulfill will of God
  3. Lead others into saving knowledge of God
  4. Perform works of benevolence
  5. Bring forth "fruits of the Spirit"

V. Growth in grace
  1. Biblical demand for growth
  2. Enemies of growth
     (1) Force within

    (2) Forces without
       a. Prince of this world
       b. World
       c. Perfection theory
  3. Aids to growth
  4. Goal of growth

CHAPTER ELEVEN

CONTINUANCE IN THE CHRISTIAN LIFE

NOW THAT WE HAVE SEEN SOMETHING OF HOW ONE ENTERS THE Christian life and becomes a child of God, let us look into the experiences one receives as a Christian. What is involved in living in fellowship with God?

I. ASSURANCE OF SALVATION

1. VARIETIES OF CHRISTIAN EXPERIENCE

All Christian experiences are not alike. Some are more emotional than others. Some are more cataclysmic than others. One who is stained and scarred with the devastating effects of sin would have a somewhat different experience in becoming a Christian than would a little child reared in a devout Christian home. The older one becomes the harder it is to break from iniquitous practices and to enter a life with God; the struggle of such a one before finally surrendering would not compare with the simple yielding of a nine- or ten-year-old child. Varying social, economic, and educational backgrounds would call for varying experiences. There are as many diversities of experiences as there are diversities of human personalities. Lydia, living in Philippi, surely did not have the same experience as the Philippian jailer (Acts 16). Billy Sunday did not have an experience identical with that of Helen Keller.

Yet, in all these varieties of spiritual experience the basic fundamental elements remain the same. In each case there is faith and there is repentance; there is justification and there is regeneration; there is sanctification and there is adoption. The willing acceptance of the grace of God brings joy, peace, and assurance to the soul. This is the normal way: a conscious fellowship with God in which the redeemed individual can gloriously sing, "Blessed assurance, Jesus is mine; Oh, what a foretaste of glory divine."

2. HOLY SPIRIT AND ASSURANCE

As one comes under the influence of the gospel he undergoes an acute consciousness of sin. This consciousness, called conviction, is produced by the Holy Spirit (John 16:8). The Holy Spirit witnesses to the unsaved that he is *not* a child of God. Then the Spirit produces regeneration, or works within the believer what

Christ has done objectively for him (John 3:5). The next work of the Spirit is to bear witness to the saved one that he is now a child of God. "The Spirit himself beareth witness with our spirit, that we are children of God: and if children, then heirs; heirs of God, and joint-heirs with Christ" (Rom. 8:16, 17). This is the inner testimony to the Christian that he *is* a child of God. The witness of the Spirit to the non-believer is conviction; the witness of the Spirit to the believer is assurance.

3. LACK OF ASSURANCE

(1) POSSIBILITY OF TRUE FAITH WITHOUT ASSURANCE

There are cases of those who have been genuinely born again but who do not possess the comforting consciousness of being a child of God. The ground of faith is the external word of promise, while the ground of assurance, as has been stated, is the internal witness of the Spirit that we have fulfilled God's conditions of redemption. Therefore the witness of the Spirit is a strengthening of faith to the point that one no longer is plagued by doubt. This witness does not constitute a new revelation; it is but the augmenting of an already existing faith. Paul, in speaking of Abraham, says, "...yet, looking unto the promise of God, he wavered not through unbelief, but waxed strong through faith, giving glory to God, and being fully assured that what he had promised, he was able also to perform" (Rom. 4:20, 21).

So even though it is the privilege of the redeemed one to know that he is saved, it is possible that he may be saved and not have the corresponding assurance. This is explicitly set forth in the Johannine writings. John says that he wrote his gospel in order that men may have eternal life by believing in Jesus as the Christ, the Son of God (John 20:31). Then he says that he wrote the first of his epistles that the believer may *know* that he has this life (I John 5:13). "It is important to distinguish saving faith from assurance of faith, for the reason that lack of assurance is taken by so many real Christians as evidence that they know nothing of this grace of God. To use once more a well-worn illustration: it is getting into the boat that saves us, and not our comfortable feelings about the boat. What saves us is faith *in Christ,* not faith in *our* faith, or faith in *the* faith."[1]

(2) REASONS FOR LACK OF ASSURANCE

What reasons may be deduced for lack of assurance on the part of a believer? Sometimes there may be sin or impurity in the life, obscuring the feeling of assurance. This sin has a neutralizing effect in the life of the believer. Sometimes the lack of assurance is due

---

[1] Augustus H. Strong, *Systematic Theology,* p. 845.

to one's not receiving the experience expected. He had preconceived feelings and sensations to be derived from his acceptance of Christ. Since these did not materialize as anticipated he now doubts his conversion. Sometimes this lack of assurance may result from his unsuccessful attempt to work out God's plan for his life. Since he has failed to perform God's will his guilt is confused with lack of assurance. Sometimes his lack may be due to spiritual perplexities, such as why the righteous suffer, or why God seemingly does not answer his prayers. These perplexing problems appear to have no answer, all of which is confused with a lack of assurance.

4. POSSIBILITY OF FALSE ASSURANCE

It is possible for a person to think that he is saved when he is not, thus leading to false assurance. Jesus makes this apparent at the conclusion of the Sermon on the Mount, when he states, "Not every one that saith unto me, Lord, Lord, shall enter into the kingdom of heaven; but he that doeth the will of my Father who is in heaven. Many will say to me in that day, Lord, Lord, did we not prophesy by thy name, and by thy name cast out demons, and by thy name do many mighty works? And then will I profess unto them, I never knew you: depart from me, ye that work iniquity" (Matt. 7:21-23). And Jesus evidently wishes to teach this in the parable of the marriage feast and the slighted invitation. To the man not having on a wedding garment the king questions, "Friend, how comest thou in hither not having a wedding-garment?" When the man is unable to reply the king commands the servants, "Bind him hand and foot, and cast him out into the outer darkness; there shall be the weeping and the gnashing of teeth. For many are called, but few chosen" (Matt. 22:11-14). According to our Lord there must be those who think they have fulfilled the conditions of salvation when they have not. A false sense of security rests in place of a true redeemed-Redeemer relationship.

5. REQUISITES TO ASSURANCE

What, then, are the spiritual requirements for a satisfying assurance?

(1) COMPREHENSION OF BASIC TRUTHS IN SALVATION

One must know and understand that all men are lost, that he at one time was lost, that Christ not only has saved him but is the only means of salvation, that faith in Christ who died in his place is the means of accepting God's grace, etc. These and other basic truths must be understood and personally accepted by the believer. This is not to maintain that he must be an expert in the field of theology and biblical interpretation. Nor does it mean that he must assent to certain dogmas in some ancient and humanly devised creed. It means that these basic truths, truths so simple that a small child is able to comprehend, must be understood.

(2) SURRENDER TO JESUS AS LORD

There must be a definite surrender to Jesus as Lord, which surrender will carry with it the eradicating power of a new affection. This new affection, Christ, will replace the love for the old sins and disobediences, and, at the same time, the guilt that accompanies them. A captivating consecration to our Lord leaves little time for agitation over lack of assurance.

II. SECURITY OF SALVATION

Many questions are asked relative to whether or not a Christian can, or will, persist in the Christian life. Is it possible for the life implanted in regeneration to fail or be extinguished?

1. MEANING OF THE DOCTRINE

This doctrine states that all who are united to Christ by faith will continue in a state of grace eternally. It is known as "eternal security of the believer," and "final perseverance of the saints," being opposite to the belief commonly called "falling from grace." It states that all who are united with God in Christ will be so forever and ever.

There are two extremes of thought deviating from this position. One is held by those who say they believe in the doctrine but who have really perverted it, maintaining that one is justified and is eternally safe regardless of what he may become in his person and character. But this is not so, for the New Testament never says that a man is saved irrespective of what he may become in character. He is saved eternally because the justifying, sanctifying, and regenerating power of God so completely changes him that he will never revert to his old way of life. Nor does the New Testament say that one will be saved whether or not he persists in faith, but that he will persist in faith and therefore be eternally saved.

The other extreme of thought opposing this position is that one may "fall from grace," that is, he may be saved at one time in life and then not saved subsequently. The author himself has heard more than one person remark, "I used to be a Christian." This view maintains that a Christian is free either to continue in grace or fall from it. His spiritual destiny lies entirely in his own hands, and he can turn in either direction at any time and at his own will. The former extreme takes the whole thing out of human hands entirely and is that fostered by the extreme Calvinists. The latter extreme makes human effort everything and is that fostered by the Arminians.

The true view lies in combining the extremes, for both the New Testament and Christian experience testify that the divine and the human aspects are vitally related to each other. Does not God take the initiative always? Does not the shepherd go to seek the lost sheep? And yet at the same time the lost son in a far country had to repent. So the lost one is more than merely a sheep; he is one who must respond. Paul admonishes us to work out our own salvation, but at the same time he affirms that God is working in us to effect his purposes and will (Phil. 2:12, 13). There is a sense in which God keeps, and there is a sense in which man keeps himself. The former is in John 17:11, 12: "Keep them in thy name. ...I kept them in thy name.... I guarded them, and not one of them perished, but the son of perdition." The latter is in I John 5:18: "he that was begotten of God keepeth himself." Just as John expresses both these ideas, so Jude expresses both also. "Now unto him that is able to guard you from stumbling..." (24). "...keep yourselves in the love of God..." (21).

God deals, and has always dealt, with man in a moral and personal way. "He does not preserve us by irresistible grace as by something which overrides our will, but by constraining grace which enlists our will. He does not preserve us in spite of transgressions and backslidings, but by renewing us unto repentance for sins and return from backslidings. His method is not that of the pantheistic view in which God's will is everything and man's nothing. Nor is it the method of the deistic view which exalts the human will to the chief place and reduces that of God to the minimum. It is the method rather which is in harmony with Christian theism. The personal God deals with personal man in a free personal manner."[2]

2. Scriptural teaching

(1) explicit in certain passages

Jesus says of his sheep that "they shall never perish, and no one shall snatch them out of my hand. My Father, who hath given them unto me, is greater than all; and no one is able to snatch them out of the Father's hand" (John 10:28, 29). Paul asserts the doctrine when, in speaking of God, he says that "whom he foreordained, them he also called: and whom he called, them he also justified: and whom he justified, them he also glorified" (Rom. 8: 30). He reaffirms this a few verses later. "For I am persuaded, that neither death, nor life, nor angels, nor principalities, nor things present, nor things to come, nor powers, nor height, nor depth, nor any other creature, shall be able to separate us from the love of God, which is in Christ Jesus our Lord" (8:38, 39). Also in Romans

---

2 Edgar Y. Mullins, *The Christian Religion in Its Doctrinal Expression*, p. 437.

he declares, "For the gifts and the calling of God are not repented of" (11:29). And in Philippians he states "that he who began a good work in you will perfect it until the day of Jesus Christ" (1:6), an avowal pregnant with confidence. The same assurance is found in the assertion: "I know him whom I have believed, and I am persuaded that he is able to guard that which I have committed unto him against that day" (II Tim. 1:12). An excellent affirmation of this same truth is in I Peter: "...who by the power of God are guarded through faith unto a salvation ready to be revealed in the last time" (1:5).

(2) IMPLICIT IN CERTAIN BIBLICAL EXPRESSIONS

The predominant term in the Gospel of John for depicting salvation is "life," or "eternal life," as it is sometimes called; the adjective "eternal" would denote the enduring quality of that life. John uses the present tense verb in conjunction with the term eternal life: "He that believeth on the Son hath eternal life" (John 3:36). The believer possesses eternal life here and now, as well as in the realm beyond. Therefore we are justified in maintaining that this significant term carries with it the implication that a Christian is as secure in his redemption now, here on earth, as he will be from physical death on. The eternal applies both to the *now* and to the *later*.

Paul talks of being "sealed" in the Spirit. The Ephesian Christians were "sealed with the Holy Spirit of promise" (Eph. 1:13); they were "sealed unto the day of redemption" in the Holy Spirit (Eph. 4:30). Just as the intercession of Jesus guarantees our eternal security, so the Holy Spirit's "sealing" is also God's promise that our salvation will be maintained here on earth and completed with the final resurrection of the body. Not only does the Spirit bear witness to the fact that we have been accepted of God; he also bears witness that we are "heirs of God, and joint-heirs with Christ" (Rom. 8:16, 17).

Paul also resorts to another term with which to depict this same thought. He affirms that this "sealing" of the Spirit "is an earnest of our inheritance, unto the redemption of God's own possession, unto the praise of his glory" (Eph. 1:14). He says it is God "who also sealed us, and gave us the earnest of the Spirit in our hearts" (II Cor. 1:22). "Now he that wrought us for this very thing is God, who gave unto us the earnest of the Spirit" (II Cor. 5:5). The Greek term translated "earnest" means pledge money, that which is put forward as a guarantee of a contract or trade agreement. The Holy Spirit's presence within us is God's guarantee that we shall enter into our inheritance at the eschaton, or final day.

(3) INFERRED FROM OTHER DOCTRINES

Certain other doctrines clearly infer the spiritual security of the believer. Union with Christ is a guarantee that the new life found in him is eternal in scope. He becomes our life, our everything; and because he lives, we shall live also (John 14:19). The one living within us is greater than the one who is in the world (I John 4:4). Election shows God's desire to bestow upon his chosen ones the influence of his Spirit in both saving them and in securing them. Regeneration effects a new creation, which is declared in justification and maintained in sanctification. Adoption also carries with it the idea of eternal security; for spiritual sonship to God would involve even a greater bond than physical sonship to mortal man, and who can revoke his physical birth? Would not God be even truer to his spiritual child? Christ's heavenly intercession for the Christian also bears great weight in this regard. The ground of our spiritual safety lies in the fact Jesus never ceases to intercede in behalf of his own. "Wherefore also he is able to save to the uttermost them that draw near unto God through him, seeing he ever liveth to make intercession for them" (Heb. 7:25). Jesus saves completely, on through life, to the very end.

3. OBJECTIONS TO THE DOCTRINE

There are some who argue against the doctrine of the eternal security of the believer, saying that it is possible for the new life begotten in regeneration to perish. Some of their arguments, with the appropriate answers, are as follows.

(1) VIOLATES MAN'S FREEDOM

It is maintained that this doctrine is inconsistent with man's freedom, that he has the right to choose to be, or not to be, a Christian at any time. But we answer by saying that it is no more so than election, or God's omniscience, or God's omnipotence. These do not violate man's freedom; nor does the fact that the true Christian is one eternally. Is this objection not based upon a misunderstanding? We are not saying that a man is saved whether he wants to be or not — far from it! We are saying that his whole being will be so revolutionized by God's redemptive process that he will choose to remain "in Christ" and thus be saved. To repent and to exercise faith, and so be converted, does not interfere with one's freedom; if, then, to cast off the serfdom of sin and to experience the glorious freedom of the sons of light does not interfere with man's freedom, why should the continuance of life in Christ do so? The radical change wrought by regeneration, justification, sanctification, and adoption should always be kept in mind when considering the idea of eternal security.

(2) ENCOURAGES IMMORALITY

It is said that this doctrine encourages one to a life of sin. If one has perfect assurance of salvation then he is at liberty to live in any manner that he desires. But such cannot be, for we have seen that this doctrine is predicated upon the fact that God saves men by seeing that they possess a completely new nature. It is concerned with the regenerate only, those whose natures have been so renewed in Christ's image that they are no longer content to rest again in sin. The regenerated man will conquer sin due to the indwelling Christ. "Howbeit the firm foundation of God standeth, having this seal, The Lord knoweth them that are his: and, Let every one that nameth the name of the Lord depart from unrighteousness" (II Tim. 2:19). From this statement of the Apostle Paul, in which he twice quotes from the Hebrew Scriptures, are discerned two factors: God's wisdom and purpose in salvation, and man's activity in holy living fulfilling that purpose. Thus we see that if God saves a man he saves him forever, for he will not revert to his old life of continuance in sin. God does this by virtue of the fact that he has placed within man an imperishable life, a guarantee that he will persevere in faith and will therefore conquer sin.

(3) TENDS TO SPIRITUAL INDOLENCE

It is declared that this doctrine encourages a life "at ease in Zion." One has merely to sit down and "wait upon the Lord." Works are either minimized or exterminated in spiritual indolence. This, too, is a perversion of the doctrine; for confidence of success does not, for the truly regenerate one, inspire indolence. The devout Christian will want to be active in the business of the kingdom. "For we are his workmanship, created in Christ Jesus for good works, which God afore prepared that we should walk in them" (Eph. 2:10). The very purpose for which we are saved is that we will be diligent for our Lord.

(4) OPPOSITE TAUGHT IN SCRIPTURES

Those of the opposite persuasion firmly believe that the Scriptures teach that one must "hold out faithful" or be lost. But most theologians will agree that the redeemed one must maintain faith or be lost; that is not the point. The point is whether or not there is something in the new nature of the Christian that guarantees his persistence in faith. The true view is that there *is* such in his renewed nature.

Some of the passages that are brought forth in an attempt to teach the possibility of apostasy, or falling away, are the following: "And ye shall be hated of all men for my name's sake: but he that endureth to the end, the same shall be saved" (Mark 13:13). "I buffet my body, and bring it into bondage: lest by any means, after that I have preached to others, I myself should be rejected" (I Cor. 9:27). " . . . by which also ye are saved, if ye hold fast the word which I preached unto you, except ye believed in vain" (I Cor. 15:2). "To him that overcometh, to him will I give to eat of the tree of life, which is in the Paradise of God" (Rev. 2:7). Revelation 2:11, 17, 26 and 3:5, 12, 21 are similar in this respect. So one *must* "hold out faithful" to be saved; but the added fact is also true: there is that vital something in the nature of the new creation that guarantees persistence in faith. Therefore the enumeration of passages teaching the necessity of perseverance in one's faith is not tantamount to proving that one may fall away into reprobation.

Other passages are also brought forward by the opposing side, two of which are in Hebrews. "A man that hath set at nought Moses' law dieth without compassion on the word of two or three witnesses: of how much sorer punishment, think ye, shall he be judged worthy, who hath trodden under foot the Son of God, and hath counted the blood of the covenant wherewith he was sanctified an unholy thing, and hath done despite unto the Spirit of grace" (10:28, 29). But this passage merely speaks of those who have had spiritual enlightenment to understand the truth and have rejected it. They have enjoyed special divine influences but are still unregenerate. The word sanctified is used to speak of an external sanctification, much like that in First Corinthians 7:14: "For the unbelieving husband is sanctified in the wife, and the unbelieving wife is sanctified in the brother." There is no thought here of one becoming a Christian merely by being in physical proximity with his Christian mate; he simply enjoys the overflow of that one's regenerate personality. Likewise is it for the term sanctified in the Hebrews passage under discussion. The second passage in Hebrews is the following: "For as touching those who were once enlightened and tasted of the heavenly gift, and were made partakers of the Holy Spirit, and tasted the good word of God, and the powers of the age to come, and then fell away, it is impossible to renew them again unto repentance; seeing they crucify to themselves the Son of God afresh, and put him to an open shame" (6:4-6). We must realize that salvation is initial, continuing, and ultimate, and that what the author is talking about is not the danger of apostasy in the usual sense of the word. It is the peril of arrested Christian growth whereby one falls short of the expected Christian development in service and in character. The word translated "fell away" is the Greek term *parapesontas,* coming from a verb which has the root idea of falling aside or of deviating from the proper road. Therefore we have the idea of "falling aside from" or "standing off from" Jesus, the very one who seeks to lead the Christian into a richer, fuller experience of what redemption actually entails. It has reference to the growth phase of the Christian life, not to the initial phase. Even the term "crucify afresh," as applied to the Hebrew Christians, means that by their "falling aside" they were identifying themselves with his crucifiers. Thus they were being part and parcel of the attitude which would negate the very purpose of his death.

(5) ACTUAL EXAMPLES CITED

Those who oppose the doctrine of the eternal security of the believer point to what they term actual examples of those who have fallen from grace. Such are Judas and Ananias. But our answer is that these men, though once outwardly reformed, were never inwardly renewed in heart and soul. It is men like David and Peter who, being genuinely children of God, repent when they find themselves ensnared in sin. The true Christian will come back; the one with only a "Christian veneer" will not come back, for he has never possessed the transforming power of Christ.

III. PRAYER

Prayer is basic and fundamental in the life of a Christian, being the very life line itself. It is the communion of the soul with God, spirit with Spirit, the saved with the Saviour. "Prayer is the very sword of the Saints."[3] Prayer is one of the greatest of spiritual realities, for there is "a breath that fleets beyond this iron world, and touches Him that made it."[4] George A. Buttrick maintains that "prayer is a rock staircase to an inviolable sanctuary, a courage to win faithfulness from sand, and a home, even amid earth's changes, in the Eternity of God."[5]

1. VARIETIES OF PRAYER

What are the various factors that enter into prayer? What are the different kinds of prayer? Some prayers may be aspiration after God, a reaching out for God. This was the prayer of the publican in the temple, "God, be thou merciful to me a sinner" (Luke 18:13), and the prayer of the psalmist, "I waited patiently

[3] Francis Thompson, "Health and Holiness."
[4] Alfred Tennyson, "Harold," III, ii.
[5] George A. Buttrick, *Prayer,* p. 23.

for Jehovah; And he inclined unto me, and heard my cry" (40:1).

Another variety of prayer is praise, or adoration, which is the recognition of God's magnificent grace and his holy character. The Psalms are replete with this concept. "Bless Jehovah, O my soul. O Jehovah my God, thou are very great" (104:1). "I will extol thee, my God, O King; And I will bless thy name for ever and ever. Every day will I bless thee; And I will praise thy name for ever and ever. Great is Jehovah, and greatly to be praised; And his greatness is unsearchable" (145:1-3).

Another element that should enter into our prayer life is that of thanksgiving, or gratitude, which is the recognition that God is the source of all our blessings. Is it not true that "every good gift and every perfect gift is from above, coming down from the Father of lights" (Jas. 1:17)? Here is the expression of our indebtedness to God for his goodness to us. "Oh give thanks unto Jehovah; for he is good; For his lovingkindness endureth for ever" (Ps. 118:1). This Psalm was always sung at the passover, and therefore must have been sung by our Lord at his last passover, the crisis period of his life. And at the tomb of Lazarus Jesus lifted up his eyes and exclaimed, "Father, I thank thee that thou heardest me" (John 11:41).

Another great element in prayer is confession. As one grows in grace and nearness to the Lord his sensitivity to sin increases. He sees his own unworthiness in the contrast between his own life and the absolute righteousness of God. Jesus teaches that we are to pray for forgiveness: "And forgive us our debts, as we also have forgiven our debtors" (Matt. 6:12). He praises the publican for pleading his own unworthiness (Luke 18:9ff.). Sin is against the living God, and there is neither peace nor power until the penitential prayer is offered. And even then the picture is not complete, for along with confession there must be resolve, a resolve to mend our blunders and to entrench our wills in a nobler way of life.

Then there is the element of petition in prayer, which, needless to say, becomes the dominant factor for so many people. There seems to be an endless chain of "things" for which to beseech God, thus making "Give me" the recurrent theme. And yet, Jesus himself taught us to pray thus: "Give us this day our daily bread" (Matt. 6:11); "Ask, and it shall be given you; seek, and ye shall find; knock, and it shall be opened unto you" (Matt. 7:7). Our asking, however, must be tempered with caution. "We should not fear to lift our earthly needs before Eternal Eyes, for we are held in Eternal Love; but we should fear the encroachment of a selfish mind. Petition is defended against that threat if first we give thanks, confess our sins, and pray for our neighbors. Then the petition may have free course. Sometimes, in sorrow, dread, or helplessness, it will be a crisis cry of creaturehood — a beating on Heaven's door with bruised knuckles in the dark. Sometimes it will be a friendship-talk with God about the affairs of every day."[6] The main thing for which we should strive is that our petitioning should grow in grace, for only then can we obey the great apostle as he admonishes: "But desire earnestly the greater gifts" (I Cor. 12:31).

The highest type of prayer is one in which we forget ourselves and plead the cause of others. The best example of intercessory praying is that of our Lord himself as found in John 17. Here he pours out his requests for those who not only *have* believed on him but for those who *will* believe. We see faces, and we bear the burdens of those faces as we approach our Father in prayer. Even our enemies must be included, for we are told to "pray for them that persecute you" (Matt. 5:44). Moses and Samuel admonish us by their very numerous examples of pleading for a faltering and backsliding Israel that we too should intercede for our burdened and bewildered neighbors. Never did Moses rise higher than when he exclaimed, "Yet now, if thou wilt forgive their sin — ; and if not, blot me, I pray thee, out of thy book which thou hast written" (Exod. 32:32). Paul could not forget his fellow Hebrews even for a moment (Rom. 9:1ff.; 10:1).

2. PURPOSE OF PRAYER

The purpose of prayer is communion with God. It is a very personal thing, dealing with all that is involved in a personal relationship of the redeemed with the Redeemer. It is spirit dealing with Spirit, making adjustments and readjustments, commitments and recommitments. "Prayer is a personal experience, not a philosophy or a theology. . . . Prayer as experience is primarily an active relationship between the individual and a power other and greater than himself, a power which he acknowledges as the solicitor of singleminded loyalty. It is the means whereby the human personality catches the spirit of the universe. At its best, prayer is man's supreme venture of faith, his whole-hearted response to the impact of God. It is a method of human adjustment to destiny."[7] Prayer does not consist in the mere repetition of stereotyped phrases and trite overtures to God. Nor does it consist of the "saying" of prayers, as by rote. Genuine praying springs from a soul intensely desirous of communicating with God about vital things, pressing matters of the spirit involved in day-to-day living.

The true motive of prayer is not that of the pagan as he be-

6 *Ibid.,* p. 263.
7 Karl R. Stolz, *The Psychology of Religious Living,* p. 257.

seeches his god in the incantations of his primitive ritual, that of persuading some unwilling deity to bestow upon him a yearned-for favor. The Christian's aim in praying is completely opposite, for it is that of beseeching God to bestow upon him any blessing that would be appropriate to divine eyes. It is not that of cajoling or coaxing God to do what he, the suppliant, wills; it is that of bringing himself to ascertain and do what God wills. This fact is easily understood when we remember that the Holy Spirit intercedes for us when we pray, since we, in our finiteness, are inadequate in communicating with God. "And in like manner the Spirit also helpeth our infirmity: for we know not how to pray as we ought; but the Spirit himself maketh intercession for us with groanings which cannot be uttered; and he that searcheth the hearts knoweth what is the mind of the Spirit, because he maketh intercession for the saints according to the will of God" (Rom. 8:26, 27). Evidently the Spirit of God takes possession of the human spirit and aids it to pray in accordance with the will of God. God's will is revealed to man as he is guided by the Spirit. It is an example of the repetitious story of God's taking the initiative, prayer being no exception. Man yearns, moves, and strives with God to bring about what God wills in and for the world.

3. SCOPE OF PRAYER

The scope of prayer is universal, for that which concerns man is automatically a subject for prayer. Anything that touches the lives of God's children is of interest to God. Any perplexing problem, any pressing decision, any difficulty, any joy, any fear, any sorrow, any crisis — all these and more are fit subjects for a discussion with God. All and each will elicit from God either a solution or help in deriving a solution. There is no problem too great to take to God in prayer; nor is there any matter too insignificant for his divine attention. "It is difficult to imagine anyone holding an intimate and loving conversation with one of the Greek gods, or even with the holy God of the Old Testament; but, for the Christian, God is the God with an eternal invitation in his heart, and prayer is the acceptance of that invitation to speak with and to listen to, God."[8] God places no restrictions upon that which motivates one to approach him in prayer; rather he welcomes the approach, whatever the motive may be.

4. ANSWER TO PRAYER

(1) NO "UNANSWERED" PRAYER

Prayer is communion with God, and in this sense there is no

8 William Barclay, *The Mind of Jesus,* p. 108.

"unanswered" prayer. The very communion of spirit with Spirit constitutes an "answer." For what should man seek more, what God can bestow or God himself? Is it not God himself? Therefore the very communion of the saved with the saving God constitutes an answer.

And yet, when most people speak of unanswered prayer, they think only of petitionary prayer, that a man asked for something and did not receive it. The prayer of thanksgiving, the prayer of aspiration, the prayer of praise, the prayer of confession — all these do not elicit from the suppliant the expressed disappointment of God's failure to respond. There are several things to be considered. First, "no" is just as much an answer as "yes," and this in spite of the fact that so many Christians cannot accept "no" for an answer. People may ask God for things which he, in his infinite wisdom, knows they should not have. Did not Jesus remind us that God gives good gifts — "how much more shall your Father who is in heaven give good things to them that ask him?" (Matt. 7:11)? God may know that it is best for us not to receive our bold requests. Second, God many times answers prayers, not as we have specifically "directed" him, but in ways that will most magnify his name and enhance his kingdom. Therefore God actually answers this or that prayer, but not in the way anticipated. This might be termed a positive answer to prayer, but positive in the realm of the unexpected. Paul pleads with God to deliver him from "the thorn in the flesh," given that he might not be overexalted. "Concerning this thing I besought the Lord thrice, that it might depart from me. And he hath said unto me, My grace is sufficient for thee: for my power is made perfect in weakness" (II Cor. 12:8, 9). God refuses his request but gives him a conquering grace instead, thereby effecting more glory to the kingdom and to his name than would occur in the fulfillment of the apostle's original plea.

> God answers sharp and sudden on some prayers,
> And thrusts the thing we have prayed for in our face.
> A gauntlet with a gift in't.
> — Elizabeth Barrett Browning

(2) CONDITIONS FOR ANSWERED PRAYER

There are certain spiritual conditions for obtaining communion with God, and therefore having one's prayers answered. First, we are to believe. "But let him ask in faith, nothing doubting" (Jas. 1:6), says James. Our Master states, "And all things, whatsoever ye shall ask in prayer, believing, ye shall receive" (Matt. 21:22). "All things whatsoever ye pray and ask for, believe that ye receive them, and ye shall have them" (Mark 11:24). This does not mean that a man can ask for anything his whims and notions may direct and then receive it; all must be in accordance with God's plan and purpose, which leads us to another, or second, condition. Every prayer must be conformable with the will of God, never at variance with it. "And this is the boldness which we have toward him, that, if we ask anything according to his will, he heareth us" (I John 5:14). Man's will must be subordinated to God's will. The third condition is that prayer must always be in the name of Jesus. "And whatsoever ye shall ask in my name, that will I do, that the Father may be glorified in the Son. If ye shall ask anything in my name, that will I do" (John 14:13, 14). "In my name" means according to his will and purpose, in direct union with him. It implies unity of thought and interest. One cannot pray in the name of Jesus and pray selfishly, for his kingdom will have priority at all times. The fourth condition is that we abide in him. "If ye abide in me, and my words abide in you, ask whatsoever ye will, and it shall be done unto you" (John 15:7). But this is very similar to the preceding condition, for again it is spiritual unity that is connoted. The fifth condition is that we pray under the guidance of the Spirit. "And in like manner the Spirit also helpeth our infirmity: for we know not how to pray as we ought; but the Spirit himself maketh intercession for us with groanings which cannot be uttered; and he that searcheth the hearts knoweth what is the mind of the Spirit, because he maketh intercession for the saints according to the will of God" (Rom. 8:26, 27). According to James the sixth condition is righteousness. "The supplication of a righteous man availeth much in its working" (Jas. 5:16).

Yet, all of these so-called "conditions" can be narrowed down ultimately to one: a complete, spiritual unity with God to the point of abject surrender to his will. God can answer our petitions only when we have moved into his realm with total surrender. We must see as he sees and think as he thinks; for only then can he respond to our supplications in a manner that does not violate his nature or counteract his purpose.

IV. MISSION OF THE CHRISTIAN

What is involved in the mission and work of a Christian? How is the life of redemption expressed in regard to the environment in which it is found? James says that the faith that does not issue in works is dead (Jas. 2:17). Of what do these "works" consist?

1. EXEMPLIFY CHRISTIAN RIGHTEOUSNESS

Not only should the believer be declared righteous by God;

he should live accordingly. His very being should radiate the life implanted in regeneration, therefore exemplifying to the world what God can do with a dedicated life. He no longer lives according to the "law of sin and of death," but according to the "law of the Spirit of life in Christ Jesus" (Rom. 8:2). He has died to sin and lives no longer therein, for he walks in newness of life (Rom. 6:2-4). He has presented the members of his body as "instruments of righteousness unto God" (Rom. 6:13). He is a disciple, a learner, in the school of Christ (Matt. 28:19). Since he is a son of God he is led by the Spirit of God (Rom. 8:14). He no longer walks "the Gentile" way of life, "alienated from the life of God," for he has put away "the old man." He has now been renewed in his spirit and has "put on the new man, that after God hath been created in righteousness and holiness of truth" (Eph. 4:17-24). He has become an imitator of God, a beloved child of God (Eph. 5:1).

2. Ascertain and fulfill will of God

According to the Scriptures the doing of God's will is a very vital matter. The man who does his will abides forever (I John 2:17). We are told to pray that his will be done (Matt. 6:10). The one who is spiritually kin to Jesus does the will of God. "For whosoever shall do the will of my Father who is in heaven, he is my brother, and sister, and mother" (Matt. 12:50). The man who does the will of God is the one who shall enter heaven (Matt. 7:21). With the matter presented so urgently the true Christian endeavors to seek God's will for his life and to perform it. Is not this in agreement with Paul when he advises the Philippians to "work out your own salvation with fear and trembling, for it is God who worketh in you both to will and to work, for his good pleasure" (Phil. 2:12, 13)? God not only works in us to save us; he also works in and through us to fulfill his purpose in the world. He continues to energize us through his Spirit that the divine life implanted may be the instrument of his will.

3. Lead others into saving knowledge of God

It should be the supreme desire of every redeemed individual that every other individual know the atoning power of Christ also. He should want to be instrumental in bringing others to Jesus, just as it is said of Andrew in regard to Peter, "He brought him unto Jesus" (John 1:42). Did not the woman at the well of Jacob go immediately and bring her villagers to Jesus, so that they could exclaim, "Now we believe, not because of thy speaking: for we have heard for ourselves, and know that this is indeed the Saviour of the world" (John 4:42)? Every Christian should be a proclaimer of good news, possessing the impulse of the woman at the well that others know Jesus also. He should want his fellow man to experience the blessings of the discipleship that he finds so rewarding. The Great Commission is for every Christian, not just those in full-time church-related vocations or those on a foreign mission field. He should possess a love for souls that is akin to that of God himself. Every Christian should be an evangelist.

4. Perform Works of Benevolence

The Christian should seek to do all the good he can to as many as he can in every way he can. Just as Jesus surveyed all around and had compassion upon them, so the Christian should aspire to be benevolent in the realm of social service. There is no antithesis between evangelistic fervor and social service; for the latter is just as spiritual, if done in the name of Christ, as the former. Helping one's fellow man is about as Christlike an activity as any to be found. Jesus commands feeding the hungry, giving drink to the thirsty, displaying hospitality, clothing the naked, and visiting the sick and imprisoned. In fact, an act of this sort is tantamount to performing it on Jesus himself. "Inasmuch as ye did it unto one of these my brethren, even these least, ye did it unto me" (Matt. 25:31-46). The parable of the Good Samaritan has this as its motive; and it is striking that this is the only parable after which Jesus exhorts, "Go, and do thou likewise" (Luke 10: 30-37). Our Lord also says, "And whosoever shall give to drink unto one of these little ones a cup of cold water only, in the name of a disciple, verily I say unto you he shall in no wise lose his reward" (Matt. 10:42). John says, "But whoso hath the world's goods, and beholdeth his brother in need, and shutteth up his compassion from him, how doth the love of God abide in him?" (I John 3:17). And James adds, "If a brother or sister be naked and in lack of daily food, and one of you say unto them, Go in peace, be ye warmed and filled; and yet ye give them not the things needful to the body; what doth it profit?" (2:16). Jesus healed maimed bodies and fed hungry multitudes. Every mountain-peak experience should lead immediately into the valley of service below. Soul winning is very important; but so is the alleviation of suffering and anguish. These are not mutually exclusive, by any means. "But be ye doers of the word, and not hearers only, deluding your own selves" (Jas. 1:22).

5. Bring Forth "Fruits of the Spirit"

The Apostle Paul makes a very vivid contrast between that which issues from the carnal life and that which issues from the spiritual life, calling the former the "works of the flesh" and the latter the "fruits of the Spirit." It is part of the mission of the Christian to produce this spiritual fruit. "But the fruit of the Spirit is love, joy, peace, longsuffering, kindness, goodness, faithfulness, meekness, self-control" (Gal. 5:22, 23). The manifestation of these nine great qualities is certain proof that one is walking in the Spirit. What a rich life indeed!

V. GROWTH IN GRACE

1. BIBLICAL DEMAND FOR GROWTH

The life implanted in regeneration needs developing and nurturing. This is not only apparent from a rationalistic standpoint; it is the assumed New Testament viewpoint. We read, "But grow in the grace and knowledge of our Lord and Saviour Jesus Christ" (II Pet. 3:18). Paul's favorite term for undeveloped Christians is "babes in Christ," whom he calls "carnal" Christians in contrast to "spiritual" Christians. These must be fed with milk, for they cannot bear meat; their strife and jealousy prove this (I Cor. 3: 1-3). Jesus exhorts Christians, "Ye therefore shall be perfect, as your heavenly Father is perfect" (Matt. 5:48). The Greek word translated "perfect" does not mean without blemish; it means complete, mature, or functional. Jesus also calls those who believe in him disciples, a term meaning learners. Therefore we are to be learners, or pupils, in the school of Christ. This learning involves the whole nature of being: mind, heart, and will; and we advance in this school just as in any other.

We have noticed that sanctification can be viewed in two respects, positional and progressive, and that the former is by far the more prominent in the Scriptures. Therefore, in a sense, progressive sanctification and growth in grace are one and the same; it is just a matter of terminology. We are told to "follow after" sanctification (Heb. 12:14) and to be sanctified "wholly" (I Thess. 5:23); but is this not tantamount to developing in grace?

2. ENEMIES OF GROWTH

What are the factors that war against spiritual growth, odds that must be surmounted if development is to materialize? They are present, both within and without. Never for a moment let the young Christian think that his struggles are over; they have really just begun! The prime difference is that now he has a nature that revolts against sin and cannot be content to dwell in its subjugation. Now he has Christ dwelling within, who will aid him in his battles against the satanic powers that would enthrall him.

(1) FORCE WITHIN

The subjective force that would restrain the Christian in his "march toward Zion" bears the biblical term flesh. This term, a special favorite of Paul, denotes human nature in its sinful and evil tendency. The Christian finds that he is never out from under this power but must always fight the "fleshly" nature of his being. This ceaseless warfare is vividly portrayed by the great apostle in Romans 8:1-13. "For they that are after the flesh mind the things of the flesh; but they that are after the Spirit the things of the Spirit.... But ye are not in the flesh but in the Spirit, if so be that the Spirit of God dwelleth in you.... So then, brethren, we are debtors, not to the flesh, to live after the flesh: for if ye live after the flesh, ye must die; but if by the Spirit ye put to death the deeds of the body, ye shall live." He also declares, "Walk by the Spirit, and ye shall not fulfil the lust of the flesh. For the flesh lusteth against the Spirit, and the Spirit against the flesh; for these are contrary the one to the other; that ye may not do the things that ye would" (Gal. 5:16, 17). The flesh cannot be struck a once-forever blow but instead must be subdued constantly. Paul glories in the fact that he has been "crucified with Christ" (Gal. 2:20), but by no means does he infer that his struggles against the flesh have ceased. Further Pauline writing is full warranty against such a misconception. In the regenerate man the Spirit predominates over the flesh, and not vice versa, as in unregenerate nature; but that very flesh must be constantly quelled, nevertheless. And only as that flesh is crushed and God's will performed will there be progress in gracious Christian living.

(2) FORCES WITHOUT

There are certain objective factors which must be reckoned with if Christian grace is to be augmented.

a. *Prince of this world*

The prince of this world is a positive deterrent to development, directing all evil forces to the detriment of Christian character. Just prior to the cross Jesus exclaims, "Now is the judgment of this world: now shall the prince of this world be cast out" (John 12:31). What Jesus means is that now, with the cross, the power of Satan is broken in the heart and life of everyone who accepts the atoning work of Calvary. Satan is still present in the world; so Jesus does not imply the devil is being cast out of the world, his sphere of influence. Does not Peter say, "Be sober, be watchful: your adversary the devil, as a roaring lion, walketh about, seeking whom he may devour: whom withstand steadfast in your faith . . ." (I Pet. 5:8, 9)? Satan wants to test all God's people, just as he wanted to test Peter. "Simon, Simon, behold, Satan asked to have you, that he might·sift you as wheat" (Luke 22:31), declares Jesus. James, along with Peter, admonishes us to resist and be steadfast. "Be subject therefore unto God; but resist the devil, and he will flee from you" (4:7). And Paul reminds us that we must withstand "the wiles of the devil. For our wrestling is not against flesh and blood, but against the principalities, against the powers, against the world-rulers of this darkness, against the spiritual hosts of wickedness in the heavenly places" (Eph. 6:11, 12). The power of this resisting comes through the blood of Christ and the witnessing of Christians (Rev. 12:11). Unless Satan is resisted there can be no growth.

b. *World*

The world, or the sphere of all evil impulses working in human society, is another adversary to spiritual development. Even Jesus did not receive a friendly welcome from the world. "He was in the world, and the world was made through him, and the world knew him not" (John 1:10). He also warns his disciples that they can expect from the world exactly the same treatment (Matt. 10:24ff.). "Woe unto you, when all men shall speak well of you" (Luke 6:26). Paul promises, "All that would live godly in Christ Jesus shall .suffer persecution" (II Tim. 3:12). But it is John who presents the most picturesque view about the Christian's true attitude toward the world (I John 2:15-17). The child of God has a power within which will help him overcome the world (I John 4:4). "For whatsoever is begotten of God overcometh the world: and this is the victory that hath overcome the world, even our faith. And who is he that overcometh the world, but he that believeth that Jesus is the Son of God?" (I John 5:4, 5). Overcoming the world is an important factor in Christian growth.

c. *Perfection theory*

The perfection theory is a foe of growth in grace. This is the theory that one may attain perfection in this life and live above sin, which perfection is obtained in a great crisis, or cataclysmic upheaval of soul. This is known as the second work of grace and is termed the "second blessing." The first work of grace is regeneration, at which one becomes a "babe" in Christ; the second work of grace is sanctification, at which time he becomes a "spiritual" Christian.

Such a theory is a detriment to growth for several reasons. It leads to a self-satisfied spirit, therefore obstructing improvement. It leads to a pharisaical attitude toward other Christians, the "carnal" ones. It has a standard of righteousness that is much too low, for what is termed perfection is far from such. Their "perfection" consists in being free from deliberate and objective acts of sin and does not take into account the subjective nature of sin as revealed by our Lord in Matthew 5:21-48. "Perfection" of this sort does not include evil promptings and sinful impulses of the inner being, deprecated so earnestly by Jesus. This theory also maintains that Christian growth may be achieved at a bound, so to speak. Spiritual maturity is no more derived in this manner than is physical and mental maturity. It is a theory that is antithetical to scriptural truth and a foe to Christian growth.

3. AIDS TO GROWTH

There are certain agencies, termed means of grace, that contribute heavily towards the augmentation of Christian character. These agencies function in growth just as in the bestowment of salvation itself. They are very familiar ones: the church, the preaching of the Word, the ordinances, the reading of the Scriptures, prayer, personal witnessing, Christian example, the influence of the Spirit, the music ministry, the Christian home, godly parents, and Christian school teachers.

As one is saved by grace, so does he develop by grace. As he is justified by grace, so does he become more Christlike by grace. Again we see that it is all of God, for God takes the initiative in everything. Now is easily discerned what Paul means when he says, "By the grace of God I am what I am: and his grace which was bestowed upon me was not found vain" (I Cor. 15:10). Where the means of grace have been minimized or stifled proper growth is lacking and a dwarfed character ensues.

4. GOAL OF GROWTH

The aim and goal of growth are a character like unto Christ. Christ is our example as well as Saviour, being the embodiment of that which God would have redeemed man to become. Jesus admonishes his disciples, "Ye therefore shall be perfect, as your heavenly Father is perfect" (Matt. 5:48). The Greek word translated "perfect" does not mean without blemish; it denotes maturity, completeness, having the ability to function. Therefore to be "perfect" means to have grown to the point of completeness, to be able to function as a Christian should. For this the believer in Christ is ever to strive and to "fight the good fight." He is to keep the ideal, Christ, ever before him, and, no matter how high he climbs, keep his eyes constantly on even more challenging heights of character achievement.

OUTLINE FOR CHAPTER TWELVE

I. Kingdom in Old Testament
   1. Grounded in sovereignty of God
   2. Theocracy of Israel
   3. Theocracy and monarchy
   4. Theocracy and messianic ideal
   5. Messianic King
II. Kingdom in New Testament
   1. Meaning of term
      (1) Definition
      (2) Mainly in Synoptics
      (3) Kingdom of heaven and kingdom of God
   2. Nature of kingdom
      (1) Founded by Christ
      (2) Spiritual in nature
      (3) Universal in scope
      (4) Present and future in time
      (5) Interrelated with church

CHAPTER TWELVE

THE KINGDOM

THROUGHOUT THE SCRIPTURES THERE IS ONE REVERBERATING THEME, the kingdom, or, as it is many times called, the kingdom of Jehovah, the kingdom of God, and the kingdom of heaven. What is the nature of this highest of all social orders, this divine society, this theocratic realm in which the ethical ideal for man attains its zenith? We shall look first at the kingdom in the Old Testament, then the kingdom in the New Testament.

I. KINGDOM IN OLD TESTAMENT

1. GROUNDED IN SOVEREIGNTY OF GOD

God's sovereignty is the basis of his kingship over all his created order. He rules as King by virtue of the fact that he has created, or brought into being, the whole physical universe. Since he has created and since he is the only God, he rules supreme. The Psalms are replete with this concept of the rule of God. "For Jehovah Most High is terrible; He is a great King over all the earth" (47:2). "Sing praises to God, sing praises: Sing praises unto our King, sing praises. For God is the King of all the earth: Sing ye praises with understanding. God reigneth over the nations: God sitteth upon his holy throne" (47:6-8). Going from the Forty-seventh Psalm to the Hundred-and-third we read: "Jehovah hath established his throne in the heavens; And his kingdom ruleth over all" (103:19). "Bless Jehovah, all ye his works, In all places of his dominion: Bless Jehovah, O my soul" (103:22). Here his "dominion" is his whole created order, over which he is supremely exalted. "Thine is the kingdom, O Jehovah, and thou art exalted as head above all" (I Chron. 29:11). The Hebrew noun generally translated "kingdom" means primarily kingship or sovereignty.

There is only one God, who is supreme, absolute, omnipresent, and omniscient. Man is subject to his moral order and must give an account of his deeds. Nations other than Israel must also receive his judgments, and he may even use these nations to chastise Israel. All in time and space are subject to his righteous rule.

2. THEOCRACY OF ISRAEL

God chooses one man, Abraham, and his descendants to be a

peculiar people, a nation with which he plans to work out his purpose for mankind. These people are the Hebrews, a branch of the Semites, with whom he enters into a covenant relationship by which they become his elect ones. The form of government for this commonwealth, as instituted by Moses their deliverer, is the "government of God," or "theocracy," a term seemingly coined by Josephus and meaning rule of God. It is the idea of divine kingship, Jehovah himself being King over Israel.

The concept of God's rule over Israel, and therefore his kingship, does not originate until Sinai, for God is not termed King until that time. "The patriarchs called Him 'Lord' and 'Shepherd,' and it is not until He has formed a people for Himself by bringing Israel up out of Egypt that He is called, Ex. 15:19, 'He who is King for ever and ever.' But the real beginning of His kingly rule was on that day on which He bound the tribes of Israel into a community by the promulgation of the law and the forming of the legal covenant: 'Then He became King in Jeshurun,' Deut. 33:5."[1] Hence the Creator of Israel is, by virtue of that creation, Israel's King. "I am Jehovah, your Holy One, the Creator of Israel, your King" (Isa. 43:15).

Other passages depicting this idea of the divine kingship are numerous. "Produce your cause, saith Jehovah; bring forth your strong reasons, saith the King of Jacob" (Isa. 41:21). "Thus saith Jehovah, the King of Israel, and his Redeemer, Jehovah of hosts: I am the first, and I am the last; and besides me there is no God" (Isa. 44:6). Thus it is seen that Jehovah's kingship is grounded in his oneness; the theocracy is based on monotheism. "Jehovah is King for ever and ever: The nations are perished out of his land" (Ps. 10:16). In Psalm 48:2 Jehovah is termed "the great King," and in Psalm 24:7-10 he is called "the King of glory."

As King, all political powers are united in him, with selected individuals being the earthly bearers of those powers, or organs through which he functions. It is, as of necessity, what might be termed church and state combined into one. Since he is King he is both Lawgiver and Judge. "For Jehovah is our judge, Jehovah is our lawgiver, Jehovah is our king; he will save us" (Isa. 33:22). All legal and civil regulations find their source in him. As King he even leads the armies of Israel. "Jehovah his God is with him, And the shout of a king is among them" (Num. 23:21). The armies of Israel are his armies. "All the hosts of Jehovah went out from the land of Egypt" (Exod. 12:41); the "hosts" of Jehovah are the armies of Jehovah.

[1] G. F. Oehler, *Theology of the Old Testament*, p. 199.

3. Theocracy and monarchy

What happens to the theocracy with the founding of the Israel-itish kingdom? There should be no mutually exclusive ideas involved, no reason why the kingdom should not be the means of confirming the theocracy. Cannot Israel's king be the earthly representative of Jehovah?

During the period of the judges the tribes show jealousy one toward another, Ephraim especially desiring the forward spot (Judg. 8:1). Yet, in spite of this jealousy, the tribes experience a need for national unity. Gideon is offered the kingship, only to refuse on the basis of God's rule over them. "And Gideon said unto them, I will not rule over you, neither shall my son rule over you: Jehovah shall rule over you" (Judg. 8:23). However, Gideon's illegitimate son, Abimelech, does rear a kingdom "over Israel" in Shechem, which lasts only three years (Judg. 9:6, 22). His sway is merely provincial and not over all Israel. Finally, during the wise leadership of Samuel the tribes at last secure a vestige of unity. At the same time they are harried by two fears: the dangers of the Ammonites and the Philistines, still not subdued, and the tyranny of Samuel's sons, Joel and Abijah, who "turned aside after lucre, and took bribes, and perverted justice" (I Sam. 8:3). Therefore in very ardent tones the people petition for a king to rule over them and to lead their armies. They request Samuel to "make us a king to judge us like all the nations" (I Sam. 8:5). Samuel interprets their request to be a denial of the sovereignty of Jehovah, thus renouncing their distinctiveness among the peoples of earth, the direct rule of God. Would not their return to God be the answer to all misfortunes, rather than the establishment of an earthly monarchy? No wonder God allays the grief of Samuel with the words, "Hearken unto the voice of the people in all that they say unto thee; for they have not rejected thee, but they have rejected me, that I should not be king over them" (I Sam. 8:7).

Yet God's rule requires human agents for its operation; so a king in perfect obedience to the theocratic principle might possibly be considered the vicegerent of Jehovah. Only his behavior as an autocrat, or despot, would defeat such an ideal. This is the principle determining Samuel's action after receiving God's permission to establish the kingdom. Saul fails to realize this ideal. There is no elaborate system of government, as we find under his successors. He lives in his ancestral home of Gibeah, with a tent for a palace and for the scene of judgment. We hear little if any of his judicial work, but quite a bit of his military campaigns. The Philistines are a constant threat. There is no information as to the methods of civil government. Though he did secure some unity of the tribes, his northern frontier seems to have been Mt. Gilboa, and Jerusalem to the south is in other hands. His reign, beginning in triumph, continues with struggle and ends in gloom. But with David, the son of Jesse, we find a man of a different stamp, for he exerts a tremendous influence on the make-up of Israel. Being the most striking personality in Israel since the days of Moses, he succeeds in establishing a kingdom which, though earthly, does not clash overmuch with the divine, but which serves in some measure to express it. With David's kingdom there is a religious note; the Psalms, not heard in Saul's reign, enhance the feeling of dependence upon God. God chooses David's house as that on which he will endeavor to build the concept of the true kingdom he desires.

The king is consecrated for his position by anointing, the rite being performed upon both Saul and David by Samuel. In fact, David is anointed again by the elders of the people when he ctually enters upon governing them. Hence the king is termed "Jehovah's anointed." This anointing is considered the symbol of endowment with the Spirit of God, thus effecting a sacred and inviolable aspect regarding his being.

It is true that Samuel does picture to the people in vivid terms the "manner of the king" that shall rule over them (I Sam. 8:11ff.), which is nothing short of a typical oriental despot, exacting service, tribute, and taxes as he wills. But do not the people desire a monarch "like the kings of the heathen nations"? Suffice it to say here, Samuel's pictorial forecast does not fully materialize until the latter part of Solomon's reign; in his declining years this son of David fulfills Samuel's very graphic presentation.

4. THEOCRACY AND MESSIANIC IDEAL

What is the significance of the kingdom in Israel? We have seen that its throne is considered as that of Jehovah. "Then Solomon sat on the throne of Jehovah as king instead of David his father, and prospered; and all Israel obeyed him" (I Chron. 29: 23). David and Solomon are merely the visible representatives of the invisible King, and as a result blessings are poured out upon them, blessings intended to be conveyed on down the dynasty. Therefore God honors the king by raising him to the highest position in this very eminent nation. He is the recipient of God's grace. He is the anointed one in a special sense, and as the theocratic king must reflect the divine majesty. His kingdom shall be forever and ever. "Thou wilt prolong the king's life; His years shall be as many generations. He shall abide before God for ever" (Ps. 61:6, 7). Psalm 72 speaks of the righteous king and says, "His name shall endure for ever; His name shall be continued as long as the sun: And men shall be blessed in him; All nations shall call him happy" (72:17). His kingdom is founded upon righteousness, and even the land is made to bloom and to prosper.

The Old Testament term "anointed one" is *Mashiach,* or Messiah. This is identical with Christ, which comes from the Greek instead of from the Hebrew. Therefore Messiah and Christ are equivalent terms, meaning Anointed One. Saul, David, and Solomon are actually anointed with oil, the first two by Samuel and the last by Zadok, and are thus God's anointed in the truest sense. "The original idea in the practice of anointing was doubtless the actual communication of supernatural qualities through contact with the unguent used. In the Old Testament usage kings, priests, and prophets were actually anointed with oil, the underlying idea being that they were thus qualified for their office. Thus the term 'anointed' came to denote metaphorically those who were set apart for some particular work, such as Cyrus, the deliverer of Israel, the Jewish patriarchs, and Israel as a nation."[2] The main idea is that the Davidic king constitutes God's anointed, around whom all the hopes and desires of the people center.

God informs Israel that when they arrive in the promised land and request a king that he, Jehovah, will select that king (Deut. 17:14, 15). He also informs them that this theocractic king shall be fully regulated in all his dealings by the law of God. "And it shall be, when he sitteth upon the throne of the kingdom, that he shall write him a copy of this law in a book, out of that which is before the priests the Levites: and it shall be with him, and he shall read therein all the days of his life; that he may learn to fear Jehovah his God, to keep all the words of this law and these statutes, to do them; that his heart be not lifted up above his brethren, and that he turn not aside from the commandment, to the right hand, or to the left: to the end that he may prolong his days in his kingdom, he and his children, in the midst of Israel" (Deut. 17:18-20).

Saul fails to live up to the theocratic ideal; therefore, at the incident of offering up his own sacrifice, rather than waiting for Samuel, the latter is compelled to inform him, "Thou hast done foolishly; thou hast not kept the commandment of Jehovah thy God, which he commanded thee: for now would Jehovah have established thy kingdom upon Israel for ever. But now thy kingdom shall not continue: Jehovah hath sought him a man after his own heart, and Jehovah hath appointed him to be prince over his people, because thou hast not kept that which Jehovah hath commanded thee" (I Sam. 13:13, 14). Also, after Saul's disobedience to God relative to his dealings with the Amalekites, God announces, also through Samuel, his rejection of Saul as king (I Sam. 15:23).

[2] H. Wheeler Robinson, *The Religious Ideas of the Old Testament,* p. 199.

Subsequent to the declaration of the cessation of Saul's dynasty is Nathan's announcement to David that his house shall reign upon the throne of his kingdom forever. "I will establish the throne of his kingdom for ever. I will be his father, and he shall be my son. . . . And thy house and thy kingdom shall be made sure for ever before thee: thy throne shall be established for ever" (II Sam. 7:12-16).

And yet this Davidic kingdom does not give much hope for expectant glorification. It is true that David extends the sway of Israel from the river of Egypt up to the Euphrates, conquering and subduing all the pagan elements around him and bringing Canaan under submission. He and Solomon produce the Golden Age of Israel's history, with their lavish building program, economic advances, and governmental improvements. It is an age in which sacred lyrical poetry reaches its zenith, for David is known as "The anointed of the God of Jacob, And the sweet psalmist of Israel" (II Sam. 23:1). Wisdom literature under Solomon springs into full bloom. An enormous palace and a lavish temple only introduce the extensive domestic enlargement program. Tribute from conquered peoples and toll from multitudes of trade caravans help to swell the treasury. It is indeed an age of splendor! Yet immediately after Solomon's era this kingdom is rent asunder and a rival kingship established in the north. The Davidic kingdom of Judah finds itself under the sway of Egypt for a while, then under the rival northern kingdom of Israel, then under Assyria, then under Babylonia. Childishness, cowardice, and idolatry are exemplified on all sides. Only a few of the kings of Judah follow the example of David and honor Jehovah, for most of them are despotic, cruel, and ostentatious, following the pagan gods borrowed from the surrounding nations. There is not even an outward pretense of following the law and will of Jehovah. This religious apostasy reaches its apex in the reigns of Ahaz and of Manasseh. Good kings like Hezekiah and Josiah are hard put to stem the tide of this moral and spiritual degeneracy.

And yet, in spite of such spiritual chaos, the Davidic king is, in the book of Jeremiah, called the signet ring upon the hand of God (22:24). And in other late passages of the Old Testament the writers see in the monarchy the hope of Israel's happiness and glory. In fact "David remained the ideal of this decaying age, David who had tended Israel with clean hands and according to the integrity of his heart. In the darkest days faith clung to the oath, sworn by God ages before to David and to his house, that the kingdom would not depart from him, that David's son would be God's son, and God his father. Thus it was a faith in things not seen, a faith in the everlasting significance of this house. It is a phenomenon without parallel in history, that even under such circumstances the confident hope of seeing the Saviour of the future born of this dishonored family is never lost."[3]

5. MESSIANIC KING

Thus Israel's faith clings tenaciously to the idea of this Davidic King, this Anointed One, this Messiah; and we see the crystallization of the messianic hope in such a coming one. Somehow or other God's promise to David through Nathan will be fulfilled, and Israel's future hope will be made complete in the branch out of the stock of Jesse (Isa. 11:1). He will be a great conqueror, reigning in glory. When he shall reign, God shall reign, for the messianic King is identified with God. He will be the administrator of Jehovah, vested with power from Jehovah, yet at the same time subordinate to Jehovah. Truly he will be Jehovah's Anointed, to whom the promise of perpetuity has been given: "I will establish the throne of his kingdom for ever" (II Sam. 7:13). "I have found David my servant; With my holy oil have I anointed him. . . . He shall cry unto me, Thou art my Father, My God, and the rock of my salvation. I also will make him my firstborn, The highest of the kings of the earth. My lovingkindness will I keep for him for evermore; And my covenant shall stand fast with him. . . . My covenant will I not break, Nor alter the thing that is gone out of my lips. Once have I sworn by my holiness: I will not lie unto David: His seed shall endure for ever, And his throne as the sun before me . . ." (Ps. 89:20-36).

Isaiah pictures this future Deliverer of the house of David in very glowing terms, which appear in chapters 7, 9, and 11. "For unto us a child is born, unto us a son is given; and the government shall be upon his shoulder: and his name shall be called Wonderful, Counsellor, Mighty God, Everlasting Father, Prince of Peace. Of the increase of his government and of peace there shall be no end, upon the throne of David, and upon his kingdom, to establish it, and to uphold it with justice and with righteousness from henceforth even for ever. The zeal of Jehovah of hosts will perform this" (Isa. 9:6, 7). A King is about to come, a Son of David, a Saviour and Redeemer. Thus he is a God-given King who will give Israel new splendor, great power, and true righteousness. Hence names are given him that reveal him to be far above anything human. There is a second passage, Isaiah 11:1-5, which is a beautiful supplement to 9:6, 7. "And there shall come forth a shoot out of the stock of Jesse, and a branch out of his roots shall bear fruit. And the Spirit of Jehovah shall rest upon him, the spirit of wisdom and understanding, the spirit of counsel and might, the spirit of

---

[3] Hermann Shultz, *Old Testament Theology*, I, 173.

knowledge and of the fear of Jehovah..." (11:1-5). Thougn the ancient house has been cut down to the root, a scion of David's line shall sprout from that noble stock. Yet it is the ethical that is stressed, for his divine capacity for the office of King rests upon the fact that the Spirit of God abides in him in the fullest measure. A third passage is Isaiah 7:14. "Therefore the Lord himself will give you a sign: behold, a virgin shall conceive, and bear a son, and shall call his name Immanuel." The term Immanuel means "God is with us," and constitutes a pledge to the people that God will not desert them. This passage from the great prophet is quoted by Matthew in 1:23 as being fulfilled in the virgin birth of our Lord.

Isaiah's contemporary, Micah of Moresheth, also depicts the coming Messiah in kingly terms. "But thou, Bethlehem Ephrathah, which art little to be among the thousands of Judah, out of thee shall one come forth unto me that is to be ruler in Israel; whose goings forth are from of old, from everlasting" (5:2). Here the Messiah is pictured as a Son of David, coming from the family birthplace, the city of David, Bethlehem. Though it may be accounted insignificant by the rest of the nation, it is the birthplace of the Messiah. The wise men of Herod the Great understand it thus; for when Herod is asked of Magi from the East where the King of the Jews is to be born, his own scribes answer immediately by quoting this famous passage from the prophet Micah (Matt. 2:1-6).

Jeremiah also tells us that this messianic King shall constitute the beginning of a new line from David, for he shall be a "shoot" or "branch" raised unto David. "In those days, and at that time, will I cause a Branch of righteousness to grow up unto David; and he shall execute justice and righteousness in the land....David shall never want a man to sit upon the throne of the house of Israel" (33:15-17). "Behold, the days come, saith Jehovah, that I will raise unto David a righteous Branch [or Shoot, or Bud], and he shall reign as king and deal wisely, and shall execute justice and righteousness in the land" (23:5). This one shall be the Prince of the kingdom expected at the end of the ages.

Zechariah represents the Messiah as a second Solomon, a Prince of Peace. "Rejoice greatly, O daughter of Zion; shout, O daughter of Jerusalem: behold, thy king cometh unto thee; he is just, and having salvation; lowly, and riding upon an ass, even upon a colt the foal of an ass" (9:9). Not as a proud warrior upon a white charger, but in a very simple and ancient manner shall he come. At Christ's entry into Jerusalem in just such a manner Matthew quotes this famous passage from Zechariah (Matt. 21:5).

In the prophecies of Daniel there is a very remarkable passage that is considered by most scholars to be messianic in nature. "I saw in the night-visions, and, behold, there came with the clouds of heaven one like unto a son of man, and he came even to the ancient of days, and they brought him near before him. And there was given him dominion, and glory, and a kingdom, that all the peoples, nations, and languages should serve him: his dominion is an everlasting dominion, which shall not pass away, and his kingdom that which shall not be destroyed" (7:13, 14). Here the "son of man" denotes the King, the Messiah, in the final era of blessedness and in the messianic kingdom of the saints. He is thought of as descending in the last days from heaven itself and revealing himself in visible form. Most scholars believe that it is here in the Hebrew Scriptures that Jesus derives the term for himself that is so prevalent in the Synoptics.

II. KINGDOM IN NEW TESTAMENT

When we come to the New Testament we see a further development of this idea of the kingdom, for the New Testament concept is based upon that of the Old. The spiritual kingdom of the Lord Jesus is the fulfillment of the theocratic kingdom of Israel, and he himself is the Saviour-King. The Greek term *basileia,* translated "kingdom" in the New Testament, corresponds to the Hebrew term *malkhûth* in the Old Testament. One has said, "Indeed in appropriating for himself the function of bringing the kingdom, in laying claim to the Messianic dignity, Jesus seized upon that in the Old Testament which enabled him at one stroke to make its whole historic movement converge upon and terminate in himself."[4]

1. MEANING OF TERM

(1) DEFINITION

What is meant by the term kingdom of God, or kingdom of heaven? Can this concept be defined? Or is it too broad for definition? Some have attempted to define it. Edgar Y. Mullins gives this statement concerning the kingdom: "A divine society wherein God and men are associated in loving fellowship; where the will of God is done by men; where love is the expression of their relations with, and conduct toward, each other; and where God graciously manifests himself in the fulness of his grace to men: this is the New Testament teaching as to the kingdom of God."[5] Albert C. Knudson sums up the teaching of Jesus relative to the kingdom in the following: "For him the Kingdom was primarily a spiritual good,

4 Geerhardus Vos, *The Kingdom and the Church*, p. 14.
5 Edgar Y. Mullins, *The Christian Religion in Its Doctrinal Expression*, p. 91.

consisting in 'eternal life'. It was universal, free from national and political limitations. It was an individual as well as a social good. It was a supramundane reality. It was embodied in his own person as future Lord and also as the Son of man who came not to be ministered unto but to minister and to give his life a ransom for many."[6] C. H. Dodd makes this statement: "The common idea ... underlying all uses of the term 'The Kingdom of God' is that of the manifest and effective assertion of the divine sovereignty against all the evil of the world."[7] Some have defined the kingdom as the rule or reign of God in the hearts of his children, as over against the realm of God. Yet it is easily seen that these concise statements concerning the nature of the kingdom are highly inadequate for a proper conception of this important figure of speech as used by our Lord; only a fuller discussion can display the many facets of its manifold nature.

(2) MAINLY IN SYNOPTICS

The terms kingdom, kingdom of God, and kingdom of heaven are predominantly Synoptic terms, being found mainly in Matthew, Mark, and Luke. They occur most frequently on the lips of Jesus, and therefore must represent an idea that figures prominently in the thinking of our Lord. The word kingdom is used on only two occasions in the Fourth Gospel, twice on one occasion and three times on the other: John 3:3, 5 and 18:36 (three times). In this latest of the four documents having to do with the life of our Lord the recurrent and corresponding term is "eternal life," or just simply "life." As this term is found many times in John, it occurs on only a few occasions in the Synoptics. And to John this term is not equated with the term kingdom of God, for it is the life one knows and experiences under the rule of God, the kingdom. It is the life inherent in the Redeemer King, implanted in the redeemed.

(3) KINGDOM OF HEAVEN AND KINGDOM OF GOD

Matthew uses the term kingdom of heaven many times and the term kingdom of God only five times. Mark and Luke use "kingdom of God" predominantly, with all three gospels using simply "the kingdom" several times each. Does Matthew mean by the "kingdom of heaven" what Mark and Luke mean by the "kingdom of God"? Yes, the two terms are used interchangeably. The following parables will verify this fact. Matthew states, "Another parable set he before them, saying, The kingdom of heaven is like unto a grain of mustard seed, which a man took, and sowed

6 Albert C. Knudson, *The Doctrine of Redemption*, p. 436.
7 C. H. Dodd, *The Parables of the Kingdom*, p. 35.

in his field: which indeed is less than all seeds; but when it is grown..." (13:31, 32). Luke states, "He said therefore, Unto what is the kingdom of God like? and whereunto shall I liken it? It is like unto a grain of mustard seed, which a man took, and cast into his own garden; and it grew..." (13:18, 19). Matthew states, "Another parable spake he unto them: The kingdom of heaven is like unto leaven, which a woman took, and hid in three measures of meal, till it was all leavened" (13:33). Luke states, "And again he said, Whereunto shall I liken the kingdom of God? It is like unto leaven, which a woman took and hid in three measures of meal, till it was all leavened" (13:20). The only material difference between the two presentations of each of these parables is in the fact that Matthew uses "kingdom of heaven" and Luke uses "kingdom of God." Since each parable has one central purpose the connotations attached to each of these two terms must be identical. And what is shown here, using these two parables, may be reduplicated time and again with other parallel Synoptic passages.

Therefore C. H. Dodd is correct when he states, "The two expressions, 'The Kingdom of God' and 'The Kingdom of Heaven,' the latter of which is peculiar to the First Gospel, are synonymous, the term 'heaven' being common in Jewish usage as a reverential periphrasis for the divine name."[8] He is referring to the fact that a righteous Jew had a reluctance to naming the name of God, or the name for God, all of which stemmed from rabbinical teaching probably based on Amos' statement that "we may not make mention of the name of Jehovah" (6:10). Matthew, though willing from the Christian standpoint, would not completely shelve this Jewish viewpoint and would have the tendency to write "kingdom of heaven" instead of "kingdom of God."

Gustaf Dolman agrees in viewing the terms as synonymous. After making a thorough study of the Galilean Aramaic in which Jesus spoke, and after examining carefully the Hebrew and Aramaic expressions translated "kingdom of God" or "kingdom of heaven," he comes to the conclusion that the term "heaven" as used by Matthew is merely a circumlocution for "God" and does not in this case have transcendental significance. "Kingdom," as used in Jewish literature and applied to God, always means kingly rule, describing the sovereignty of the King, not his territory. "The two expressions are absolutely synonymous, anything that can be read into the one must also be read into the other, and any attempt to differentiate between the two or to give a more transcendental significance to 'Kingdom of Heaven' is doomed to shipwreck on the rock of Dolman's argument."[9]

8 *Ibid.*, p. 21.
9 Norman Perrin, *The Kingdom of God in the Teaching of Jesus*, pp. 23, 24.

However, Professor A. B. Bruce gives another possible slant to Matthew's aberration in terminology. "Mark and Luke call it the kingdom of God. Matthew almost uniformly calls it the kingdom of heaven. The expression suggests the thought that the kingdom is an ideal hovering over all actual societies, civil or sacred, like Plato's Republic, to be found realized in perfection nowhere on this earth, the true home of which is in the supersensible world. In all probability, the title was used alternatively by Jesus for the express purpose of lifting the minds of the Jewish people unto a higher region of thought than that in which their present hopes as members of the theocratic nation moved."[10] In other words, Jesus uses the term heaven to add to the spiritual conception of the kingdom and to help remove it from a mundane, provincial connotation.

There are some who are attempting to establish the view that the terms kingdom of heaven and kingdom of God are not synonymous. They say that the former is visible, earthly, and local, while the latter is invisible, heavenly, and universal. The former is to be identified with the kingdom of ancient Israel, is present in mystery form now, containing both good and bad, and is the future earthly millennial kingdom in which Christ reigns in person. This view is completely without formulation. It places both saved and unsaved in the kingdom; for it consists of all "professing Christians," thus making it identical with modern Christendom. Jesus definitely did not teach such, nor would agree with such. The whole theory is based on a false assumption, that Jesus came to earth primarily concerned with the re-establishment of Israel's ancient political kingdom. It is an endeavor to interpret the kingdom of God in terms of the ancient Jewish state instead of the true Israel, the true sons of Abraham, the people of faith. In his *Christ's Kingdom and Coming* Jesse Wilson Hodges states, "Christ's kingdom is definitely spiritual and redemptive both in its immediate and in its ultimate objectives."[11] The student is referred to this book for a fuller refutal of this dualistic view of the kingdom.

2. Nature of kingdom

(1) founded by christ

The kingdom, as founded by our Lord, is the prime motive of his advent. The opening sermon of his ministry is: "The time is fulfilled, and the kingdom of God is at hand: repent ye, and believe in the gospel" (Mark 1:15). The goal of his activity is the kingdom, as is seen in the prayer he teaches his disciples. "Thy

[10] A. B. Bruce, *The Kingdom of God*, p. 58.
[11] Jesse W. Hodges, *Christ's Kingdom and Coming*, pp. 21, 22.

kingdom come. Thy will be done, as in heaven, so on earth" (Matt. 6:10). Our wills are to become identified with his in the kingdom he has come to usher in. All the New Testament writers are thoroughly convinced that some new and wondrous thing has entered where man dwells, and it has entered through the presence of Christ. Paul says, "For the grace of God hath appeared, bringing salvation to all men..." (Titus 2:11). Because of this great event the author of Hebrews enjoins us, "Let us therefore draw near with boldness unto the throne of grace, that we may receive mercy, and may find grace to help us in time of need" (4:16). The Levitical religion keeps men at a distance from God, but no longer is this necessary. John expresses this contrast between old and new. "For the law was given through Moses; grace and truth came through Jesus Christ" (John 1:17). Jesus himself declares that the one who is but little in the kingdom of heaven is greater than John the Baptist, and of all those born of women none is greater than John (Matt. 11:11). Something new has happened, an epoch-making event with far-reaching consequences! The kingdom is here!

It is true that the name employed by our Lord for this new phenomenon is an old one. But this is good, for it introduces the new concept with the least amount of shock to old associations. "Kingdom" is a familiar term to his hearers and depicts affinity and not antagonism. It will be good for permanent use, since it is not a transient term. Their hopes have been built around that very term; now these hopes can become a reality. Therefore Jesus uses the term with full consciousness of its significance, both for those in the past and for his followers in the future.

We have already seen that the Scriptures represent Christ's offices as prophet, priest, and king, and that he combines all of these Old Testament functions in himself in an ideal reality. Here we are concerned with the third of these offices, for his founding of the kingdom rests upon his all-important kingship. The sovereignty of the divine-human Redeemer is the basis of this new advent of the glory of God.

(2) SPIRITUAL IN NATURE

Contrary to the statements of men like Weiss and those that have followed him through the years, Jesus' original intent is that of setting up a purely spiritual kingdom. Weiss, in his *Leben Jesu*, would make us think that Jesus reverses his original plan, that he comes with youthful enthusiasm to set up a theocratic kingdom of Israel with himself as king, but that due to the unexpected turn in events he finds a cross instead of a throne. Therefore he turns to a spiritual dominion of universal scope instead. Weiss has had his followers, with varied additions or alterations, through the years. But what of his theory? Jesus knows full well from his baptism and temptation on that his kingdom will be a spiritual one. The very opening statements of the Sermon on the Mount, the Beatitudes, show this (Matt. 5:3-12). His defense of his disciples for feasting rather than fasting demonstrates the identical thing (Matt. 9:14, 15). Though his thoughts and plans may alter slightly due to outward events, they are present in his mind, in germ at least, from the very start of his ministry.

Thus the great prophecy of Daniel is fulfilled: "And in the days of those kings shall the God of heaven set up a kingdom which shall never be destroyed, nor shall the sovereignty thereof be left to another people; but it shall break in pieces and consume all these kingdoms, and it shall stand for ever" (2:44). Both Jesus and John the Baptist come preaching that the kingdom is at hand: "Repent ye; for the kingdom of heaven is at hand." John the Baptist in Matthew 3:2 and Jesus in Matthew 4:17 proclaim identically the same words, the latter after the former is delivered up to prison. Yet even John the Baptist himself does not possess the same concept of this kingdom as does Jesus, as John's final words from prison show: "Art thou he that cometh, or look we for another?" (Matt. 11:3). The Jews want a Messiah who will bring back the Golden Age of David and Solomon, one who will set up an earthly, Jewish, Palestinian kingdom and reverse the Rome-Jerusalem order of power. With a cataclysmic display of might he will break the power of all the enemies of the Jews, much in the manner of the imprecatory Psalms, and make Jerusalem supreme among the nations and ruler over all the earth.

Peter, as well as John the Baptist, evidently shares this prevailing view. He indeed declares Jesus to be the Christ, for which he receives the Lord's blessing; but he immediately reveals the typical, Jewish-encrusted view of Messiahship. When Jesus declares that he must be crucified and die and be raised up, Peter refutes such a thought vehemently. There is no place in his theology for a suffering and dying Messiah, even though such is portrayed graphically in Isaiah 53. (All this is discerned in Mark 8:27ff.) And when, at the height of his popularity, they endeavor to make Jesus king, he slips from their midst and withdraws to be alone (John 6:15). He has not come to be that kind of king. And when James and John are desirous of the enviable positions at either side of Jesus' throne, they too have in mind the restored Davidic throne in Jerusalem (Mark 10:35ff.). Jesus' humble birth in Bethlehem is in full accord with his meek ride into Jerusalem upon a lowly beast of burden. At both events he is called King: by the Magi from the East at his birth (Matt. 2:2) and by the street throng of

Jerusalem at his triumphant entry (Luke 19:38). In his kingdom there must be no pomp and circumstance for the purpose of impressing the world, only humility and personal righteousness. Pilate, being in doubt as to his true identity, asks Jesus at the trial if he is the king of the Jews, to which Jesus replies, "My kingdom is not of this world: if my kingdom were of this world, then would my servants fight, that I should not be delivered to the Jews: but now is my kingdom not from hence." Pilate again asks if he is a king, to which he replies, "Thou sayest that I am a king. To this end have I been born, and to this end am I come into the world . . ." (John 18:33ff.). Evidently Pilate follows this up with the superscription over the cross: "Jesus of Nazareth, the King of the Jews" (John 19:19).

Jesus' conception of a completely spiritual, universal kingdom, as over against a mundane, exclusively Jewish one, so unnerves the Jews that they rebel at such a thought. The old conception is so engrained in their thinking that even after the resurrection Cleopas and his unnamed friend walking from Jerusalem to Emmaus can say, "But we hoped that it was he who should redeem Israel" (Luke 24:21). And even on the day of the ascension his disciples look at him and say, "Lord, dost thou at this time restore the kingdom to Israel?" (Acts 1:6), evidently thinking of the restoration of the old Davidic kingdom on an even more grandiose scale. Jesus endeavors to make them conceive of a kingdom free from national, racial, and political limitations, one embodied in himself as future Lord and present Son of man. In fact, he very seldom applies the term Christ, or Messiah, to himself, for it brings to the Jewish mind a concept far from what he desires. So he chooses the obscure title Son of man, as found in the famous passage of Daniel 7:13ff., and pours into this unexpected term the concept of himself that he wishes the world to have, which concept, by the way, includes the Suffering-Servant idea of Isaiah 53. Therefore, when he speaks of dying, it is no wonder his followers exclaim, "We have heard out of the law that the Christ abideth for ever: and how sayest thou, The Son of man must be lifted up? who is this son of man?" (John 12:34).

(3) UNIVERSAL IN SCOPE

The spiritual aspect of the advent of our Saviour determines the spiritual nature of his kingdom. But along with the spiritual nature of the kingdom goes a correlative idea: it is universal and not limited in scope. Jesus comes to save all who will accept him, not just national Israel, as is forcefully seen in an incident at Nazareth, his home town. There he enters the synagogue and reads a portion of the great prophet who, probably more than any other Old Testament writer, has sensed Israel's great responsibility to a needy world. This passage is now our Isaiah 61:1ff. "The Spirit of the Lord is upon me, Because he anointed me to preach good tidings to the poor: He hath sent me to proclaim release to the captives, And recovering of sight to the blind, To set at liberty them that are bruised, To proclaim the acceptable year of the Lord" (Luke 4:18, 19). The reading is followed by his one comment: "To-day hath this scripture been fulfilled in your ears." His mission is a ministry of grace to sorrowing mankind. Luke's placing of this incident in the forefront of his gospel shows that Jesus' doctrine moves on the plane of spirituality and universality from the very start. Jesus' ministry soars into a higher region than merely that of a restored theocratic kingdom of national Israel. No wonder the people marvel at "the words of grace which proceeded out of his mouth" (Luke 4:22).

The kind of people to whom he preaches, the strata of society to whom he ministers, and the variety of the persons to whom he issues his gracious invitation — these are indicative of the universality of his kingdom. He preaches his kingdom to the poor (Matt. 11:5); he comes to call sinners, not the "righteous" (Matt. 9:13); he comes seeking lost ones (Luke 19:10). Publicans, harlots, and sinners constitute the greatest group pressing into the kingdom, a fact which astounds the "righteous" and reputable Pharisees. "The kingdom of God was being made a cave of Adullam, whither every one that was in distress or deep in moral debt resorted. The city of God was being taken possession of by 'dogs'; whose proper place was without; it was, as it were, being stormed by rude, lawless bands, and taken from those who thought they had an exclusive right to it. What a violence! What a profanation! Perhaps so; but one thing is clear: those persons who by their passionate earnestness were storming the kingdom would not suppose that *they* had any right to it. They listened to Christ's call, because they gathered from His preaching that the kingdom was a gift of grace, meant, in fact, God's sovereign, unmerited love to unworthy men, blessing them with pardon, and so gaining power over their hearts. And they felt that it did gain power, and that the dominion was real. Forgiven much, they loved much. Christ also was aware of the fact, and that was one of His reasons for seeking citizens of the kingdom in such a quarter; and that He did seek them there, for such a reason, shows very plainly what His idea of the kingdom was: *a kingdom of grace in order to be a kingdom of holiness.*"[12]

Nothing shows the universality of the kingdom, that it is not bound by race, nation, or any other provincial limitation, more

---

[12] Bruce, *op. cit.,* p. 54.

than the very words of Jesus himself. "Ye are the salt of the earth"; "Ye are the light of the world" (Matt. 5:13, 14) ; "The field is the world" (Matt. 13:38) . The children of the kingdom are to have a salting and enlightening influence upon the world, with the word of the kingdom sown throughout that world. Jesus' final injunction embraces all mankind: "Go ye therefore, and make disciples of all the nations..." (Matt. 28:19) . These significant utterances extend over too extensive a horizon to make Jesus merely a patriotic Jew concerned only with his countrymen and with the consummation of national Israel.

(4) PRESENT AND FUTURE IN TIME

It is very obvious from a study of the New Testament that the kingdom of God is both a present reality and a future hope. With the coming of Jesus the kingdom comes, is newly come. There is a Greek word which depicts this idea quite clearly, *kairos,* which, though translated with the English "time," actually means the appointed time, the appointed season. Therefore, with the coming of Christ comes the *kairos;* God has inaugurated his rule. But parallel with this magnificent fact is the depressant thought that Satan's power has not yet been completely overthrown, so that the supreme establishment and triumph of God's kingdom is still to be consummated. The kingdom is embodied, so to speak, in Jesus — as Son of man on earth, therefore present, and as future Lord in heaven, therefore to be consummated at a later date. In a sense, and paradoxically speaking, the future has become present and yet has not ceased to be future. The kingdom is present and immanent, yet also future and supramundane; it is here, yet it also will be. The harmony of these two concepts is grounded in the very teaching of Jesus himself. In him rest both the inauguration of the kingdom and the consummation of the kingdom.

There are passages which seem to show that the kingdom is present, here and now, for it comes with the early appearance of Jesus. "But if I by the Spirit of God cast out demons, then is the kingdom of God come upon you" (Matt. 12:28) . The verb, as used here in the Greek, expresses in a very forcible way the fact that the kingdom of God has actually arrived. Daniel 7:22 reads, "...and the time came that the saints possessed the kingdom." Is not the advent of Jesus the fulfillment of the Daniel passage? Another indication of the present reality of the kingdom is found in Jesus' introductory preaching: "The time is fulfilled, and the kingdom of God is at hand: repent ye, and believe in the gospel" (Mark 1:15) . The Greek verb again depicts the presence of the kingdom. Still another passage showing the presence of the kingdom is that concerning Jonah and the Queen of the South. "The men of

Nineveh shall stand up in the judgment with this generation, and shall condemn it: for they repented at the preaching of Jonah; and behold, a greater than Jonah is here. The queen of the south shall rise up in the judgment with this generation, and shall condemn it: for she came from the ends of the earth to hear the wisdom of Solomon; and behold, a greater than Solomon is here" (Matt. 12:41, 42). The Greek term translated "greater" is in both cases a neuter adjective and would be better translated "greater something." Translating the term as "greater" would require a masculine adjective in the original language. Another pertinent passage is one given in answer to a query from the Pharisees: "The kingdom of God cometh not with observation: neither shall they say, Lo, here! or, There! for lo, the kingdom of God is within you" (Luke 17:20, 21). The term translated "within you" might also be translated "in the midst of you"; but still the idea is the same. The kingdom is a present reality.

Just as there are passages which show that the kingdom is present, there are others which show that it has a future characteristic also. True, there is no explicit statement such as, "The kingdom of God will come," as a counterpart of the statement, "The kingdom of God has come." Yet we do find the following sayings. "There are some here of them that stand by, who shall in no wise taste of death, till they see the kingdom of God come with power" (Mark 9:1). The perfect participle represents an action as already complete from the standpoint of the main verb. It is not that they will see the kingdom coming, but that they will see that it has already come. Another pertinent passage is found in Matthew. "And I say unto you, that many shall come from the east and the west, and shall sit down with Abraham, and Isaac, and Jacob, in the kingdom of heaven" (8:11). There is also the famous saying at the Last Supper. "But I say unto you, I shall not drink henceforth of this fruit of the vine, until that day when I drink it new with you in my Father's kingdom" (Matt. 26:29).

Of a truth, then, the kingdom, future and at the same time present, is a mystery. To grasp this mystery one needs spiritual perception. "Ordinary things can only be either future or already present. Purely future things cannot sally forth from their future and be operative here and now. Marvels can be both and do both. This is the very reason that they are marvels."[13] So it is with the kingdom as Jesus reveals it. However, there are some who reject the idea that the kingdom is present and view it only as future. One of these is Rudolf Bultmann, who "sets his face firmly against all who would see an element in the teaching of Jesus in which the King-

---

[13] Rudolf Otto, *The Kingdom of God and the Son of Man*, p. 73.

dom is present; on this point the arguments and evidence adduced by Dodd, Jeremias, Kümmel et al. leave him quite cold."[14] For him the kingdom is like a train entering the station, but yet not having reached the platform. Albert Schweitzer is another who believes the kingdom to be altogether future.[15]

(5) INTERRELATED WITH CHURCH

What is the relation of the kingdom to the church? Are these synonymous terms; and if not, do they overlap in meaning? It is true that the social ideal of the New Testament is found in both of these great concepts. Yet the term kingdom is mainly a Synoptic term, being found repeatedly on the lips of our Lord. The term church is found mainly in Acts and in the epistles, Jesus having used it sparingly. It is a great Pauline term.

The terms are not identical. If the term church is used in a local sense it is a much narrower one than kingdom. If it is used in a universal sense it is as broad, but it is still not identical. The kingdom is the reign of God in the lives of his people, and through them in the whole world; the church is the ideal assembly of all true believers. The kingdom is the rule of God; the church consists of the people under God's rule. The kingdom is grounded in the sovereignty of God, while the church is God's own community of the redeemed, obedient to their sovereign King. The persons involved are the same, as even the underlying principles are the same. But the concepts which these terms embrace are different. The effective instrument of God for carrying on the business of the kingdom in the world is the church. Or, to express it differently, the local church is the divinely appointed means for extending the kingdom of Christ in the world. John Bright is right when he affirms, "There is no tendency in the New Testament to identify the visible church with the Kingdom of God. The church that makes such an identification will soon begin to invite God to endorse its own very human policies and practices, will equate the people of God with those nice people who share its particular beliefs and participate in its services, and will reckon the advance of the Kingdom in terms of its numerical growth. But it will not be the New Testament Church."[16]

The very term kingdom suggests a society, and that society is designated by the term church. The first occurrence of the name of this society on the lips of Jesus is in the statement directed to Peter at Caesarea Philippi, "I will build my church" (Matt. 16:

---

14 Perrin, *op. cit.*, p. 114.
15 See "The Kingdom of God" in C. H. Dodd's *The Parables of the Kingdom*, for a fuller discussion of the present and future aspects of the kingdom.
16 John Bright, *The Kingdom of God*, p. 236.

18) . It is to be a society elective in nature. It is to be furnished with symbolic rites, which will serve as bonds of union and of fellowship. "The identity of Church and kingdom is not absolute but relative only. The two categories do not entirely coincide, even when the Church as a visible society is all it ought to be; its members all truly Christian in faith and life. The kingdom is the larger category. It embraces all who by the key of a true knowledge of the historical Christ are admitted within its portals."[17] Thus we see that in the mind of Jesus the kingdom is a spiritual commonwealth including all those adopting certain principles and motives in life and meeting the moral and spiritual requirements which he lays down, while the church is a society based upon the principles of the kingdom in which the members are held together by outward ties of fellowship. The term kingdom is definitely the more prominent one in the mind of Jesus; the term kingdom occurs one hundred and twelve times in the gospels, while the word church occurs on only two occasions (and that not at all in the Gospel of John). And yet Jesus knows that the common spiritual life of the kingdom needs to be fostered by the fellowship resulting from an organized society of believers. This is the church.

[17] Bruce, *op. cit.*, pp. 265-6.

OUTLINE FOR CHAPTER THIRTEEN

I. Significance
 1. English word church
  (1) Derivation
  (2) Usages
 2. New Testament word for church
  (1) Meaning
  (2) Usages
   a. Local
   b. General
    (a) Generic
    (b) Collective
    (c) Universal
 3. New Testament concepts of church
  (1) Body of Christ
  (2) Congregation of the faithful
  (3) Fellowship of the Spirit

II. Administration
 1. Monarchical
 2. Episcopal
 3. Presbyterial
 4. Congregational
  (1) Precedent in Scripture
  (2) Supreme headship of Christ
  (3) Equality of all believers
  (4) Salvation by grace through faith
  (5) Freedom and responsibility of believer

III. Membership
 1. Regeneration
 2. Baptism

IV. Officers
 1. General officers
  (1) Apostles
   a. Those called apostles
   b. Qualifications of an apostle
    (a) Call and commission
    (b) Witness of resurrection
    (c) Signs of an apostle
    (d) Authority and privileges
  (2) Prophets
  (3) Evangelists
  (4) Teachers

2. Local officers
   (1) Elders, bishops, pastors
       a. Meaning of terms
          (a) Elder
          (b) Bishop
          (c) Pastor
       b. Nature of the office
          (a) Qualifications
          -(b) Duties
          (c) Appointment
          (d) Authority
   (2) Deacons
       a. Meaning of term
       b. Origin of office
       c. Qualifications
       d. Duties
V. Work and Worship
   1. Evangelism and missions
   2. Benevolence and humanitarianism
   3. Social and domestic righteousness
   4. Edification and growth
   5. Worship and praise

CHAPTER THIRTEEN

THE CHURCH

LET US LOOK AT THE CHURCH IN ITS MEANING, CONSTITUTION, ACTIVITY, and ordinances. All but the last named will be considered in this chapter, the last in the subsequent chapter. This doctrine of the church, called ecclesiology, is one of great interest and moment because of the varied views that are prevalent among scholars and church leaders.

I. SIGNIFICANCE

1. ENGLISH WORD CHURCH

(1) DERIVATION

The English word church is very similar to the Scottish word *kirk* and to the German word *Kirche,* although it is probably derived from the old Saxon words *circe, cirice,* or *cyrace* (different forms of the same word). These in turn were probably derived from the Greek term *kuriakon,* which was used by Greek Christians to denote the house of worship. It is a known fact that the Teutonic races received their first knowledge of Christianity from the Greek Christians. The Greek word *kuriakon* is merely the neuter adjective of the Greek word for Lord (found many times in the New Testament). Therefore it means pertaining to the Lord, or the Lord's house or place. In all the early literature of the Greek Christians this neuter adjective was used like a noun (by adding the article) and applied to the house of worship. Usage was then transferred to those worshipping in the building, or the assembly of the people themselves. Then usage spread rapidly to the various meanings applied to the term through the centuries.

(2) USAGES

What are the various usages of the English word church prevailing in the Christian literature of the day? It is applied to a particular body of Christians organized for the purpose of worship. This is the local church, the most common use of the term in the New Testament. It is also used for the general body, or sum total, of all Christians. This is the universal church, as the word is used a few times in the New Testament. To these two modern uses, identical with those found in the New Testament, are added three uses that have evolved during the centuries. It is applied to the building where a local assembly meets for the purpose of worship, the original meaning of *kuriakon*. It is also applied to a denomination of Christians with the same doctrines, organization, etc., and embracing the local bodies of that order. It is also used as an adjective, as in the following: "church meeting," "church polity," "church history," "church order," and "church affairs."

2. New Testament Word for Church

(1) MEANING

The New Testament word translated church is *ekklēsia,* which is derived from two words, *ek* meaning "out" and *kaleō* meaning "to call." Therefore it originally designated the assembly of citizens "called out" from their houses to the gathering place for the purpose of discussion of public business. The "called-out ones" were those summoned to attend these gatherings. Then the term passed over into the New Testament documents and designated the assembly of those gathered together for public worship, or those called out to assemble for Christian purposes. It is very similar in meaning to the Old Testament term translated congregation and is used in the New Testament in both the local and the general sense.

(2) USAGES

a. *Local*

Most of the time *ekklēsia* is used in the New Testament it designates a local assembly of Christian believers. This is the local church. Some examples are as follows. Immediately after Luke tells us that Ananias and Sapphira are struck dead because of their deceit, he states, "And great fear came upon the whole church, and upon all that heard these things" (Acts 5:11). In connection with the death of Stephen Luke states, "And there arose on that day a great persecution against the church which was in Jerusalem" (Acts 8:1). Acts 11:22 talks of the church at Jerusalem, while Acts 11:26 talks of the church at Antioch. Luke states that during Paul's first missionary journey "they had appointed for them elders in every church" (Acts 14:23). "And when he had landed at Caesarea, he went up and saluted the church" (Acts 18:22). "And from Miletus he sent to Ephesus, and called to him the elders of the church" (Acts 20:17). The plural form also is used for church in the local sense. "Now concerning the collection for the saints, as I gave order to the churches of Galatia, so also do ye" (I Cor. 16:1). Second Corinthians 8:1 speaks of "the churches of Macedonia." There are many other examples, but these will suffice.

b. *General*

We now look at the word *ekklēsia* as used in a more general sense. It is hard to ascertain as to whether the local sense gave rise to the general, or the general to the local, or whether the two senses arose simultaneously in the first century. This is immaterial. The main fact is that when we leave the conception of the local assembly the word takes on a meaning that becomes more and more general. Therefore the general sense seems to divide itself into three categories: the generic, the collective, and the universal.

(a) The generic sense is rejected by many scholars, relegating the passages used to support it to either the local or the universal sense; but it should probably be recognized. It constitutes the first rung of the ladder away from the local sense. Examples are as follows. Paul is speaking to Timothy about "how men ought to behave themselves in the house of God, which is the church of the living God, the pillar and ground of the truth" (I Tim. 3:15). Our Lord probably has this in mind when he advises, "And if he refuse to hear them, tell it unto the church: and if he refuse to hear the church also, let him be unto thee as the Gentile and the publican" (Matt. 18:17). "And God hath set some in the church, first apostles, secondly prophets, thirdly teachers..." (I Cor. 12:28). The idea in these passages is any church, the church that may be reached. It is just one shade away from the definitely local sense and is still open to debate.

(b) The collective sense is that of the mass of professing Christians more or less widely extended, or the sum total of Christians in the world, or in any territory. Sometimes this is called the "church visible." The church mentioned as the object of Paul's pre-Christian wrath would be an example. "But Saul laid waste the church, entering into every house, and dragging men and women committed them to prison" (Acts 8:3). Paul himself says, "I persecuted the church of God" (I Cor. 15:9). Other passages are Galatians 1:13 and Philippians 3:6. Paul persecuted the Christians wherever he found them, not just at Jerusalem; he was on his way to Damascus for that very purpose when he was converted. Some passages represent the church as more or less extended abroad, and so reveal the collective sense. "So the church throughout all Judea and Galilee and Samaria had peace, being edified" (Acts 9:31). This refers to all the Christian people through these regions. Paul addresses the Christians at Rome, "Gaius my host, and of the whole church, saluteth you" (Rom. 16:23). He also states, "Give no occasion of stumbling, either to Jews, or to Greeks, or to the church of God" (I Cor. 10:32). Here the collective number of professing Christians is the sense conveyed.

(c) The universal sense gives the broadest use of the word church, denoting the whole body of true believers in Christ of all ages, whether alive or having died and gone on to be with Christ. The book of Ephesians uses the word only in this sense. It is found also in Colossians 1:18, 24, and in Hebrews 12:23. Paul states that Christ is "head over all things to the church, which is his body, the fulness of him that filleth all in all" (Eph. 1:22, 23). He also desires that the manifold wisdom of God "might be made known through the church" (Eph. 3:10). The writer to the Hebrews definitely includes those Christians that have passed on: "to the general assembly and church of the firstborn who are enrolled in heaven" (Heb. 12:23). In the famous passage from the lips of our Lord, "upon this rock I will build my church" (Matt. 16:18), the universal sense seems to be the best interpretation; for he apparently denotes the whole body of the redeemed of all ages. In the New Testament there are definitely more examples of the use of the word church in the local sense than there are in the universal sense, but this does not warrant the thought that the New Testament writers have only an incidental interest in the universal concept of the church. It is just that their aims and motives in writing called for more uses of the term in the local sense.

3. NEW TESTAMENT CONCEPTS OF CHURCH

There are certain New Testament concepts of the church that are too broad to be denoted by one word, such as *ekklēsia*.

(1) BODY OF CHRIST

The church is not an institution, such as the home, or the state, or the school, and therefore should never be called an institution. It is an organism, characterized by spiritual life. It is alive and dynamic. It cannot be defined in human terms, as simply an aggregate of individuals brought together for spiritual purposes. It is the body of Christ, and believers are to know a common life in the body of Christ. They have been baptized into Christ. They have put on Christ. He is the head of the church; therefore they live under him. They consititute his chosen and commissioned ones, to whom are given the keys of the kingdom. This great teaching is found in Ephesians, Colossians, and First Corinthians.

Paul says that God "put all things in subjection under his feet, and gave him to be head over all things to the church, which is his body, the fulness of him that filleth all in all" (Eph. 1:22, 23). "And he is the head of the body, the church" (Col. 1:18). There is a transcendent element in the church, for it is composed of those whom Christ has saved and through whom he reveals God. Union with Christ presupposes the church, for this union alone transforms sinners and thus makes possible the spiritual fellowship among Christians that is the organizing principle of the church. The church is no humanitarian organization, for Christ lives within it. "For as the body is one, and hath many members, and all the members of the body, being many, are one body; so also is Christ. For in one Spirit were we all baptized into one body, whether Jews or Greeks, whether bond or free; and were all made to drink of one Spirit. For the body is not one member, but many" (I Cor. 12:12-14). We become members of his body, the church, by his own gracious act, not by what we do. We do not create the church; it is the body of Christ, and we are simply added to it.

(2) CONGREGATION OF THE FAITHFUL

The church is composed of believers in Christ, those who have life by faith in him. The church is the congregation, or assembly, of these faithful ones. This view of the church, with emphasis upon preaching, worship, prayer, baptism, and the Lord's Supper, is found in Acts, Galatians, and Romans. It is the congregation of the faithful.

When a man believes he receives the grace of God and is justified; he becomes a child of God by sheer grace. Yet this is not just an individual matter, for he becomes part of the assembly of the faithful. God chose Abraham and his descendants for a purpose, making a covenant with them, calling them his holy nation. He made a new covenant with spiritual Israel, composed of believers in Christ, for a purpose. "Ye did not choose me, but I chose you, and appointed you, that ye should go and bear fruit, and that your fruit should abide" (John 15:16). Every "you" in this passage is in the plural in the Greek. Also, in Paul's phrase "Christ in you, the hope of glory" (Col. 1:27), the "you" is in the plural. This is none other than the church, the congregation of the faithful. Especially is this concept seen in Acts, where the church is pictured simply as those who believe. "And the Lord added to them day by day those that were saved" (Acts 2:47). "But many of them that heard the word believed; and the number of the men came to be about five thousand" (Acts 4:4). "And the multitude of them that believed were of one heart and soul" (Acts 4:32). "And believers were the more added to the Lord, multitudes, both of men and women" (Acts 5:14). The words believe and faith are used to depict the relationship of the redeemed one to Christ. "We are to imagine, then, a little community confessing Jesus as Messiah and Lord, vividly aware of an 'upsurge of a new-life,' living together like a big family, devoting themselves to preaching the Word, celebrating their rite of table-fellowship with their living Lord, and looking for his advent in glory."[1] This is the congregation of the faithful.

(3) FELLOWSHIP OF THE SPIRIT

The church is composed of those who have fellowship in the Spirit, a concept of the church found mainly in the book of Acts. The church is where the Spirit is, active with power, which is the condition subsequent to Pentecost. "And they were all filled with the Holy Spirit, and began to speak with other tongues, as the Spirit gave them utterance" (Acts 2:4). This pouring out of the Spirit upon the church is the fulfillment of Jesus' prophecy: "But ye shall receive power when the Holy Spirit is come upon you" (Acts 1:8). It is also, according to the Apostle Peter, the fulfillment of Joel's prophecy (Acts 2:16-21). Because of the presence of the Holy Spirit Peter is no longer the vacillating one but is the fearless preacher instead (Acts 4:8). Praying and being filled with the Holy Spirit give the disciples power to speak the word of God boldly (Acts 4:31). It is to the Holy Spirit that Ananias and Sapphira lie concerning the price of the parcel of land sold to give money to the common fund in the church at Jerusalem (Acts 5:1-11). Peter and John were sent to Samaria that the ones there accepting the word of God might receive the Holy Spirit (Acts 8:14-17). The Holy Spirit sent Paul and Barnabas on their missionary journey (Acts 13:2, 4). According to Acts the distinctiveness of Christianity lies in the great change produced in the individual believer by the Holy Spirit and in the vitalizing power of the Spirit pervading the church. This great book informs us that "the company of disciples, upon whom the Holy Spirit had descended, together with their first converts, comprised a new religious group who shared a common loyalty. The twelve apostles formed the human center of the group. But it was not a merely human fellowship. It was, rather, the sharing of a common life whose source was in God."[2] Truly this was the fellowship of the Spirit.

II. ADMINISTRATION

Church administration may also be designated by the terms church government, church polity, church order, church organization, or church constitution. Every group of believers in Christ calling itself a church has some form of government. These forms

---

[1] A. M. Hunter, *Introducing New Testament Theology*, p. 78.
[2] L. S. Thornton, *The Common Life in the Body of Christ*, pp. 5, 6.

are generally classified by four types: monarchical, episcopal, presbyterial, and congregational.

1. MONARCHICAL

This form of church government places the ultimate authority in the hands of one man, hence the name monarchical (pertaining to the rule of one). The supreme example of this type is the Roman Catholic Church, with the Pope at Rome as its head. That he speaks with authority, or *ex cathedra* (from the chair), and, when he does so, is infallible, is a Roman Catholic tenet maintained since 1870. It is held that the Pope is the successor to Peter and is the vicegerent of Christ. This church claims to be the one universal, or catholic church, a world-church idea with Rome as the center. Hence we have the name Roman Catholic Church.

2. EPISCOPAL

This type of church government is also called the prelatical, since it is governed by prelates, or the clergy. Since those who govern are usually the bishops, this type of government is termed episcopal; for the Greek term for bishop in the New Testament is *episkopos. Episkopos* also means overseer, which falls in line with this view. The bishop, presiding over a certain area or district, is officially superior to the other ministers in that area. It is maintained that the power to ordain and the right to rule belong to the office of bishop, or *episkopos.* This modern concept of a ruling bishop is contrary to the view of the term as found in the New Testament. The Methodist Church would be an example of episcopacy.

3. PRESBYTERIAL

This type of church government is that controlled by elders. The term elder, as found in the New Testament, translates the Greek term *presbuteros,* hence the name presbyterial, pertaining to elders, or presbyters. Presbyterianism recognizes two types of elders, preaching and ruling. These meet to form the Session of the Church, the body transacting the business of the church, even to the admission and dismissal of the members. The next higher ranking body is the Presbytery, then the Synod, then the General Assembly. Decisions can always be appealed to the higher authoritative body, the adjudication of the General Assembly being final. The Presbyterian Church constitutes an example of presbyterianism.

4. CONGREGATIONAL

This type of church government is also called the independent type, for it is maintained that each local church is independent of the authority of every other local church and of any governing body or prelate. As the presbyterial is the representative type of government, so the congregational is the democratic type. Hence it is also called the democratic, for it is maintained that all governing power should lie in the hands of the members themselves. Baptists constitute an example of this type.

Those that adhere to the congregational type and believe that everything must be decided in a democratic manner look with disfavor upon governing bodies formulating rules or laws for the local churches to follow. These local churches are independent of each other. Even within the local church itself every issue must be decided by majority vote. The pastor and the deacons have no more ecclesiastical authority than the youngest of members. Each has only one vote in the deciding of any issue, and the majority rules. This democratic power cannot be delegated or transferred, nor is it ever made representative. It is held by the members themselves, who are regenerated, baptized individuals, each old enough to request voluntarily his membership on the basis of a conversion experience. This would necessarily exclude infant baptism, or pedobaptism. It would exclude "being born" into a church. It would exclude a world-church idea, as is found in Roman Catholicism, which holds that all local churches are subject to the authority of the Pope at Rome. It would exclude a national-church idea, as is found in certain nations or provinces, which holds that all members of the church in that nation or province are bound together in one organization holding jurisdiction over the local churches.

There are several good reasons for favoring the congregational type of church government. These are as follows.

(1) PRECEDENT IN SCRIPTURE

The New Testament churches were organized according to this democratic fashion, and do not the Scriptures constitute the only sufficient rule in regard to faith and practice? The method and practice of the apostles themselves, who knew our Lord personally, and who wrote the sacred documents comprising our New Testament, would constitute a precedent of extreme worth. There is no evidence in the New Testament of "ruling elders," or "bishops," who direct the affairs of the church. There is no official class who rules. Even our Lord himself, in one of the only two occasions in which he mentions the church by terming it church, advises that it be made the last source of appeal (Matt. 18:15-17). If two brothers disagree, and other means of reconciliation fail, let them take it to the church — the members in democratic meeting. It is the "multitude of the disciples" who choose the first seven deacons at Jerusalem, not some ruling class of bishops (Acts 6:1-6). In the great Jerusalem Controversy, as recorded in Acts 15, concerning whether or not Gentiles should be required to become Jews before they can become Christians, the final decision is made by "the whole church" (Acts 15:22). Also, any advice Paul presents to the early Christians in his epistles, is given to the whole church, not to some august assemblage selected from its midst. He claims that his apostolic position gives him the authority to exhort and instruct a church, but he never extends this authority to the degree of coercing a church, or of dictating to it in any way. "Since Christ the Lord rules, there are no rulers. There are indeed persons to whom an official duty has been allocated, the episcopoi who are mentioned only on one single occasion by Paul. But this differentiation of the gifts of grace (charismata) does not create any difference in jurisdiction or rank. Paul knows nothing of Presbyterian or Episcopal Orders."[3]

(2) SUPREME HEADSHIP OF CHRIST

Christ is the head of every Christian. He is the only Lord of every believer. In regard to the church it is inconsistent to believe this spiritually and then to follow another conviction practically; for to submit to the authority of pope, bishop, priest, or council is to do the latter. To whatever extent this is done the believer negates the headship of Christ. Therefore a democratic form of government seems imperative.

(3) EQUALITY OF ALL BELIEVERS

Every believer stands equally before Christ. Every child of God has become so by grace. The ground is level at the foot of the cross. This fact as of necessity calls for a democratic setup; nothing else is permissible. There can be no spiritual hierarchy. There can be no division into "clergy" and "laity," for this is the first step toward a hierarchy. In Christ there is no Jew or Gentile, bond or free, male or female (Gal. 3:28). "There is no respect of persons with God" (Rom. 2:11).

(4) SALVATION BY GRACE THROUGH FAITH

Salvation by grace through faith calls for a democratic church. The other concept of salvation, erroneously evolving through the centuries, is that of priestly mediation through what are termed sacraments (from seven in the Roman Catholic Church down to two in others). It is maintained that grace is mediated through

3 Emil Brunner, *The Christian Doctrine of the Church, Faith, and the Consummation*, III, 43.

these sacraments. This is the sacerdotal, or priestly, concept of salvation. It is the "pipe-line" concept, as though salvation were like a fluid flowing through a pipe. As this concept historically arose, the church became less and less democratic, the two errors flourishing together.

(5) FREEDOM AND RESPONSIBILITY OF BELIEVER

The freedom and responsibility of the believer rest upon the fact that the Holy Spirit dwells in every Christian, thus making him not only free to express the Spirit's leading and guidance but responsible to do so. He must express the will of God for his life as revealed by the Holy Spirit. "Work out your own salvation with fear and trembling" (Phil. 2:12). This would be impossible in an episcopal type of government, or government by an official class, for it effaces the freedom of the individual. It avows the Spirit's guidance supremely in the bishops or ruling elders.

III. MEMBERSHIP

Who should belong to the church? What constitutes membership? Who can qualify? There are two qualifications: regeneration and baptism, or spiritual new birth and symbolical new birth.

1. REGENERATION

Regeneration, or the new birth, is a prime requisite for church membership. Only those should be received into the church who give evidence of having received Christ as Saviour. There must be a spiritual entrance into communion with the death and resurrection of Christ. This requisite evolves from the fact that the church is a spiritual organism, with the members being members of the body of Christ. "For in one Spirit were we all baptized into one body.... For the body is not one member, but many" (I Cor. 12:13, 14). It is not an organization; it is not an institution; it is a living organism composed of redeemed individuals. Only those animated by the presence of Christ should be members of his body. The work of the church is spiritual, which work can be carried on only by spiritual individuals. How can an unregenerate individual draw lost souls to the regenerating Christ?

The New Testament makes it clear that only regenerate individuals were admitted to the church. Most, if not all of the original one hundred twenty who constituted the nucleus of the church at Jerusalem were probably personal disciples of Jesus. The book of Acts makes it clear in practically every case of those added to this one hundred and twenty that there was a voluntary acceptance of the gospel and a conversion experience. "They then that received his word were baptized" (Acts 2:41). "And the

Lord added to them day by day those that were saved" (Acts 2:47). "But many of them that heard the word believed, and the number of the men came to be about five thousand" (Acts 4:4).

Since the church must include only regenerate individuals, only those who have reached the age of determining whether or not this regeneration has taken place, and who can profess such as having taken place, should seek membership in the church. This profession and request for membership must be personal and voluntary. No one else can make the decision and no coercion can be applied. Therefore infant baptism is immediately ruled out. One is not "born" into the church. He does not become a member by the sole virtue of having entered the world. Every man must hear, repent, and believe. Personal choice must be present, else the act is neither moral nor spiritual.

2. BAPTISM

Baptism constitutes the second requisite for church membership. It constitutes the formal profession to the world that one has entered into Christ's death and resurrection. It is a symbol to the world that regeneration has ensued. It is the symbol of having been buried with Christ and having risen with him to new life. "Baptism is the sign, common to all the Christian Churches, of membership in the church."[4]

Paul presents a marvelous picture of baptism in Romans 6:1ff., in which he shows the symbolism in immersion and how it is the picture of one who has been buried to the old life of sin and has risen to a new life in Christ. It is based on the assumption that every Christian has been baptized, and that by being immersed. "We were buried therefore with him through baptism into death: that like as Christ was raised from the dead through the glory of the Father, so we also might walk in newness of life" (Rom. 6:4).

The book of Acts shows that in the apostolic church baptism preceded church membership. "They then that received his word were baptized: and there were added unto them in that day about three thousand souls" (Acts 2:41). When the people of Samaria believed the preaching of Philip "they were baptized, both men and women" (Acts 8:12). The Ethiopian eunuch was baptized immediately following his acceptance of Jesus (Acts 8:38). Likewise, the Apostle Paul was immediately baptized (Acts 9:18). Peter commanded that those of Cornelius' household at Caesarea be baptized, since they had received the Holy Spirit (Acts 10:48). Other cases could be added.

4 *Ibid.,* p. 53.

DOCTRINES OF THE CHRISTIAN RELIGION

"In the New Testament we have no account of any being members of churches except such as were considered to be truly regenerated believers and had actually submitted to the rite of baptism. Now the Baptist churches insist as one of their fundamental principles that only truly regenerated believers in Christ, after having been properly baptized on profession of their faith in the Lord, should be received as members of the church. There is some diversity of opinion as to the method of a statement of Christian experience from applicants for membership, and of course mistakes are sometimes made; but in the main, and to the extent of human knowledge, Baptist churches earnestly adhere to this as one of their fundamental principles, viz., a converted and baptized membership."[5]

IV. OFFICERS

The subject of the officers of the church is a very difficult one, a difficulty based on various factors. For one, it is so easy to carry one's own bias and predisposition over into the interpretation. Modern connotations are driven back into the first century to infiltrate the New Testament concepts. Also, the New Testament does not give an abundance of information on the subject of the officers of the church. Third, some terms are ambiguous relative to translation. For instance, sometimes the Greek word for apostle can better be translated messenger, and sometimes the Greek word for deacon with the word servant. Last, classification of all the terms is very elusive, an unbending classification being almost impossible. The terms sometimes overlap each other. Yet, in spite of all this, an attempt at classification will be made; and the main division will be between that of general officers and that of local and permanent officers. The former class seems not to have pertained to the local church.

1. GENERAL OFFICERS

(1) APOSTLES

The word apostle means one sent, or messenger, and therefore, in the biblical sense, implies one sent of God. Everyone who believes in Jesus and follows him is called a disciple, which means learner. From all Jesus' disciples he selects twelve apostles, sending them forth with a specific mission. Besides these there are others in the New Testament who are also called apostles. The apostles seem to possess great authority among the churches, their preaching being readily received and their advice willingly heeded. They found many of the churches and guide them through perilous days.

[5] Edwin Charles Dargan, *Ecclesiology*, pp. 167-8.

a. *Those called apostles*

The original twelve apostles are selected by Jesus early in his ministry and are trained by our Lord prior to his departure. After the fall of Judas one named Matthias is selected by lot to take his place among the original twelve, but nothing is heard of him after his selection (Acts 1:23-26). Paul terms himself, and is likewise termed by Luke in the book of Acts, an apostle, avowing he owes his call directly to Christ himself. Acts 14:14 uses the expression "the apostles, Barnabas and Paul." It will be noticed that Barnabas is placed first; and it will also be noticed that the title apostle is distinctly used for Barnabas, thus allaying any suspicion that he is called this purely because of his association with the eminent Paul. In Romans 16:7 Paul states, "Salute Andronicus and Junias, my kinsman, and my fellow-prisoners, who are of note among the apostles." All of these named make the apostles mentioned in the New Testament seventeen in number.

b. *Qualifications of an apostle*

(a) An apostle must have received a special call and commission. We know that Jesus himself calls the original twelve apostles and Paul. Matthias is specially selected from the two men set aside as qualified to replace Judas. Paul and Barnabas seem to have been set apart in a special way for missionary service by the church at Antioch (Acts 13:2). The commission given the apostles is to preach and teach the gospel and to found churches.

(b) An apostle must be able to testify personally to the reality of the resurrection of Jesus. It is required of Matthias (Acts 1:22). We may reasonably assume it for Barnabas (Acts 4:33, 36) and Andronicus and Junias (Romans 16:7). Paul definitely claims it for himself (I Cor. 9:1; 15:8, 9).

(c) He must have "the signs of an apostle." This evidently refers to the ability to work miracles and to the spiritual activity of an empowered messenger. "Truly the signs of an apostle were wrought among you in all patience, by signs and wonders and mighty works" (II Cor. 12:12). Paul informs the Corinthians, "If to others I am not an apostle, yet at least I am to you; for the seal of mine apostleship are ye in the Lord" (I Cor. 9:2).

(d) He enjoys certain authority and privileges. This is seen in the prominence given to the twelve by our Lord and in his special training of them for leadership. It is also discerned in the manner in which the disciples recognize and accept their leadership after Jesus ascends back into heaven.

(2) PROPHETS

The prophets are not officers elected by the churches, but rather they seem to be men especially inspired of God for the benefit of the churches. In both passages where lists of officers are mentioned they are placed next in rank to apostles, thus placing them next in rank to those appointed by our Lord himself. It could be that all apostles are prophets, but certainly not vicé versa. They are inspired men of God used of God to make known new truth or better insight into known truth. This may not involve foretelling the future, as in Acts 11:28 and in 21:10, 11. Thus the prophet's function in the New Testament era is much the same as that in the Old Testament era.

(3) EVANGELISTS

We are limited in our discussion relative to evangelists due to the scarcity of scriptural evidence. They appear to have been traveling preachers, authorized in their work by the apostles and the churches. Thus they were preachers without apostolic rank, and, possibly, without prophetic inspiration. In Acts 21:8 we read of "Philip the evangelist, who was one of the seven." This refers to one of the seven deacons listed in Acts 6:1-6 and is probably the same Philip who preached throughout Samaria (Acts 8:4-8) ; and to the Ethiopian treasurer (Acts 8:26-40). Paul exhorts Timothy to "do the work of an evangelist" (II Tim. 4:5). In Paul's list of officers in Ephesians 4:11 evangelists are mentioned next in order to prophets.

(4) TEACHERS

Here again we have to deal with only a few passages, but somewhat more than for evangelists: Acts 13:1; I Corinthians 12:28, 29; Ephesians 4:11; I Timothy 2:7; II Timothy 1:11; 4:3; Hebrews 5:12; James 3:1. If these passages are studied it will be observed that the term teacher does not seem to refer to a specific office, per se, but rather that teaching was a function connected with other offices. Probably elders, prophets, and evangelists, as well as many others, taught. James does not wish that many aspire to be teachers due to the heavy responsibility upon those who have this function. "Be not many of you teachers, my brethren, knowing that we shall receive heavier judgment" (Jas. 3:1). The writer to the Hebrews states that, considering the time they have been Christians, they ought to be teachers; instead they themselves need to be taught. "For when by reason of the time ye ought to be teachers, ye have need again that some one teach you the rudiments of the first principles of the oracles of God" (Heb. 5:12).

2. LOCAL OFFICERS

We turn now to the local and permanent officers of the church, those functioning within the local church rather than generally.

(1) ELDERS, BISHOPS, PASTORS

Although three separate terms are used in the New Testament it is generally admitted that the same office is intended by all three titles. Both Paul and Peter understood it thus. "It is a fact now generally recognized by theologians of all shades of opinion that in the language of the New Testament the same office in the church is called indifferently bishop, elder, or presbyter."[6]

a. *Meaning of terms*

(a) The term elder is used many times in the gospels to designate certain officials among the Jews, as in Luke 20:1 — "the chief priests and the scribes with the elders." Sometimes it is used in the New Testament to designate simply an old person, as in I Timothy 5:1, where Paul admonishes his young friend, "Rebuke not an elder, but exhort him as a father; the younger men as brethren." This also seems to be the case in I Peter 5:5. The literal meaning of the Greek term so translated is elder one, or older one. But the main use of the term elder is for a specific church officer, which term occurs more frequently than its cognates, bishop and pastor. This more frequent use of the word elder may be due to its existing familiarity on the part of the Jews. The term carries with it the respect due to age, as its meaning and use would imply. It connotes experience, wisdom, and maturity. It is found in Acts 11:30; 14:23; 15:2, 4, 6, 22, 23; 16:4; 20:17; 21:18, and in other books also.

(b) The term bishop translates a Greek term meaning overseer; and it would not be a bad idea to translate the Greek term as such in the translations of the New Testament, since the term bishop *connotes* much more in modern use than the term *denotes* in strict New Testament usage. It received these added connotations as it progressed through church history. The term bishop, or overseer, refers more to the functions of the office than to the character of the office, as would be the case for "elder." It refers more to authority and rule than would "elder." Paul tells the elders of the Ephesian church, "Take heed unto yourselves, and to all the flock, in which the Holy Spirit hath made you bishops..." (Acts 20:28). Here, according to the author, Luke, elders and bishops are used interchangeably. In I Timothy 3:1-7 Paul outlines the qualifications for a bishop, as also in Titus 1:7-9. In I Peter 2:25 it is used of Christ, where the term pastor is also used of him, "the Shepherd and Bishop of your souls."

(c) The term pastor, used for an officer of the church, is found in only one place in the New Testament, Ephesians 4:11, when

6 Joseph Barker Lightfoot, *St. Paul's Epistle to the Philippians*, p. 95.

Paul mentions it as one of the groups receiving gifts from the ascended Christ. It is a term meaning shepherd, and thus involves the personal and spiritual concern that an elder (or bishop) would have for his flock. The surprising thing is that the word pastor, most commonly used today of this set of three synonyms, is found in only one place in the New Testament designating this office. The term most used in modern parlance is least used in the Bible. It probably arose from the unscriptural connotations surrounding the terms elder and bishop. Yet, in spite of all this, there are passages where the term pastor is not used but where the work of a pastor, or shepherd, is alluded to, thus substantiating the term itself. Jesus instructs Peter to "tend my sheep" (John 21:16). Paul tells the Ephesian elders to "feed the church of the Lord" (Acts 20:28). Peter instructs the elders, "tend the flock of God" (I Pet. 5:2). So the term implies the spiritual care of the people, like the care a shepherd would give his sheep. Jesus refers to himself, and is referred to, as a shepherd (John 10:11; Heb. 13:20, and I Pet. 2:25).

b. *Nature of the office*

(a) The qualifications for this office are important. Paul outlines them both to Timothy and to Titus (I Tim. 3:1ff.; Titus 1:7ff.). Peter also enumerates them (I Pet. 5:1ff.). They must stand high morally, be blameless, be above reproach, and be free from grievous faults. They must be leaders, knowing how to manage spiritual matters. They must be able to teach and must at all times set a spiritual example for others.

(b) The duties of this office are oversight and direction of the spiritual affairs of the church. This is seen in the root meaning of the term translated bishop, which is overseer. This term is *episkopos,* from which is derived the English term episcopal. Other duties are teaching and preaching to the church, thus edifying the church (I Tim. 3:2; 5:17). I Timothy 5:17 is the verse used as a basis for differentiating between "ruling elders" and "teaching elders," but without warrant in interpretation.

(c) The appointment to this office seems to be by election of the church. Yet, in the first New Testament instance of the appointment of elders Paul and Barnabas seem to have the upper hand. "And when they had appointed for them elders in every church, and had prayed with fasting, they commended them to the Lord, on whom they had believed" (Acts 14:23). Also, Titus is directed to appoint elders in every city (Titus 1:5). Along with appointment to office there appears to be some ceremony of induction into office, which seems to consist of the laying on of hands by the elders (I Tim. 4:14).

(d) The authority of this office is another matter of little evidence. However, the people are advised to respect this authority. Paul says, "But we beseech you, brethren, to know them that labor among you, and are over you in the Lord, and admonish you; and to esteem them exceeding highly in love for their work's sake" (I Thess. 5:12, 13). The writer to the Hebrews makes it stronger. "Obey them that have the rule over you, and submit to them: for they watch in behalf of your souls, as they that shall give account; that they may do this with joy, and not with grief" (Heb. 13:17).

(2) DEACONS

The deacons comprise the second group of local and permanent officers, and again the New Testament evidence is small.

a. *Meaning of term*

The term deacon translates a Greek term meaning servant or minister. The term is often used in the New Testament just simply in such a manner, and must be so translated. Examples of these are as follows: "Not so shall it be among you: but whosoever would become great among you shall be your minister" (Matt. 20:26). "Then the king said to the servants, Bind him hand and foot..." (Matt. 22:13). Many other examples of the same could be cited. To translate these with the word deacon would be to violate the meaning intended by the writer. There are two passages where the word deacon is the best rendering, however. In Philippians 1:1 Paul speaks of "the bishops and deacons." In I Timothy 3:8, 12 Paul again uses the term, this time giving the qualifications for the office. Even in Acts 6:1-6, where we read of the choosing of the first seven deacons at Jerusalem, the men set aside are not termed such, but rather "seven men of good report." Therefore it should always be remembered that the name deacon means servant.

b. *Origin of office*

The origin of the office of deacon is found in the choosing of the seven in Acts 6:1-6. It is true that they are not called such, but the usual interpretation of this passage is that these are the first to assume the office of deacon. These men are set aside to attend to the distribution of the common fund of the church, so that the twelve apostles can give all their time to the proclamation of the Word of God.

c. *Qualifications*

The qualifications for deacons are found in Paul's instructions to Timothy (I Tim. 3:8-13). They are to be serious men and not double-tongued. They are not to use much wine and are not to be covetous regarding money. They are to have a strong faith. Also, they are to have only one wife and to rule their houses well. Acts 6:1-6 tells us they are to be men of good reputation.

d. *Duties*

The duties of deacons mainly concern financial matters and the care of the needy. They are to look after the business affairs of the church and are to see that the widows and orphans have food and clothing. Justin Martyr states that early in the second century they ministered at the Lord's Supper, thus showing an early function at this sacred duty.

V. WORK AND WORSHIP

The church has a responsibility in this world toward God and man. The worship services and the ordinances express the Godward side, while the benevolent activities represent the manward side. Yet, at the same time, these two phases overlap. The cup of cold water must be given in the name of Christ (Matt. 10:42). Truly, "the field is the world" (Matt. 13:38). So the Godward phase and the manward phase overlap in evangelism and in missions.

The duty of the church, to propagate the principles of Christianity throughout the world, has been remarkably accomplished when we consider the hindrances and marring due to human sin and doctrinal perversion. Sin has mingled with the forces of Christ to thwart and neutralize the proclamation of the gospel. Selfishness and ulterior motives have many times blinded the eyes of those who might have accepted, or been helped spiritually. A study of church history verifies this tragic admission. Yet, in spite of this, the church has been and is at work in the world in regard to sinning and suffering humanity.

The church has a tremendous responsibility upon its shoulders, a responsibility placed there by our Lord himself. Part of this responsibility is assumed on the local church level and part cooperatively, depending upon whichever is more feasible. Generally a combination of efforts will accomplish much more in missionary and benevolent work than could be achieved through each local church working independently. Mission boards, associations, and conventions constitute examples of cooperative efforts. Yet, it must always be remembered, these combined efforts are purely voluntary. There must never be a mandatory element in the request for combined effort, only a suggestion which may or may not be accepted. Even the similarity to an hierarchical system must be avoided, for the independence of the local church must be maintained.

1. EVANGELISM AND MISSIONS

The main duty of the church is to win the lost, whether they are near or far and whether they have heard or have not heard the gospel. The good news, the glad tidings of great joy, must be proclaimed throughout the world. This is, or at least should be, the primary concern of the church. The heart of the New Testament is evangelism and missions; the prime interest of our Lord is identically the same. He tells Zacchaeus, "For the Son of man came to seek and to save that which was lost" (Luke 19:10). He says to those around him, "I came that they may have life, and may have it abundantly" (John 10:10). The Great Commission is rooted and grounded in our Lord's desire that fallen man be reconciled to God, for the marching command to the church is found in this great statement of Jesus just prior to his ascension (Matt. 28:19, 20). The early church accepted the challenge, and the winning of the lost, both Jews and Gentiles, proceeded at a rapid pace. The whole book of Acts depicts this great initial missionary advance. Jewish and Roman persecutions did not deter it; rather they augmented it. It was the heresy and ease that followed the persecutions which deterred it. The modern missionary movement, commencing with Carey, spread throughout the world; yet the church today is failing to do vitally what it should in regard to evangelism and missions.

There are three primary facts that are clearly taught in the Scriptures. Man is a sinner and in need spiritually; Christ is the sufficient answer to that need; the church is the instrumentality for these to come together. This is the spiritual outreach of the church, as differentiated from the humanitarian outreach depicted in the benevolent work of the church, to be discussed subsequently. The spiritual duty of the church must be placed above the purely humanitarian, which is the reason this phase of the church's work is discussed first of all. Man's need as a sinner must be placed above man's need as a sufferer. The former concerns his eternal soul; the latter concerns his temporal mind and body. The former concerns his relation to God; the latter concerns his relation to self. What greater proof do we need than this that the prime concern of the church should be a lost humanity?

Yet history itself adds to the proof. All along the centuries it can be easily discerned that the churches that have grown and been influential are the ones that endeavored to win the lost. The great revivals of the ages have been motivated by this urgent need of man and the resultant response of the church. Whenever the church has become secularized, rich, opulent, at ease, and favoring a priestly viewpoint, thus dissipating her energies, she has suffered. But when she has remained true to the evangelistic and missionary pursuits as advocated by the Lord Jesus, she has grown and been blessed.

2. Benevolence and humanitarianism

Though subordinate in importance to the work just discussed, the pursuit of the lost for Christ, the work of building up the brokenhearted has a place of great significance in the work of the church. Jesus fed the hungry and healed the sick. He made the lame to walk and the poor to rejoice. Human welfare demanded a large slice of his time, for he had compassion upon all he surveyed. He did this in the name of the kingdom; we must do it in the name of our Lord.

James says, "Pure religion and undefiled before our God and Father is this, to visit the fatherless and widows in their affliction" (Jas. 1:27). He also queries, "If a brother or sister be naked and in lack of daily food, and one of you say unto them, Go in peace, be ye warmed and filled; and yet ye give them not the things needful to the body; what doth it profit? Even so faith, if it have not works, is dead in itself" (2:15-17). Only after the Good Samaritan parable does Jesus say, "Go, and do thou likewise" (Luke 10:37). In the judgment parable Jesus places condemnation upon those who have not fed the hungry, given drink to the thirsty, and clothed the naked (Matt. 25:41-46).

Children's homes, homes for unwed mothers, hospitals, Christian schools — all should be institutions through which the church can manifest the Spirit of Christ. The church cannot neglect such and be true to the Scriptures. Yet, at the same time, all must be done in the name of Christ. He must be glorified in both the cause and the motive. The personal contact in the name of Christ is the all-important feature. Sometimes those within the church itself need the benevolence, especially the sick and the aged; sometimes it is those without who need help. Christian schools have been, and still are, a great means of reaching out in a humanitarian way in the name of Christ, at the same time constituting a forceful means of teaching the great doctrines and principles of the faith. All this is involved in the church's benevolent and humanitarian role.

3. Social and domestic righteousness

The church cannot be indifferent toward the social evils that are rampant in the world today, evils and vices that definitely call for a militant spirit. There is no "social" gospel, but there is a social aspect to the gospel. It produces regenerate and transformed individuals who cannot countenance social immorality. The church must cry out against divorce, against the sale and use of alcoholic beverages, against unchaste living, against immoral entertainment, against gambling, and such like. Merely to refrain from such social ills is not sufficient; a militant crusade against them is all that will suffice. There are still temples to be cleansed with a braided whip (Matt. 21:12, 13). There are still "scribes and Pharisees, hypocrites," who must be dubbed "sons of hell" to their face (Matt. 23:15). People must still be reminded that the marriage vow is not a temporary arrangement but a permanent partnership, and that Jesus said, "What therefore God hath joined together, let not man put asunder" (Matt. 19:6). These are all vital issues affecting man as a social group. The church cannot afford to be silent.

4. EDIFICATION AND GROWTH

The church in its outreach must not forget to look in upon its own; the members themselves must not be forgotten. Babes in Christ must grow into full Christian maturity, being fed with the meat of the Word, not just the milk (I Cor. 3:1, 2). Growth in grace of those who have already professed faith should be the order of the day. The edification of the saints must never be neglected in the full-scale pursuit of other duties. Christian lives need to be nurtured into wondrous replicas of the marvelous personality of the Master himself. New converts must not be simply "dipped and dropped"; they must be enlisted into the full program of the church. The youngsters should be privileged to have the best teachers in the whole Sunday School.

If the church is to be God's kingdom agency in the world the members must be trained, prepared, and taught for this vital task. The teacher and leader of others must be qualified. Therefore a great part of the energy of a church must be directed in the development of its own efficiency as a moral and spiritual force in the midst of mankind. Yet, at the same time, this developing of the members for the sake of others produces more spiritual personalities for those members. The process feeds back upon itself, is self-stimulating in its results. There is a development of religious principles and sentiments, a development of humble piety, a development in the grace of giving.

5. WORSHIP AND PRAISE

Worship is not mere entertainment, the passing of time surrounded and engulfed by a ritual. It is not mere objective participation in successive acts and events. It is the giving of honor to

God, the rendering of "worthship" to our Creator and Redeemer; and he deserves all we can give — and more! It is drawing close to God, the communion of spirit with Spirit. It is man speaking to God and God to man. It is one of God's great means of developing the spiritual life of the worshiper. It is the time of spiritual eating and drinking.

It is the Holy Spirit who inspires the church in worship. "We know not how to pray as we ought; but the Spirit himself maketh intercession for us with groanings which cannot be uttered; and he that searcheth the hearts knoweth what is the mind of the Spirit, because he maketh intercession for the saints according to the will of God" (Rom. 8:26, 27). Other passages showing the Spirit's leadership in worship are I Corinthians 14:15; Ephesians 5:18-20; and Acts 4:31. When the Spirit leads in the worship service there will be warmth and feeling. The praise, the prayer, the giving, and the exhortation will have meaning and purpose. Without the Spirit's guidance there will be dullness and coldness.

As one proceeds from the Old Testament to the New there is a marked difference in the elements of worship. In the former there is sacrifice; in the latter there is teaching and preaching. In the former there is ritual; in the latter ritual is practically absent. In the New Testament spirituality is the keynote, not the objective act of sacrifice. Besides, Christ has fulfilled all sacrifice. Ritual fulfills a need as long as it leads to Christ. When it is substituted for true worship it becomes an end in itself, constituting more a curse than a blessing.

Christ worshiped. "And he came to Nazareth, where he had been brought up: and he entered, as his custom was, into the synagogue on the sabbath day..." (Luke 4:16). "As his custom was" — those words reveal that he was an habitual attendant at the synagogues. Twice he cleansed the temple, and that vehemently, of the unspiritual ones who had defeated the purpose of those holy precincts. Its purpose was for prayer and worship, not the traffic of those who wanted it to be the seat of a lucrative racket. On the mountain tops and by the sea, sometimes alone and sometimes with others, he worshiped. After the first Lord's Supper he and his disciples sang a hymn.

Prayer, praise, Scripture, and exhortation — these are the four cardinal elements of worship. These the church must foster.

OUTLINE FOR CHAPTER FOURTEEN

I. General View
   1. Definition of term
   2. Number
   3. Purpose
      (1) Erroneous view
      (2) True view
   4. Observers

II. Baptism
   1. Scriptural obligation
      (1) Intention of Christ
      (2) Practice of apostles
   2. Mode
      (1) Meaning of Greek term
         a. In lexicons
         b. In New Testament
         c. In other writings
      (2) Practice in history
      (3) Views of those who practice pouring or sprinkling
         a. Statements of affusionists
         b. Arguments of affusionists
   3. Meaning
      (1) Not regenerative
         a. Statements of those holding regenerative view of baptism
         b. Scriptures employed in effort to vindicate regenerative baptism
      (2) Symbolical only
         a. Symbol of death and resurrection of Christ
         b. Symbol of purpose of that death and resurrection: deliverance from sin to new life
         c. Symbol of that purpose fulfilled in life of one being immersed
         d. Symbol of manner in which new life is bestowed: union with Christ
   4. Administrator
   5. Recipient
      (1) New Testament teaching
      (2) Arguments used for infant baptism
         a. Circumcision
         b. "Household" passages
         c. Other passages
         d. Early rise, continuance, and extensive growth

   e. Church authority
   f. Regenerative baptism
III. Lord's Supper
   1. Scriptural teaching
      (1) Instituted by Jesus
      (2) Analogous to passover meal
   2. Mode
      (1) The elements
      (2) Both elements essential
      (3) Function of assembled church
      (4) Frequency of observance
   3. Meaning
      (1) Roman Catholic
      (2) Lutheran
      (3) Calvinistic
      (4) Zwinglian
         a. Symbol of death of Christ for our sins
         b. Symbol of appropriation of benefits of that death for
            believer
         c. Symbol of means of that appropriation: union with Christ
   4. Administrator
   5. Prerequisites to participation
      (1) Regeneration
      (2) Baptism
      (3) Church membership

CHAPTER FOURTEEN

THE ORDINANCES

I. GENERAL VIEW

ALL THROUGH CHRISTIAN HISTORY THESE SACRED RITES HAVE BEEN THE battleground for controversy, great and fierce debates. When it is realized that the very sacredness of the subject under dispute constitutes the motive of the disagreement, we are more prone to be lenient in our denunciation. The very fact that they belong to the Lord, not to men, makes sincere Christians jealous in regard to their personal interpretations of them.

1. DEFINITION OF TERM

What are the ordinances? The word itself comes from the Latin *ordo,* a row, or order. *Ordinare,* the verb, means to place in the right row, or order, from which is derived the meaning to establish, or to command. Therefore "ordinance" denotes something established, or commanded, and, when applied to baptism and the Lord's Supper, denotes something commanded of our Lord.

Many denominations have steered clear of the term sacraments as applied to these two sacred observances, though the term is used by the Roman Catholics, Lutherans, and many others. The word possesses a magical, mystical connotation derived from the "transfer-of-grace" principle not accepted by those who insist upon the "symbolical-only" theory. The word sacrament as originally used by the early Christians presented the other side of the picture expressed by the word ordinance, i.e., the voluntary acceptance of the authority expressed by "ordinance." The *sacramentum* was the sacred oath of allegiance of the Roman soldier to his commander; thus sacrament was the sacred consecration of the Christian to his Lord. But soon it came to mean merely a holy thing, and from this to mean something through which grace is mediated. Because of this derived connotation, coming later through the centuries, many have refrained from using the term sacrament.

The word ordinance is very commonly used among Protestants today, and it is well that it should be. However, the term is not found in the New Testament as applied to these two great observances. According to the King James Version Paul does say, "Now I praise you, brethren, that ye remember me in all things, and keep the ordinances, as I delivered them to you" (I Cor.

11:2). But the Greek word here is *paradoseis,* and should be translated "traditions" instead. The King James Version itself translates the same Greek word with the English word "tradition" in Matthew 15:2, 3, 6. So there is no reference in the First Corinthians passage to baptism and the Lord's Supper, but merely to customs and proprieties. In spite of all this there is no objection to using the term ordinance as a designation for these two rites.

2. NUMBER

There are two ordinances: baptism and the Lord's Supper. A few sects practice footwashing as an ordinance, which would make three instead of two. Primitive (or Hardshell) Baptists and Dunkards are among these groups. This view is based upon a literal interpretation of John 13:12-17, especially verses 15 and 17. "For I have given you an example, that ye also should do as I have done to you" (John 13:15). "If ye know these things, blessed are ye if ye do them" (John 13:17). Jesus meant that we should follow his example of humble service. If he had meant that this should be a third ordinance, the apostles would have understood it as such; but there is no evidence whatsoever of footwashing as an ordinance in the early church. Besides, the act of washing the feet of another would have no essential connection with the gospel, while baptism and the Lord's Supper essentially represent the gospel. The Roman Catholic Church and the Greek Orthodox Church observe seven sacraments, including what they term baptism, confirmation, the Eucharist, matrimony, penance, holy orders, and extreme unction.

3. PURPOSE

(1) ERRONEOUS VIEW

The Romanist theory is that the act itself, in some way or another, confers a blessing; just the mere performance automatically transmits grace to the receiver and holiness is produced. The elements are not merely the symbols for union with Christ but the means of maintaining that union. It is the "pipe-line" theory of grace being "fed" to the believer. But it is maintained that objective acts in and of themselves do not bring grace, since there is nothing miraculous about them. The blessing received is spiritual, resulting from a true religious experience occurring at the time of the ordinance. There is nothing at all mystical about the act itself.

(2) TRUE VIEW

The whole tenor of the New Testament leads us to view these

rites as visible and outward signs of the indwelling Christ, symbols of a saving gospel experienced by the participant. They are overt representatives of the redemptive power of Christ in the life of the believer. They are symbolic acts which Christ has commanded Christians to observe and keep, setting forth abstract truths in a visible form. They have no power within themselves either to effect salvation or to maintain it, but are God-ordained institutions recognizing the lordship of Christ.

4. Observers

The observers, or keepers, of these sacred rites are to be Christians, and Christians only. In fact, only to the one in Christ are they meaningful; for they symbolize spiritual truth, and only the born-again individual can discern spiritual truth (I Cor. 2:14, 15). They are Christian ceremonies, rightly marking the true disciples of the Lord Jesus.

So everyone, indiscriminately, cannot partake of these two rites, only believers. And yet even Christians, indiscriminately, cannot observe them. A believer by himself cannot observe them. Nor is the fact that he finds himself in the company of other Christians sufficient warrant for him and his Christian friends to observe or to administer them; a chance meeting of Christians does not constitute a reason for observance. Nor does just being an ordained minister, or a priest, grant this privilege. Nor does the privilege to administer these rites come by virtue of authority handed down in apostolic succession — from Jesus to Peter and on down. Besides, by what right would one today claim apostolic succession and thereby prove his right?

Who or what constitutes the seat of authority for administering and deciding when and to whom to administer these sacred acts? The churches themselves decide this; the local bodies of believers retain this prerogative. These two rites are church functions. If this or that particular scriptural passage cannot be adduced to warrant this statement, it is maintained that it is perfectly apparent from the entire purport of New Testament teaching. "We must take one of three positions in regard to the matter, namely, that of apostolic succession in bishops, or that of general and ill-defined performance, or that of church observance. Only a few choose the middle one of these, and the question practically narrows itself to a choice between apostolic succession in bishops and the responsible action of the local churches."[1] It is very obvious that the latter is the New Testament way.

[1] Edwin Charles Dargan, *Ecclesiology*, p. 279.

DOCTRINES OF THE CHRISTIAN RELIGION

II. BAPTISM

1. SCRIPTURAL OBLIGATION

Did Christ mean for the act of baptism to be carried on by the church down through the ages? Did he mean for this objective and ceremonial act to be perpetuated through the years? What is the basis of obligation? It is grounded upon two factors.

(1) INTENTION OF CHRIST

The desire of Christ our Lord, that the newly professed believer be baptized, is shown from various angles. Jesus sets the example for us by being immersed in the Jordan by John the Baptist. "Then cometh Jesus from Galilee to the Jordan unto John, to be baptized of him. But John would have hindered him, saying, I have need to be baptized of thee, and comest thou to me? But Jesus answering said unto him, Suffer it now; for thus it becometh us to fulfil all righteousness. Then he suffereth him" (Matt. 3:13-15). Jesus tells us later that John's baptism is sanctioned of God (Matt. 21:25-27); so he submits to John's baptism "to fulfil all righteousness"— not because of repentance for the forgiveness of sin! His baptism is a part of his ministry of redemption here upon earth, the initial phase, in fact. It constitutes public entrance into his ministry, and, therefore, in a way, is equivalent to the believer's entrance upon his Christian life. The Father speaks from heaven and places his approval upon the baptism of the Son (Matt. 3:17).

So Jesus sets the example for all Christians of all ages by being immersed of John in the Jordan. But evidently he wishes to teach his disciples to use baptism as the initiatory rite also, for the Pharisees "heard that Jesus was making and baptizing more disciples than John (although Jesus himself baptized not, but his disciples)" (John 4:1, 2). He instructs his followers to make baptism the ceremony symbolic of their entrance into his kingdom and service. This is made very vivid and explicit by Jesus' command in the Great Commission: "Go ye therefore, and make disciples of all nations, baptizing them into the name of the Father and of the Son and of the Holy Spirit" (Matt. 28:19). Baptism is placed midway between the making of the disciple and the teaching of that disciple.

(2) PRACTICE OF APOSTLES

The apostles seem to understand that Jesus means for baptism to be the initiatory rite. Three thousand converts are immediately baptized after Peter's great sermon on the Day of Pentecost (Acts 2:41). Philip's Samaritan converts are baptized (Acts 8:12). The Ethiopian treasurer is baptized (Acts 8:38). Saul of Tarsus is baptized at Damascus immediately after receiving his sight on the visit of Ananias (Acts 9:18). Cornelius is baptized (Acts 10:48). Lydia is baptized (Acts 16:15). The Philippian jailer is baptized (Acts 16:33). Twelve converts are baptized at Ephesus (Acts 19:5).

That baptism was universally practiced by the apostles and the early Christians relative to the new converts is the basis of Paul's vivid picture of baptism in Romans 6:1-11. Though Paul's immediate reason for presenting this portrayal of baptism by immersion is an argument against antinomianism, it still presents in his mind the importance of this initiatory function. At first glance it might seem that Paul in I Corinthians 1:13-17 is placing baptism on a low esteem; he is not, however, for he is arguing against using it as a basis of loyalty of the one being baptized for the one baptizing. The loyalty must go to Christ alone. Yet, though mistaken in such thinking, the Corinthians show a high regard for baptism. Even the obscure passage in I Peter 3:21 shows baptism as a duty in the mind of the Christian. Therefore the apostles continued the teaching and will of Christ in regard to baptism.

2. MODE

We now take up the mode, or form, of baptism. Three forms are found in use today throughout the world: sprinkling, pouring, and immersion. Which is the New Testament form?

(1) MEANING OF GREEK TERM

The Greek verb translated "I baptize" in the New Testament is *baptizō*. One should really say transliterated, rather than translated, for our English word baptize is derived directly from the Greek word used by the New Testament writers; therefore it is not, strictly speaking, a translation. To use the English word dip, or plunge, or immerse, would be to translate, for this is the English equivalent of the Greek term *baptizō*.

a. *In lexicons*

Professor J. H. Thayer gives this meaning for *baptizō* in his *Greek-English Lexicon of the New Testament:* "Properly to dip repeatedly, to immerse, submerge." The second meaning he gives is: "To cleanse by dipping or submerging, to wash, to make clean with water." The third meaning is: "Metaphorically to overwhelm. ..." Then he states, "In the New Testament it is used particularly of the rite of sacred ablution, first instituted by John the Baptist, afterwards by Christ's command received by Christians and adjusted to the contents and nature of their religion, viz., our immersion in water, performed as a sign of the removal of sin, and administered to those who, impelled by a desire for salvation, sought admission to the benefits of the Messiah's kingdom."[2] Thayer's work was a revision of Grimm's working over of an edition in Latin by a man named Wilke. Thayer was a Congregationalist and the last two named were German Lutherans. Therefore the definitions of these men are not bound by denominational preference but are derived from purely academic study and interpretation.

W. F. Arndt and T. W. Gingrich in their *Greek-English Lexicon of the New Testament* give the following for *baptizō:* "dip, immerse." They state that in non-Christian literature it is used for "plunge, sink, drench, overwhelm, etc."[3]

b. *In New Testament*

Not only do the lexicons give the meaning of "baptize" to be "dip, plunge, or immerse"; it is used that way throughout the New Testament. Every time the word is employed it is with this meaning only. Attempts have been made to prove otherwise, that it may just as well mean sprinkling; but these attempts have always failed. Though there are some places where only the act is mentioned, there are many others where the details given would allow only immersion. To derive any other meaning for the Greek word than immersion would be inappropriate.

Mark says that Jesus "was baptized of John in the Jordan." Then he adds, "and straightway coming up out of the water ..." (1:9, 10). Here immersion is plainly required. So it is with the baptism of the Ethiopian treasurer by Philip in Acts. "And as they went on the way, they came unto a certain water; and the eunuch saith, Behold, here is water; what doth hinder me to be baptized? And he commanded the chariot to stand still: and they both went down into the water, both Philip and the eunuch; and he baptized him. And when they came up out of the water, the Spirit of the Lord caught away Philip" (8:36, 38, 39). The Fourth Gospel also has a pertinent passage: "And John also was baptizing in Aenon near to Salim, because there was much water there" (John 3:23). This could mean none other than that there was sufficient water for immersion. Paul's epistles contain two passages, Romans 6:1-4 and Colossians 2:12, which picture baptism as a burial and resurrection. To contend for anything but immersion in these two passages would be to do violence to scriptural evidence.

There are other Greek words for sprinkling which the New Testament writers could have used for baptism, had they only

2 Joseph H. Thayer, *A Greek-English Lexicon of the New Testament,* p. 94.

3 W. F. Arndt and T. W. Gingrich, *Greek-English Lexicon of the New Testament,* p. 131.

wished. These are *rantizō,* I sprinkle; *rantismos,* sprinkling; *proschusis,* pouring upon; and *epicheō,* I pour on. All these terms are employed in the New Testament but never for the rite of baptism; only *baptizō* is used thus. If sprinkling or pouring had been the mode desired for the sacred rite the writers would have used these other terms instead of *baptizō.*

c. *In other writings*

When we turn to literary Greek the story is the same. *Baptizō* is always used with the meaning of plunge or dip. Many examples could be called up, but one will suffice. Strabo tells of a certain lake in his *Geography,* Book XII, Chapter 5, Section 4: "The water solidifies so readily around everything that is immersed [baptized] into it, that they draw up salt crowns when they let down a circle of rushes." The same is true for all the early Christians writing in Greek; they employ the term just as it is used in the New Testament, always with the meaning of immersion. So it is with the Latin writers later, for they use Latin terms meaning to dip.

(2) PRACTICE IN HISTORY

The practice in history is not a conclusive argument for immersion, just a supplemental one, for it is to the New Testament that we must go for definite evidence of the proper mode of baptism. Yet the argument from history confirms the New Testament view.

Writings show that during the New Testament period and the subsequent apostolic age immersion was the mode of baptism used. During the patristic period, or period of the church fathers, A.D. 100-604, immersion was still practiced; but other customs were emerging. Trine immersion, or immersion three times successively, was becoming prevalent. Also, sprinkling was permitted in special cases. A quotation from the *Didaché* manifests this. "Now concerning baptism, baptize thus: Having first taught all these things, baptize ye in the name of the Father, and of the Son, and of the Holy Ghost in living (running) water, and if thou hast not living (running) water, baptize in other water, and if thou canst not in cold then in warm; but if thou hast neither, pour thrice upon the head in the name of the Father, and of the Son, and of the Holy Ghost" (Chapter VII). This quotation shows that immersion was the usual form of baptism, but that an emergency would allow pouring. Yet it is obvious that "baptize" and "pour" are not synonymous at all. Thus we see affusion, or pouring, emerging at this early age, although up to this time *only* immersion was the mode. This *Didaché,* or *The Teaching of the Twelve Apostles,* was written during the second century. Other authors, or writings, of this age could be quoted, but all with one effect: to show that immersion was the usual custom, that trine immersion was quite prevalent, and that pouring was creeping in. Yet there is no more scriptural evidence for trine immersion than there is for pouring. Immersion *three times* is not taught in the Scriptures.

In the medieval period trine immersion continued to be the usual practice, this being discerned in various writings. Many baptisteries have been discovered, baptisteries of all ages, some of which are in the catacombs of Rome. Many were of good size. More advances were made during this period toward affusion (or pouring) and sprinkling as the mode of baptism instead of immersion. Yet the famous Dean Stanley can say, "For the first thirteen centuries the almost universal practice of baptism was that of which we read in the New Testament, and which is the very meaning of the word 'baptize,' — that those who were baptized were plunged, submerged, immersed into the water."[4] This statement comes from a famous church historian, an English Churchman. When the Protestant Reformers came along affusion had been the substitute form for two hundred years. The easier method gained over the more difficult. Infant sprinkling (or aspersion) gained ground. Persons that were sick could be sprinkled much more easily than immersed. During the Reformation period both methods (affusion and immersion) were practiced by both Protestants and Catholics. Protestants continued to be divided, while the Romanists switched completely to sprinkling. The reader is referred for further study to *Act of Baptism* by Henry L. Burrage and to *Archaeology of Baptism* by W. N. Cote.

(3) VIEWS OF THOSE WHO PRACTICE POURING OR SPRINKLING

We see from the previous discussion that baptism by immersion was the first and exclusive practice, and that pouring and sprinkling gradually acquired great weight. Yet, we might ask, what do men say that accept a way other than immersion?

a. *Statements of affusionists*

"For several centuries after the establishment of Christianity, baptism was usually conferred by immersion; but since the twelfth century the practice of baptizing by affusion has prevailed in the Catholic Church, as this manner is attended with less inconvenience than baptism by immersion." This statement is by a Catholic, Cardinal Gibbons, in *Faith of our Fathers,* p. 275. "In respect to the form of baptism, it was, in conformity with the original institution and the original import of the symbol, performed by im-

[4] Arthur P. Stanley, *Christian Institutions,* p. 21.

mersion, as a sign of entire baptism into the Holy Spirit, of being entirely penetrated by the same." This is a Lutheran, the great church historian Neander, in his *Church History*, Vol. I, p. 310. "The word baptize signifies to immerse, and it is certain that immersion was the practice of the ancient church." This is by John Calvin, forerunner of the Presbyterians, in his famous *Institutes of the Christian Religion*, Book IV, Chapter XV, Section 19. In regard to Romans 6:3, John Wesley, the famous founder of Methodism (though he himself never left the Church of England), says in his *Notes on the New Testament*, "We are buried with him, alluding to the ancient manner of baptizing by immersion." Other examples, of these denominations and of other denominations, could be cited; but these will suffice.

b. *Arguments of affusionists*

Those today who object to immersion as the mode of baptism do so on one of the following grounds: they totally deny immersion, or they partially deny it, or they concede to it but try to justify themselves on the change. It will be readily seen that the preceding quotations are those of this third group, which is by far the largest. The first two groups make no concession whatever.

The first group, small in number, endeavors to prove that *baptizō* does not mean immerse, or that it means pour or sprinkle. The second group endeavors to prove that immersion was not the only act of baptism in the New Testament period and immediately following, but that there were other forms also in use. The third, by far the largest, admits that immersion was the original and exclusive mode of baptism but that sprinkling and pouring are justified also. This justification is made on an appeal to the authority of the church or is made simply on the basis of convenience. Many quotations might be adduced to illustrate these two grounds of argument. For further study the pupil is referred to Edwin C. Dargan's *Ecclesiology*.

3. MEANING

The meaning of baptism will be discussed negatively and positively — what it is not and what it is, and in this order.

(1) NOT REGENERATIVE

Baptism does not effect or produce salvation. It is not regenerative in consequence. The mere act itself does not convey spiritual grace, nor does it produce any spiritual change in the one being baptized. It does not save; it does not even help to save. It should not be termed, therefore, a sacrament, for this term implies the mediation of grace.

a. *Statements of those holding the regenerative view of baptism*

Many denominations, however, hold to the mediation-of-grace view, entirely or in part. The Roman Catholic view is seen in a declaration at the Council of Trent: "If any one saith that by the said sacraments of the New Law grace is not conferred through the act performed (ex opere operato), but that faith alone in the divine promise suffices for the obtaining of grace, let him be anathema" (Session vii, Canon 8). Hence, baptism is essential to salvation. The view of the English Church is seen in the Anglican Catechism in answer to the question, "Who gave you this name?" The answer required is: "My sponsors in my baptism, wherein I was made a member of Christ, the child of God and an inheritor of the kingdom of heaven." The view of the Lutheran Church is seen in the Augsburg Confession, Article IX: "Of baptism they teach that it is necessary to salvation, and that by baptism the grace of God is offered; and that children are to be baptized, who by baptism being offered to God, are received into God's favor." The Presbyterian view is found in *Systematic Theology*, Vol. 3, pp. 579-604, by Charles Hodge, where he states, "Baptism is, however, not only a sign and seal, it is also a means of grace, because in it the blessings which it signifies are conveyed, and the promises of which it is the seal are assured or fulfilled to those who are baptized, provided they believe." The phrase "means of grace" brings this view mighty close to the Anglican and Lutheran view. The Methodist view is that baptism is symbolical and declarative only, "a sign of regeneration and profession." Yet the Methodists retain the word sacrament. The Disciples of Christ and the Church of Christ evolved from the Campbellite movement. The view of Campbell was that New Testament baptism "was not *a* baptism, but *the baptism of repentance.* It was not for remission of sins, but for *the* remission of sins. The fixtures of language could not more safely secure the intention of the institution. It was not because your sins had been remitted, but it is for and in order to the remission of sins." Thus we have the view that baptism is one of the conditions for the remission of sins.

b. *Scriptures employed in effort to vindicate regenerative baptism*

There are certain scriptural passages that are repeatedly called forth in an endeavor to prove regenerative baptism. One is Mark 16:16: "He that believeth and is baptized shall be saved; but he that disbelieveth shall be condemned." John 3:5 is another passage: "Verily, verily, I say unto thee, Except one be born of water and the Spirit, he cannot enter into the kingdom of God." In Acts 2:38 we have Peter's declaration on the Day of Pentecost: "Repent ye, and be baptized every one of you in the name of Jesus Christ unto the remission of your sins; and ye shall receive the gift of the Holy Spirit." Acts 22:16 gives Paul's description of Ananias' coming to him after his conversion, stating to him, "And now why tarriest thou? arise, and be baptized, and wash away thy sins, calling on his name." In Ephesians 5:26 are the words: "that he might sanctify it, having cleansed it by the washing of water with the word." In Titus 3:5 are the words: "not by works done in righteousness, which we did ourselves, but according to his mercy he saved us, through the washing of regeneration and renewing of the Holy Spirit." In I Peter 3:21 is a famous passage: "which also after a true likeness doth now save you, even baptism."

The Mark 16:16 passage reveals that when the matter is stated negatively there is no mention of baptism, leaving faith only as the deciding factor. Besides, this verse has much textual criticism against its being a part of the original Gospel of Mark.

Jesus' words to Nicodemus in John 3:5 are used symbolically. One is regenerated, born spiritually, by the Spirit of God. The water *might* be thought of as the symbol of this great change. So *if* the passage refers to baptism, as many commentators believe it does, it is purely symbolical.

Peter's famous words on the Day of Pentecost (Acts 2:38) are to be taken as symbolical also. He talks of being baptized "unto the remission of your sins." The Greek preposition *eis,* translated "unto," does not mean effecting remission of sins but due to remission of sins. Baptism is God's express sign of the remission of sins. Ananias' words to Paul (Acts 22:16) are to be taken symbolically. He asks Paul to be baptized as a sign of the removal of his sins. Paul's passage in Ephesians 5:26 may or may not refer to baptism. He speaks of "the washing of water with the word." The Greek word translated "washing" is really "laver" and is the same word used in the Titus 3:5 passage. This is a symbolical reference to cleansing, which would be true whether it referred to baptism or not. Therefore Titus 3:5 yields to the same method of interpretation, the symbolical.

In the I Peter 3:21 passage are the words "which also after a true likeness doth now save you, even baptism." The words "after a true likeness" are very important. Baptism is a symbolism of the true salvation; it is not that by which salvation is granted.

There are two ways that these passages may be interpreted, literally or symbolically. They are far better understood in the latter sense. To take them literally would be to contradict the remaining portion of the New Testament; for besides these seven passages where "baptism," "washing," or "water" are mentioned in connection with salvation there are countless other passages which condition salvation solely on repentance and faith. "Sirs, what must I do to be saved? And they said, Believe on the Lord Jesus, and thou shalt be saved" (Acts 16:30, 31). This example can be followed by countless others equally as good. The Bible plainly teaches that regeneration is necessary apart from any law, ceremony, or deed, and that the only condition of salvation is a purely spiritual one. Salvation is man's spirit in relationship with God as Spirit. To make salvation dependent upon any objective act, or upon a ceremony, would be completely antithetical to the spiritual import of what it means to be saved. This would be legalism, which is exactly what Jesus forcefully opposed in his teaching while here upon earth. The tenor of the New Testament is against legalistic tendencies that would thwart the spiritual essence of Christianity. Jesus opposed those who would make keeping the law the condition of salvation; Paul opposed those who would make circumcision a prerequisite to becoming a Christian; and such like.

The entire New Testament abounds in symbolical language. Paul states, "Or are ye ignorant that all we who were baptized into Christ Jesus were baptized into his death?" (Rom. 6:3). One cannot literally be baptized into Christ or into his death; therefore it is an absurdity to interpret this passage other than symbolically. The preposition translated "into" in both these cases is *eis*, the same one Peter uses in Acts 2:38 and which is translated "unto": "Repent ye, and be baptized every one of you in the name of Jesus Christ unto the remission of your sins." This also is used symbolically.

Jesus says to a paralytic on a stretcher, "Son, thy sins are forgiven" (Mark 2:5). He says to a sinful woman, "Thy faith hath saved thee; go in peace" (Luke 7:50). He says to the thief on the cross, "Today shalt thou be with me in Paradise" (Luke 23:43). Baptism is mentioned in none of these utterances. Salvation has always been, and will always be, by grace through faith. In Old Testament times it is so; before Pentecost and after Pentecost it is so. God did not make baptism a condition of salvation from Pentecost on, as though this arbitrary requirement came into being at that time. Acts 10:43; 13:38, 39; 16:31 show that salvation after Pentecost is by grace through faith, just as well as before Pentecost. Pentecost itself did not alter the conditions of salvation, as though God would arbitrarily work one way during one period and in a different way during another.

(2) SYMBOLICAL ONLY

The act of baptism is symbolical only. The experiences of grace are inward; it is there that spirit meets Spirit. The heart is regenerated and made new in Christ, and a union with Christ is effected. All this is expressed or declared to the world in the act of baptism, which represents what has previously transpired: the entrance of the believer into the communion of Christ's death and resurrection.

a. *Symbol of death and resurrection of Christ*

Just prior to his death Jesus says, "But I have a baptism to be baptized with; and how am I straitened till it be accomplished!" (Luke 12:50). This is one of the passion sayings of Jesus, definitely referring to his death. Paul talks of "having been buried with him in baptism, wherein ye were also raised with him through faith in the working of God, who raised him from the dead" (Col. 2:12). He also states, "Or are ye ignorant that all we who were baptized into Christ Jesus were baptized into his death?" (Rom. 6:3). Therefore baptism is a picture of Jesus' death, burial, and resurrection.

b. *Symbol of purpose of that death and resurrection: deliverance from sin to new life*

The most pertinent verse on this score is that of Romans 6:4: "We were buried therefore with him through baptism into death: that like as Christ was raised from the dead through the glory of the Father, so we also might walk in newness of life." Christ's death and resurrection were for the purpose of freeing the sinner from death and granting him eternal life. This fact is also discerned in Colossians 2:12, 13: "having been buried with him in baptism, wherein ye were also raised with him through faith in the working of God, who raised him from the dead. And you, being dead through your trespasses and the uncircumcision of your flesh, you, I say, did he make alive together with him, having forgiven us all our trespasses."

c. *Symbol of that purpose fulfilled in life of one being immersed*

Paul says in Galatians, "For as many of you as were baptized into Christ did put on Christ" (3:27). And at the conclusion of his great portrayal of baptism in Romans 6 he states, "Even so reckon ye also yourselves to be dead unto sin, but alive unto God in Christ Jesus" (6:11). As the water rolls over the one being immersed it signifies that the old nature has been laid aside and is dead, buried in the grave with Christ. As he emerges from the water there is signified the possession of new life with Christ. "For ye died, and your life is hid with Christ in God" (Col. 3:3).

d. *Symbol of manner in which new life is bestowed: union with Christ*

"For if we have become united with him in the likeness of his death, we shall be also in the likeness of his resurrection" (Rom. 6:5). It is very striking that the Greek word translated "united" is the same one used in secular Greek literature for the man and the horse united in the Centaur, a Greek legendary figure. This union with Christ is seen in the fact that the one act of immersion depicts the death and resurrection of both the believer and Christ. "For ye died, and your life is hid with Christ in God" (Col. 3:3).

4. ADMINISTRATOR

Due to the many factors involved there is considerable difference of opinion relative to the agent, or administrator, of the rite of baptism. The matter is affected by whether or not the baptizer has recognized church authority. It includes whether or not he must be an immersed believer. It involves the view of baptismal succession, the view of the church, the view of the ordained, and the view of the officers of the church. It is also entangled by the significance attached to the act of baptism, whether it is regenerative or symbolical only.

Let it be said first that the authority does not lie with the recognized ministry, or ordained ones. They do not have the authority, invested in them at the time of laying on of hands, to baptize when or where or whom they may deem fit. This would give an official class within the church the authority to conduct the ordinances or any other ecclesiastical function at will. This would give rise to "clergy" and "laity," terms used in the Roman Catholic Church but foreign to New Testament terminology.

But not only do the ordained ones, or recognized ministers, lack the authority residing within themselves to administer baptism as they see fit; they also do not possess a monopoly on performing this rite. Ordination, or laying on of hands, is not a New Testament prerequisite to being the agent in baptism.

What is the answer? It seems to be twofold. First, the administrator of baptism should be an immersed believer. He himself should believe and should have signified that belief by immersion. Otherwise his conduction of this important rite would be a mockery. Second, the church must decide who is to do the baptizing. It is a church ordinance, and as such is subject to the decision of the church. The church itself possesses the authority to decide the "who" and the "whom" of baptism. Baptism is not only the means of signifying one's belief in Christ but also of identifying one's self with a particular community of believers. This was true in New

Testament times and is equally true today. It is not an individual act; it is a church act, and as such must be administered by the church. The church decides who the administrator will be. It is generally the recognized fact that this is to be the pastor of the church; but in case the church is without a pastor it may designate who is to perform this rite. In fact it is the duty and responsibility of the church to decide any issue relative to baptism according to its own convictions due to scriptural evidence.

"Church succession" is not a requisite for the agent in baptism. An unbroken chain of churches back to the New Testament times, or a line of ordained ministers back to that time, is not required in the case of baptism. In the first place, how could it be proved? In the second place, this is ecclesiastical legalism. Church authority is not derived in this manner; it, too, is spiritual. Under this system, if a man were to be permitted to baptize, the succession of churches down to the one that baptized him would have to be traced out.

5. RECIPIENT

Who may be baptized? The only person who should be baptized is one who has heard the gospel, repented, believed, and confessed that belief. In other words, only one who has been regenerated and has passed from death unto life and is old enough to know and state that fact possesses the right to be baptized.

(1) NEW TESTAMENT TEACHING

If the acts of baptism of John the Baptist are studied in the gospels it will be observed that these are always performed upon those of sufficient maturity to testify of an inward change. "They were baptized of him in the river Jordan, confessing their sins" (Matt. 3:6). From this passage it is noted that those being baptized are old enough to confess their sins. "And all the people when they heard, and the publicans, justified God, being baptized with the baptism of John" (Luke 7:29). The phrase "justified God" shows maturity on the part of the ones being baptized. Other passages could also be brought forth to strengthen this statement relative to John's baptism (Acts 11:16; 13:24; 19:4).

But what about Christian baptism? There are many passages to be studied. "After these things came Jesus and his disciples into the land of Judaea; and there he tarried with them, and baptized" (John 3:22). "When therefore the Lord knew that the Pharisees had heard that Jesus was making and baptizing more disciples than John (although Jesus himself baptized not, but his disciples), he left Judaea, and departed again into Galilee" (John 4:1, 2). Here we see that the ones being baptized are disciples, and the word disciple is never used in the Scriptures for an infant. In

337

the Great Commission Jesus himself commands us to baptize disciples (Matt. 28:19). On the Day of Pentecost many are baptized. "They then that received his word were baptized: and there were added unto them in that day about three thousand souls. And they continued stedfastly in the apostles' teaching and fellowship, in the breaking of bread and the prayers" (Acts 2:41, 42). Only mature Christians could "continue" in the things Luke mentions here. Acts 8:12 states that those who believed due to Philip's preaching "were baptized, both men and women." Many other passages could be brought forth and studied; but in none are infants mentioned as the subjects of baptism, and in many or most it must of necessity be believers who can testify of their belief (Acts 8:36, 38; 9:18; 10:44, 48; 16:14, 15; 16:33, 34; 18:8; 19:5; I Cor. 1:14-16).

In three of these passages — Lydia (Acts 16:14, 15), the Philippian jailer (Acts 16:33, 34), and Stephanas (I Cor. 1:14-16) — the fact of household baptisms is mentioned. That these passages are used by pedobaptists (baptizers of infants) as one of their strongest arguments will be discussed later. Suffice it to say here that every indication leads to the conclusion that those passages do not refer to infant baptism but refer only to the baptism of those capable of making a profession of repentance and faith. The conclusion drawn is that the passages of the New Testament describing the act of baptism, when subjected to exhaustive study and thought, lead in all cases to believers' baptism.

There are a few passages which speak of baptism doctrinally that also support the view just discussed. Romans 6:1-4 pictures the Christian's being buried with Christ through baptism unto death and being raised to walk in newness of life, which would apply only to mature Christians who submit to baptism as a sign of their new life in Christ. So it is with the picture in Colossians 2:12 and also in I Peter 3:21. The doctrinal passages, therefore, lead to the conclusion that only believers' baptism is taught and practiced in the New Testament.

(2) ARGUMENTS USED FOR INFANT BAPTISM

There are many arguments used by the pedobaptists to defend their position.

a. *Circumcision*

Some turn to the Scriptures and bring up circumcision, stating that in the Old Testament children were members of the congregation (or church) by virtue of circumcision at the age of eight days. They maintain that since the old covenant and the new covenant are both covenants of grace, and since the seal of the old covenant was circumcision, the seal of the new covenant is baptism. Baptism is merely substituted for circumcision; so the child becomes a member of the church at baptism. But we answer by saying that the conclusion drawn from the premises is incorrect. The argument is based on an analogy that cannot stand; for the congregation of Israel was not identical with the Christian church, and baptism was never substituted for circumcision.

b. "Household" passages

The pedobaptists also appeal to the "household baptism" passages in the Scriptures to support their view. These are three in number: Lydia's household in Acts 16:14, 15; the Philippian jailer's household in Acts 16:33, 34; Stephanas' household in I Corinthians 1:14-16. Pedobaptists explain the scarcity of these passages on the brevity of the history, but believe that "household" includes the children also. Let it be said in answer that the word infants is not used at all. Also, if infant baptism were taught and practiced elsewhere in the Scriptures these three passages could be used as supporting evidence; but they prove nothing in and of themselves. When it says a family was baptized it means one of two things: either all were mature enough to believe, did so, and were baptized; or else all who were old enough to believe did so and were baptized. Therefore it is maintained that these passages do not include the infants of the household.

c. Other passages

The pedobaptists also turn to various other passages of Scripture in an endeavor to sustain their view. "Suffer the little children, and forbid them not, to come unto me: for to such belongeth the kingdom of heaven" (Matt. 19:13-15). But nothing is said here concerning baptism. Besides, Jesus means that one must become humble and believing, as a little child, in order to enter the kingdom. It is a teaching analogy used by our Lord, not a categorical statement relative to baptism.

There are two passages that the pedobaptists apply in a similar way in an endeavor to prove their point. One is the Great Commission in Matthew 28:19, and the second is Peter's statement in Acts 2:38, 39. In the Great Commission Jesus instructs us to "make disciples of all the nations, baptizing them...." It is argued that "all nations" includes even the children. But in the same breath Jesus says that we are to teach them; how could this be possible for very little children? In the Acts 2:38, 39 passage Peter tells the crowd at Pentecost, "Repent ye, and be baptized every one of you...." It is argued that "every one" includes children; for in the following statement Peter says, "For to you is the promise, and to your children, and to all that are afar off, even as many as the Lord our God shall call unto him." But the command to repent prior to the baptism would knock out any thought of including children in that rite; and besides, all Peter means by "children" is posterity, those coming in later generations.

In Paul's famous passage, I Corinthians 7:12-14, where he states that an unbelieving spouse is sanctified in the mate, he adds, "else were your children unclean; but now are they holy." The pedobaptists insist that "holy" involves church membership and, as a consequence, baptism. In the Greek "holy" means sanctified; therefore this line of reasoning applied to the whole passage would make the unbelieving wife or husband also sanctified, and therefore in line for church membership and baptism.

Another passage used by the pedobaptists is Ephesians 6:1: "Children, obey your parents in the Lord: for this is right." It is maintained that in this passage "children" are thought of as church members, but this is not necessarily so. Paul talks first to wives, then to husbands, then to children, and then to servants, thus involving the whole domestic circle. It is not necessary to suppose that all were Christian, or that he thought of all as being Christian.

d. Early rise, continuance, and extensive growth

The pedobaptists argue that the early rise of infant baptism points to apostolic approval, which assumption is based on a so-called patristic evidence (teaching of the early church fathers). The custom may have been in existence during the time of Tertullian, about A.D. 160, but this is doubtful. The first undisputed reference to it was made by Cyprian in A.D. 253, which statement shows that it was in existence prior to that date. But it is maintained that a two-hundred-year span back to the apostles is too long a time to draw such an inference; nor does it take us back to New Testament evidence even then.

The continuance of the custom and its great prevalence today are used as proof that it must be right and should not be abandoned. But this could be said of many other erroneous doctrines and beliefs. Mohammedanism has spread tremendously, but its vast expansion is certainly no proof of its validity.

e. Church authority

The church says it is right and proper to baptize infants; this in itself is all that is necessary. Such an argument is used by Roman Catholics but not by Protestant pedobaptists. This same line of reasoning is used by the Catholics in many other regards, for instance, purgatory. It is as false in one respect as another. Is not the "tradition of the church" of Roman Catholics analogous to the "tradition of the elders" of the Jews as denounced so vehemently by Jesus in the fifteenth chapter of Matthew?

f. *Regenerative baptism*

Those who believe in regenerative baptism argue that it is just as effective for children as for adults, and just as needful. The Roman Catholics form the main group here, although the Episcopalians and Lutherans hint at it. The Catholic argument is that children come under the sway of original sin and are born in a defiled state, needing baptism to enter the kingdom. The Church of Christ (derived from the Campbellites) is strong for regenerative baptism but disagrees with the Roman Catholic Church in line of argument for infant baptism. So regenerative baptism tends to infant baptism, which is a good example of how one erroneous doctrine calls for another.

III. LORD'S SUPPER

The second ordinance instituted by our Lord while here upon earth is the Lord's Supper. Many of the principles discussed already in connection with baptism apply equally well to this second rite.

Sometimes the ordinance is called communion; but such is not an adequate name, for it applies to only one aspect of the rite. It is found in I Corinthians 10:16: "The bread which we break, is it not a communion of the body of Christ?" The Greek word translated "communion" is better translated "participation," for the ordinance concerns not so much communion one with another (or fellowship) as communion with the Lord.

Another name sometimes used for this rite is eucharist, which is derived from the Greek word *eucharistēsas*, translated "gave thanks," in Jesus' words concerning the cup in Matthew 26:27. Later in Christian history the two elements came to be regarded as thank-offerings, thereby making the term eucharist even more appropriate. However, this concept is purely unscriptural, thus making this term undesirable also.

The Roman Catholic term mass, their term for the Lord's Supper and one of their seven sacraments, is unscriptural and unwarranted. It is a contraction of the Latin *missa est,* a phrase equivalent to "it is over" and used as a dismissal formula. The term sacrament should not be used for the Lord's Supper any more than it should for baptism, although many denominations use this term instead of "ordinance." The Bible refers to the Lord's Supper as "the breaking of bread." (Acts 2:42 and Acts 20:7). This is a good scriptural term which, for some reason or other, has not caught on. The term Lord's Supper is still the best available for this rite.

1. SCRIPTURAL TEACHING

(1) INSTITUTED BY JESUS

The following scriptural passages depict the institution of the Lord's Supper: Matthew 26:26-29; Mark 14:22-25; Luke 22:17-20; and I Corinthians 11:23-26. The Matthew passage and Mark passage are similar to each other; the Luke passage and the First Corinthians passage are similar one to the other. The Matthew passage is as follows: "And as they were eating, Jesus took bread, and blessed, and brake it; and he gave to the disciples, and said, Take, eat; this is my body. And he took a cup, and gave thanks, and gave to them, saying, Drink ye all of it; for this is my blood of the covenant, which is poured out for many unto remission of sins. But I say unto you, I shall not drink henceforth of this fruit of the vine, until that day when I drink it new with you in my Father's kingdom." The bread represents his body and the wine his blood, a symbolical representation; Jesus definitely does not speak literally.

Paul's account, which is very similar to that of Luke, is as follows: "For I received of the Lord that which also I delivered unto you, that the Lord Jesus in the night in which he was betrayed took bread; and when he had given thanks, he brake it, and said, This is my body, which is for you: this do in remembrance of me. In like manner also the cup, after supper, saying, This cup is the new covenant in my blood: this do, as often as ye drink it, in remembrance of me. For as often as ye eat this bread, and drink the cup, ye proclaim the Lord's death till he come."

From these passages we see that Jesus instituted and gave the Lord's Supper to his apostles and through them to all of his disciples through the ages. It is truly the Lord's Supper. Just how or where Paul "received of the Lord" is hard to determine, but it must have been through some special revelation. Paul also quotes Jesus as using the phrase "as often as ye drink it," thereby revealing his desire that we should perpetuate the rite.

Therefore Jesus instituted the rite and meant for it to be observed until his second coming. In fact, only after his death could its purpose as a commemorative feast be meaningful. The uniform practice, as seen in the New Testament and early churches, in keeping this important rite shows that the disciples so understood Jesus' remarks relative to the Supper. "And they continued stedfastly in the apostles' teaching and fellowship, in the breaking of bread and the prayers" (Acts 2:42).

(2) ANALOGOUS TO PASSOVER MEAL

It was during the passover, or paschal, meal that Jesus delivered to the apostles the Lord's Supper. He instructed two of his apostles to prepare for the passover in an upper room. On the appointed evening, the fifteenth day of the Jewish month Nisan, Jesus met with the twelve to partake of the paschal lamb, the unleavened bread, the wine, and the bitter herbs. Toward the end of the meal, "and as they were eating," he instituted the Lord's Supper, which was probably after Judas had left the company for the purpose of betraying him.

What the passover was to the Jew the Lord's Supper is to the Christian, and more! The passover was a memorial feast, a yearly reminder that God had delivered them out of bondage in Egypt. God did not want them to forget for a moment that he had passed over their houses in Egypt, the houses with the blood of the lamb on the doorposts and the lintel, and had not killed their firstborn, but had killed the firstborn in every Egyptian house. The Lord's Supper is a memorial feast also, a memorial of the fact that Jesus has redeemed us out of the bondage of sin into the glorious light of his eternal love. In regard to eating the bread Jesus says, "This do in remembrance of me" (I Cor. 11:24); in regard to drinking the cup he says, "This do, as often as ye drink it, in remembrance of me" (I Cor. 11:25). The whole rite is a memorial of Calvary and its redeeming power. In addition, Paul remarks, "For our passover also hath been sacrificed, even Christ" (I Cor. 5:7). He is our Paschal Lamb, and the Lord's Supper is our paschal meal. It is our redemption feast. Paul's use of the word "our" shows that the Lord's Supper is the New Testament antitype of the Old Testament prototype, the passover. According to John's gospel Jesus was crucified on the day the paschal lamb was slain, the fourteenth day of Nisan, the day of preparation. Paul's naming Jesus our passover correlates with the Johannine view.

Yet there is another way that the Lord's Supper is correlative to the Jewish passover. The passover not only looked back to the great deliverance from Egypt; it also looked forward to a new deliverance by the Messiah for whom they looked in anticipation. There was an eschatological aspect to the paschal meal. Likewise with the Lord's Supper, for in the observance of it the participants do "proclaim the Lord's death till he come" (I Cor. 11:26) — preach Calvary till the second advent. This also has an eschatological aspect.

2. MODE

(1) THE ELEMENTS

The followers of Christ are to partake of both the bread and the cup. The bread used by Jesus was doubtless the unleavened bread of the passover meal, as the wine he used was doubtless the fermented juice of the grape. But this does not mean that we must of necessity use unleavened bread, nor does it mean that we cannot use the unfermented juice of the grape. Unleavened bread is what Jesus had at hand, and his phrase "fruit of the vine" in Matthew 26:29 would include unfermented juice as well. The bread and the cup are symbolical only. To insist on literalism would be tantamount to legalism.

(2) BOTH ELEMENTS ESSENTIAL

Christ says, in speaking of the cup, "Drink ye all of it" (Matt. 26: 27). Yet the Roman Catholic Church withholds the cup from the laity; only the priest partakes of it, which has been the case since the Council of Constance, 1415. The communicant receives only the bread, which Catholics term the "host," or "wafer consecrated in the Eucharist." The Roman Church withholds the cup in spite of the fact that it believes both elements actually become the body and blood of Christ. This withholding is directly a disobedience of the command of Christ when he says, "Drink ye all of it." Mark tells us that "they all drank of it" (Mark 14:23). Such withholding would imply that the communicant receives only a portion of the benefits of the death of Christ. The Greek Orthodox Church does not withhold the cup from the laity as the Roman Church does; the bread and wine are mixed and given by means of a spoon.

(3) FUNCTION OF ASSEMBLED CHURCH

The Lord's Supper was never intended to be administered as an individual act. Rather, it was intended as something for the church assembled. Luke says in the "we" section of Acts, "And upon the first day of the week, when we were gathered together to break bread, Paul discoursed with them" (20:7). The same idea is found in the longer passage, I Corinthians 11:17-34. This would indicate that the Lord's Supper is not intended as a solitary observance for individuals. Nowhere in the New Testament do we find the Lord's Supper celebrated in each family by itself. No individual has a right to partake of it alone, nor does a minister have the similar right to administer it at the sickbed. When Paul gives his instructions in I Corinthians 11 he is talking to "the church of God which is at Corinth" (I Cor. 1:2).

(4) FREQUENCY OF OBSERVANCE

Since the New Testament gives no specific direction as to how often the Lord's Supper should be observed, each local church should decide the issue. We have biblical examples of what appear to be daily and weekly observances. "And day by day, continuing stedfastly with one accord in the temple, and breaking bread..." (Acts 2:46). "And upon the first day of the week, when we were gathered together to break bread..." (Acts 20:7). Jesus' phrase, "as often as ye drink it" (I Cor. 11:25), is the nearest approach to any instruction relative to frequency, and this statement is certainly not definite. Some churches observe the rite on every Lord's day; some observe it every three months; some observe it every six months; and some go for longer periods yet.

3. MEANING

There are four main views that have been attached to the Lord's Supper through the centuries. Every present-day denomination holds to one of these four views, with modifications here or there.

(1) ROMAN CATHOLIC

The Roman Catholic view, commonly called transubstantiation, is that the substance of the bread and the wine is actually changed into the body and blood of Christ. This was formally enunciated in 1551 in the Decrees and Canons of the Council of Trent, at which time all other views were condemned. The decree concerning this "sacrament" is long, but a significant statement is as follows: "And because that Christ our Redeemer declared that which he offered under the species of bread to be truly his own body, therefore, has it ever been the firm belief in the Church of God, and this holy Synod doth now declare it anew, that by the consecration of the bread and of the wine a conversion is made of the whole substance of the bread into the body of Christ our Lord, and of the whole substance of the wine into the substance of his blood; which conversion is by the Holy Catholic Church suitably and properly called transubstantiation." This is the belief that the bread and wine are changed by sacerdotal consecration into the very body and blood of Christ, thus reënacting Christ's atoning sacrifice. The partaking of these elements mediates saving grace from God to the communicant.

Our reply is that this view constitutes a false interpretation of Scripture, for it rests upon a literal interpretation of the figurative language in our Lord's institution of this important rite. When Jesus said, "This is my body," he meant, "This is a symbol of my body." Transubstantiation is as preposterous today as it was absurd for the initial event that first evening. It is absurd that a priest should change a small wafer and a small bit of wine into the real body and blood of Christ, and it is even more absurd to think that an unfit priest could work a divine miracle such as this. "There is no word of a sacramental magic happening, of a 'miracle' either in the account of the first Lord's Supper or in Paul — who is indeed the only person who gives instruction about the Lord's Supper (I Cor. 10:16, 17). How could there be the thought of any such thing, seeing that in the first celebration of the Supper the broken body and the shed blood were still present, unbroken and unshed in the bodily presence of Jesus?"[5] Besides, such a view changes that which was meant for a symbolism into an object of worship, not to mention the fact that it contradicts the evidence of our senses. If we cannot trust our senses here, how can we trust them anywhere? It denies the "once and for all" view of Christ's sacrifice, implying the necessity for a priestly repetition of this atoning act, or implying that further sacrificial acts are necessary in a supplemental sense. This view of what the Catholics call the Mass, or Eucharist, must of necessity be dismissed.

(2) LUTHERAN

The Lutheran view, commonly called consubstantiation, is that the body and blood of Christ are truly present in the elements of bread and wine and are therefore taken by the communicant. The communicant eats the true body and drinks the true blood of Christ in the bread and wine; yet these elements, in contrast to the view of transubstantiation, do not cease to be material. This is clearly stated in the Augsburg Confession, Article X: "Of the Supper of the Lord they teach that the body and blood of Christ are truly present and are there communicated to those that eat in the Lord's Supper." The later German edition adds after the words, "are truly present," the words, "under the form of bread and wine." Later statements yet attempt to elaborate the view and to contrast it with opposing doctrines (Roman Catholic and Reformed). This view also led to further argumentation as to the mode of the Lord's presence in the elements. It is held by the Lutherans and High Church Episcopalians.

Our reply to this view is that it is as unscriptural as the Roman view and leads to psychological questionings and unnecessary mysteries. Explanations are of necessity highly involved and unsatisfactory. This belief cannot be separated from the sacramental system of which it is a part; for it makes materialistic elements the means and condition for receiving Christ, thus violating the simple doctrine of justification by faith alone. The rite becomes a means of salvation, a means of grace. This view, like that of transubstantiation, requires a priestly, or sacerdotal, order to consecrate the elements. The miracle demanded is practically the same as in the Roman view. The whole theory tends toward ritualism.

[5] Emil Brunner, *The Christian Doctrine of the Church, Faith, and the Consummation*, III, 61, 62.

(3) CALVINISTIC

The Calvinistic view is that the body and blood of Christ are dynamically present in the elements of bread and wine. This view mediates between that held by Luther and that held by Zwingli and was the view of the Reformed Churches as distinguished from the Lutheran Church in the Reformation. It is held by some Presbyterians and some Episcopalians. A good statement of this view is as follows: "While Calvin denied the real presence of the body and blood of Christ in the eucharist, in the sense in which that presence was asserted by Romanists and Lutherans; yet he affirmed that they were dynamically present. The sun is in the heaven, but his light and heat are present on the earth; so the body of Christ is in heaven, but from that glorified body there radiates an influence other than the influence of the Spirit (although through his agency) of which believers, in the Lord's Supper, are the recipients. In this way they receive the body and blood of Christ, or their substance or life-giving power."[6] Therefore it is plainly discerned that this view argues for the miraculous even in this "dynamic presence" of the body and blood of Christ.

Our reply is that this view is too vacillating, too wavering. Its lack of definiteness necessitates its nonacceptance. We turn now to the simplest view of all.

(4) ZWINGLIAN

This view, that the two elements are symbolical of the body and blood of Christ offered up as a sacrifice for our sins, is the view held by most evangelical Christians and is the one that most nearly fits all the conditions surrounding this important rite. Zwingli, a contemporary of Martin Luther, opposed Luther hotly on his view of the Lord's Supper.

This view is commemorative, since it looks back to his death. "This do in remembrance of me" (Luke 22:19). As the passover was commemorative of a great deliverance for Israel, so the Lord's Supper is commemorative of a great deliverance for the Christian, a spiritual deliverance from sin by the death of the Son of God. It is related to the present, since it is a proclamation of Christ's death till he comes. "For as often as ye eat this bread, and drink the cup, ye proclaim the Lord's death till he come" (I Cor. 11:26). It is a public proclaiming, a means of confessing Christ and of witnessing to our faith in the saving power of his death. It is anticipatory, since it looks forward to the coming perfection of life in the kingdom of God. It looks toward future glory, the great festival, "the marriage supper of the Lamb" (Rev. 19:9). "But I

6 Charles Hodge, *Systematic Theology*, III, 611ff.

say unto you, I shall not drink henceforth of this fruit of the vine, until that day when I drink it new with you in my Father's kingdom" (Matt. 26:29).

The Lord's Supper has no regenerative power, it possesses no sanctifying grace. There is nothing magical or mystical about its nature. It is a symbol of the relation of the believer to Christ, who alone does the sanctifying. The outward tokens devised by Christ himself are the symbols of the atoning power and forgiving love of his great sacrifice, which was once and for all efficacious. The sacrifice cannot be, and does not have to be, reënacted by priests down through the centuries. This view is made explicit in the Heidelberg Catechism and is held by Baptists, by some Presbyterians, and generally by Methodists.

The Lord's Supper seems to convey a threefold symbolism.

a. Symbol of death of Christ for our sins

Concerning the bread Jesus says, "This is my body, which is given for you," and concerning the cup, "This cup is the new covenant in my blood, even that which is poured out for you" (Luke 22:19, 20). Paul says, "For as often as ye eat this bread, and drink the cup, ye proclaim the Lord's death till he come" (I Cor. 11:26). His blood seals the new covenant between God and man, the covenant upon which our salvation depends. It is the blood of the atoning death of our Lord, poured forth that we might live. His death constitutes the giving of his life "a ransom for many" (Matt. 20:28), of which the Lord's Supper is an eternal and proclaiming witness. "Body and blood, then, represent and fitly symbolize two different aspects of sacrifice, — namely the dedicated victim and the sacrificed life."[7] Therefore we see that Jesus himself regarded his death as the climax of his great redemptive act and the crowning glory of his atoning work. It is the supreme sacrifice eternally remitting sin. The Lord's Supper attests to this central place of his death in the mind of Jesus.

b. Symbol of appropriation of benefits of that death for believer

Jesus says, "This is my body, which is for you" (I Cor. 11:24). Paul says, of Jesus, "For our passover also hath been sacrificed, even Christ" (I Cor. 5:7). Just as the paschal lamb symbolized for the Israelites deliverance from the bondage of Egypt, so the Lord's Supper symbolizes for the Christian deliverance from the bondage of sin, which is the appropriation of the benefits of his death.

7 L. S. Thornton, *The Common Life in the Body of Christ*, p. 331.

c. *Symbol of means of that appropriation*: *union with Christ*

Through union with Christ one appropriates the saving benefits of his death; this also is symbolized in the Lord's Supper. Paul states, "The cup of blessing which we bless, is it not a communion of the blood of Christ? The bread which we break, is it not a communion of the body of Christ?" (I Cor. 10:16). The word translated "communion" is *koinōnia*, which is usually translated "fellowship" in the New Testament. Here it can easily be translated "participation," as it is in the marginal reading of the American Standard Version. So what Paul is virtually saying is: "does it not symbolize the participation in?" This union with Christ is also signified in the statement: "Verily, verily, I say unto you, Except ye eat the flesh of the Son of man and drink his blood, ye have not life in yourselves" (John 6:53). This spiritual union with Christ is symbolized in the Lord's Supper.

4. ADMINISTRATOR

All the decisions relative to the administration of the Lord's Supper should rest with the church, including the one who leads in the service as well as the ones who assist. Normally it is understood that the pastor assumes the leadership in observance and is aided by the deacons. However, in case there is temporarily no pastor, the church can appoint one of its members to direct the observance. As in baptism, merely the laying on of hands in ordination to the ministry does not invest with authority to administer the Lord's Supper, much less bestow a monopoly over deacons and unordained members to do so The church must decide in all cases relative to administration.

5. PREREQUISITES TO PARTICIPATION

Jesus did not give the Supper to the world at large, but only to his disciples. Then what are the requirements for its celebration?

(1) REGENERATION

The Lord's Supper is symbolical of spiritual life in the believer, the one partaking. Therefore, to be partaken of by one who is spiritually dead, one who is "dead through . . . trespasses and sins," would be a desecration of that which is holy. As the physically dead do not need physical food, the spiritually dead do not need the food symbolical of the sacrificial and atoning death of our Lord. There is no evidence in the New Testament of the Supper being administered to unbelievers. Wherefore whosoever shall eat the bread or drink the cup of the Lord in an unworthy manner, shall be guilty of the body and the blood of the Lord. But let a man prove himself, and so let him eat of the bread, and drink of the cup. For he that eateth and drinketh, eateth and drinketh judgment unto himself, if he discern not the body" (I Cor. 11:27-29). How could one not a Christian "discern the body"? This would necessitate saving faith, which he does not possess.

(2) BAPTISM

It appears from various New Testament readings that the apostles celebrating the Lord's Supper had been baptized. Peter, in speaking to the one hundred and twenty soon after Jesus' ascension, says, "Of the men therefore that have companied with us all the time that the Lord Jesus went in and went out among us, beginning from the baptism of John, unto the day that he was received up from us, of these must one become a witness with us of his resurrection" (Acts 1:21, 22). Then they select one to take Judas' place. The phrase "from the baptism of John" is very significant. Christ is baptized by John, and it is very probable that he selects for his apostles only those who likewise have submitted to John's baptism. And he definitely recognizes John's baptism as being ordained of God (Matt. 21:25).

Besides this fact, Jesus places baptism as first in prominence after profession of faith. "Go ye therefore, and make disciples of all the nations, baptizing them into the name of the Father and of the Son and of the Holy Spirit: teaching them to observe all things whatsoever I commanded you" (Matt. 28:19, 20). Make disciples, then baptize — this is the order in the command of Christ. If it is argued that there is no formal command in the Bible to admit only those who have been baptized to the Lord's Supper, it can also be stated that there is no formal command that only the regenerate may be baptized. In both cases we must judge from the practice of the apostles as that practice is discerned in the New Testament. Statements such as the following show this: "They then that received his word were baptized.... And day by day, continuing stedfastly with one accord in the temple, and breaking bread..." (Acts 2:41, 46).

(3) CHURCH MEMBERSHIP

The Lord's Supper is a church rite, to be observed by the assembled church. Therefore does it not follow that church membership is a prerequisite to participation? Luke speaks of "the first day of the week, when we were gathered together to break bread" (Acts 20:7). Paul's admonition to the Corinthians in regard to the Lord's Supper is directed to the whole church (I Cor. 11). The Lord's Supper is a symbol of fellowship, fellowship with the Lord and with one another. "We, who are many, are one bread, one body: for we all partake of the one bread" (I Cor. 10:17).

OUTLINE FOR CHAPTER FIFTEEN

I. Covenant in Old Testament
  1. Promises of covenant
  2. Enactment of covenant
     (1) Decalogue
     (2) Book of the Covenant
     (3) Ritual
  3. Ratification of covenant
  4. Characteristics of covenant
     (1) Grounded in historic deliverance
     (2) Motivated by love
     (3) Effected with corporate Israel
     (4) Distinguished by mutual obligations
     (5) Characterized by the ethical and spiritual as well as the ritualistic and ceremonial
     (6) Represented by symbols
        a. Pillar
        b. Circumcision
        c. Ark of the covenant
  5. Breaking of covenant
II. Covenant in New Testament
  1. In Synoptics
  2. In Hebrews
  3. In fulfillment of Jeremiah's prophecy
     (1) Subjective in nature
     (2) Communal in result
     (3) Abundant in forgiveness
     (4) Eternal in scope
  4. In Jewish rejection of Jesus

CHAPTER FIFTEEN

THE COVENANT

THE BASIC STRUCTURE IN BOTH THE OLD AND THE NEW TESTAMENT
is the covenant relationship: in the Old, a covenant between God
and Israel, and in the New, a covenant between God and the
individual Christian through Christ.

What is a covenant? It is an agreement between two parties, a
compact of a contractual character. The parties, or covenanters,
may be of equal rank, or one may be stronger than the other. The
conditions may be mutually drawn up or may be formulated completely by one side. A covenant between God and his created ones
is always of the latter nature, with God setting both the conditions
of acceptance and the consequences of violation.

I. COVENANT IN OLD TESTAMENT

The Hebrew word *berith* is best translated covenant, as it is in
most of the late English translations. It is this that constitutes the
uniqueness of the Hebrew religion as revealed in the Old Testament, which would be better termed the Old Covenant, as the New
Testament would be better depicted as the New Covenant. The
term Testament is derived from the Latin word *testamentum,*
which in the Latin Vulgate is used to translate *berith* in the
Hebrew Scriptures. The English word covenant most adequately
translates the Hebrew term *berith,* which term is probably derived
from a verb meaning to cut. Therefore "to make a covenant" is
usually "to cut a covenant," i. e., to kill a victim, or victims, in
order to form the agreement. At any rate, "to cut a covenant" became a common idiom in Hebrew terminology.

This covenant may be between equals, as between Abraham and
Abimelech. "So they made a covenant at Beersheba: and Abimelech
rose up, and Phicol the captain of his host, and they returned into
the land of the Philistines" (Gen. 21:32). The covenant between
David and Jonathan was between equals. "Then Jonathan and
David made a covenant, because he loved him as his own soul"
(I Sam. 18:3). Jacob made a covenant with Laban, for the latter
said, "And now come, let us make a covenant, I and thou; and
let it be for a witness between me and thee" (Gen. 31:44). The
marriage relation was, and is, a covenant between equals. Two
tribes may enter into a covenant for trade relations, or for the
purpose of amity, or for the purpose of marriage. But there is

also the covenant between unequals, as the covenant between an elected king and his people. The victor may make a covenant with the defeated, to spare him or to provide him a place to live. Joshua made a covenant with the people of Gibeon. "And Joshua made peace with them, and made a covenant with them, to let them live: and the princes of the congregation sware unto them" (Josh. 9:15). Ahab made a covenant with the defeated Benhadad (I Kings 20:34).

Yet, the most important fact is that God made a covenant with Israel. This, too, is a covenant between unequals; for God set all the conditions, the conditions on his part and the conditions on Israel's part. Therefore the suggestions made by the English word covenant must not be pressed too far — an agreement on equal terms. True, there are conditions on both sides, but God himself formulated both sets of them. Israel willingly accepted what God offered.

From the days of Sinai on the relation between Jehovah and the children of Israel was covenantal. At that time the national faith was formally ratified and established with a ceremony. This covenant was based on the fact that Jehovah had redeemed and blessed his people; his power and wisdom had been signally displayed. Upon this fact rested Israel's faith in him. This covenant relation was established at Sinai, but we see forerunners (also called covenants, but containing the basic elements encountered in the covenant at Sinai) as far back as the days of Abraham. These are not separate covenants, as some theologians would have us believe. They are one and the same as that encountered at Sinai; for the Old Testament reveals but one. The book of Hebrews justifies this view; this writer speaks of Christ as "the mediator of a better covenant, which hath been enacted upon better promises. For if that first covenant had been faultless, then would no place have been sought for a second" (Heb. 8:6, 7). "That first covenant" — this term is singular, not plural.

1. PROMISES OF COVENANT

God spoke to Abraham in covenantal terms several times. In Haran of Padan-Aram God said to him, "Get thee out of thy country, and from thy kindred, and from thy father's house, unto the land that I will show thee: and I will make of thee a great nation, and I will bless thee, and make thy name great; and be thou a blessing: and I will bless them that bless thee, and him that curseth thee I will curse: and in thee shall all the families of the earth be blessed" (Gen. 12:1-3). Later on we read, "In that day Jehovah made a covenant with Abram, saying, Unto thy seed have I given this land, from the river of Egypt unto the great river, the river Euphrates" (Gen. 15:18). Later God said, "I am God Almighty; walk before me, and be thou perfect. And I will make my covenant between me and thee, and will multiply thee exceedingly. And Abram fell on his face: and God talked with him, saying, As for me, behold, my covenant is with thee, and thou shalt be the father of a multitude of nations. Neither shall thy name any more be called Abram, but thy name shall be Abraham; for the father of a multitude of nations have I made thee. And I will make thee exceedingly fruitful, and I will make nations of thee, and kings shall come out of thee. And I will establish my covenant between me and thee and thy seed after thee throughout their generations for an everlasting covenant, to be a God unto thee and to thy seed after thee. And I will give unto thee, and to thy seed after thee, the land of thy sojournings, all the land of Canaan, for an everlasting possession; and I will be their God" (Gen. 17:1-8). Immediately after this declaration concerning the covenant God designated circumcision as its sign and promised Isaac, the son of promise, as its means of fulfillment.

God spoke unto Isaac practically the same words of promise that he gave to Abraham, thus reiterating the covenantal blessings previously given. "Go not down into Egypt; dwell in the land which I shall tell thee of: sojourn in this land, and I will be with thee, and will bless thee; for unto thee, and unto thy seed, I will give all these lands, and I will establish the oath which I sware unto Abraham thy father; and I will multiply thy seed as the stars of heaven, and will give unto thy seed all these lands; and in thy seed shall all the nations of the earth be blessed; because that Abraham obeyed my voice, and kept my charge, my commandments, my statutes, and my laws" (Gen. 26:2-5).

God also spoke unto Jacob, Isaac's son, and renewed the covenant promise, at Bethel on the way to Haran and again at Bethel on the return trip. At the latter time he said, "Thy name is Jacob: thy name shall not be called any more Jacob, but Israel shall be thy name: and he called his name Israel." To this God further added, "I am God Almighty: be fruitful and multiply; a nation and a company of nations shall be of thee, and kings shall come out of thy loins; and the land which I gave unto Abraham and Isaac, to thee I will give it, and to thy seed after thee will I give the land" (Gen. 35:10-12).

2. ENACTMENT OF COVENANT

These promises to the patriarchs Abraham, Isaac, and Jacob came to fruition in the phenomena of Sinai. Here Israel became Jehovah's people, and Jehovah became their God. This relation became explicit in the form of a *berith*, or covenant, which covenant has as its foundation God's great historic redemption of his people by a mighty act out of Egypt. God redeemed; then God covenanted. "The new order is inaugurated and made valid by a great covenant, made between Yahweh on the one hand and the people on the other. They are treated as a single whole, and, for the first time, we have emerging the conception of Israel as a national entity."[1]

The simplest form of this covenant is a review of God's requirements, which tends to make this historic covenant approach the idea of a command rather than an agreement. God commanded; Israel accepted. However, even then there were conditions on both sides. "This day Jehovah thy God commandeth thee to do these statutes and ordinances: thou shalt therefore keep and do them with all thy heart, and with all thy soul. Thou has avouched Jehovah this day to be thy God, and that thou wouldest walk in his ways, and keep his statutes, and his commandments, and his ordinances, and hearken unto his voice: and Jehovah hath avouched thee this day to be a people for his own possession, as he hath promised thee, and that thou shouldest keep all his commandments; and to make thee high above all nations that he hath made, in praise, and in name, and in honor; and that thou mayest be a holy people unto Jehovah thy God, as he hath spoken" (Deut. 26:16-19).

Israel had been redeemed out of Egypt. Israel possessed a consciousness of salvation, rooted in which is the idea of being in a covenant relation with the one who had redeemed her, Jehovah God. "This embraced all. Other redemptive ideas were but deductions from this, or arose from an analysis of it. The idea of the covenant is, so to speak, the frame within which the development goes on; this development being in great measure a truer understanding of what ideas lie in the two related elements, Jehovah on the one side and the people on the other, and in the nature of the relation. This idea of a covenant was not a conception struck out of the religious mind and applied only to things of religion; it was a conception transferred from ordinary life into the religious sphere."[2]

There are three sections to the biblical account of the acceptance of the covenant at Sinai: the Decalogue, or Ten Commandments, in Exodus 20:3-17; the Book of the Covenant in Exodus 20:22-23:19; the covenant ceremony, or ritual, in Exodus 24:1-11. All three of these elements are of extreme importance.

(1) DECALOGUE

The Ten Commandments became the foundation stone of

[1] T. H. Robinson, "The History of Israel," *A Companion to the Bible*, p. 213.
[2] A. B. Davidson, *The Theology of the Old Testament*, p. 239.

Israel's ethics, for it was the ethical nature of the covenant relation with Jehovah that made the Hebrew religion unique. Jehovah is a moral God, a righteous God, a holy God, one who demanded that his peculiar people be of the same character. This is the nature of the Decalogue as the basis of the covenant, for here we find that God required that Israel worship him, Jehovah alone, and that his Name be honored. Even the introduction to the Decalogue is a reminder of the fact that it was Jehovah who delivered from Egypt, the house of bondage. Since he is the only God, he is a jealous God, demanding all Israel's affection. As a consequence there were to be no images, no other gods. The first four commandments have to do with man's relation to God; the last six have to do with man's relation to man. Therefore, Israel's social ethics were derived from this very same covenant relationship. The Decalogue takes an upward look, but it also takes an outward look.

These Ten Commandments were presented to Israel, via Moses, at Sinai on tables of stone — given twice, in fact. "For the law was given through Moses" (John 1:17). The book of Exodus reads, "And Jehovah said unto Moses, Come up to me into the mount, and be there: and I will give thee the tables of stone, and the law and the commandment, which I have written, that thou mayest teach them. And Moses rose up, and Joshua his minister: and Moses went up into the mount of God.... And Moses went up into the mount, and the cloud covered the mount.... And Moses entered into the midst of the cloud, and went up into the mount: and Moses was in the mount forty days and forty nights" (Exod. 24:12-18). There God gave him directions and specifications for many things: the ark, the tabernacle, the furnishings for the tabernacle, the garments of the priests and of the high priest, etc. But especially did God present Moses with an unusual object. "And he gave unto Moses, when he had made an end of communing with him upon Mount Sinai, the two tables of the testimony, tables of stone, written with the finger of God" (Exod. 31:18).

Moses immediately descended from the mount with the divinely engraved stones, only to find the children of Israel engaged in a religious orgy of the most degrading sort. Not having seen Moses for well over a month, and not being satisfied with the spiritual and imageless presence of God, they begged Aaron to construct for them a golden calf. This he did, probably having learned the art well in Egypt, land of the golden bull Apis and the golden calf Mnevis. Constructed with golden earrings and implemented with an altar before it, the calf became the center of a corrupt rite, to which was attached the name of Jehovah! This religious amalgamation of Egyptian ritual and the worship of Jehovah is but a foretoken of the spiritual deviations to be entered into by the

Israelites later in the promised land. When Moses observed this wanton revelry he became indignant, casting the tablets upon the ground to their utter destruction, "tables that were written on both their sides; on the one side and on the other were they written" (Exod. 32:15).

With this God directed Moses to secure two more tables of stone and to reascend the mount. "Hew thee two tables of stone like unto the first: and I will write upon the tables the words that were on the first tables, which thou brakest.... And he hewed two tables of stone like unto the first; and Moses rose up early in the morning, and went up unto Mount Sinai, as Jehovah had commanded him, and took in his hand two tables of stone" (Exod. 34:1-4). God immediately revealed to Moses in a very striking statement the nature of the Almighty One with whom Israel had covenanted. "And Jehovah passed by before him, and proclaimed, Jehovah, Jehovah, a God merciful and gracious, slow to anger, and abundant in lovingkindness and truth; keeping lovingkindness for thousands, forgiving iniquity and transgression and sin; and that will by no means clear the guilty, visiting the iniquity of the fathers upon the children, and upon the children's children, upon the third and upon the fourth generation" (Exod. 34:6, 7). Moses immediately bowed and worshiped, making supplication for the rebellious people. God proclaimed, "Behold, I make a covenant: before all thy people I will do marvels, such as have not been wrought in all the earth, nor in any nation" (Exod. 34:10). He warned them not to make a covenant with the people of the land they were about to invade: the Amorite, the Canaanite, etc. "Take heed to thyself, lest thou make a covenant with the inhabitants of the land whither thou goest, lest it be for a snare in the midst of thee" (Exod. 34:12). The covenant with Jehovah was sufficient and complete; any other covenant would lead to idolatry and apostasy. After reviewing with Moses the laws of the covenant God commanded Moses, "Write thou these words: for after the tenor of these words I have made a covenant with thee and with Israel. And he was there with Jehovah forty days and forty nights; he did neither eat bread, nor drink water. And he wrote upon the tables the words of the covenant, the ten commandments" (Exod. 34:27, 28). Here the Decalogue is practically identified with the covenant itself.

(2) BOOK OF THE COVENANT

The Book of the Covenant, as recorded in Exodus 20:22-23:19, was another element in this covenantal relation between Jehovah and Israel. It is far from a code of laws interposed with ritual. It is moral to the core, containing many of the great ethical demands of the eighth-century prophets. Jehovah demanded ethical living, and his ethical requirements could not be depicted in ten pithy statements; a fuller description was necessitated, which is contained in the Book of the Covenant. This is God's mandatory righteousness, as in differentiation from his condemnatory righteousness or from his redemptive righteousness. In the Book of the Covenant the importance of brotherly principles of conduct is highly stressed, for all Israelites were members of the social group, or community, which owed supreme allegiance to Jehovah. This allegiance is a basic feature of the covenant he offered to Israel, and which Israel accepted.

(3) RITUAL

The ritual, or ceremony, which accompanied the acceptance of the covenant can be easily discerned in Exodus 24:1-11. Moses related to the people all the words and ordinances of Jehovah, to which the people gave ascent. He then built an altar and twelve pillars. On the altar burnt-offerings were offered, also peace-offerings of oxen. God was thought of as on one side and the people on the other side of the altar. The blood was drained into bowls; half was sprinkled on the altar. "And he took the book of the covenant, and read in the audience of the people: and they said, All that Jehovah hath spoken will we do, and be obedient" (Exod. 24:7). Then after their formal acceptance of all the terms of the covenant, Moses sprinkled the remaining half of the blood over the people. This blood is called "the blood of the covenant." Moses, Aaron, Nadab, and Abihu, and seventy elders of Israel "beheld God, and did eat and drink" (Exod. 24:11). The common life, established by this covenant, had found expression in eating and drinking.

This very impressive ritual sealed the covenant between Jehovah and Israel. " 'The blood is the life' (Lev. 17:11, 14), the vital essence. Two parties, at present independent one of another, are to be united in a single whole; and, to secure the desired union, a third party is introduced. Its life is taken from it and made available for the other two. Both come under it, both are included in it; the same vital essence now covers and embraces the two. They are thus no longer independent entities, they are one, finding their unity with each other in their unity with that third party whose blood now covers them both. Till this point is reached, however near they might have been brought to one another, they are merely contagious; now they are continuous, and form parts of a single indivisible whole. We might almost say that now Yahweh is Himself included in Israel: henceforward it will connote not merely a human community, but one of which He is a member."[3]

These three phases — Decalogue, Book of the Covenant, and ritual — constitute the full establishment of the covenant. This covenant made and "cut" at Sinai thus became the foundation stone for all subsequent relations between Jehovah and Israel — both theological and ethical.

3. RATIFICATION OF COVENANT

Due to the direct command of God the covenant was ratified at historic Shechem. What was accepted at Sinai (or Horeb) was reaccepted at a point midway between Mt. Ebal (3085 ft.) and Mt. Gerizim (2849 ft.). Between these twin peaks, at Shechem (meaning ridge), the people were to assemble themselves for a ceremony similar to that at Sinai, all according to the command of God as found in Deuteronomy 27. "And Moses and the elders of Israel commanded the people, saying, Keep all the commandment which I command you this day. And it shall be on the day when ye shall pass over the Jordan unto the land which Jehovah thy God giveth thee, that thou shalt set thee up great stones, and plaster them with plaster: and thou shalt write upon them all the words of this law, when thou art passed over" (Deut. 27:1-3). These stones were to be set up at Mt. Ebal, the mount of curses. An altar was to be erected, upon which burnt-offerings and peace-offerings were to be sacrificed, and a meal was to be eaten. Mt. Gerizim, the twin peak, was the mount of blessing. Half the tribes were to be assembled at Mt. Ebal and half at Mt. Gerizim, the former for the curse of the law and the latter for the blessing of the law. Obedience to the requirements of the covenant would bring blessings (Deut. 28:1-14), while failure to fulfill them would bring curses (Deut. 28:15-68). (Notice to what greater lengths God goes to depict the result of breaking the covenant than to what he goes to depict the result of obeying it — 54 verses to 14 verses!)

The actual ratification in obedience to this command occurred immediately after the capture of Ai. The center of the whole assembly was the ark of the covenant, as would be expected. Half the tribes were placed in front of Mt. Ebal and half in front of Mt. Gerizim, while the elders, the officers, the judges, the Levites, and Joshua stood between the two divisions of tribes. Joshua then read the law (curses and blessings) before all the people (Josh. 8:30-35). Again God vividly reminded his people of this all-important spiritual contract, for here there was a generation later than the one which had accepted the covenant at Sinai.

3 W. O. E. Oesterly and T. H. Robinson, *Hebrew Religion*, pp. 156-7.

4. CHARACTERISTICS OF COVENANT

What are the characteristics of the covenant that God made with Israel? What is its nature?

(1) GROUNDED IN HISTORIC DELIVERANCE

It was based on an historic redemption out of Egyptian slavery. This redemption must never be forgotten; it must be sealed in an objective, concrete deed of partnership bearing the highly significant truth that Israel belonged to God due to God's great act of salvation. "I am Jehovah thy God, who brought thee out of the land of Egypt, out of the house of bondage" (Exod. 20:2). Immediately after this significant statement the Ten Commandments are enumerated.

(2) MOTIVATED BY LOVE

The motive of this covenant was love. Therefore the relation of Jehovah to Israel was a moral one, not a natural one. God chose Israel, and Israel accepted God's offer. In the pagan worship of other Shemites the god was a natural father of the people; but not so here. The word covenant is not found in Joel, Amos, Micah, Obadiah, Zephaniah, or Habakkuk, though the idea expressed by the term is certainly there. Yet the great prophet of love, Hosea, uses the term. "They have transgressed my covenant, and trespassed against my law" (Hos. 8:1). To transgress the covenant is to do violence to the love of Jehovah for Israel. This same motive of love will also be found as the force behind the new covenant through Christ.

(3) EFFECTED WITH CORPORATE ISRAEL

The covenant was made with corporate Israel, not with individuals. We must remember that this is the covenant in the Old Testament, in which the individuals share as members of the whole nation. Jehovah delivered the nation from Egypt, all the tribes as a unit. It was with this unit that he covenanted at Sinai. It was the nation for whom he fought and the nation to whom he supplied manna and quail and water. It was the nation whom he led by a pillar of fire and a pillar of cloud. The whole unit of twelve tribes constituted "a kingdom of priests, and a holy nation" (Exod. 19:6), and the ordained priests and high priest were merely representative. Jehovah was King, King of Israel. "I am Jehovah, your Holy One, the Creator of Israel, your King" (Isa. 43:15). Yet this must not be pushed too far; God did deal with individuals in many instances. God's dealings with Abraham, the "friend of God," show this. It is also seen in the Psalms and in Proverbs. But individual responsibility, as propounded by Jeremiah and Ezekiel, is relatively late in Israel's history. The remnant idea comes much later than Sinai.

(4) DISTINGUISHED BY MUTUAL OBLIGATIONS

There was an obligation upon Israel and also an obligation upon God. The former obligation is that Israel should serve God, and this service was without right or claim. "See, I have set before thee this day life and good, and death and evil; in that I command thee this day to love Jehovah thy God, to walk in his ways, and to keep his commandments and his statutes and his ordinances, that thou mayest live and multiply, and that Jehovah thy God may bless thee in the land whither thou goest in to possess it" (Deut. 30:15, 16). There were to be no other gods and no covenants with neighboring people. They were to love God and to cleave unto him (Deut. 30:20). The Decalogue and the Book of the Covenant were to be strictly adhered to.

Yet God also had an obligation — a self-imposed one. He was to guide them in the desert and to be their inspiration and divine aid in war. He promised to drive out the inhabitants of Canaan from before them. He would place blessings upon Israel and curses upon Israel's enemies. He would multiply them as the sand of the sea. He promised that the fruits of their cattle and of their land would be plenteous. He would judge them and would make his will known to them. He would see that vengeance was taken for wrong.

(5) CHARACTERIZED BY THE ETHICAL AND SPIRITUAL AS WELL AS THE RITUALISTIC AND CEREMONIAL

The fundamental principles of the covenant developed along two lines: the ethical and spiritual, as proclaimed by the prophets, and the ritualistic and ceremonial, as adhered to by the priests. The former is expressed in the demand for righteous living and the latter in the act of sacrificial worship. These do not develop in a co-ordinate manner; often there is the feeling of antithesis. Yet at times both come together in one man — as in Samuel and in Ezekiel. The main thing is that both trace their origin to the covenant and to its demands. Both increase and develop side by side, the prophets (*Nebiim*) and the law (*Torah*).

(6) REPRESENTED BY SYMBOLS

There were symbols representing the covenant relationship.

a. *Pillar*

Sometimes a pillar was erected as a sort of silent third party, a witness. When Moses built the altar for the burnt-offerings and the peace-offering he also erected twelve pillars, one for each of the twelve tribes entering into the covenant (Exod. 24:4). When Jacob made a covenant with Laban he set up a stone as a pillar (Gen. 31:44-52). Joshua, before he died, made a covenant with the people of Israel that they would keep the Sinaitic covenant; for this he set up a pillar (Josh. 24:19-28).

b. *Circumcision*

The rite of circumcision was a symbol of the covenant. It represented the putting off of the natural life of the flesh and the putting on of the spiritual things of God. It became the constant symbol of covenant obligations and, at the same time, covenant promises. It was performed on the Hebrew boy (and also upon slaves) when eight days old. It was based on the idea that the natural life is corrupted with impurity and that this impurity must be removed from the lives of those entering into a covenant with the pure and righteous God. One was therefore bound to obedience of the covenant, because he bore the covenant sign in his body. This also necessitated a blameless walk before God (Gen. 17:1ff.). Therefore circumcision became the symbol of the renewal of the heart, which is brought out by the phrase "uncircumcision of heart," attributed to those not receiving the blessings and the things of God (Lev. 26:41; Jer. 9:25).

c. *Ark of the covenant*

The ark of the covenant was also a symbol. In it were placed the tables engraved with the Decalogue, the very foundation of the covenant. This ark was not conceived as an image of Jehovah, or as an idol, or even as a symbol of his presence. He was thought of as actually residing there, that it was his dwelling place. He was especially localized there, and yet at the same time he was not confined to this small chest. It was consistently termed the ark of the covenant, another visible means whereby the relationship involved in the covenant would be constantly brought to mind. If the most important thing *in* the ark was the tables of testimony, the most important part *of* the ark was the mercy seat, or the *kapporeth*. God told them that he would meet them there, and commune with them from above the mercy seat (Exod. 25:22). Here the highest act of Old Testament atonement was executed. It was kept in deep darkness, where only the high priest entered once a year; even then he enveloped himself in a cloud of incense as he raised the curtain to enter this most holy place.

5. Breaking of covenant

Israel violated the covenant, just as God had prophesied to

Moses in Moab that they would. "Behold, thou shalt sleep with thy fathers; and this people will rise up, and play the harlot after the strange gods of the land, whither they go to be among them, and will forsake me, and break my covenant which I have made with them. Then my anger shall be kindled against them in that day, and I will forsake them, and I will hide my face from them, and they shall be devoured, and many evils and troubles shall come upon them; so that they will say in that day, Are not these evils come upon us because our God is not among us?" (Deut. 31:16, 17). Then God told Moses to write a song, which would be his witness at a future date of that which he foretold relative to Israel's apostasy and breach of the covenant — his "I told you so" for tomorrow! God reiterated, "Then will they turn unto other gods, and serve them, and despise me, and break my covenant" (Deut. 31:20). This song, known as the Song of Moses (Deut. 32:1-43), is written in Hebrew poetry.

Jeremiah, who started prophesying in 626 B.C., is God's man who reveals in unquestionable terms that Israel broke the covenant. This is in addition to the prophets before him who had hammered at the tragedy of Israel's unfaithfulness toward the covenant. Elijah, in answer to God's query relative to his presence in a cave at Sinai subsequent to his flight from Mt. Carmel, stated, "I have been very jealous for Jehovah, the God of hosts; for the children of Israel have forsaken thy covenant..." (I Kings 19:10). Hosea declared, "...because they have transgressed my covenant, and trespassed against my law" (8:1).

Jeremiah reminded his people repeatedly that they had transgressed the covenant. "The house of Israel and the house of Judah have broken my covenant which I made with their fathers" (11:10). After reviewing the desolation to come upon the house of the king of Judah and upon Jerusalem, Jeremiah informed them, "And many nations shall pass by this city, and they shall say every man to his neighbor, Wherefore hath Jehovah done thus unto this great city? Then they shall answer, Because they forsook the covenant of Jehovah their God, and worshipped other gods, and served them" (22:8, 9). But the greatest passage from this prophet of troublous times is found in 31:31-34. Its entirety must be presented. "Behold, the days come, saith Jehovah, that I will make a new covenant with the house of Israel, and with the house of Judah: not according to the covenant that I made with their fathers in the day that I took them by the hand to bring them out of the land of Egypt; which my covenant they brake, although I was a husband unto them, saith Jehovah. But this is the covenant that I will make with the house of Israel after those days, saith Jehovah: I will put my law in their inward parts, and in their heart will I write it; and I will be their God, and they shall be my people. And they shall teach no more every man his neighbor, and every man his brother, saying, Know Jehovah; for they shall all know me, from the least of them unto the greatest of them, saith Jehovah: for I will forgive their iniquity, and their sin will I remember no more." Israel had failed tragically to meet the obligations expected and laid out in the covenant; therefore the relationship was broken. God's prophecy had been fulfilled!

We have seen that in the covenant between God and Israel God took the initiative, drawing near to man to bless him, which is none other than grace, the bestowal of his favor, the giving of his fulness. We have seen that man was expected to acknowledge this, to understand what was being offered, to comprehend God's desire and attitude and aim, and to accept this bestowal with gratitude and deep humility. Israel acknowledged and accepted, and the covenant was sealed.

Within this framework, however, man was not expected to be perfect, free from sin. His career would not be free from imperfections; there would be voluntary sins, sins that definitely would be construed as great evils. The aim of the covenant would be to decrease these, both in frequency and intensity, to overcome them more and more. But the relationship would *not* be severed by them: the sacrificial system allowed for their expiation, even to the point of providing an all-sweeping forgiveness on the Day of Atonement. What, then, would cause a suspension of the covenant? Unbelief, as found during the wilderness wanderings; and idolatry, the worship of "no gods"; and apostasy, the leaving of Jehovah for pagan abominations. These demanded the cutting off of the people, for they violated the basic attitude of the soul toward God, which undergirded the whole covenant relationship.

It will be immediately discerned that the most appropriate term with which to express this drawing near of Jehovah to Israel is grace, and that the best term with which to denote man's response to God's approach is faith. The covenant was made with Israel as a whole, and individuals were blessed by being members of the group. Since the individual was a member of the group, and was therefore within the covenant, it was assumed that he had the right attitude toward God and toward the covenant. If by his conduct he showed he did not possess this attitude he was cut off. To be righteous was to have a right attitude toward God's covenant, which meant to accept it wholeheartedly with faith. But this is nothing but imputed righteousness, or righteousness reckoned for faith. Therefore it is discerned that grace, faith, and righteousness are the keynotes in the Mosaic covenant. Idolatry was denial of Jehovah as alone God of Israel, or lack of faith in Jehovah as the redeeming one. Since this placed the sinning one outside the covenant, he was without the realm where God's grace was operative. This is why sins of ignorance or sins of weakness could be atoned for in the Mosaic sacrificial system, but willful sins, or high-handed sins, could not. The latter undermined the whole covenant relationship and therefore left no basis for atonement.

But the prophets viewed Israel as flagrantly sinful, incurably sinful. The covenant had been broken! The preaching of repentance, the only hope of avoiding a national calamity, was not heeded! They seemed to be incapable of repenting. Jeremiah exclaimed, "And if thou say in thy heart, Wherefore are these things come upon me? for the greatness of thine iniquity are thy skirts uncovered, and thy heels suffer violence. Can the Ethiopian change his skin, or the leopard his spots? then may ye also do good, that are accustomed to do evil. Therefore will I scatter them, as the stubble that passeth away, by the wind of the wilderness. This is thy lot, the portion measured unto thee from me, saith Jehovah; because thou hast forgotten me, and trusted in falsehood" (13: 22-25). Therefore, only in a new covenant, that Jehovah would surely bring, could there be the bestowal of righteousness and the forgiveness of sin (Jer. 31:31-34).

II. COVENANT IN NEW TESTAMENT

The Greek term *diathēkē* is translated with "testament" twelve times and with "covenant" eighteen times in the King James Version of the New Testament. Would not one English word, consistently used, have been better? Yes, and that word is "covenant," which is equivalent to the Old Testament Hebrew term *berith*. The American Standard Version uses "covenant" in all thirty of those instances but two (Heb. 9:16, 17). There are some, however, who maintain that the term covenant is just as inadequate with which to translate the Greek term *diathēkē* as the term testament. Frank Stagg says, "The Greek term diathēkē is not adequately translated by either 'testament' or 'covenant.' It is a covenant between God and man, but the covenant is unilateral. It is not an agreement worked out between God and man. God alone determines the nature, the grounds, the demands, and the provisions of the covenant. It is not coercive upon man, for man remains free to enter into the covenant or not; but the covenant is strictly God's covenant offered to man. In a real sense it is a 'will' or 'testament' in that it is God's 'will' offered to man. The term 'New Testament' is a serviceable one, and no real gain would derive from the substitution of 'New Covenant,' as is frequently suggested. The 'New Testament' is concerned with the 'will' of God or the unilateral covenant, not a contract or agreement, which God has offered man in Jesus Christ."[4] Another scholar reminds us that "the new covenant, like the old, will rest upon the initiative and authority of God. Man's faith will be a response to what God does, not a bilateral bargain between equal partners. That is the meaning of the words, 'I will make....' "[5] But notice that these men use the word covenant, not the word testament, with which to discuss this vital relationship between God and his people.

Christ, the Son of God, is the means of the fulfillment of Jeremiah's prophecy, for it is he who brings the new covenant. This new covenant is not made with a nation, or with a corporate group; it is made with the individual. The repentant individual enters into a covenant with God through Christ, who, by pouring out his blood, sealed the covenant between that one and God. Yet, being accepted by the individual, it issues in a body, the body of Christ, the church.

1. In Synoptics

The words of our Lord at the Last Supper are quite lucid. "This cup is the new covenant in my blood, even that which is poured out for you" (Luke 22:20). Not only does the King James Version use "new testament" here; it also employs the word "shed," which is much too mild a word for the Greek term. His blood was literally "poured out," which is what the Greek denotes. As the blood of animals was poured out at Sinai to seal the old covenant, the blood of the Lamb of God was poured out at Calvary to seal the new covenant. The cup represents his blood, as the bread his body.

2. In Hebrews

The book of Hebrews contrasts the old covenant with the new, telling us that the latter is a better covenant. "But now hath he obtained a ministry the more excellent, by so much as he is also the mediator of a better covenant, which hath been enacted upon better promises. For if that first covenant had been faultless, then would no place have been sought for a second" (8:6, 7). The author of Hebrews then quotes the entire "new covenant" passage from Jeremiah, after which he says, "In that he saith, a new covenant, he hath made the first old. But that which is becoming old and waxeth aged is nigh unto vanishing away" (8:13). The new has replaced the old, for the old is broken. The author of Hebrews even quotes a part of Jeremiah's passage the second time in his desire to demonstrate the fulfillment in Christ (10:16, 17).

[4] Frank Stagg, *New Testament Theology*, p. 2.
[5] Bernhard W. Anderson, *Understanding the Old Testament*, p. 353.

So he tells us that it is a better covenant and that Christ is the Mediator of it. He tells us also that Christ, the Mediator, sealed the new covenant with his death, thus effecting the salvation of those under the old covenant and also those under the new (9: 15-22). It is the blood of the covenant with which the believer is sanctified, or made holy (10:29). This covenant will not be broken, for it is eternal (13:20).

3. IN FULFILLMENT OF JEREMIAH'S PROPHECY

Let us look briefly at Jeremiah's "new covenant" passage in order to see the characteristics of it as fulfilled in Christ

(1) SUBJECTIVE IN NATURE

"I will put my law in their inward parts, and in their heart will I write it" (31:33). It will not be written upon slabs of stone, but upon slabs of the heart. It will constitute an inner change that underlies the covenantal relationship. Circumcision of heart will replace circumcision of flesh. God says, "They shall all know me, from the least of them unto the greatest of them" (31:34). This "know" is not just an intellectual knowledge; it is a knowledge of heart, mind, will, and spirit. It is not knowledge about God; it is knowledge of God. "The new society, which was to enshrine the relation of God to man and to build up the new order in obedience to its God, was to consist of the men who were circumcised in heart. The basis for the divine and enduring life was not the accident of having been born into Judaism: it was the birth into faith and a new obedience."[6]

(2) COMMUNAL IN RESULT

"I will make a new covenant with the house of Israel, and with the house of Judah" (Jer. 31:31). Yes, but in accord with the spiritual nature of the new covenant it will be with true Israel, the true sons of Abraham, the church. Does not Paul make this clear when he says, "For they are not all Israel, that are of Israel: neither, because they are Abraham's seed, are they all children: but, in Isaac shall thy seed be called" (Rom. 9:6, 7)? He also states, "For ye all are one man in Christ Jesus. And if ye are Christ's, then are ye Abraham's seed, heirs according to promise" (Gal. 3:28, 29). The community formed is the church, true Israel, spiritual sons of Abraham. Through individual regeneration to a community of saved and redeemed souls — this is the aim. Through the old covenant Israel became God's chosen people. Through the new covenant Christians, true Israel, are now God's chosen people.

6 A. C. Welch, *The Religion of Israel Under the Kingdom*, p. 239.

"Ye did not choose me, but I chose you, and appointed you . . ." (John 15:16). Christians are the elect ones, chosen ones, today; the "you" in the above passage is plural in the Greek, not singular. It is the church that Jesus is referring to. "And I will be their God, and they shall be my people" (Jer. 31:33).

(3) ABUNDANT IN FORGIVENESS

Forgiveness is the highlight of the new relationship. "I will forgive their iniquity, and their sin will I remember no more" (Jer. 31:34). Ezekiel's foretelling is apropos: "A new heart also will I give you, and a new spirit will I put within you; and I will take away the stony heart out of your flesh, and I will give you a heart of flesh. And I will put my Spirit within you, and cause you to walk in my statutes, and ye shall keep mine ordinances, and do them" (36:26, 27). Christ, with the new covenant, brings this forgiveness; for he says, "This is my blood of the covenant, which is poured out for many unto remission of sins" (Matt. 26:28). "Behold, the Lamb of God, that taketh away the sin of the world!" (John 1:29).

(4) ETERNAL IN SCOPE

This new covenant will be an everlasting one. The prophecy of Hosea will be fulfilled: "And I will betroth thee unto me for ever; yea, I will betroth thee unto me in righteousness, and in justice, and in lovingkindness, and in mercies" (2:19). Another great prophet spoke for God: "In overflowing wrath I hid my face from thee for a moment; but with everlasting lovingkindness will I have mercy on thee, saith Jehovah thy Redeemer. For this is as the waters of Noah unto me; for as I have sworn that the waters of Noah shall no more go over the earth, so have I sworn that I will not be wroth with thee, nor rebuke thee. For the mountains may depart, and the hills be removed; but my lovingkindness shall not depart from thee, neither shall my covenant of peace be removed, saith Jehovah that hath mercy on thee" (Isa. 54:8-10). This new covenant will be as stedfast as God's promise after the flood not to destroy the earth again by water. The basis of this eternal stability is that God not only requires a new nature in his people but he will effect that new nature. Yet this effecting will not be the result of magic; they will come in genuine repentance from sin and a turning to God. Repentance of people, forgiveness of God — this is the order. Did not God say to Jeremiah, "Yea, I have loved thee with an everlasting love: therefore with lovingkindness have I drawn thee" (31:3)? This everlasting love will be expressed in an everlasting covenant; for Jeremiah states elsewhere, "And I will make an everlasting covenant with them, that I will not turn away from following them, to do them good; and I will put my fear in their hearts, that they may not depart from me" (32:40). An everlasting love (Jeremiah) plus an everlasting lovingkindness (Isaiah) equals an everlasting covenant (Jeremiah and Hebrews). The author of Hebrews declares that through the new covenant brought by the blood of Christ comes "the promise of the eternal inheritance" (9:15), which blood is also the "blood of an eternal covenant" (13:20).

4. IN JEWISH REJECTION OF JESUS

The Jewish opposition toward our Lord and all that he came to earth to accomplish is rooted in a tragic failure to recognize the fact that the old covenant was broken and that Christ is the fulfillment of Jeremiah's most significant utterance, the proclamation of a future new covenant. The rejection by the Jews was due to their false security in that which had been replaced by something superior. "For if that first covenant had been faultless, then would no place have been sought for a second" (Heb. 8:7). "In that he saith, A new covenant, he hath made the first old. But that which is becoming old and waxeth aged is nigh unto vanishing away" (Heb. 8:13).

The first covenant was broken; Jesus was the advent of a new covenant. Yet, evidently, the Jews who would not accept him but argued and carped at his teaching and his offers and his love, were pinning their hopes on a blood descent from Abraham. "We are sons of Abraham" had been their cry. "We have been born into the covenant; we are heirs through blood of all that it offers." They failed to realize that, having miserably failed to meet the requirements of the Mosaic covenant — though warned and entreated by faithful men of God — this covenant of old was broken; they were outside its scope and blessings. John the Baptist adamantly warned them, "Bring forth therefore fruit worthy of repentance: and think not to say within yourselves, We have Abraham to our father: for I say unto you, that God is able of these stones to raise up children unto Abraham" (Matt. 3:8, 9). Blood descent from the exalted patriarch means nothing now. Twice in the eighth chapter of John we find the Jews informing Jesus that they are lineal descendants of Abraham. "We are Abraham's seed" (8:33). "Our father is Abraham" (8:39). They mean by this that they are heirs of the covenant made with Abraham, which is their proudest boast. How mistaken they are! Jesus endeavors to make them realize that if they were true sons of Abraham they would do the works of Abraham. Instead, they do the works of the devil, so are sons of the devil. The devil is a murderer and a liar, and so are they (John 8:39-44). This would definitely place them without the pale of the old covenant. In Matthew 23:15 Jesus calls the carping Jews "sons of hell." This also places them outside the territory of the old covenant. The history of the old covenant has necessarily terminated; the history of a new covenant has begun. The Jews who were rejecting Jesus failed to realize this. Thus came a false security through depending upon a blood descent from the noted patriarch of old, which is still discerned in the phrase B'nai B'rith, the Jewish men's brotherhood. Just as the Protestants have the Masons and the Catholics the Knights of Columbus, the Jews have their B'nai B'rith — sons of the covenant! But this refers to a covenant broken and replaced by a new and better one.

How similar to the false security of many who "profess" Christianity today. They, too, are depending upon the external, the objective. They have stated they believe; they have been baptized; they have their name upon a church roll; they go through the motions of worship; they enter into the ritual; they contribute financially — but their name is not in the Lamb's Book of Life (Rev. 20:12, 15). There is no saved-Saviour relationship. These are the ones Jesus evidently has in mind when he states, "Not every one that saith unto me, Lord, Lord, shall enter into the kingdom of heaven; but he that doeth the will of my Father who is in heaven. Many will say to me in that day, Lord, Lord, did we not prophesy by thy name, and by thy name cast out demons, and by thy name do many mighty works? And then will I profess unto them, I never knew you: depart from me, ye that work iniquity" (Matt. 7:21-23). It may be these Jesus is warning when he states, "And why call ye me, Lord, Lord, and do not the things which I say?" (Luke 6:46).

It is still the circumcision of the heart that counts, not the circumcision of flesh; this is true in the new as well as the old covenant. It is the subjective relationshp that is vital, not the objective adornments. "I will put my law in their inward parts" (Jer. 31:33) — this is vitally necessary to enter into the new covenant.

OUTLINE FOR CHAPTER SIXTEEN

I. Death

II. Sheol
   1. Old Testament term
   2. Characteristics

III. Hades
   1. New Testament term •
   2. Relation to Sheol

IV. Intermediate State
   1. Various views
   2. Conditions immediately after death
      (1) Presence of Christ
      (2) No "soul-sleeping"
      (3) Nó purgatory
      (4) No limbo

V. Millennium
   1. Schools of interpretation
      (1) Premillennialism
      (2) Postmillennialism
      (3) Amillennialism
      (4) Combination view
   2. Dangers in interpretation

VI. Return of Christ
   1. Nature
   2. Time
   3. Reasons
      (1) World judgment
      (2) Kingdom consummation
      (3) Cosmic transformation

VII. Resurrection
   1. Scriptural account
   2. Nature
   3. Source
   4. Pharisees, Sadducees and resurrection
   5. Greeks and resurrection

VIII. Judgment
   1. Scriptural account
      (1) Old Testament
      (2) New Testament

2. Nature
   (1) Inevitable
   (2) Personal
   (3) Universal
   (4) Thorough
3. Judge
4. Subjects
   (1) All mankind
   (2) Evil angels
5. Object
6. Necessity
   (1) Responsibility of man
   (2) Conscience in man
   (3) History
   (4) Christian theism

IX. Final State of Righteous
   1. New Testament terms
   2. Objective environment
      (1) Place
      (2) Location
   3. Essential character
      (1) Reward
      (2) Relief
      (3) Realization
      (4) Activity
      (5) Progress

X. Final State of Unrighteous
   1. New Testament terms
   2. Characteristics
      (1) Place
      (2) State
      (3) Valley of Hinnom
      (4) Degrees of condemnation

XI. False Theories of Final Things
   1. Annihilationism
      (1) Forms of theory
      (2) Arguments against
   2. Restorationism
      (1) Forms of theory
      (2) Arguments against

CHAPTER SIXTEEN

FINAL THINGS

THE DOCTRINE OF FINAL THINGS BEARS THE NAME ESCHATOLOGY, which is derived from two Greek words: *eschatos*, last, and *logia*, study; therefore it is the study of last things. Generally it has been recognized as involving phenomena from death on; but this concept is seen to be inadequate, for theologians such as C. H. Dodd have insisted that it also includes certain aspects of the present Christian life. The Christian, with his citizenship already in heaven, is even in this life realizing many of the aspects normally relegated to the hereafter.

I. DEATH

The word "death" translates the Greek word *thanatos*, which is the term Paul uses when he queries, "Who shall deliver me out of the body of this death?" (Rom. 7:24), and when he says, "For the wages of sin is death" (Rom. 6:23). Death is the penalty resulting from sin. Originally there seems to be innocence and childlike walking with God; for man has been created "good," conforming to the divine aim of God. Yet this good has not developed into something self-determined, for man little realizes his blessedness. It is a childlike naïveté. And since there is no sin there is no guilt. It is an undisturbed and peaceful union with God.

But this peaceful union with God does not continue, for man violates God's only prohibition and enters at once on the path of death. "In the sweat of thy face shalt thou eat bread, till thou return unto the ground; for out of it wast thou taken: for dust thou art, and unto dust shalt thou return" (Gen. 3:19). "Behold, the man is become as one of us, to know good and evil; and now, lest he put forth his hand, and take also of the tree of life, and eat, and live for ever — therefore Jehovah God sent him forth from the garden of Eden" (Gen. 3:22, 23). Death follows the decision of man to exercise his will against God's will. This penalty falls upon all men, for death takes place when the spirit of life sustaining man is withdrawn by God.

Death, as thus imposed, places man outside fellowship with the living God; and this dire consequence is universal in scope. "Therefore, as through one man sin entered into the world, and death through sin; and so death passed unto all men, for that all sinned" (Rom. 5:12). Paul also talks of the unsaved as being "dead through your trespasses and sins" (Eph. 2:1). But the soul does not suffer cessation of being; there is a state of banishment from God into a miserable existence.

Only the Christian has victory over death, for it is the man in Christ who experiences a reversal of the decree of Eden. In Christ death is obliterated. In Paul's great passage on the resurrection he avows, "Death is swallowed up in victory. O death, where is thy victory? O death, where is thy sting? The sting of death is sin; and the power of sin is the law: but thanks be to God, who giveth us the victory through our Lord Jesus Christ" (I Cor. 15:54-57). The physical organism expires, but the expiration is a victory; defeat has been transformed into triumph. The new life found in Christ will transcend the gates of mortal death and stretch out into God's vast eternity.

II. SHEOL

The Old Testament information about life after death is extremely meager. In fact there is a rather gloomy aspect toward it, for in the Old Testament the promises of God mainly concern this life and the richness to be found here in a vital communion with Jehovah God. The temporal good is stressed above the eternal. This centers largely in the fact that God does not unfold the great truths about the future life in the Old Testament period that he reveals later in the New Testament era. The "fulness of time" brings greater vistas to man.

The early part of the Old Testament has little, if any, to say about resurrection, judgment, or life after death, all of which sheds light on why the Sadducees of Jesus' time do not accept belief in the resurrection. Dominated by an extreme conservatism they accept as the oracles of God only the Torah, the first five books of the Hebrew Scriptures: Genesis through Deuteronomy. But these books mention nothing of man's being raised up, as is recorded in the late books of the Old Testament. But the Pharisees, accepting all the books of the Hebrew Canon, would have such passages in their Scriptures. Martha, in speaking of her brother Lazarus, says, "I know that he shall rise again in the resurrection at the last day" (John 11:24).

1. OLD TESTAMENT TERM

Since, for the Hebrew, the future life is merely a weakened shadowy existence to which all must eventually enter, it is to be avoided as long as possible. The term applied to this subterranean region to which the dead resort in misery and gloom is "Sheol," an English transliteration of the Hebrew term itself. This is as it should be, for there is no other English term equivalent to the

Hebrew. The King James Version translates "Sheol" with "hell," which is very unfortunate; for its New Testament counterpart is "Hades" and not "Gehenna." "Gehenna" is a New Testament term rightly translated "hell." Thus the confusion! To use "hell" in the Old Testament for "Sheol" makes the latter equivalent in the mind of the reader to the New Testament term hell. But it is equivalent to "Hades" (used three times on the lips of Jesus), not to "hell" (used many times on the lips of Jesus).

The word Sheol may have been derived from a Hebrew verb "to ask," in which case it would appear that the place of the dead is insatiable in its demands. "Let us swallow them up alive as Sheol, And whole, as those that go down into the pit" (Prov. 1:12). (Incidentally, the King James Version translates the word Sheol in this verse with "grave," thus showing the relationship in the Hebrew mind of going down into the "grave" and down into "Sheol.") "Sheol and Abaddon are never satisfied; And the eyes of man are never satisfied" (Prov. 27:20). In contrast, later scholars believe the word Sheol is derived from a verb meaning to be hollow. This would be in accord with the German *Höhle,* a cavern, and with *Hölle,* hell.

2. CHARACTERISTICS

What are some of the aspects of this Old Testament region of departed souls? It is depicted as under the earth, in the depths. "But if Jehovah make a new thing, and the ground open its mouth, and swallow them up, with all that appertain unto them, and they go down alive into Sheol; then ye shall understand that these men have despised Jehovah" (Num. 16:30). "For a fire is kindled in mine anger, And burneth unto the lowest Sheol" (Deut. 32:22). It is shown to be a region of thickest darkness. Job states, "Are not my days few? cease then, And let me alone, that I may take comfort a little, Before I go whence I shall not return, Even to the land of darkness and of the shadow of death; The land dark as midnight, The land of the shadow of death, without any order, And where the light is as midnight" (10:20-22). Departed souls seem to be gathered together in tribes in Sheol. "And Abraham gave up the ghost, and died in a good old age, an old man, and full of years, and was gathered to his people" (Gen. 25:8). Sheol is deprived of all that belongs to life in the fullest sense. "Unless Jehovah had been my help, My soul had soon dwelt in silence" (Ps. 94:17). "For the living know that they shall die; but the dead know not anything, neither have they any more a reward; for the memory of them is forgotten. As well their love, as their hatred and their envy, is perished long ago; neither have they any more a portion for ever in anything that is done under the sun.... there is no work, nor device, nor knowledge, nor wisdom, in Sheol, whither thou goest" (Eccles. 9:5, 6, 10). However, consciousness is not destroyed in Sheol, for the individual can be aroused from his slumber-like existence. Concerning the king of Babylon Isaiah states, "Sheol from beneath is moved for thee to meet thee at thy coming; it stirreth up the dead for thee, even all the chief ones of the earth" (Isa. 14:9). Deceased Samuel, aroused by the necromancer of Endor, asks Saul, "Why hast thou disquieted me, to bring me up?" (I Sam. 28:15). Yet, notwithstanding the Samuel incident, it appears impossible to return to this earth from Sheol. "As the cloud is consumed and vanisheth away, So he that goeth down to Sheol shall come up no more. He shall return no more to his house, Neither shall his place know him any more" (Job 7:9, 10). Evidently there are no variations in rewards or in punishments for those in Sheol. "There the wicked cease from troubling; And there the weary are at rest, There the prisoners are at ease together; They hear not the voice of the taskmaster. The small and the great are there: And the servant is free from his master" (Job. 3:17-19). The only passages that seem to negate such a condition are those of Isaiah 14:15 and Ezekiel 32:23, where the fallen conquerors are relegated to the uttermost depths of Sheol. Since rewards and retributions due to the Mosaic law have their sphere entirely in this life, there is neither blessedness nor its negative counterpart in Sheol. Even the translation of Elijah proves nothing; such a special ascension seems to indicate that a highly favored man might be exempt from the curse of death. Though Sheol is unknown to mortal man, it is open before God. "Sheol is naked before God" (Job 26:6). Therefore God can save from Sheol. "But God will redeem my soul from the power of Sheol; For he will receive me," says the psalmist (Ps. 49:15). Those who enter Sheol are called shades, as in the Hebrew of Job 26:5; and none escape the destiny of becoming shades. "What man is he that shall live and not see death, That shall deliver his soul from the power of Sheol?" (Ps. 89:48).

III. HADES

1. NEW TESTAMENT TERM

The Greek word corresponding to the Hebrew Sheol is Hades, which seems to mean "the unseen." It is found in classical Greek writing, for which see *Odyssey,* Book XI; or *Iliad,* Books VI and IX; or *Agamemnon,* by Aeschylus. It is found in the Septuagint, the Greek translation of the Hebrew Scriptures produced in Alexandria, Egypt, 285 B.C., where it translates "Sheol." Therefore in the thinking of the Septuagint translators "Hades" conveys a meaning identical to "Sheol" in the Hebrew Scriptures. Does not this throw light on the connotation of the term Hades as used by Jesus on at least three occasions? How unfortunate that here also, on all three occasions, the King James Version translates the term with "hell," instead of "Hades." Jesus distinctly uses "Hades" in all three statements, not "hell." He uses the term Gehenna, or hell, many times, however. This lack of differentiation between the two terms by the King James Version has led to perverted thinking on the part of many people relative to the afterlife. And not only does Jesus employ the term Hades; it is also found in several places in Acts and Revelation.

2. RELATION TO SHEOL

The word Hades, as found in the New Testament, is used much as Sheol in the Old Testament. Jesus uses the term in three recorded incidents, all in the Synoptic gospels. He states that Capernaum shall not be exalted to heaven, but shall go down into Hades (Matt. 11:23). (This agrees completely with Ezekiel's famous passage in which all the mighty and strong ones of Egypt, Assyria, Persia, Edom, etc. are seen in Sheol [Ezek. 32:17-32].) Second, Jesus also declares that the gates of Hades shall not prevail against his church (Matt. 16:18). The meaning conveyed seems to be that the church will not be swallowed up by the gates of Hades — or overcome by its power; the church shall not cease to exist, for there will always be Christians in the world. Third, Jesus uses the term in the famous passage in Luke's gospel concerning the rich man (known to many as Dives due to the influence of the Latin Vulgate) and Lazarus, the beggar (16:19-31). In all three of these Synoptic incidents the King James Version translates the Greek term with the English "hell" rather than with the English term Hades; but this third incident is the most unfortunate, for it has produced a most disastrous effect on the thinking of people relative to the afterlife. This is probably due to the many evangelistic sermons that have been preached on this spectacular text, depicting the rich man in hell and the beggar and Abraham in heaven.[1]

Peter uses the term twice in his great discourse on the Day of Pentecost, once citing an Old Testament passage where Sheol is used in the Hebrew, and once where he is not quoting but is himself speaking. The quoted passage is from Psalm 16:10. "Because thou wilt not leave my soul unto Hades, Neither wilt thou give thy Holy One to see corruption" (Acts 2:27). The second

---

[1] See John A. Broadus' *Commentary on the Gospel of Matthew*, p. 359, and Edgar Y. Mullins' *The Christian Religion in Its Doctrinal Expression*, p. 459, for a fuller treatment of the term Hades as used by Jesus.

use is found four verses later in the same chapter of Acts: "he foreseeing this spake of the resurrection of the Christ, that neither was he left unto Hades, nor did his flesh see corruption." Unfortunately, the King James Version translates in both incidents with the word hell.

In the book of Revelation the term is used four times, all of which are translated "hell" in the King James Version: 1:18; 6:8; 20:13; and 20:14. The word Gehenna, or hell, is not found a single time in the book of Revelation; in fact it occurs only once in the entire New Testament outside the Synoptic gospels: James 3:6. The word Hades as used in these passages fits in exactly with the thought the writer is endeavoring to convey, as well as with the remainder of the New Testament.

IV. INTERMEDIATE STATE

Does the Bible speak of a middle state for the deceased, a state between mortal death and the resurrection-judgment event? What is the immediate condition of the deceased? The New Testament is not clear on this subject.

1. VARIOUS VIEWS

Augustus H. Strong[2] taught an intermediate state and a disembodied soul, as did also Edgar Y. Mullins.[3] James Denney is another who believed that the resurrected body is not put on till judgment day. He admits that the New Testament holds itself quite in reserve relative to any definite concepts about the interval between death and the resurrection-judgment event, revealing very little about the consciousness, the mutual communication, the work, the joys, or the sufferings of the departed ones. He says there are those who believe "that Paul shrank in horror from the vague conception of a disembodied existence, and that in the desire to escape from it his faith produced the idea of a new body to be assumed, not at the day of judgment, but in the very instant of death." He believes "this is a misinterpretation, and that St. Paul held from first to last the same faith, that the new body was a resurrection body, and was not put on till the judgment-day."[4]

George B. Stevens of Yale maintained that the New Testament does not convey precise teaching on this subject. Concerning Paul and the intermediate state he says, "He has certainly developed no doctrine concerning it, and it is a perplexing question as to what

2 Augustus H. Strong, *Systematic Theology*, p. 998.

3 Edgar Y. Mullins, *The Christian Religion in Its Doctrinal Expression*, pp. 459-60.

4 James Denney, *Studies in Theology*, p. 247.

his statements most naturally imply. His expectation of the nearness of the parousia naturally accounts for his entire neglect of this subject. Even if his principles required the assumption of a middle state, the conception of such a state would remain comparatively unimportant for him in view of the speedy culmination of human history in the resurrection and judgment." Yet Stevens maintains that Paul does look upon the resurrection and judgment as definite future events occurring after our Lord's return. What then does Paul teach as to the state of the dead between physical death and the resurrection? Stevens states, "The apostle has given no answer, beyond expressing the confident hope that the believer enters at death into fellowship with Christ. In what state or sphere this fellowship will be realized previous to the bestowal of the resurrection-body, and to the final award of the judgment day, we are left to conjecture. We thus see that Paul has expressed the Christian hope of immediate entrance into fellowship with Christ at death, without in any way adjusting this hope to his doctrine of the resurrection from the realm of the dead at the second advent. His doctrine of the resurrection and the judgment seem clearly to presuppose some sort of preliminary state between death and the completion of personal life in the resurrection; but the hope of being at once with Christ, together with the expectation of the Lord's speedy return, has deterred the apostle's mind from developing any doctrine of the middle state which his principles so obviously require."[5] Thus it is apparent that Stevens believes Paul failed to develop the doctrine clearly, but he seems to imply that Paul's teaching advocates a disembodied condition prior to the resurrection.

W. D. Davies, R. H. Charles, and Frank Stagg are among those who maintain that Paul teaches that the redeemed attain the spiritual body immediately after mortal death and that there is no disembodied condition. W. D. Davies says that there is "no room in Paul's theology for an intermediate state of the dead."[6] The famous eschatologist R. H. Charles also adheres to the "immediate" view. He believes that the analogy of the seed in the pertinent I Corinthians 15 passage "points not to a period externally determined and at some possibly remote age, but to the hour of departure of the individual believer," and "that with the death of the present body the energies of the human spirit are set free to organize from its new environment a spiritual body — a body adapted to that environment. Thus in a certain sense the resurrection of the faithful would follow immediately on death, and not be adjourned to the parousia." Charles believes that the

---

[5] George B. Stevens, *The Pauline Theology*, pp. 358-9.
[6] W. D. Davies, *Paul and Rabbinic Judaism*, p. 318.

II Corinthians 5 passage also shows that this was Paul's real view.[7] Frank Stagg maintains that the New Testament never speaks of a "disembodied state." He states, "There are isolated verses which may imply a disembodied state, but this is by no means certain. Never does a biblical writer envision a person as disembodied." He cites the examples of Moses and Elijah at the transfiguration, able to dwell in tents (Luke 9:33) ; the rich man in Hades, wanting water for his tongue (Luke 16:24) ; and Paul's horror at the thought of being "unclothed"— without a body (II Cor. 5:1-8) . Stagg maintains that the "spiritual body" will be the immediate replacement for the "natural body."[8]

2. CONDITIONS IMMEDIATELY AFTER DEATH

There are certain scriptural teachings that throw light on what the believer can expect immediately after death. In speaking of Abraham, Isaac, and Jacob, Jesus states, "God is not the God of the dead, but of the living" (Matt. 22:32) . Lazarus is "carried away by the angels into Abraham's bosom" (Luke 16:22) . Jesus says to the repentant thief on the cross, "To-day shalt thou be with me in Paradise" (Luke 23:43) . Paul speaks of a desire "to depart and be with Christ; for it is very far better" (Phil. 1:23) . He also maintains "that if the earthly house of our tabernacle be dissolved, we have a building from God, a house not made with hands, eternal, in the heavens" (II Cor. 5:1) . And he avows that nothing "shall separate us from the love of Christ" (Rom. 8:35-39) . Did not Jesus himself promise, "I am with you always, even unto the end of the world" (Matt. 28:20) ? What do these and other correlative passages teach?

(1) PRESENCE OF CHRIST

The Christian at death goes directly into the presence of Christ, there to experience a blessed, joyous fellowship with his Redeemer. Christ says to the repentant thief, "To-day . . ." (Luke 23:43) . For Lazarus to be in Abraham's bosom means that he is associating with the great patriarch and progenitor of the Hebrew people — the acme of bliss to the Hebrew mind (Luke 16:22) . Paul says that to depart and be with Jesus would be much better (Phil. 1:23) . There is supreme spiritual happiness with Jesus, for nothing can separate the believer from his love (Rom. 8:35-39) . He will be in the presence of his Lord always.

(2) NO "SOUL-SLEEPING"

At death the redeemed one does not enter a state of uncon-

7 R. H. Charles, *Eschatology*, p. 318.
8 Frank Stagg, *New Testament Theology*, pp. 322-3.

sciousness. Many times the Bible speaks of death as "sleep," but never does it say the deceased one sleeps. Abraham and Lazarus are very active in their post-mortem state (Luke 16:19ff.). Does not our Lord remind the disciples, "God is not the God of the dead, but of the living" (Matt. 22:32)? Geerhardus Vos believes that Paul makes explicit statements about the state after death "which positively exclude its having been to his mind a state of unconsciousness, such as, apart from dreams, physical sleep ordinarily induces. In 2 Cor. v the whole train of Paul's reasoning is based on the thought that there will be a differentiation in feeling (that is, a perceptible difference in the self-reflexive consciousness) in the state after death. Whether he feels clothed with a body or feels naked will be an object of perception to him. To the unconscious dead there is not and cannot be any distinction between the one state and the other; all things are alike to them."[9]

(3) NO PURGATORY

There is no such state as purgatory awaiting the deceased Christian. This Roman Catholic dogma teaches that only the perfected saint escapes purgatorial suffering. The unperfected saint suffers sufficiently to "work off" his residue of unpurged sin, after which he goes to be with Jesus. He is purified from his venial sins, or undergoes the temporal punishment still remaining after the guilt of mortal sin has been forgiven. Such teaching is derived mainly from two sources: the tradition of the Catholic Church (quotations of men like Augustine, Cyprian, and Tertullian) and a quotation from Second Maccabees, one of the fourteen books of the Apocrypha (the books written in the interbiblical period and contained in the Roman Catholic Scriptures but not in the canonical Scriptures of evangelical Christians). Reference is sometimes made to First Corinthians 3:13, 14. The name purgatory comes from the word purge.

(4) NO LIMBO

This, another Roman Catholic dogma, refers to the place on the border of hell or heaven where "unbaptized" infants are relegated (limbo of infants), or to the temporary abode of the righteous ones dying before the coming of Christ to the earth (limbo of the fathers, or limbo of the patriarchs). The name is derived from *limbus,* meaning border. Evangelical Christians do not accept belief in either purgatory or limbo.

V. MILLENNIUM

"Millennium" comes from two Latin words, *mille* (thousand) and

---

9 Geerhardus Vos, *The Pauline Eschatology,* p. 144.

anni (years). From the two corresponding Greek words is derived the word chiliad; so chiliasm and millennialism are one and the same, both philologically and historically. The thousand-year reign of Christ with the martyred saints is mentioned in only one place in the New Testament, Revelation 20:1-10. This passage is highly apocalyptic, which means that it is a most figurative and poetic one.

1. SCHOOLS OF INTERPRETATION

The various schools of interpretation relative to the millennium center in whether Christ shall come again prior to, or subsequent to, this period, or whether or not the term is to be taken literally or figuratively.

(1) PREMILLENNIALISM

The premillennialists hold that Christ's second coming (or parousia) will precede the period known as the millennium. They believe that when he returns the world generally will be under the power of evil, the Antichrist holding sway. At this time there will be a notable victory over Christ's enemies, the Antichrist being destroyed. The living Christians will be caught up to meet the Lord in the air. The first resurrection will occur, which is that the dead in Christ will arise with him. There will be a judgment of the nations. The risen saints will reign with Christ during the millennium. Satan, who has been bound these thousand years, will be loosed, and wickedness will flare up again. Then there will be a resurrection of the wicked, which will be succeeded by the final judgment and eternal rewards. The chief Scripture passages used in support of the premillennial view are as follows: Matthew 24 and 25; I Thessalonians 4:13-18; II Thessalonians 2:1-12; I Corinthians 15:20-24; and Revelation 20:1-6. Some Old Testament prophecies are also brought forward.

(2) POSTMILLENNIALISM

The postmillennialists hold that there will be a thousand-year period also, but maintain that Christ will come at the end of this period instead of at the beginning. During this period Christianity will triumph over the earth due to the gradual spread of the gospel and the application of the teaching of Jesus. At the end of the period the conflict between the forces of righteousness and the forces of evil will be renewed. Then Christ will return, and the resurrection of the righteous and the wicked will occur, which will be followed by the final judgment and eternal rewards.

The chief Scripture passages used in support of the postmillennial view are as follows: Matthew 16:27; Matthew 25:31-33; John

5:28, 29; II Thessalonians 1:6-10; II Peter 3:7, 10; Revelation 20:1-10; and Revelation 20:11-15.

(3) AMILLENNIALISM

The a-prefix is derived from a Greek prefix normally meaning without. However, it does not connote such in this case, for this would mean no millennium. On the contrary, the amillennialists interpret the term spiritually and believe it to symbolize the present Christian era in which Christ reigns triumphantly with his followers now. The term martyrs, applied to these followers, would refer to martyrs in reality or in spirit. Satan is bound now in the sense that Christ gives victory over evil to all his followers. The first resurrection is the spiritual resurrection from spiritual deadness in which one is made alive through the Holy Spirit. It is over these spiritually raised ones that the second death, or eternal punishment, has no power. The second resurrection is the final one for both the righteous and the unrighteous, occurring when Jesus comes again. Then comes the judgment, with rewards for the righteous and punishment for the wicked.

The statement of Frank Stagg is elucidating in this respect. "It is not likely that the author of Revelation intended that the thousand years be taken literally. . . . To understand the 'millennium' not as a literal period of a thousand years but as a dramatic portrayal of the triumph through the life-giving of Christ and his people accords with the nature of apocalyptic and the message of the entire New Testament. Apocalyptic is a dramatic-poetic type of literature with its own way of conveying its message. To take it seriously and honestly one must not take literally apocalyptic imagery that was never meant to be taken literally." He also states, "Consensus of scholars by no means amounts to proof, but at this point critical scholarship is virtually agreed. The position that the language of the whole book of Revelation is to be taken as symbolic and not literal was assumed by so balanced a scholar as Conner, *The Faith of the New Testament*, p. 493."[10]

(4) COMBINATION VIEW

The view of Professor Augustus H. Strong, Baptist theologian of the nineteenth and early twentieth centuries, is so distinctive that it must also be presented, for it is a combination of both the premillennarian and postmillennarian views. It is maintained that Christ will come in a spiritual sense at the beginning of the millennium, reigning with his saints spiritually in the advancement

[10] Stagg, *op. cit.*, pp. 317-8.

of his kingdom, with his visible and literal coming at the end of the thousand years.

This theory is based on a twofold use in the Scriptures of four significant terms: death, judgment, coming of Christ, and resurrection. There is a spiritual death and also a physical and literal death; there is a spiritual judgment and also an outward and literal judgment; there is a spiritual and invisible coming of Christ (at destruction of Jerusalem, at Pentecost, at death) and also a visible and literal coming; there is a spiritual resurrection and also a physical and literal resurrection. Scripture passages are given for each of these eight phases.

It is maintained that Revelation 20:4-10 is to be interpreted as highly figurative, teaching "not a preliminary resurrection of the body, in the case of departed saints, but a period in the later days of the Church militant when, under the special influence of the Holy Ghost, the spirit of the martyrs shall appear again, true religion be greatly quickened and revived, and the members of Christ's churches become so conscious of their strength in Christ that they shall, to an extent unknown before, triumph over the powers of evil both within and without." It is therefore held that this passage does not refer to the second advent of Christ and to the resurrection connected with it, but rather to "great spiritual changes in the later history of the church," which will precede the second advent and resurrection.[11] Although this view is purported to be a combination of both the "pre" and the "post" views, it leans heavily toward the "post" view.

2. DANGERS IN INTERPRETATION

The term millennium occurs in only one place in the Scriptures, Revelation 20:4-10, a passage penned in highly apocalyptic language. Such a passage should always be interpreted with the remainder of the Bible in mind. It is always hazardous to give too much prominence to one passage of Scripture, that is, to take one passage — and that a highly figurative one — and build a whole system of eschatology around it. This tends toward majoring on the minor. If a whole system of theology *must* be built around one word, or term, why not take a significant term used by our Master, such as "the kingdom," and construct the system around it? In fact, the parousia, or future coming of Christ, should occupy the central place in a study of the future life, not the millennium.

The passage in which the term millennium occurs is found in a very late book of the New Testament Canon. Peter, Paul, James, Philip, and various other prominent preachers of the first Chris-

11 Strong, *op. cit.*, pp. 1013-4.

tian century may never have heard of the term. Yet they did a marvelous work for Jesus; witness Peter's sermon on Pentecost and the souls added to the church as a result! If the term millennium were so important that it should today "split the camp," would not our Lord have spoken of it often? He never mentioned the term.

Passages in Revelation that are highly symbolical are fused in with others that are literal. Along with this John passes from heaven to earth and back again at will. This adds to difficulty in interpretation.

No one theory of interpretation solves all the problems. One view may overload its program of the future with subordinate details. One may fail to comply with the note of expectancy in Christ's return. One may make literal passages subordinate to a highly figurative one. If one system were able to satisfy completely there would be no cause for disagreement.[12]

VI. RETURN OF CHRIST

Relative to the return of Christ, or the parousia, there is also divergence of opinion; therefore a tolerant spirit should always be manifested. An intolerant attitude is a negation of one of the cardinal principles of Christianity itself.

1. NATURE

The final advent of Christ will be visible and outward, a fact easily discerned in the scriptural comparison of the manner of Christ's departure with the manner of his return. "This Jesus, who was received up from you into heaven, shall so come in like manner as ye beheld him going into heaven" (Acts 1:11). The words "in like manner" mean visibly and in the air. The visible return is also easily discerned in statements such as: "And they shall see the Son of man coming on the clouds of heaven with power and great glory. And he shall send forth his angels with a great sound of a trumpet, and they shall gather together his elect from the four winds, from one end of heaven to the other" (Matt. 24:30, 31); "For the Lord himself shall descend from heaven, with a shout, with the voice of the archangel, and with the trump of God" (I Thess. 4:16); "Behold, he cometh with the clouds; and every eye shall see him, and they that pierced him; and all the tribes of the earth shall mourn over him" (Rev. 1:7).

These passages are not to be interpreted in a metaphorical or spiritual sense, though this might be the tendency for some people.

12 The reader is referred to E. A. McDowell, *The Meaning and Message of the Book of Revelation,* and Ray Summers, *Worthy Is the Lamb,* for a full treatment of the book of Revelation.

The present spiritual comings of our Lord do not exhaust the ideas in these verses; his final advent will not be purely subjective and spiritual but will be external and visible. His arrival to judge the world will be similar to his previous advent, except that its glories will far exceed a manger for a crib and a stable for a nursery.

The best term with which to describe this final parousia of our Lord is cataclysmic. It will be sudden in appearance, violent in upheaval, and far-reaching in scope. Clouds of glory and trumpet blasts will herald his approach. The glory of the Lord will be seen, much as on the Mount of Transfiguration. "But the day of the Lord will come as a thief; in the which the heavens shall pass away with a great noise, and the elements shall be dissolved with fervent heat, and the earth and the works that are therein shall be burned up" (II Pet. 3:10). What a contrast this presents alongside the first advent of our Lord, one of extreme humiliation! He was born in a stable and placed in a manger. He was reared in a carpenter's shop. He had nowhere to lay his head but lodged here and there with friends. His triumphant entrance into the Holy City was upon a lowly beast of burden. He died upon an ignominious cross and was placed in a borrowed tomb.

2. Time

Neither Christ nor his apostles reveal definitely when the return will be; the time is with God the Father alone. "But of that day or that hour knoweth no one, not even the angels in heaven, neither the Son, but the Father. Take ye heed, watch and pray: for ye know not when the time is" (Mark 13:32, 33). "And he said unto them, It is not for you to know times or seasons, which the Father hath set within his own authority" (Acts 1:7). "But the day of the Lord will come as a thief" (II Pet. 3:10). Therefore we see that the apostles know not the time of the coming again of our Lord; and it is even hidden from Christ himself during the incarnation. Therefore anyone attempting to set the exact time and season of the final advent of Christ assumes to know what Christ says no one will know! This, coupled with the complete discomfiture of those in the past who have set dates (as the Millerites, etc.), only to be proved completely in error, should steer discerning people away from those who exclaim, "I know the date! I know the hour!"

3. Reasons

What are the reasons for Christ's return? There seem to be at least three.

(1) WORLD JUDGMENT

Christ came the first time to save the world, not to judge it. "For God sent not the Son into the world to judge the world; but that the world should be saved through him" (John 3:17). "I came not to judge the world, but to save the world" (John 12:47). All the power necessary for salvation was released at Calvary and at the open tomb. Christ will come again to judge the world. "And he gave him authority to execute judgment, because he is a son of man" (John 5:27). "The word that I spake, the same shall judge him in the last day" (John 12:48). "But when the Son of man shall come in his glory, and all the angels with him, then shall he sit on the throne of his glory: and before him shall be gathered all the nations: and he shall separate them one from another, as the shepherd separateth the sheep from the goats" (Matt. 25:31, 32). The remainder of this last graphic passage shows the results of the judging process as carried out by our Lord on the day of judgment.

And when Jesus comes to judge it will be too late to repent! His wonderful salvation may be accepted prior to his coming to judge, but not subsequently. Paul declares in his great Athenian discourse in the midst of the Areopagus that God now "commandeth men that they should *all everywhere* repent: inasmuch as he hath appointed a day in which he will judge the world in righteousness by the man whom he hath ordained; whereof he hath given assurance unto all men, in that he hath raised him from the dead" (Acts 17:30, 31). To say that Christ saves a remnant now, the elect, the church, and that he will save a greater number after he returns again, overawing them in might and in power, is to wind up with two methods of redemption: one now by persuasion through the spiritual power of the gospel and another later by an overwhelming impression of majesty. There is no biblical foundation whatsoever to warrant such thinking. The latter method of salvation would result in submission to God due to a subservient fear and cringing allegiance rather than to the acceptance of the redeeming and outpouring love of Calvary.

(2) KINGDOM CONSUMMATION

Jesus will come to bring to completion that which is now incomplete. He will perfect the imperfect. Those who, with Paul, say, "For now we see in a mirror, darkly; but then face to face" (I Cor. 13:12), will have their conviction realized. Jesus finishes the Great Commission with the words: "and lo, I am with you always, even unto the end of the world" (Matt. 28:20). The Greek phrase translated "the end of the world" really means the consummation of the age. Therefore Jesus gives the Great Commission to command attention and enjoin efforts until the eschaton, the fulfillment of the present age.

The kingdom of God (or, as in Matthew's gospel, the kingdom of heaven) has both a present and a future connotation, a fact expressed in many statements of our Lord. "The time is fulfilled, and the kingdom of God is at hand: repent ye, and believe in the gospel" (Mark 1:14). "But if I by the Spirit of God cast out demons, then is the kingdom of God come upon you" (Matt. 12:28). To these passages showing a present connotation may be added others depicting a future aspect. "Then [at the judgment] shall the King say unto them on his right hand, Come, ye blessed of my Father, inherit the kingdom prepared for you from the foundation of the world" (Matt. 25:34). "But I say unto you, I shall not drink henceforth of this fruit of the vine, until that day when I drink it new with you in my Father's kingdom" (Matt. 26:29). "Then [right after the judgment] shall the righteous shine forth as the sun in the kingdom of their Father" (Matt. 13:43). At the consummation the present aspect of the kingdom will merge into the future, thus becoming one, as it is essentially even now.[13]

The Son, come to earth incarnate, offers redemption to lost humanity. As a result all authority over the human race is given to him. "All authority hath been given unto me in heaven and on earth" (Matt. 28:18). "...even as thou gavest him authority over all flesh" (John 17:2). This authority envisions the complete realization of the salvation of men. Some day it will be universally recognized "that in the name of Jesus every knee should bow, of things in heaven and things on earth and things under the earth, and that every tongue should confess that Jesus Christ is Lord, to the glory of God the Father" (Phil. 2:10, 11). The deliverance of the kingdom to the Father, along with the abolishing of death, is part of the consummation. "Then cometh the end, when he shall deliver up the kingdom to God, even the Father; when he shall have abolished all rule and all authority and power. For he must reign, till he hath put all his enemies under his feet. The last enemy that shall be abolished is death" (I Cor. 15:24-26). When the work of redemption is accomplished, he restores the kingdom to the Father, having brought the redeemed back into the submission and fellowship of God.

(3) COSMIC TRANSFORMATION

There are passages which seem to denote a future cosmic sig-

---

[13] The reader is referred to *The Day of His Coming*, by Gerhard Gloege, pp. 137-47, for a fuller discussion of the present and future aspects of the kingdom.

nificance to Christ's second coming. "For the earnest expectation of the creation waiteth for the revealing of the sons of God. For the creation was subjected to vanity, not of its own will, but by reason of him who subjected it, in hope that the creation itself also shall be delivered from the bondage of corruption into the liberty of the glory of the children of God. For we know that the whole creation groaneth and travaileth in pain together until now" (Rom. 8:19-22). Parallel with this mournful utterance of creation is man's groaning within himself, waiting for the redemption of his body (Rom. 8:23). Peter speaks similarly when he enjoins us to be "looking for and earnestly desiring the coming of the day of God, by reason of which the heavens being on fire shall be dissolved, and the elements shall melt with fervent heat. But, according to his promise, we look for new heavens, and a new earth, wherein dwelleth righteousness" (II Pet. 3:12, 13). This may be identical to John's new heaven and new earth as envisioned on Patmos (Rev. 21:1ff.). Whatever the answer, there is a cosmic renewal to be expected in the eschaton.[14]

VII. RESURRECTION

1. SCRIPTURAL ACCOUNT

Both the Old Testament and the New Testament clearly enunciate a resurrection in which the just and the unjust are involved. To the just it will be a resurrection unto rewards, with a body fitted for the uses of the sanctified spirit. To the unjust it will be a resurrection unto condemnation, with all that pertains to perdition.

There are many passages relative to the resurrection. "And many of them that sleep in the dust of the earth shall awake, some to everlasting life, and some to shame and everlasting contempt" (Dan. 12:2). "The hour cometh, in which all that are in the tombs shall hear his voice, and shall come forth; they that have done good, unto the resurrection of life; and they that have done evil, unto the resurrection of judgment" (John 5:28, 29). "Having hope toward God ... that there shall be a resurrection both of the just and unjust" (Acts 24:15). This last statement is in Paul's address to Felix in answer to the orator Tertullus. And to Agrippa he queries, "Why is it judged incredible with you, if God doth raise the dead?" (Acts 26:8).

One of the pertinent passages relative to the resurrection is the fifteenth chapter of First Corinthians, where Paul discusses at length both the fact of the resurrection and the nature of the

14 The reader is referred to *Them He Glorified*, by Bernard Ramm, pp. 105-8, for a fuller treatment of the idea of cosmic redemption.

resurrection body. "But if there is no resurrection of the dead, neither hath Christ been raised: and if Christ hath not been raised, then is our preaching vain, your faith also is vain" (I Cor. 15:13, 14). "So also is the resurrection of the dead. It is sown in corruption; it is raised in incorruption: it is sown in dishonor; it is raised in glory: it is sown in weakness; it is raised in power: it is sown a natural body; it is raised a spiritual body" (I Cor. 15:42-44). "We all shall not sleep, but we shall all be changed, in a moment, in the twinkling of an eye, at the last trump: for the trumpet shall sound, and the dead shall be raised incorruptible, and we shall be changed" (I Cor. 15:51, 52). "Who shall fashion anew the body of our humiliation, that it may be conformed to the body of his glory" (Phil. 3:21). "And the sea gave up the dead that were in it; and death and Hades gave up the dead that were in them: and they were judged every man according to their works" (Rev. 20:13). Notice that this verse says **Hades**, not hell, as it is incorrectly translated in the King James Version.

2. NATURE

Christ's resurrection was a bodily one; ours will also be as much. Yet it is realized that this phase of the doctrine is fraught with many problems. After physical death the body soon decays, disintegrating into the mere chemical elements comprising it. Only the bones remain, and with sufficient time and certain conditions these also will deteriorate. Some bodies are cremated. Paul concerns himself with this puzzling fact in the fifteenth chapter of First Corinthians. There he states that it is sown a natural body and raised a spiritual body, completely adapted to the spiritual realm in which it will spend eternity. This body of corruption will be raised in incorruption. This body of dishonor will be raised in glory. "It is sown in corruption; it is raised in incorruption: it is sown in dishonor; it is raised in glory: it is sown in weakness; it is raised in power: it is sown a natural body; it is raised a spiritual body" (I Cor. 15:42-44).

The great apostle even detects a connection between the old body and the new; the old body is sown and the new stems from it. As the grain is sown and the plant comes from it, so the physical is sown and the spiritual springs up. Yet, in spite of the relativity there is a contrast; it is the contrast that always subsists between the physical and the spiritual, between the earthly and the heavenly. This body is characterized by mortality and corruption, the resurrection body by immortality and glory. Our new body will be like that of Christ, for he shall "fashion anew the body of our humiliation, that it may be conformed to the body of his glory" (Phil. 3:21).

3. SOURCE

Paul, being a good Pharisee prior to his Damascus road experience, would be one anticipating a resurrection of both the just and the unjust. He adheres to this as a Christian also, as is seen in his address to Felix in the book of Acts. Yet in his epistles his discussion of the resurrection is mainly concerned with the Christian resurrection, grounded on union with Christ (I Cor. 15). The one "in Christ" shall arise by virtue of Christ's resurrection. Christ *is* the resurrection; for he says to Martha, "I am the resurrection, and the life: he that believeth on me, though he die, yet shall he live; and whosoever liveth and believeth on me shall never die" (John 11:25, 26). From him stem all resurrections, for he is the first-fruits of the resurrection. "But now hath Christ been raised from the dead, the first-fruits of them that are asleep. For since by man came death, by man came also the resurrection of the dead. For as in Adam all die, so also in Christ shall all be made alive" (I Cor. 15:20-22). In the sixth chapter of John's gospel Jesus states that he will raise up the believer at the last day; he declares this four times (John 6:39, 40, 44, 54), the basis for such a promise being his statement in the eleventh chapter, "I *am* the resurrection."

A study of the pungent sermons found throughout the book of Acts reveals this very significant truth; for these sermons, stressing highly the resurrection of Christ, make it the basis of the gospel appeal. It becomes the cornerstone of the preaching of the early apostles; practically every address brings it to the forefront. Because of the resurrection he lives, and because he lives the believer shall arise and be with him eternally! His breaking the bonds of death, along with establishing his authority over it, becomes the basis of the future resurrection of every child of God. Immediately subsequent to the resurrection "shall come to pass the saying that is written, Death is swallowed up in victory" (I Cor. 15:54). When the dead hear the voice of the Son of God they will arise, some to life, some to condemnation (John 5:28, 29).

4. PHARISEES, SADDUCEES AND RESURRECTION

The Apostle Paul had been trained as a Pharisee, one of the sects of the Jews prior to and coincident with the time of Christ (Phil. 3:5). The Pharisees believed in the resurrection, basing their belief on passages found in the late sections of the Hebrew Scriptures, such as the twelfth chapter of Daniel. The Pharisees accepted as the Word of God exactly the same books that make up the Christian's Old Testament. The Sadducees, another sect of the Jews, did not believe in the resurrection. "And there come unto him Sadducees, who say that there is no resurrection" (Mark 12:18). They were ultra-conservative in what they regarded as the oracles of God, accepting only the first five books, or the Torah, as inspired. But these books do not speak of the resurrection, so the Sadducees were bereft of such a doctrine. Martha, in stating, "I know that he [Lazarus] shall rise again in the resurrection at the last day" (John 11:24), reveals the fact she has been trained as a Pharisee.

5. GREEKS AND RESURRECTION

To the Greeks of Paul's day the idea of the resurrected body was a philosophical anomaly. Their conception of salvation argued for the escape of the soul from an inherently evil body, thereby relegating the body to a useless category. It is the immortality of the soul, without the resurrection of the body, that constitutes salvation. Athens, in Achaia, was the very seat of this Greek method of thought. Therefore the Apostle Paul proceeds wonderfully with his address in the midst of the Areopagus of Athens until he mentions the resurrection of Jesus from the dead. "Now when they heard of the resurrection of the dead, some mocked; but others said, We will hear thee concerning this yet again. Thus Paul went out from among them" (Acts 17:32, 33). The resurrection is antithetical to anything these Stoic philosophers have heard; so Paul's stay at Athens is brief. Yet the New Testament in every instance refutes such a Greek method of thinking and states that the true conception of life is human nature in its entirety, as body and spirit.

Bernard Ramm is right in his conclusion: "According to both the Old and New Testaments the body is an integral, dignified part of the total self. The human person is a unity and a totality of the material and the spiritual. Consequently the strict dualisms of Plato, Descartes, and religious liberalism are unbiblical. The latter went astray in looking at the human body almost as a hangover from man's brute ancestry and therefore deplored any doctrine of the resurrection as gross materialism. . . . In the biblical doctrine of the whole man — including the body — we find the foundations for a doctrine of the resurrection."[15]

VIII. JUDGMENT

Throughout the Scriptures all punishments of individuals, or of a nation as a whole, are represented as acts of the judgment of

---

[15] *Ibid.*, p. 96.

God. Yet these are both imperfect and incomplete, ιor there will someday be a final and complete vindication of God's righteousness. The very principle of judgment rests upon God's creation of man as a free moral agent capable of choosing right or wrong, with the attendant consequences thereof. But these consequences are not wholly reserved to the final denouement; no one can do good or evil without somehow, immediately and in this life, being rewarded with good or evil accordingly. Thus it is in a moral realm. Yet such a process of attendant reward or punishment must of necessity be incomplete. Say it were otherwise, that man is completely, objectively, and openly rewarded subsequent to every deed. This would lead to ethical obedience due to fear, or due to the wisdom of following the pragmatical, not due to the love of the right and the good per se, or because of love toward the Creator and Redeemer. The moral freedom of man would be reduced almost to coercion. So the full reward of deeds does not follow immediately the executing of the act, right or wrong.

1. SCRIPTURAL ACCOUNT

The judgment of God has a central place in both the Old Testament and in the New, yet with a different emphasis. In the former the emphasis is upon judgment in this life; in the latter it is judgment at the denouement that is in the forefront.

(1) OLD TESTAMENT

The flood of Genesis 6-8 is God's judgment upon the universal sin and degradation of mankind. "And God saw the earth, and, behold, it was corrupt; for all flesh had corrupted their way upon the earth" (Gen. 6:12). The destruction of Sodom and Gomorrah constitutes a judgment of God because of heinous sin. "Then Jehovah rained upon Sodom and upon Gomorrah brimstone and fire from Jehovah out of heaven" (Gen. 19:24). Judgments are pronounced upon Egypt at the time of the Israelite exodus by means of the ten plagues (Exod. 7-12). The Babylonian captivity also comprises a judgment of God upon his own people. "And Jehovah, the God of their fathers, sent to them by his messengers, rising up early and sending, because he had compassion on his people, and on his dwelling-place: but they mocked the messengers of God, and despised his words, and scoffed at his prophets, until the wrath of Jehovah arose against his people, till there was no remedy. Therefore he brought upon them the king of the Chaldeans, who slew their young men with the sword in the house of their sanctuary, and had no compassion upon young man or virgin, old man or hoary-headed: he gave them all into his hand" (II Chron. 36:15-17). This judgment has the dual purpose of punishing and purging the chosen ones that they might then continue fulfilling the purpose of God. Amos' picture of "the day of Jehovah" is certainly one of judgment. "Woe unto you that desire the day of Jehovah! Wherefore would ye have the day of Jehovah? It is darkness, and not light . . ." (Amos 5:18-20) .

(2) NEW TESTAMENT

Under the new covenant the emphasis is upon the final judgment. It is true that the destruction of Jerusalem, as predicted by our Lord in the Little Apocalypse (Matt. 23, Luke 21, Mark 13) and as occurred in A.D. 70 by the armies of Rome, falls under the category of a judgment of God against the Jews in this life. Yet most references to judgment in the New Testament pertain to the final eschaton, or to the judgment day itself, which is easily discerned from passages such as Matthew 25. "But when the Son of man shall come in his glory, and all the angels with him, then shall he sit on the throne of his glory: and before him shall be gathered all the nations: and he shall separate them one from another, as the shepherd separateth the sheep from the goats; and he shall set the sheep on his right hand, but the goats on the left. Then shall the King say unto them on his right hand, Come, ye blessed of my Father, inherit the kingdom prepared for you from the foundation of the world. . . . Then shall he say also unto them on the left hand, Depart from me, ye cursed, into the eternal fire which is prepared for the devil and his angels. . . . And these shall go away into eternal punishment: but the righteous into eternal life" (31-34, 41, 46) .

2. NATURE

This final judgment will consist of an objective and visible event. It will not be an endless procedure, but a definite and specific occurrence which is to ensue at a particular time in the future. The following characteristics are relative to this final judgment.

(1) INEVITABLE

It is something to be expected. "Out of sight and out of mind" does not relegate the judgment to the status of a non-entity. It is to be prepared for. Luke says that when Paul "reasoned of righteousness, and self-control, and the judgment to come, Felix was terrified" (Acts 24:25) . The author of the book of Hebrews tells about "a certain fearful expectation of judgment" (10:27) . He also promises, "And inasmuch as it is appointed unto men once to die, and after this cometh judgment . . ." (Heb. 9:27) .

(2) PERSONAL

Everyone will stand before God for a reckoning. "So then each one of us shall give account of himself to God" (Rom. 14:12). The individual account will not be lost in the multitude; it will retain its individuality. There will be nothing gained by proxy, nothing acquired by substitution; nor will there be any transfer of merit, or exchange of grace. "For we must all be made manifest before the judgment-seat of Christ; that each one may receive the things done in the body, according to what he hath done, whether it be good or bad" (II Cor. 5:10).

(3) UNIVERSAL

Just as sin is universal, with every individual standing in dire need of a Saviour, so the judgment has a universal sweep also. None will escape its reckoning. "All that are in the tombs" shall come forth for an accounting (John 5:28, 29). "For we must all be made manifest before the judgment-seat of Christ" (II Cor. 5:10). Each will stand under the blazing light of God's righteous adjudication.

(4) THOROUGH

Every deed, every word, every thought, and every motive will be brought to light. "And I say unto you, that every idle word that men shall speak, they shall give account thereof in the day of judgment" (Matt. 12:36). "Wherefore judge nothing before the time, until the Lord come, who will both bring to light the hidden things of darkness, and make manifest the counsels of the hearts" (I Cor. 4:5).

3. JUDGE

God in the person of Jesus Christ will be the judge. The Saviour, who is now being accepted or rejected, will one day judge all men. "For we must all be made manifest before the judgment-seat of Christ" (II Cor. 5:10). God commands all to repent, "inasmuch as he hath appointed a day in which he will judge the world in righteousness by the man whom he hath ordained; whereof he hath given assurance unto all men, in that he hath raised him from the dead" (Acts 17:31). In Hebrews we read that God is judge of all: "and to God the Judge of all" (Heb. 12:23); yet the judging activity is performed through the Son. This is similar to creation, where God does the creating, yet the Son is the mediating agent (John 1:3, 10; Col. 1:16). John expresses this judging activity of the Son by proclaiming its source: "For neither doth the Father judge any man, but he hath given all judgment unto the Son"

(John 5:22). "And he [the Father] gave him authority to execute judgment, because he is a son of man" (John 5:27).

Christ was God in the flesh, fully divine and at the same time genuinely human. Therefore he is able to respond with the requisites of true judgment: both mercy and justice. He is able to incorporate in his decisions both the love of God and the law of God. It is not sin that most sympathizes with sin; it is purity and righteousness that are able to discern the need and to understand the weakness of the impure and of the unrighteous. Christ, "touched with the feeling of our infirmities" and "tempted like as we are," yet being sinless and perfect in righteousness (Heb. 4:15), is able to execute perfect judgment. "He will judge the world in righteousness by the man whom he hath ordained; whereof he hath given assurance unto all men, in that he hath raised him from the dead" (Acts 17:31).

4. SUBJECTS

Those being judged at the eschaton fall into two categories.

(1) ALL MANKIND

All mankind will be judged; none will be exempt. "We all shall not sleep, but we shall all be changed, in a moment, in the twinkling of an eye, at the last trump: for the trumpet shall sound, and the dead shall be raised incorruptible, and we shall be changed" (I Cor. 15:51, 52). "For we must all be made manifest before the judgment-seat of Christ; that each one may receive the things done in the body, according to what he hath done, whether it be good or bad" (II Cor. 5:10).

(2) EVIL ANGELS

"For if God spared not angels when they sinned, but cast them down to hell, and committed them to pits of darkness, to be reserved unto judgment. . . ." (II Pet. 2:4). (The word translated "hell" is Tartarus, a word used in Greek philosophy and religion for a place of punishment under the earth. For example, the Titans are said to have been sent there. This is the only place in the New Testament where the word is found, and even here it is a form of the verb "to send to Tartarus" rather than the substantive. It is rightly translated "hell," as is also the usual New Testament word, Gehenna.) "And angels that kept not their own principality, but left their proper habitation, he hath kept in everlasting bonds under darkness unto the judgment of the great day" (Jude 6).

These passages show us that evil angels will be judged, while others show that good angels will be at the judgment in ministering capacities. "The Son of man shall send forth his angels, and they shall gather out of his kingdom all things that cause stumbling, and them that do iniquity, and shall cast them into the furnace of fire: there shall be the weeping and the gnashing of teeth" (Matt. 13:41, 42). "But when the Son of man shall come in his glory, and all the angels with him, then shall he sit on the throne of his glory: and before him shall be gathered all the nations" (Matt. 25:31, 32).

5. OBJECT

The object of the judgment is not to determine the character of the ones being judged. Since God already possesses that knowledge he does not have to ascertain such, much as a man might be ascertained guilty or not guilty in a modern law court. The omniscient Judge knows fully the conditions of every moral creature. Men are already inwardly judged when they die; they are outwardly judged at the final day.

The object of the judgment is the revealing of the character formed upon earth, and the assignment of rewards or punishments corresponding. "For we must all be made manifest before the judgment-seat of Christ; that each one may receive the things done in the body, according to what he hath done, whether it be good or bad" (II Cor. 5:10). In Romans men are said to treasure up for themselves "wrath in the day of wrath and revelation of the righteous judgment of God; who will render to every man according to his works" (2:5, 6). Our Lord tells us, "But there is nothing covered up, that shall not be revealed; and hid, that shall not be known" (Luke 12:2).

The Greek term translated "to judge" means to separate, to discriminate, being derived from a term for sieve. Therefore judgment is God's great sifting process, much as sheep are separated from goats (Matt. 25). God discriminates between the righteous and the unrighteous in an eternally severing event; but this is simply to make manifest that which, in essence, has previously existed. Therefore works, or deeds, become involved in the criterion of judgment because they are the visible outgrowth of character. They are the offspring of God's grace that has saved; therefore men are judged by the use they make — through deeds — of the redeeming grace of God.

A somewhat similar picture is presented in the latter part of the twentieth chapter of Revelation. "And I saw the dead, the great and the small, standing before the throne; and books were opened: and another book was opened, which is the book of life: and the dead were judged out of the things which were written in the books, according to their works. And the sea gave up the dead that were in it; and death and Hades [not "hell," as translated in the King James Version, for the Greek word is Hades, not Gehenna] gave up the dead that were in them: and they were judged every man according to their works.... And if any was not found written in the book of life, he was cast into the lake of fire" (20:12-15). This passage concretely shows that one enters heaven or hell according to the presence or absence, respectively, of his name in the Lamb's Book of Life. Then "the books," already differentiated from "the book," are employed as the basis of conferring relative rewards or condemnations.

Hic jacet in expectatione diei supremi.... Qualis erat, dies iste indicabit. "Here lies, in expectation of the last day.... Of what sort he was, that day will show." This epitaph has an aura of theological truth.

6. Necessity

The incomplete nature of the principle of justice consistently operative in the historical order constitutes the necessity of a final judgment. The kingdom of God demands finality in its various aspects. The crime that is hidden upon earth must be revealed and brought to light. The goodness that is thwarted and oppressed here must be recompensed there. God's justice must have a supreme, objective, and final vindication in every aspect; otherwise it is only approximate. This it finds in the final judgment.

"It is claimed that we are being judged now, that laws execute themselves, that the system of the universe is automatic, that there is no need for future retribution. But all ages have agreed that there is not here and now any sufficient vindication of the principle of eternal justice. The mills of the gods grind slowly. Physical immorality is not proportionately punished. Deterioration is not an adequate penalty. Telling a second lie does not recompense the first. Punishment includes pain, and here is no pain. That there is not punishment here is due, not to law, but to grace."[16]

Several things may now be observed relative to the necessity of the judgment.

(1) RESPONSIBILITY OF MAN

Man is responsible to God because God created him, is now preserving him, and, if man has accepted the reconciliation proffered, has redeemed him. He lives in God's created order, subject to his laws, both natural and moral; "for in him we live, and move, and have our being" (Acts 17:28). Man is a free moral agent, with the right of choice, even to accepting or rejecting God's gracious

16 *The Expositor,* March 1898.

offer of redemption. He is accountable to God *in toto*. Nor does salvation by grace diminish such a responsibility; justification by grace through faith does not abrogate the law. "Do we then make the law of none effect through faith? God forbid: nay, we establish the law" (Rom. 3:31). To say that salvation by grace extenuates man's responsibility to moral law and to God who redeemed him is a travesty against God's revealed truth. This theological aberration, prevalent during apostolic times, goes by the name antinomianism, which the man from Tarsus controverts in the sixth chapter of Romans. Antinomianism is based on a false idea of what salvation by grace really denotes. The child of God is not released from any obligation to keep the moral law; on the contrary, he is strengthened by renewing grace to the point that he is able to fulfill that very law itself. "For what the law could not do, in that it was weak through the flesh, God, sending his own Son in the likeness of sinful flesh and for sin, condemned sin in the flesh; that the ordinance of the law might be fulfilled in us, who walk not after the flesh, but after the Spirit" (Rom. 8:3, 4). So God's gift of grace does not decrease man's responsibility to God; rather, it augments it. God deals with man by grace; he will judge him accordingly.

(2) CONSCIENCE IN MAN

The conscience, endowed upon man by God during creation itself, is a witness to the moral order in the universe. Therefore the verdict of the conscience is a verdict of God, implying and pointing toward a final verdict on a day of reckoning. Wrongdoing is accompanied by "a certain fearful expectation of judgment" (Heb. 10:27).

(3) HISTORY

Corporate crimes fill the pages of history, crimes of ruling powers where the innocent suffer and bear the brunt of grief. And the influence of such offenses extends from generation to generation — both as regards the suffering itself and as regards the ill example. The choosing of low standards and of immoral acts by social groups must be dealt with justly. We are told not to avenge ourselves, but rather to forgive; therefore God's climactic action, bringing into being an equitable adjustment, is very apropos.

(4) CHRISTIAN THEISM

God is a person. He is a moral being, perfectly righteous and completely holy. We live in a universe of freedom and obligation, a realm of moral ideals and ethical demands. Since God is righteous and holy, he desires the same of those who are in relationship with him. There is an interaction of moral personalities with a moral God. The human soul searches for an understanding of the moral order, an effort God will not ignore. There is a seeking of purpose in the whole design. This is teleology, and teleology implies judgment. Judgment is the time when all loose ends are tied together. It is the climax of a world drama and God's answer to the moral-immoral struggle. It is the victory so plainly discerned in the book of Revelation.

We are not to suppose that the moral condition of the world is that of "an endless suspense, in which good and evil permanently balance each other, and contest with each other the right to inherit the earth. Such a dualistic conception is virtually atheistic, and the whole Bible could be read as a protest against it. . . . It would be impossible to overestimate the power of the final judgment, as a motive, in the primitive church. On almost every page of St. Paul, for instance, we see that he lives in the presence of it· he lets the awe of it descend into his heart to keep his conscience quick; he carries on all his work in the light of it; 'before our Lord Jesus, at His coming' — that is the judgment by which he is to be judged, that is the searching light in which his life is to be reviewed."[17]

IX. FINAL STATE OF RIGHTEOUS

The final state of the righteous is that of perfection for those who are sanctified. It is the holy life of earth brought to completion in heaven. It is communion with God and other sanctified spirits at the level of fulness, a blessedness par excellence that is without end.

1. NEW TESTAMENT TERMS

The final state of the saved is usually depicted by the scriptural term of heaven. Jesus remarks, "Rejoice, and be exceeding glad: for great is your reward in heaven" (Matt. 5:12). He also tells us that the Father is there. "Even so let your light shine before men; that they may see your good works, and glorify your Father who is in heaven" (Matt. 5:16).

But there are other biblical terms that are also employed to portray this state. One is eternal life. "And these shall go away into eternal punishment: but the righteous into eternal life" (Matt. 25:46). Another is glory. Peter says that he is "a fellow-elder, and a witness of the sufferings of Christ, who am also a partaker of the glory that shall be revealed" (I Pet. 5:1). This is the same glory into which Christ was received up (I Tim. 3:16). Another term

17 Denney, *op. cit.*, pp. 240-1.

is sabbath rest. "There remaineth therefore a sabbath rest for the people of God" (Heb. 4:9). Another term is resurrection. "For in the resurrection they neither marry, nor are given in marriage" (Matt. 22:30). Still another is kingdom. Jesus declares, "I shall not drink henceforth of this fruit of the vine, until that day when I drink it new with you in my Father's kingdom" (Matt. 26:29).

2. OBJECTIVE ENVIRONMENT

The Bible speaks many times in glowing terms of heaven. Isaiah 65:17-25; Romans 8:18-25; Revelation 21:1-22:5; John 14:1-4 — these and other passages present the following conclusions.

(1) PLACE

It is a locality as well as an inward state. This is shown in Jesus' words, "I go to prepare a place for you" (John 14:2). It also is shown from the fact of the resurrection body of Jesus and the corresponding bodies of his followers. Jesus will "fashion anew the body of our humiliation, that it may be conformed to the body of his glory" (Phil. 3:21). Listen to the words of our Master: "And I say unto you, that many shall come from the east and the west, and shall sit down with Abraham, and Isaac, and Jacob, in the kingdom of heaven: but the sons of the kingdom shall be cast forth into the outer darkness: there shall be the weeping and the gnashing of teeth" (Matt. 8:11, 12). How can one "sit down" with the patriarchs of old except in a place, and how can anyone be "cast forth" except from a place?

(2) LOCATION

Since heaven is a place it must of necessity have a location. Where is its locale? There are scriptural evidences that point to the fact that the earth itself *may* be the future location. If so, of course, the earth will not be of its present nature. "For the earnest expectation of the creation waiteth for the revealing of the sons of God. For the creation was subjected to vanity, not of its own will, but by reason of him who subjected it, in hope that the creation itself also shall be delivered from the bondage of corruption into the liberty of the glory of the children of God. For we know that the whole creation groaneth and travaileth in pain together until now" (Rom. 8:19-22). This would agree with Jesus' remark in the Sermon on the Mount, "Blessed are the meek: for they shall inherit the earth" (Matt. 5:5). Also, in John's vision on Patmos the heavenly city descends to earth (Rev. 21:1, 2). In Second Peter we are told that "the heavens shall pass away" and that "the earth and the works that are therein shall be burned up" (3:10). Then, after speaking of "the coming of the day of God," Peter remarks,

"But, according to his promise, we look for new heavens and a new earth, wherein dwelleth righteousness" (3:13).

Yet, there are other passages that speak of "down out of heaven." John's heavenly city is one "coming down out of heaven from God" (Rev. 21:2). Jesus himself is the bread coming down out of heaven. "I am the living bread which came down out of heaven: if any man eat of this bread, he shall live for ever" (John 6:51). Jesus ascended from Mt. Olivet up into heaven. "And it came to pass, while he blessed them, he departed from them, and was carried up into heaven" (Luke 24:51). When Stephen was stoned he looked up into heaven and saw Jesus on the right hand of God. "Behold, I see the heavens opened, and the Son of man standing on the right hand of God" (Acts 7:56).

Even *if* the earth, made new again and completely changed by fire, should be the location of the redeemed in the new age, the saved ones will probably not be confined to it. If earth is to be our abode, there could be excursions throughout the whole universe. Paul speaks, "Unto a dispensation of the fulness of the times, to sum up all things in Christ, the things in the heavens, and the things upon the earth" (Eph. 1:10). Would not a future with no end, yet filled with activity and development, require a wide range for the spiritual powers involved? Our glorified bodies may be able to move throughout the universe at the immediate motive of our glorified wills. Yet all this, to a considerable degree, is purely conjecture. Heaven may in reality be far distant from this earth. When Jesus speaks of heaven his words imply that it is presently existent as well as expectantly future. The "prepared place" of which Jesus speaks in John 14:2 may be already prepared. If so, how would this fit in with the promise of "a new heaven and a new earth," as found in Revelation 21:1? The Scriptures do not fully explain, and we do not have the right to make more of a distinction than they would justify.

3. ESSENTIAL CHARACTER

So much for the objective environment of heaven. What about the inward aspect, the essential character of heaven? Several factors should be considered.

(1) REWARD

Since this reward is according to works, there will of necessity be variation. Not all will be rewarded to the same degree. "Behold I come quickly; and my reward is with me, to render to each man according as his work is" (Rev. 22:12). "And the dead were judged out of the things which were written in the books, according to their works" (Rev. 20:12). The parable of the pounds teaches rewards according to faithfulness and work. "Take away from him the pound, and give it unto him that hath the ten pounds" (Luke 19:24); such is the dire consequence to the man who kept his pound in a napkin. Besides the extra pound the man with ten pounds received ten cities; the man with five pounds received five cities. The parable of the talents in Matthew manifests the same idea as the parable of the pounds, that the rewards will be according to ability. "To each according to his several ability" is the phrase used (25:15).

(2) RELIEF

Relief from the adverse conditions of this life constitutes the negative phase of heaven. The thorns and thistles, brought on because of man's sin (Gen. 3:18), will be completely removed. All mourning and tears, all sorrow and pain, all death and adversity will be removed. God himself "shall wipe away every tear from their eyes; and death shall be no more; neither shall there be mourning, nor crying, nor pain, any more: the first things are passed away" (Rev. 21:4). All the conditions that make life grueling will be appropriately absent.

(3) REALIZATION

In heaven we shall experience the fulfillment of every incomplete spiritual aspiration. Knowledge will be richer. "For now we see in a mirror, darkly; but then face to face: now I know in part; but then shall I know fully even as also I was fully known" (I Cor. 13:12). Worship will be in an ideal state. "And the throne of God and of the Lamb shall be therein: and his servants shall serve him; and they shall see his face; and his name shall be on their foreheads" (Rev. 22:3, 4). Communion with God will be perfect. "Behold, the tabernacle of God is with men, and he shall dwell with them, and they shall be his peoples, and God himself shall be with them, and be their God" (Rev. 21:3). Holiness will characterize the heavenly saints. "And there shall in no wise enter into it anything unclean, or he that maketh an abomination and a lie: but only they that are written in the Lamb's book of life" (Rev. 21:27). The glory of heaven will far transcend the spiritual glory experienced by the Christian while in this life. "For I reckon that the sufferings of this present time are not worthy to be compared with the glory which shall be revealed to us-ward" (Rom. 8:18). We will be in the very presence of Jesus. "And if I go and prepare a place for you, I come again, and will receive you unto myself; that where I am, there ye may be also" (John 14:3). "And so shall we ever be with the Lord" (I Thess. 4:17).

(4) ACTIVITY

There will be ceaseless service to God, the acme of the abundant life; and the abundant life means activity. Praise and adoration will be involved in every phase of it. "After these things I heard as it were a great voice of a great multitude in heaven, saying, Hallelujah; Salvation, and glory, and power, belong to our God: for true and righteous are his judgments" (Rev. 19:1, 2). And yet there will be other activity also, activity bringing in its wake no weariness and no fatigue.

(5) PROGRESS

The redeemed one will be complete when he enters heaven in the sense that he will be free from sin; but this will not stop his development or progress. This is illustrated in the fruit tree — the perfect bud, the perfect blossom, the perfect fruit. Each is perfect; yet there is progress, for the first two are not final. Perfection does not rule out growth. This is seen in the life of Jesus. He was sinless, yet he grew. "And Jesus advanced in wisdom and stature, and in favor with God and men" (Luke 2:52). The hindrance to growth is sin; when the redeemed individual is placed in an environment free from sin, there is a marked incentive to growth. Paul is doubtlessly referring to the eternal order in his statement relative to knowledge in the thirteenth chapter of First Corinthians. "For we know in part, and we prophesy in part; but when that which is perfect is come, that which is in part shall be done away.... For now we see in a mirror, darkly; but then face to face: now I know in part; but then shall I know fully even as also I was fully known" (13:9-12). Our knowledge then will be more direct than now, for we shall be face to face. Yet our knowledge will not be omniscient, for only God is omniscient.

X. FINAL STATE OF UNRIGHTEOUS

The final state of the lost is the absence of all good — both physical and spiritual. It is the misery of one banished from God eternally, the separation of one from the company of the redeemed and all that is holy. It is tantamount to abiding forever under God's curse, rather than amidst his blessings as an heir of spiritual glory. It is the spending of eternity with the devil and his angels, never to behold the face of God.

1. NEW TESTAMENT TERMS

The final state of the lost is usually depicted by the scriptural term of hell. Jesus warns, "And if thy right eye causeth thee to stumble, pluck it out, and cast it from thee: for it is profitable for thee that one of thy members should perish, and not thy whole body be cast into hell" (Matt. 5:29). The same term is similarly used in the very next verse, the thirtieth. Jesus also admonishes, "And be not afraid of them that kill the body, but are not able to kill the soul: but rather fear him who is able to destroy both soul and body in hell" (Matt. 10:28). He asks the Pharisees how they expect to "escape the judgment of hell" (Matt. 23:33).

But there are other biblical terms that are also used to portray this state, terms that represent the same thing, some of which are even more graphic than the word hell. One is eternal fire. "Then shall he say also unto them on the left hand, Depart from me, ye cursed, into the eternal fire which is prepared for the devil and his angels" (Matt. 25:41). Another term is outer darkness. "And I say unto you, that many shall come from the east and the west, and shall sit down with Abraham, and Isaac, and Jacob, in the kingdom of heaven: but the sons of the kingdom shall be cast forth into the outer darkness: there shall be the weeping and the gnashing of teeth" (Matt. 8:11, 12). This abominable final state is also called destruction. "Enter ye in by the narrow gate: for wide is the gate, and broad is the way, that leadeth to destruction, and many are they that enter in thereby" (Matt. 7:13). It is termed eternal punishment. "And these shall go away into eternal punishment" (Matt. 25:46). It is described as eternal destruction from the face of the Lord. ". . . who shall suffer punishment, even eternal destruction from the face of the Lord and from the glory of his might" (II Thess. 1:9). It is called second death. "But for the fearful, and unbelieving, and abominable, and murderers, and fornicators, and sorcerers, and idolaters, and all liars, their part shall be in the lake that burneth with fire and brimstone; which is the second death" (Rev. 21:8).

2. CHARACTERISTICS

(1) PLACE

Hell is a place as well as a state, as was discerned also in the case of heaven. That hell is a place is necessary to the doctrine of the supremacy of God. In the kingdom of God there is harmony, which entails submission to the will of God; and those who do not submit must be banished from the realm of his holiness. Therefore a place must be provided for the unrighteous ones commensurate with their chosen path of degradation.

(2) STATE

Hell is a state characterized by the antithesis of all the attributes of heaven. It is the negation in the soul of all that heaven offers.

Heaven is reward, and hell is punishment. Heaven is gain, and hell is loss. Heaven is the acme of Christian experience, and hell is the epitome of perdition. Heaven is the fulfillment of love, and hell is the consummation of selfishness. Heaven is Christ-centered, and hell is Satan-centered. Heaven is peace, and hell is frustration.

Man was made for eternal fellowship with God and for obedience to all the moral laws of God's universe. God is righteous; therefore the soul that consorts with God must also be righteous. If this high state is impossible for man to fulfill, God will provide the means; and salvation through faith in Christ is just such a means. Unbelief, or lack of faith, leaves man in a state of unrighteousness. He is separated from God, with no vestige of fellowship. His power of obedience is paralyzed, and estrangement between his spirit and God is the stark reality. Antagonism and rebellion are the order of the day. He finds himself in God's universe but at the same time alienated from God and at variance with every phase of the divine plan. The result, morally and spiritually, is hell, the outcome of unbelief and sin. "But for the fearful, and unbelieving, and abominable, and murderers, and fornicators, and sorcerers, and idolaters, and all liars, their part shall be in the lake that burneth with fire and brimstone" (Rev. 21:8). "And then will I profess unto them, I never knew you: depart from me, ye that work iniquity" (Matt. 7:23). "And be not afraid of them that kill the body, but are not able to kill the soul: but rather fear him who is able to destroy both soul and body in hell" (Matt. 10:28). "And if thine eye causeth thee to stumble, pluck it out, and cast it from thee: it is good for thee to enter into life with one eye, rather than having two eyes to be cast into the hell of fire" (Matt. 18:9).

(3) VALLEY OF HINNOM

During the days of the divided kingdom there was a valley southeast of Jerusalem where child sacrifice was practiced, little children being thrown into the fiery arms of the idol Moloch. God, speaking through Jeremiah, proclaimed his regard for this place. "And they have built the high places of Topheth, which is in the valley of the son of Hinnom, to burn their sons and their daughters in the fire; which I commanded not, neither came it into my mind. Therefore, behold, the days come, saith Jehovah, that it shall no more be called Topheth, nor The valley of the son of Hinnom, but The valley of Slaughter: for they shall bury in Topheth, till there be no place to bury" (Jer. 7:31, 32). Jeremiah started prophesying in 626 B.C., during the reign of Josiah, who outlawed this pagan place of sacrifice and prohibited this vicious practice. "And he defiled Topheth, which is in the valley of the children of Hinnom, that no man might make his son or his daughter to pass through the fire to Molech" (II Kings 23:10). Josiah attempted to wipe out this depraved form of worship that had so engrained itself in the life of Jerusalem during the days of the two preceding kings, Manasseh and Amon. Of Manasseh the Bible states, "And he made his son to pass through the fire" (II Kings 21:6). Even prior to this, in the days of Ahaz, it was practiced. "Moreover he burnt incense in the valley of the son of Hinnom, and burnt his children in the fire" (II Chron. 28:3). After Josiah outlawed the valley in order to prevent these pagan religious orgies, the ravine became the trash heap of Jerusalem, where the refuse, dead animals, and bodies of criminals smoldered continually. The fire and the worm never ceased their ravaging activity.

The "valley of Hinnom" in the Hebrew language of the Old Testament is *ge'hinnom,* which in the Greek of the New Testament becomes Gehenna. This is the term Jesus and the New Testament writers use to depict the place of eternal punishment for the unsaved. Jesus himself uses the term on many occasions, for the extreme degradation of the valley of Hinnom is the best symbol at his command with which to portray the dreadfulness of the place of eternal condemnation. The best English word with which to translate Gehenna is hell, as is done in practically all English versions. False conceptions in eschatology arise when Sheol in the Old Testament and Hades in the New Testament are also translated with the word hell, rather than being simply transliterated with the words Sheol and Hades themselves. "Hell" is unfortunately employed in the King James Version to translate all these terms. Even though Jesus uses the term Gehenna, the name of this terrible valley southwest of Jerusalem, with which to represent and describe hell, the latter is as real a place as the former. It is a place "where their worm dieth not, and the fire is not quenched" (Mark 9:48). It is a place of "outer darkness," characterized by "the weeping and the gnashing of teeth" (Matt. 8:12).

In II Peter 2:4 we find the statement that God cast sinful angels down to hell. The Greek word in this passage is not the usual word for hell, the one employed continually by Jesus, Gehenna. It is the word Tartarus (actually a form of the verb "to commit to Tartarus"), which is found throughout secular Greek writings as the place of punishment for the wicked. This is the only occasion the term is found throughout the New Testament. It is rightfully translated hell, however.

(4) DEGREES OF CONDEMNATION

Just as there are diversities of reward in heaven, so are there diversities of punishment in hell. Not all the wicked will suffer to the same extent in their final state. In concluding the parable of

407

the faithful and unfaithful servants Jesus states, "And that servant, who knew his lord's will, and made not ready, nor did according to his will, shall be beaten with many stripes; but he that knew not, and did things worthy of stripes, shall be beaten with few stripes" (Luke 12:47, 48). This clearly implies variations in punishment. In another passage he heaps woes upon the cities of Chorazin, Bethsaida, and Capernaum because they failed to accept him and his teaching, which constitutes the sin against light. Concerning the first and second cities he proclaims, "But I say unto you, it shall be more tolerable for Tyre and Sidon in the day of judgment, than for you" (Matt. 11:22). And concerning Capernaum he likewise states, "But I say unto you that it shall be more tolerable for the land of Sodom in the day of judgment, than for thee" (Matt. 11:24). The penalty will vary according to the light that was available. Whatever the meaning of "many stripes" and "few stripes," and whatever is designated by "more tolerable," there is sufficient reason to believe that there will be variations of condemnation.

There is one thing of which we can be certain: God, in his judging, will do right. He will take into consideration the light that a man possessed, the degree to which he accepted and lived according to that light, the use of his naturally endowed powers, his acceptance of opportunities, the favorable or unfavorable elements in his environment, and every other condition that might bear upon human responsibility in a moral and ethical universe. Difficulties that the human mind might conceive as thwarting or inhibiting justice will be fully eradicated or sublimated by God at the final hour. God will both reward and punish, whichever the case may require, according to his infinite knowledge, justice, and grace.

XI. FALSE THEORIES OF FINAL THINGS

There are certain false theories that deny eternal punishment. These theories seem to fall into two categories: annihilationism and restorationism.

1. ANNIHILATIONISM

Annihilationism holds to the view that the unsaved do not suffer eternally but are annihilated, ceasing to exist. This view also goes by the name of conditional immortality, holding that the soul becomes immortal only by union with Christ and the divine life imparted by him due to faith. Otherwise the soul, because of sin, will one day cease to exist, being apart from the life-giving qualities of the Saviour. Thus acceptance of the grace of Christ is the condition of immortality. This theory has occurred in various modes.

(1) FORMS OF THEORY

The oldest expression of the theory is that at death the soul ceases to exist. Another form this theory has assumed is that of the gradual weakening of the powers of the wicked until cessation of being ensues. Another form is that there is a set punishment proportionate to the deeds, and after this comes annihilation; this is possible any place between death and the judgment. A fourth form holds that men become responsible in a new way for their disobedience and failure to accept the gift of Christ; therefore they must be held in being until the judgment, after which they are cast into the lake of fire and brimstone. A fifth form puts the annihilation in the distant future after the judgment, thus allowing time for the full punishment meted out at that time.

(2) ARGUMENTS AGAINST

All these argumentations are based on pertinent words found in the Scriptures, such as: death, destruction, perdition, lost, etc. It will be readily discerned, however, that the terms have been misinterpreted. One example will suffice. "But the heavens that now are, and the earth, by the same word have been stored up for fire, being reserved against the day of judgment and destruction of ungodly men" (II Pet. 3:7). Other passages where the term "destruction" is used demonstrate clearly that it does not mean annihilation.

The idea of annihilation is one drawn from metaphysics, not from the Old and New Testaments. It is man's speculation superimposed upon biblical truth. It is even contrary to all rational and moral considerations that argue for the immortality of the soul. It lowers the dignity of human nature and places it upon the level of the brute. It does violence to the doctrine of the incarnation.

2. RESTORATIONISM

Restorationism holds that all or some of the wicked will be saved after death. This theory has also appeared in different modes throughout the years.

(1) FORMS OF THEORY

One of the forms is that death itself produces a change of character that will permit fellowship with God. This would result in the salvation of every individual; therefore this view of the theory could be called universal restoration, or, simply, universalism. This view is rarely held today. Another form of the theory is that the gospel is preached to the spirits of those dying without hearing the gospel, giving them a chance to repent and accept. This second probationary period terminates at the judgment. A third form is similar to the second except that the probationary period is extended unto the indefinite future, with some accepting and some not. Those not accepting are finally lost. A fourth form is similar to the third, except that God will use stronger and stronger means of persuasion until all are saved. This would be universal salvation, or universalism, also.

(2) ARGUMENTS AGAINST

Again Scripture is alluded to in order to support restorationism. One example will suffice. "For as in Adam all die, so also in Christ shall all be made alive" (I Cor. 15:22). But the word "all" refers only to the ones about whom he is speaking, the believers in Christ. Many other passages are also cited, but all are misinterpreted, just as this one. The interpretation placed upon these passages by the advocates of restorationism is offset by countless other passages where the true view is very obvious. Advocates of restorationism also use arguments from the nature of God, the nature of man, and the nature of the moral kingdom; but these reasonings are also erroneous.

Restorationism is in direct conflict with the teaching of Jesus, whose terms are clear and definite in regard to final states. He uses words which reveal the irrevocableness of both rewards and condemnations, and the tenor of the remaining parts of the New Testament is in accord with his teaching. The nature of hell, the nature of heaven, the sinfulness of sin, the cost of the atonement — all these precipitate a denial of any view of restorationism.

BIBLIOGRAPHY

Anderson, Bernhard W. *Understanding the Old Testament*. Englewood Cliffs, N. J.: Prentice-Hall, 1957.

Arndt, W. F. and Gingrich, T. W. *Greek-English Lexicon of the New Testament*. Chicago: University of Chicago Press, n.d.

Aulén, Gustaf. *Christus Victor*. New York: Macmillan, and London: S.P.C.K., 1951.

Baillie, D. M. *God Was In Christ*. London: Faber and Faber, and New York: Scribner, 1948.

Baillie, John. *The Idea of Revelation in Recent Thought*. New York: Columbia University Press, 1956.

———. *Our Knowledge of God*. London: Oxford, and New York: Scribner, 1959.

Barclay, William. *Jesus As They Saw Him*. New York: Harper, 1962.

———. *The Mind of Jesus*. New York: Harper, 1961.

Barth, Karl. *Dogmatics in Outline*. New York: Harper, 1949.

———. *The Word of God and the Word of Man*. New York: Harper, 1928.

Berkhof, Louis. *Systematic Theology*. Grand Rapids: Eerdmans, 1942.

Berkouwer, G. C. *The Person of Christ*. Grand Rapids: Eerdmans, 1954.

Bright, John. *The Kingdom of God*. Nashville: Abingdon, 1953.

Broadus, John A. *Commentary on the Gospel of Matthew*. "American Commentary Series."

Bruce, A. B. *The Kingdom of God*. Edinburgh: T. & T. Clark, 1890.

Bruce, F. F. *The Acts of the Apostles*. London: Tyndale, 1951.

Brunner, Emil. *The Christian Doctrine of the Church, Faith, and the Consummation*. Tr. David Cairns. London: Lutterworth, and Philadelphia: Westminster, 1962.

———. *The Mediator*. Philadelphia: Westminster, 1947.

———. *Revelation and Reason*. Philadelphia: Westminster, 1946.

Burrows, Millar. *An Outline of Biblical Theology*. Philadelphia: Westminster, 1946.

Burton, Ernest De Witt. *The Epistle to the Galatians*. "The International Critical Commentary." Ed. C. A. Briggs. Edinburgh: T. & T. Clark, 1920.

Buttrick, George A. *Prayer*. Nashville: Abingdon, 1942.

Campbell, John McLeod. *The Nature of the Atonement*. London: Macmillan, 1886.

Charles, R. H. *Eschatology*. New York: Schocken, 1963.

Conner, W. T. *Christian Doctrine*. Nashville: Broadman, 1937.

Dargan, Edwin Charles. *Ecclesiology*. 1905.

Davidson, A. B. *The Theology of the Old Testament*. Edinburgh: T. & T. Clark, 1904.

Davies, W. D. *Paul and Rabbinic Judaism*. London: S.P.C.K., 1955.

Denney, James. *Studies in Theology*. London: Hodder & Stoughton, 1895.

Dodd, C. H. *The Authority of the Bible*. London: Nisbet, 1928.

———. *The Bible Today*. New York: Cambridge University Press, 1947.

———. "The Life and Teaching of Jesus." *A Companion to the Bible*. Ed. T. W. Manson. Edinburgh: T. & T. Clark, 1947.

———. *The Parables of the Kingdom*. Herts, England: Nisbet, and New York: Scribner, 1935.

Ferré, Nels F. L. *The Christian Faith.* New York: Harper, 1942.
Findlay, G. G. *Fellowship in the Life Eternal.* Grand Rapids: Eerdmans, 1955.

Gloege, Gerhard. *The Day of His Coming.* Philadelphia: Fortress, 1963.

Herrmann, Wilhelm. *Der Begriff der Offenbarung.* 1887.
Hodge, Charles. *Systematic Theology.* Grand Rapids: Eerdmans, reprint.
Hodges, Jesse Wilson. *Christ's Kingdom and Coming.* Grand Rapids: Eerdmans, 1957.
Hunter, A. M. *Introducing New Testament Theology.* Philadelphia: Westminster, 1957.

Knudson, Albert C. *The Doctrine of God.* Nashville: Abingdon, 1930.
———. *The Doctrine of Redemption.* Nashville: Abingdon, 1933.

Ladd, George E. *The Gospel of the Kingdom.* Grand Rapids: Eerdmans, 1959.
Leitch, Addison H. *Interpreting Basic Theology.* Des Moines: Meredith, 1961.
Lightfoot, Joseph Barker. *St. Paul's Epistle to the Philippians.* Grand Rapids: Zondervan, reprint.

Mackintosh, H. R. *The Doctrine of the Person of Jesus Christ.* Edinburgh: T. & T. Clark, 1912.
McDowell, E. A. *The Meaning and Message of the Book of Revelation.* Nashville: Broadman, 1951.
Mullins, Edgar Y. *The Christian Religion in Its Doctrinal Expression.* Nashville: Broadman, 1917.

Oehler, G. F. *Theology of the Old Testament.* New York: Funk & Wagnalls, 1883.
Oesterley, W. O. E., and Robinson, T. H. *Hebrew Religion.* London: S. P. C. K., 1930.
Orr, James. *God's Image in Man.* Grand Rapids: Eerdmans, 1948.
Otto, Rudolf. *The Kingdom of God and the Son of Man.* London: Lutterworth, and Boston: Beacon, 1938.

Perrin, Norman. *The Kingdom of God in the Teaching of Jesus.* London: SCM, and Philadelphia: Westminster, 1963.

Ramm, Bernard. *Them He Glorified.* Grand Rapids: Eerdmans, 1963.
Robinson, H. Wheeler. *The Christian Experience of the Holy Spirit.* London: Nisbet, 1928.
———. *Inspiration and Revelation in the Old Testament.* Oxford: Clarendon, 1946.
———. *The Religious Ideas of the Old Testament.* London: Duckworth, 1913.
Robinson, T. H. "The History of Israel." *A Companion to the Bible.* Ed. T. W. Manson. Edinburgh: T. & T. Clark, 1947.
Rowley, H. H. *The Rediscovery of the Old Testament.* Philadelphia: Westminster, 1946.

Sanday, William, and Headlam, A. C. *Commentary on the Epistle to the Romans.* "The International Critical Commentary." Ed. C. A. Briggs. Edinburgh: T. & T. Clark, 1905.
Scott, E. F. *The New Testament Idea of Revelation.* New York: Scribner, 1935.
Shultz, Hermann. *Old Testament Theology.* Edinburgh: T. & T. Clark, 1892.
Stacey, W. David. *The Pauline View of Man.* New York: St. Martin's, 1956.
Stagg, Frank. *New Testament Theology.* Nashville: Broadman, 1962.
Stanley, Arthur P. *Christian Institutions.* 1881.
Stevens, George B. *The Pauline Theology.* New York: Scribner, 1892.
———. *The Theology of the New Testament.* New York: Scribner, 1899.

Stewart, James S. *A Man in Christ.* New York: Harper, 1935.

Stolz, Karl R. *The Psychology of Religious Living.* Nashville: Abingdon, 1937.

Strong, Augustus H. *Historical Discourse.* Valley Forge: Judson, 1900.

————. *Systematic Theology.* Valley Forge: Judson, 1912.

Summers, Ray. *Worthy Is the Lamb.* Nashville: Broadman, 1951.

Taylor, Vincent. *The Atonement in New Testament Teaching.* London: Epworth, 1940.

————. *Jesus and His Sacrifice.* New York and London: Macmillan, 1937.

Temple, William. *Nature, Man and God.* London: Macmillan, and New York: St. Martin's, 1949.

Thayer, Joseph H. *A Greek-English Lexicon of the New Testament.* Grand Rapids: Zondervan, reprint.

Thornton, L. S. *The Common Life in the Body of Christ.* London: Black, and Naperville: Allenson, 1942.

Tillich, Paul. *Systematic Theology.* Chicago: University of Chicago Press, 1951.

Vos, Geerhardus. *The Kingdom and the Church.* Grand Rapids: Eerdmans, 1958.

————. *The Pauline Eschatology.* Grand Rapids: Eerdmans, 1952.

Vriezen, Theodore C. *An Outline of Old Testament Theology.* Oxford: Blackwell & Mott, 1958.

Welch, A. C. *The Religion of Israel Under the Kingdom.* Edinburgh: T. & T. Clark, 1912.

Wendt, Hans. *The Teaching of Jesus.* Edinburgh: T. & T. Clark, 1892.

Wolf, William J. *No Cross, No Crown.* Garden City, N. Y.: Doubleday, 1957.

INDEX OF SUBJECTS

Major subjects treated are indicated in the index by SMALL CAPITALS.

Works
  and the church, 316-319
  and debt, 236
  and faith, 226

and rewards, 402
Worship, 319, 320
Wrath of God, 185

INDEX OF NON-ENGLISH TERMS

Adam (Heb.), mankind, 203
Anēr (Gr.), mankind, 203
Anthrōpos (Gr.), mankind, 203
Aphesis (Gr.), forgiveness, 231
Baptizō (Gr.), baptize, 327
Basar (Heb.), flesh, 128
Basileia (Gr.), kingdom, 285
Berith (Heb.), covenant, 352
Christus Victor (Lat.), a theory of the atonement, 174, 175
Dianoia (Gr.), mind, 132
Diathēkē (Gr.), covenant, 365
Dikaiōsis (Gr.), justification, 234
Elohim (Heb.), God, 115
Glossolalia (Lat.), speaking in tongues, 110, 111
Hagiasmos (Gr.), sanctification, 246
Hilasmos (Gr.), expiation, 185
Hilastērion (Gr.), expiation, 185
Huiothesia (Gr.), adoption, 238
Huper (Gr.), for, on behalf of, 187
Imago Dei (Lat.), image of God, 83, 140
Ish (Heb.), man, 203
Kardia (Gr.), heart, 130

Katallagē (Gr.), reconciliation, 239
Kenosis (Gr.), emptying, 88
Leb (Heb.), heart, 130
Logos (Gr.), word, 76, 83, 84
Metamelomai (Gr.), repent, 220
Metanoia (Gr.), repentance, 220
Nephesh (Heb.), soul, 125
Nous (Gr.), mind, 131
Palingenesia (Gr.), regeneration, 243
Paraclete (Gr.), Comforter, 101, 105
Parousia (Gr.), second coming of Christ, 385-389
Phrēn (Gr.), mind, 132
Pistis (Gr.), faith, 224, 225
Pneuma (Gr.), spirit, 99, 125, 133, 135, 136
Psuchē (Gr.), soul, 126, 135, 136
Ruach (Heb.), spirit, 125
Sarx (Gr.), flesh, 128, 136
Shema (Heb.), refers to Deut. 6:4-5, 113
Sōma (Gr.), body, 132, 136
Suneidesis (Gr.), conscience, 133
Thelēma (Gr.), will, 133
Torah (Heb.), law, 19, 56, 57, 281

INDEX OF AUTHORS

Abelard, Pierre (Peter), 174
Aeschylus, 376
Alger, W. R., 47
Anderson, Bernhard W., 366
Anselm, 170, 175
Aquinas, Thomas, *see* Thomas Aquinas
Aristotle, 138
Arius, 85, 122
Arndt, W. F., 328
Augustine, 138, 155
Aulén, Gustav, 174, 175

Baillie, D. M., 75, 76, 88, 178, 198, 232
Baillie, John, 23, 25, 29, 32, 250
Barclay, William, 83, 267
Barr, Allan, 82
Barth, Karl, 16, 18, 33, 180
Berkhof, Louis, 15, 22

Berkouwer, G. C., 76, 77
Boyce, James P., 138
Bright, John, 85, 295
Broadus, John A., 377
Browning, Elizabeth Barrett, 268
Browning, Robert, 6, 31, 134
Bruce, A. B., 288, 292, 296
Bruce, F. F., 111
Brunner, Emil, 17, 23, 307, 309, 346
Bultmann, Rudolf, 294
Burrage, Henry L., 330
Burrows, Millar, 128, 207, 243
Burton, E. D., 235
Bushnell, Horace, 173, 174
Buttrick, George A., 264, 266

Calvin, John, 155, 331, 347
Campbell, J. M., 174, 238, 332

INDEX OF SCRIPTURE REFERENCES

230.0
Ste